D0548692

HANDBOOK ON URBAN PLANNING

Jacket photograph: Denver Aerial. The snow-capped Rockies form a spectacular backdrop for the shining new skyscrapers of downtown Denver.

At the far left is the Queen City's classic Civic Center. In the center foreground is the gold-domed State Capitol. The thirteenth step of the west side of the Capitol is exactly one mile (5,280 feet) above sea level.

Denver's tallest buildings are Brooks Towers, 42 stories, in the background center, and the 31-story Security Life Building at the right center. (Photo courtesy Denver Colorado Convention and Visitors Bureau)

HANDBOOK ON URBAN PLANNING

EDITED BY

WM. H. CLAIRE

VAN NOSTRAND REINHOLD COMPANY
NEW YORK CINCINNATI TORONTO LONDON MELBOURNE

Van Nostrand Reinhold Company Regional Offices:
New York Cincinnati Chicago Millbrae Dallas

Van Nostrand Reinhold Company International Offices:
London Toronto Melbourne

Copyright © 1973 by Litton Educational Publishing, Inc.

Library of Congress Catalog Card Number: 73-2574
ISBN: 0-442-21563-0

All rights reserved. No part of this work covered by the
copyright hereon may be reproduced or used in any form
or by any means—graphic, electronic, or mechanical, including photocopying, recording, taping, or information storage
and retrieval systems—without permission of the publisher.

Manufactured in the United States of America

Published by Van Nostrand Reinhold Company
450 West 33rd Street, New York, N.Y. 10001

Published simultaneously in Canada by Van Nostrand Reinhold Ltd.

15 14 13 12 11 10 9 8 7 6 5 4 3 2 1

Library of Congress Cataloging in Publication Data

Claire, William H
  Handbook on urban planning.

  Includes bibliographical references.
  1. Cities and towns—Planning—1945-
—Addresses, essays, lectures. I. Title.
HT166.C52   309.2'62   73-2574
ISBN 0-442-21563-0

ABOUT THE AUTHORS

WILLIAM H. CLAIRE, AIP, F.ASCE, Director of Planning, Charles Gathers & Associates, Denver architects and planners, graduated University of Colorado (B.S. in Arch. Eng.) 1936. Four years U.S. Corps of Engineers in World War II followed by planning, architectural, and engineering positions with H. W. Lochner & Co, Chicago, C. F. Braun & Co, Alhambra, Calif., and as Assistant Executive Director of the Community Redevelopment Agency of the City of Los Angeles during the 1950s. He started his own firm, Wm. H. Claire & Associates, in Los Angeles in 1959 in planning, urban renewal, and transportation consulting work in California, Oklahoma, Florida, Puerto Rico, Mexico, and London, England, the latter on the London Traffic Survey being retained by Engineering Service Corp., Los Angeles. He was with Interstate General Corp., San Juan real estate developers, and Harland Bartholomew & Associates in Washington, D.C., and Memphis during the late 1960s; registered professional engineer (civil) in California, Colorado, Illinois, and Tennessee; Chairman, Executive Committee, Urban Planning and Development Division, ASCE 1963-64, and received ASCE Harland Bartholomew Award in 1971. Editor, ASCE *Urban Planning Guide,* published 1969; author of numerous professional articles, and lecturer in planning and renewal at several universities.

K. WOODROW BENCKERT studied engineering at Lafayette College (Easton, Pa.), Lehigh University, Pennsylvania State College, and Temple University. Personnel management and labor relations courses were studied at George Washington University. He enlisted in the U.S. Navy 1944, took naval indoctrination and Gyro School courses and served to 1946 as a Lieutenant Senior Grade. His next formal training was the Utility Executive Course, University of Michigan (1961). He was, from 1932 to 1950, with the Bell Telephone Co. of Pennsylvania. From 1950 to 1953 he was with the Department of Agriculture in Washington, D.C., as Chief of the Telephone Engineering Division and from 1953 to 1963 was employed by General Telephone Co. of Michigan as Chief Engineer and later as Operating Vice-President. He was President, Puerto Rico Telephone Co. 1963 to 1968, and President, IT&T World Directories, Inc. from 1968 to 1971. He is presently (1972) Special Assistant to Group Executive-ICO (IT&T subsidiary) and Chairman of the Board, Puerto Rico Telephone Co., since 1968. He is a Member, Executive Board of U.S. Independent Telephone Assn., Chairman, ComSat Committee of U.S. Telephone Assn., Member, Independent Telephone Pioneer Association, and a Professional Engineer in Pennsylvania. He served in Scarsdale as Chairman of committees on Airport Development and City Planning, is a Member of Newcomen Society of North America, and a Member of the National Defense Executive Reserve.

HERBERT A. GOETSCH has been Commissioner of Public Works of the City of Milwaukee, Wisconsin, since 1963. He received his B.S. and M.S. degrees in civil engineering from the University of Wisconsin and is a Registered Professional Engineer in Wisconsin. His previous positions include that of City Engineer of the city of Milwaukee, and Expressway Engineer of Milwaukee County. He is a National Director of APWA. He is a Fellow of ASCE and past chairman of the Urban Planning and Development Division. He is also a member of NSPE, AWWA, and SAME. During World War II he served in the U.S. Army Corps of Engineers and Military Intelligence in Europe. He has presented many papers before technical, professional, and educational groups. He was selected as one of the Top Ten Public Works Men-of-the-Year in 1968 and has received a Distinguished Service Citation from the University of Wisconsin.

HAROLD M. MAYER, Ph.D., AIP, is University Professor of Geography at Kent State University, since 1968, and also is Senior Research Fellow of the university's Center for Urban Regionalism. He received the B.S. from Northwestern University, M.S. from Washington University, St. Louis, and Ph.D. from the University of Chicago. Between 1940-1950 he was occupied in full-time city planning, except briefly during the war. He was Research Planner with the Chicago Plan Commission, Chief, Division of Planning Analysis of the Philadelphia City Planning Commission, and Director of Research of the Chicago Plan Commission. In 1950 he joined the faculty of the Department of Geography of the University of Chicago, with which he was associated during the following eighteen years. He has also served as consultant to planning organizations, civic organizations, and commercial, industrial, and transportation firms in the United States, Canada, and abroad. Among official positions, he served as a member of the first Chicago Regional Port District Board and as Commissioner of the Northeastern Illinois Planning Commission. He is author of *The Port of Chicago and the St. Lawrence Seaway,* coeditor of *Readings in Urban Geography,* and coauthor of *Chicago: Growth of a Metropolis,* as well as author of over 100 articles in scientific, technical, and planning journals.

RUSSELL H. RILEY studied Civil Engineering at the University of Illinois and received a B.S. in Landscape Architecture at Iowa State College. He was Field Engineer with A. D. Taylor in Orlando, Florida. He has been with Harland Bartholomew and Associates since 1929; Partner 1934 to 1961; Managing Partner 1961 to 1964; Consultant since 1964. He has been Assistant Director of St. Louis Regional Planning Commission 1933 to 1938. He directed preparation of comprehensive plans and special studies in more than 60 American and Canadian cities and counties. He is the author of several articles on comprehensive planning and zoning in professional magazines, and Chairman of the Executive Committee of Urban Planning and Development Division of ASCE from 1964 to 1965. He is a member of ASCE, AIP and ASLA; a Life Member of MSPE; and a Registered Professional Engineer in Missouri.

PREFACE

Urban planning is one of the most pressing subjects of the times with the majority of the people living in urban areas in North America and Europe and those areas continuously growing.

The lag in effective planning for this growth is a concern of the five authors of this handbook and their efforts herein are aimed at reducing and eventually eliminating that lag. One reason for the lag is not knowing where to start or how to proceed and the handbook endeavors to supply the knowledge for each, step by step.

There is a note of caution, in fairness to readers, that should humbly be recorded: there are techniques described in the book that apply less or not at all to other than Canada and the United States, with the possible exceptions of Australia, New Zealand, and a few other countries of the world.

The motivation of the authors also includes their desire to place in the hands of planners (professional and lay) a positive and useful book (a) to offset the dire predictions of the future, so in vogue, with principles, objectives, methods, and standards of planning that will ensure a hopeful instead of a hopeless future, (b) to recognize the order and abundance that exists and to capitalize on them for the benefit of all, and (c) to instill a faith in man's ability to solve any problem he makes.

Several uses are intended for the handbook in the fields of education, professional planning, and political science in Canada, the United States, and other American nations. The usefulness of the book in academic circles is proposed in urban planning courses but in a different sense than most such works. The growing importance of urban planning has brought the need for a wider spectrum of scientific disciplines to understand the subject and engage in the work as support professionals. Consequently, the public official, architect, landscape architect, engineer, economist, sociologist, psychologist, journalist, artist, lawyer, doctor, accountant, geographer, and businessman will find the handbook performing a specific function as an adjunct to their knowledge and as a reference work

guiding their endeavors. Professional planners in consulting firms, in planning departments of all types of government, and related public and private agencies and associations
or societies will find the book a ready guide and reference tool in their continuous
decision-making process of planning.

Reaching political scientists and politicians is an aim of the handbook and is meant
as a general reference in urban planning and development to be used by planning
commissioners, city councilmen, commissioners of parks, schools, utilities, housing
authorities, renewal agencies, county officials, and state and federal legislators and other
officials.

There are millions of persons in North America in poverty, in substandard housing,
and in no position to help themselves in many cases. There are also hundreds of millions
with a standard of living better than kings of only a few centuries in the past. This is the
great challenge of the times—for the free-enterprise system to bridge the gap between
poverty and affluence with plenty for all—plenty enough for a fulfilling life.

THE EDITOR

CONTENTS

FIGURES

TABLES

HANDBOOK ON URBAN PLANNING

1 PLANNING— THE OPTIONS AHEAD

Wm. H. Claire

The deep desire in the minds and hearts of most people to enjoy a full life in a state of orderliness and progress is a fundamental tenet of this handbook. The foundation of this desire is set forth as a series of general and specific objectives formulated in terms of realistic goals to overcome current problems as well as other obstacles in the path toward such goals. As large and complicated as the problems are, they are surmountable. They are man-made; they are the results of change, and the opportunities to solve present problems lie in the fact that every problem finds its solution as additional changes are made.

This chapter covers some of the more pressing issues an urban planner deals with and recommends a stance for him toward them. The issues are change, rights, order, obstacles, and objectives. Also in this chapter are references relating the other chapters to these issues.

CHANGE—A WAY OF LIFE

Change is a way of life in North America and undergirded the reasons for development of the New World. The people of the United States in less than 200 years have created the highest standard of living in the history of man—highest in material goods, highest in personal freedom, and highest in opportunities. Yet the rapid pace of development has left some serious unfinished business. The majority of Americans are not satisfied that poverty still persists, even though it lessens as the years pass; that job opportunities are not equitably available to all; that educational benefits are not yet equally distributed.

There were approximately 3,000,000 United States citizens when the country was born in 1776. They grew with 35 million immigrants to 105 million by 1921, when the Congress all but closed the door on immigration. During those 145 years a combination of favorable factors brought about tremendous development—a free-enterprise system with unheard of opportunities for any who were willing to work, a wealth of natural resources, a diversity of ingenuity, and from many cultures a spirit of liberty and a zeal for improvement. This was the period that saw the start of the industrial revolution.

The impacts of these on the new American nation rapidly affected the use of land. What started as an agrarian economy gradually, at first, shifted from a rural to an urban economy, and later, with the advent of the industrial revolution, at an increased tempo, to an industrial and urban economy [Figure 1-1]. The use of land per capita grew with the growth of capital as more space was required for farming, national forests and parks, grazing lands, forest preserves, and many other uses. This trend is still in force, a fact the planner should fully recognize as plans for urban areas, counties, and regions are formulated today.

Impact of Change

The impact of change on the economy since the beginning of labor unions has been to correct intolerable working conditions at poverty level salaries resulting in a series of raises in wages. The resulting higher cost of production has been passed on to the consumer in the form of higher prices. These trends stimulated a rash of labor-saving devices culminating in automation of industry as it is practiced today. Foreign competition at wage scales only a fraction of those in America and a free trade international policy are causing more changes and adjustments in the economy. A reorientation away from the obsession of accumulation of material things beyond certain necessities, particularly with the younger generation, is a change of the times having a profound effect on these economic problems.

Transportation changes, too, have created great expansion of the country and many shifts in the methods of transport through the years [Figure 1-2]. The mobility of Americans is manifested in the tremendous increase in use of all types of transportation through the decades since the industrial revolution and new trends that the planner must recognize in his work are now emerging.

The author's estimates of future use of transportation modes is an attempt to translate trends and pressures for change to better and less polluted forms of conveyance into projections of what the planner should include in his considerations of urban functions in the future. These projections most probably will need refinement and adjustment as still unforeseen factors impinge on these matters in the years ahead.

Another economic phenomenon in America is decentralization of business and industry since World War II. Several pushing and pulling forces are at work here. The pushing forces are big city high rents or taxes, lack of expansion space, congestion, pollution, and high wages—all pushing the businessman or manufacturer away from conditions that complicate his business and price his products above that of his competi-

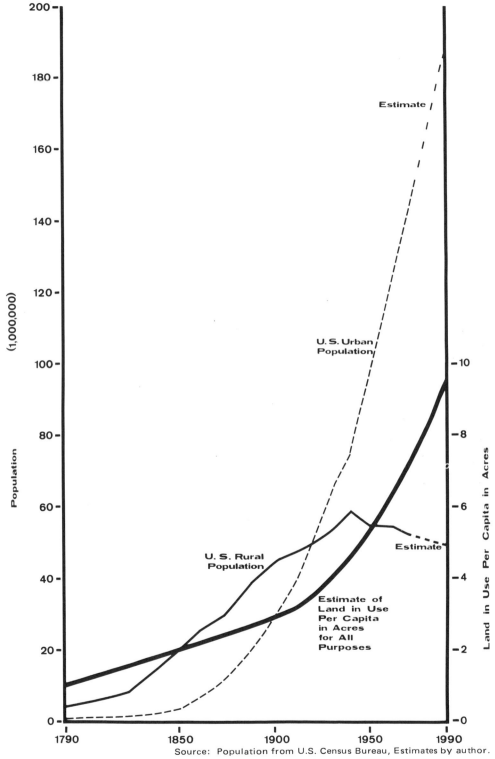

Source: Population from U.S. Census Bureau, Estimates by author.

Figure 1-1 Estimated U.S. population and urban land occupied 1790 to 1990.

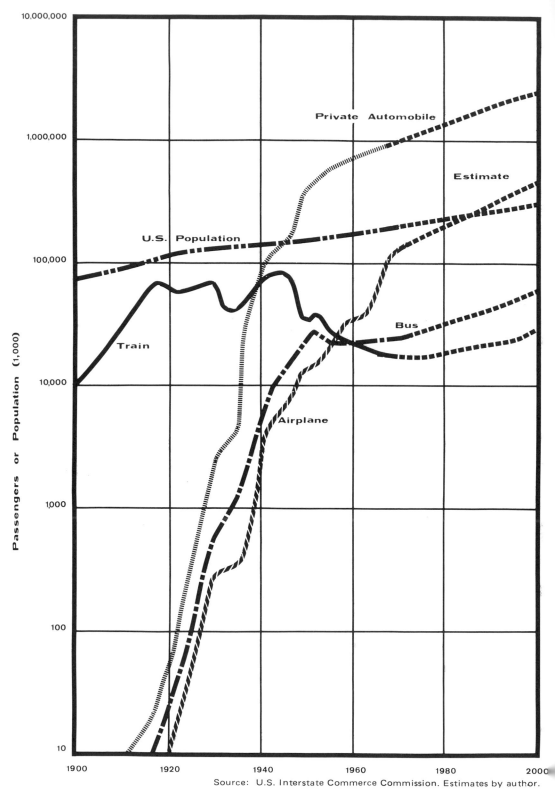

Figure 1-2   U.S. modes of passenger travel 1900 to 2000.

tion. The pulling forces are the developing areas of the country in search of jobs with enticements of low taxes, plenty of inexpensive land, clean air, cheaper labor, and living amenities for management and labor. This decentralization offers many opportunities to solve physical, social, and economic problems as may be seen in subsequent chapters on planning commercial and industrial areas (Chapter 5) and urban renewal of older and vacated sections of inner cities (Chapter 11).

Still one other trend deserving mention is the rash of business mergers in recent decades. Economies in management, accounting, maintenance, servicing, and the like are possible with bigness. Elimination or reduction of competition is another impetus to this trend and its eventual effect on urban planning and development is manifest in terms of shifting of business and industrial locations and requirements of more and larger sites for these activities (as described more fully in Chapter 5).

The impact of change on the mental life or outlook of the individual is just beginning to get the attention needed. On the active side people need an opportunity to express themselves, to get another chance when they make mistakes, to be justly compensated for useful work, to get recognition for an unusual effort, to excel in something, and hence to feel a sense of accomplishment in these efforts. On the more passive side the people need an anchor of security, some beauty and inspiration, someone to turn to for advice, a refuge in a catastrophe. Mobility of people, whether self-motivated or not, complicates or erodes a feeling of well-being. Some changes relieve pressures for certain persons and intensify them for others. The changes caused by urban renewal, for example, have an effect of confusion and frustration for some, and relief and betterment for most, when the process is finished. The planning process should include, through care and understanding, a thorough analysis of the effects of substantial change on the individual.

Rate of Change

What emerges as the population exceeds 200 million? —An increase in the rate of change for one important thing. This is the result of better communications, use of computers, more widespread knowledge, faster transportation. The rapid rate of change increases the flexibility needed to solve the problems of urban planning. The challenge is to the planners in using impending changes to improve urban plans. The changes necessary to provide half again as many homes as there are now before the end of the century form the opportunities the planner may use toward a better environment, physically, socially, and economically. It entails largely a matter of orderliness through planning, instead of the crash-program type of development too common in the past and to a lesser extent in the present.

THE RIGHT OF THE PEOPLE TO ORDERLINESS

The Great Seal of the United States of America has on it a Latin inscription that exemplifies the spirit of the country—*Novus Ordo Seclorum,* New Order of the Age. And so it was and so it is still. One distinct prospect of the New Order of the Age that is a bright hope in solving present problems is the right of the people to orderliness. This has an individual aspect and a group aspect having the power to coerce leaders into the action required.

Constitutional Rights

The New Order, aware of its imperfections, is in the process of reasserting itself, righting the wrongs of too rapid growth, searching for a new and better orderliness that is the right of the people in a free society. The authors of the Constitution of the United States of America recognized this right in these immortal words:

> "We the People of the United States, in Order to form a more perfect Union, establish Justice, insure domestic Tranquillity, provide for the common defence, promote the general Welfare, and secure the Blessings of Liberty to ourselves and our Posterity, do ordain and establish this Constitution for the United States of America."

The capitals are in the original, as they are also in the following excerpt: "Article I, Section 8: The Congress shall have Power To lay and collect Taxes ... and provide for ... the general Welfare of the United States."

Certainly "welfare" as used in the Constitution includes orderliness, clean air and water, freedom from excessive noise and other disturbances. But these amenities have been neglected in the rush of expansion and lack of orderliness prevails in the lives of far too many urban inhabitants. General welfare should be interpreted by the planner as protection and enhancement of the public welfare as planning decisions are made.

Community Pressures and Local Government

Through the years the grouping of individuals to make a showing of greater strength collectively rather than individually to bring pressure on local government to right wrongs or champion a worthy cause has evolved to a point of creating extremely complicated and numerous pressure groups for one cause or another.

Some of these groups operate on a national scale with local chapters which have an effect on local government. To many politicians, planning commissioners, and professional planners there is often a frustrating reaction to the diversity and seemingly chaotic proliferation of groups of one kind or another. However, there is a pattern and purpose to these groups, and they influence decision-making. Most of them are sincere, with worthwhile goals that defend individual rights from some inequity or another regarding housing, schools, highways, or such things as frequency of waste collection. These are the little-known arms of the Constitution bringing to daily recognition of local government the individual rights of this or that citizen or group.

These groups, often referred to as the power structure, and their general thrust are usually effective supporters of good planning and community betterment programs. The power in these groups is there to respond to and encourage community leadership to protect the right of the people to orderliness. There are more details on such socioeconomic groups in the next chapter.

Planning Commission and Leadership

Here is where orderliness should begin; where public and private groups and individuals should look for direction. The planning commission by itself is usually a recommending body that forwards plans to a legislative body for adoption, if necessary, depending upon the type of plan under consideration.

Planning commissioners are usually appointed by the mayor and confirmed by the city council and customarily serve without pay as a civic duty or honor that frequently also provides exposure to the public, a help in the commissioners' business.

This book describes these processes in considerable detail in Chapters 2 and 13 and here the general relationship between the planning commission and the local leadership is touched on in regard to the right of the people to orderliness. Leadership is the key word and the responsibility lies with the mayor and with the burdens he usually bears. But this is his role, that of leader, and there is no higher office in the community for the people to turn to. This is where the truth of the facts as they are should be disseminated and discussed; where orders for the formulation of plans to be made should originate; where enthusiasm for coordination and understanding should emanate; where fair and unbiased implementation of the plans should be insisted on; and finally, where the vision of how the plans fit into the broader metropolitan, county, regional, or state plans is expected.

Earning the Right to Orderliness

Hand in hand with the privilege of liberty is the obligation to nurture it, strengthen it, and guard it. No one is exempt from this call, if orderliness is to prevail and the free society remain free. The United States and Canada are countries of conscientious people, for the most part, who recognize injustice, inequities, and lack of orderliness and who want to correct these impediments to fulfillment for all. A better order of things and procedures is the hope of a free society, and every man that has this hope in him and practices it daily is earning his right to orderliness and liberty.

Esthetics and Planning

One aspect of orderliness is beauty, a blessing opulent in nature and rare in American cities. Planning can help this problem too.

Early planning efforts in America near the end of the nineteenth century were concerned to a considerable degree with esthetics, in grand boulevards, elaborate parkway systems, street trees, vistas of public buildings, and other urban beauty features. These worthy efforts were often frowned upon and considered frills by hard-headed city fathers who were responsible for conjuring up the tax revenue for acquisition of vast park sites and maintenance cost of extensive landscaped areas of the city.

Planning shifted away from the "impractical" esthetic considerations to more pragmatic matters of traffic, public facilities, and land use. Esthetics was all but squeezed out of the picture completely. Recreation and parks were the only threads of continuity that kept esthetics in the planning process at all during the first half of the twentieth century. Recently, a surfeit of ugliness and emphasis on a new set of values is bringing esthetics back into its proper place in planning. The urban renewal program helped this along by permitting a certain share of the site improvement budget to include artwork— sculpture, mosaics, decorative walls, landscaping, and the like. The boom in ecology is often expressed in terms of the beauty of nature, more natural surroundings within the city, and lately this is supplemented by such considerations as the esthetics of bridges and other public works. Still other manifestations of the need for the beautiful are a part of planning. Beauty is order and orderliness requires esthetics in planning. Beauty is a necessity to human well-being.

SOCIAL AND ECONOMIC ASPECTS OF PHYSICAL PLANNING

The social and economic factors the planner is confronted with in the modern urban area are increasingly important to him in solving most physical planning problems. His need for knowledge in these other disciplines forces his reliance on others for the comprehensive planning that has become his responsibility.

Urban or regional planning should be the profession that assembles for analysis, interprets, and recommends all the pertinent social and economic facts and goals as a basis for comprehensive planning decisions and evaluates the advantages and disadvantages of alternatives. The sociologist, psychologist, political scientist, geographer, economist, architect, engineer, and others represent the disciplines to be consulted by the planner and from whom data is obtained, but the planner should have the overall responsibility of interpretation and coordination of these data.

This chapter touches on some of the attitudes the planner encounters in his work and recommends appropriate postures he should assume and actions he should pursue regarding them. The socioeconomic order and its mutual relationship to physical planning is becoming more involved with the ecology of the region in which a plan is being formulated.

ECOLOGY, PAST AND PRESENT

There is more orderliness in the social and economic structures of urban life in the United States and Canada than one might gather from the news media. Order is not usually newsworthy but disorder is. Millions of persons going to work each day is not news but 500 laid off is. Billions of automobile trips by the people annually is not news but thousands of them ending in fatalities is. The thesis here is not to put down the news media nor to take morbid statistics lightly but to appreciate the order that prevails and upon which better order and ways of living together can evolve through sound planning.

An even more convincing example of order than the job or automobile trip is ecology, the science of organisms and their relationships to their environments. The order in nature is a wonder to behold. The annual budding of trees in the spring is an example of order that is evidence of an infallible system of life recycling. The regeneration of birdlife and the abundance of food for its sustenance is another case in point where order prevails in a marvelously delicate system. These and other ecological evidences of order are full of instruction for the planner. He may learn how complete and comprehensive is each ecological system and how he may apply such facts to his own problems. He may learn how organisms function, what they need in plant and animal environments without the presence of man, and what his effect has been on them. He may learn what adjustments should be made now by man for all life to live in harmony. This is particularly critical now for the planner as population increases are resulting in less land area per person and necessitating greater care of what is done with the land [see Figure 1-3].

Environment—What Planning Is All About

Points of view persist, mostly among the more affluent segments of society, that environment is not as important as planners claim; that a look at the successful who worked their way out of the slums is proof that the slums remain only because those who remain in them have no interest in bettering their lot; that no matter what environment such people were placed in, they would make a slum of it in time. This handbook takes the stand that these points of view are applicable in a very limited number of cases; that an adverse environment is a potential breeding place for discontent, crime, disease, ignorance, poverty, and despair; that, on the contrary, an appropriate environment fosters content, order, health, enlightenment, wealth, and inspirational living.

Ecology and Urban Planning

The urgency behind the swift pace of development of America was and is largely profit motivated, an urge that brings a continually higher standard of living coupled with a pace that promotes continually more involvement, hence more problems. One of the most serious of these problems is the effect over 200 millions of Americans and to a lesser extent more then 20 millions of Canadians have on their respective total environments in an ecological sense and especially on their urban environments.

The present book is confined to urban planning, but the position of urbanization in the total environment and influences of urbanization on rural land and the whole ecology are of concern to such planning. As aggravated and costly as these problems are, they are solvable. This handbook is aimed at helping to solve large problems requiring solutions of great magnitude. The New Order of the Age is having growing pains but is still very much alive and to rescue ecology is an important objective of planning.

Future Development Decisions and Ecology

The secret of solving a problem is matching the magnitude of it with a solution of equal or greater size, as mentioned above; the vast changes ahead to provide for population increases provide opportunities to right some of the wrongs of an ecological

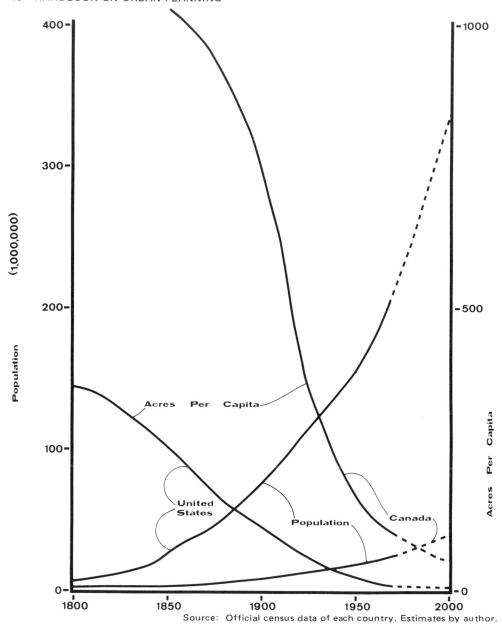

Source: Official census data of each country. Estimates by author.

Figure 1-3 Estimated Canadian and U.S. open space per person 1800 to 2000.

nature. How provision for an additional hundred million Americans by the end of this century is planned for can solve or compound ecological problems, and nearly all of the addition will be urban.

The foresight of the planner must be a warning beacon or prodding tool to restructure government to cope with an additional hundred million persons. Any decisions of the scope required and far-reaching effects that result should carefully be coordinated with efforts of the ecologist regarding adequate agricultural land of the appropriate type and location, provision for sufficient quantities and complete treatment of water, and an integration of urban with other land uses in a manner that protects each.

The enormity and intricacy of the decisions that are needed to develop everything for a population half again as large as at present, requires the highest type of intelligent coordination of all concerned to rescue and restore the ecology and simultaneously provide efficient urbanization.

OBSTACLES OR FACTORS AFFECTING GROWTH AND HOW TO COPE WITH THEM

Whatever decisions are made for future urban development and whatever plans that development is based upon, there will be certain factors influencing growth that will need to be taken into account in them. These factors may be physical, a lake or mountain range, as examples; social, birth control or migration in or out; they may be economic, such as a building boom or a shift in types of employment in an urban area.

The description of their influence on urban planning and how to plan for them is an essential step in the planning process, and such factors are treated especially in Chapters 4 through 7. Often, a list of these factors is taken into consideration in planning objectives.

PLANNING OBJECTIVES

The simplest definition of planning objectives in urban planning in a republic is what the people want. Finding out what the people want is not so simple. Yet this should be a planner's solemn obligation—first to learn the desires of the people.

Elected officials of the city, county, or region being planned should be considered the key group, whose opinions should reflect the needs and wants of the people who elected them, a primary source of public opinion information the planner should seek and that should influence his planning.

Formulation

A list of objectives is included here as a reminder or checklist and should be augmented as necessary to meet the situation at hand. No two urban areas would be likely to have the same ones. The goals could be titled planning objectives during plan formulation and development objectives when the plan is ready for implementation, but they should remain basically the same in each case. This approach indicates the planning process continues after implementation begins. The general planning or development objectives are as follows:

1.   Provide for anticipated land uses of various types in appropriate locations and arrangements with respect to each other as the demand in the foreseeable future indicates.

2. Reserve adequate space in appropriate locations for movements of persons and objects in a transportation system and utilities systems to serve proposed land uses.
3. Analyze natural resources and plan their proper utilization.
4. Protect valuable surface or underground resources from obstruction to access for use or extraction.
5. Preserve available sources of water and add to them where necessary to supplement supply.
6. Arrange for adequate open space in natural conditions where appropriate for man and other living creatures [Figure 1-3].
7. Establish legal means by which the above objectives are guaranteed.
8. Provide for additions or revisions of the above objectives as subsequent events require.

The above list is broad and general in nature, but does not include specifics of housing, business, industry, and the like covered in respective chapters on these subjects later. Objectives are only as effective as the support they receive from the people and their representatives.

Dissemination and Support

This is an essential part of the whole planning process and is covered in detail in Chapter 13. Widespread notification to the people in newspapers, pamphlets, schools, and discussion groups is an effective way of fostering support of the objectives. As tentative objectives become more thoroughly understood and modified in accord with points obtained from meetings and public hearings, they are ready for finalization and adoption.

Basis for Planning Decisions

Once the objectives are adopted they are ready for their principal role as the foundation for the urban plan. The many decisions in the plan formulation period should be checked step by step with the objectives and rechecked as deeper analyses reveal reasons for altering the objectives. A reliable set of objectives should be general enough to be free of contradictions of details and comprehensive enough to include an interpretation of details with sufficient latitude to cover all the possibilities of development that might be encountered. If this ideal is attained, revisions of the objectives should be at a minimum. However, there is always the possibility of such a complete shift in conditions that considerable changes in objectives could result.

GETTING THE MOST FROM THIS HANDBOOK

Key to Answers

A complete index of items and materials is included at the end of the book. Additional reading may be found in a bibliography at the end of each chapter or in footnotes. The source of direct quotes may be found in a numbered footnote at the bottom of the page where the quote occurs. References in the text of the handbook to tables and figures are shown in [brackets] for ready identification.

Planning in the United States and Canada

While the handbook is geared to United States and Canadian consumption, most parts should serve in other American countries, and virtually any nation in the free world where individual property rights are guaranteed by the government.

Certain revisions in subsequent editions indicated as necessary may increase the usefulness of the book and, together with appropriate translations, broaden its application and foster more uniformity in planning techniques. This latter feature will become more pertinent as the world of business and diplomacy shrinks the Earth even more in the future.

Planning for Built-up Urban Areas

The present book recognizes that built-up areas present the greatest challenge to government and planning—to overcome the mistakes of the past, maintain efficiency and order in the present, and accommodate anticipated growth. Principles, methods, and standards are included in subsequent chapters together with the objectives in this and other chapters in the hope of achieving orderly growth toward complete correction of current problems and smooth-running urban systems. Most of the expected development will in all probability occur within or adjacent to present urban areas and the book is written with this in mind.

Planning for New Towns

The foregoing remark about most new development being in or adjacent to built-up areas should not be construed as precluding New Towns. Without a doubt New Towns will be legion. In fact the lessons learned in New Towns will benefit planning and development practices in built-up areas. New Towns can and should be the test tube of the exciting social and economic inventions that form the city of the future and finally release man from the ugly, the congested, the costly, the depressing, and point the way to the efficient, natural, harmonious urban environment he is capable of creating.

SUMMARY

Summarizing this chapter, this handbook is intended as a positive practical set of instructions on how to plan urban areas. There is no fear on the part of its authors that the country is going to be drugged to extinction, cobalt-bombed to bits, starved to death from overpopulation, or perish from pollution. Instead, the brains, brawn, bravery, and best in the great majority of people will prevail to make old and new cities better and better through the years. The current cliché that anyone who is optimistic just ignores the horrible facts, should be counteracted by the knowledge that nearly everyone wants to lead a normal, sensible, happy life, with plenty of fun and good times and plenty of meaningful work of a rewarding and satisfying nature and that, in this awareness of the work ahead to correct present problems, they will be corrected.

2 GOVERNMENTAL AND SOCIOECONOMIC STRUCTURES

Wm. H. Claire

The matrix of official and unofficial groups the planner works with or for is the subject of several books, and this chapter is intended to sort out and describe some of the principal ones as they influence planning without claim of thoroughness of detail. The chapter considers in three sections relationships of the planning function to governmental structures and the socioeconomic structures, and some points on opportunities as to how these can strengthen one another in a direction of benefit to all.

The power structure, an important part of these matters, should be recognized for what it is, how it is changing, and how the planner is affected in the transition. Gone are the one-man power structures of the past. It would be jumping at conclusions to rate one-man power structures as evil or even undesirable in most instances. The same is true of modern multifaceted power structures. Often the power structure is a small group of heads of families with large real estate holdings or businesses. Occasionally a college or university or some organization important to the economy of the city or town is the force in the background, and in some cities labor unions. Whatever its make-up, it is a factor in getting planning completed and implemented.

PLANNING AND GOVERNMENTAL STRUCTURES

There were over 91,000 governmental units in the United States in 1960, two-thirds of which were single-function units, such as school boards, sanitary districts, etc.[1] Growth since then has pushed this well over 100,000. These are the jurisdictions the planners are called upon to plan for and within.

A government of, by, and for the people in a free society has the people to regulate and check it, and not always the best trained or knowledgeable. Politics attracts a wide variety of types of people. The saying that a republic or a democracy is cumbersome, inefficient, wasteful, and slow, but is the best form of government in the world, still applies but needs to be reexamined. Now it is clear that a peaceful (for the most part so far) revolution is growing, and impatience to right wrongs sooner, more efficient systems pressing in to replace inefficiencies, outrage aimed at delay and wastefulness, and ecological disorders are demanding attention.

The backers of the revolution through the political process are mostly the young, with others, of course, and the impact they are having on the old line politician and public administrator, including the planner, should lead toward the needed big solutions to the big problems. This chapter is a reminder of the flexibility of new ways in which cities are and will be planned. The voting age reduced to eighteen, attitudes toward war, the search for a more simplified way of life, in short, a new look at values and priorities are behind this peaceful revolution.

Within this background, the place of the planner in various governmental settings is sketched below and in subsequent chapters as the framework within which plans are being formulated.

Local Governments

There are more than 35,000 municipal and township governments[2] and 3,049 county governments in the United States, as well as a larger number of other types of local governments, such as airport commissions, water districts, housing authorities, and the like. Most of the 35,000 do planning in one form or another, but not all of them have formal planning commissions (see Chapter 12).

COUNCIL AND PLANNING COMMISSION   Towns and cities are established by state enabling legislation in the United States and provincial or Dominion law in Canada. Most municipalities in the United States have the mayor-council form of government operating as an executive-legislative team, but recent decades have seen the rise in utilization of the council-manager method of home rule. Here the council is elected by the residents as in the mayor-council system, and the councilmen then elect one of their own members as mayor and head of the council. The council then appoints a city manager and in this manner it is intended that a nonpolitical, trained professional manages the city. Somewhat the same objective rule is possible by means of a chief city administrative officer who reports directly to the mayor in the mayor-council system.

State enabling legislation is also the legal source of planning commissions, and a

1. International City Management Association, Chicago.
2. *1969 Statistical Abstract of the United States,* U.S. Dept. of Commerce, Bureau of the Census, p. 405.

variety of statutes, depending upon which state is being considered, cover the manner in which the commissions operate and the territory for which they have permissive or obligatory planning functions. The first planning commission in the United States was formed in Hartford, Connecticut, in 1907.

The planning commission is usually appointed by the mayor and confirmed by the city council, as mentioned in the previous chapter, and the planning commissioners have the responsibility of hiring the planning director and getting a plan formulated with the director's staff or with the help of planning consultants. Towns too small to justify a full-time planning director or staff may retain consultants for all their planning and zoning work or delegate it to the city engineer, public works director, or others.

One of the first orders of business is for a planner to investigate the planning enabling statutes and other requirements and limitations. Most statutes of this type make obligatory the formulation of a general plan and of what it should consist, as well as other duties, such as zoning administration. This latter often is so time-consuming that little actual planning work gets done. Other related statutes that should also be checked by the planner involve, for example, housing, urban renewal, public works, annexation, and others.

ANNEXATION   Annexation studies should be a high-priority goal for the planner. This may be his only means of planning comprehensively enough to prepare for orderly growth as other methods, described below, fall short of this goal. Annexing should be handled with deliberation, however; it can be a two-edged sword. Adding adjacent territory to a city by annexation adds also to the responsibility of providing city services to the territory.

Some of the principal aims of annexation are to increase the tax base, achieve greater governmental efficiency, prepare rural fringe areas for urbanization, assure orderly development, and to plan adjacent areas integrally with the city. The planning commission (or its planner) is charged with the responsibility of getting the facts on each of the above points and making annexation recommendations to the council or local governing body.

ASSESSMENT   The assessed valuation of an area to be planned is a basic consideration for the plan. The sources of tax revenue should be explored and the tax base determined as the foundation upon which improvements proposed in a plan are based. The uniformity of property assessment is the underlying key to the assessment techniques in an area and the capability of the tax base to provide funds for proposed improvements. An overview of taxable property in the country as a whole in comparison to the state or province should give a general indication of how up-to-date assessments are [Figure 2-1]. Then a comparison of the state assessments per capita with those in the area being planned affords still another and closer check. The estimated assessed value of property [Figure 2-1] is the source of funds for needed improvements of the future.

COORDINATION   One requirement the planner should fulfill, whether a statutory obligation or not, is coordinating with other governmental jurisdictions in and around the

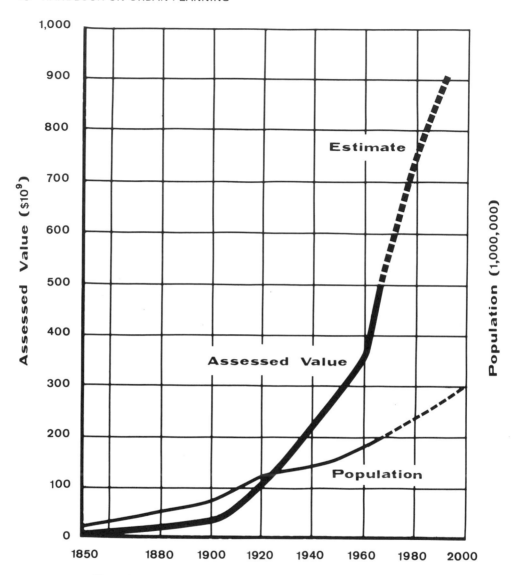

Figure 2-1 Assessed value of taxable property in the U.S. 1850 to 2000.

city, such as the board of education, utilities both public and private, the state highway department, welfare organizations, and the county or other larger jurisdiction of which the city is a part. Some of the more pertinent details of these coordinating processes are described in Chapters 3 through 10 and Chapter 12.

County and Metropolitan Governments

The 3,049 United States counties, like cities, exist by virtue of state enabling legislation and the governmental and planning functions in counties are determined in like manner. Counties usually are governed by elected commissioners, supervisors, or members of a quarterly court and in turn elect their own chairman or president. The county commissioners appoint citizens to commissions to supervise the county (planning, public works, parks, etc.) and they in turn hire the planning director and other staff to carry on the work. Provinces of Canada are not organized into counties, as in the United States, but form districts within provinces as convenient areas to study and direct.

The growing awareness of the advantages to be gained by consolidation of city and county governments is a hopeful sign of reducing governmental entities and realizing more efficient public administration of urban areas. Only four United States counties have consolidated their governments with the major city therein to date, but many more are studying the idea. The four are Baton Rouge, Indianapolis, Jacksonville, and Nashville. Each of them claims reduction in overlapping services, greater operating efficiency, and less cost of government. Indianapolis is able to manage better with 500 less personnel as a result of consolidation.

The consolidated city-county government idea grew out of the broader concept of metropolitan government, a necessity in this era of sprawling urbanization and the need to control it through planning to achieve orderly growth.

METROPOLITANIA   The metropolitan form of government was first born (at least in the Western Hemisphere) by vote of the people in the metropolitan area of Toronto, Ontario, in 1953. The objective of the new government originally was metropolitan-wide planning to resolve difficulties the burgeoning metropolis was having with such services as water supply, waste control, highways, transit, and overlapping governmental units. Now other facilities and services are being added with encouraging results.

About a decade later, Miami and Dade County formed the first United States metropolitan government after a few fitful starts, and now others are studying the idea (see Chapter 12 on metropolitan and regional planning).

Resistance to the idea developed as a matter of a false sense of loss, in many cases since positions of authority or salary were in jeopardy of elimination. Compounding this difficulty is the fact that no two counties have the same set of circumstances or needs. There is no simple political solution to consolidation in spite of the glowing advantages to be gained. The answer lies in long-term education of the public through the schools and press and positive factual and unemotional information on the subject. However, urbanization problems grew in spite of the resistance to consolidation, and another means of coping with the problems without the demise of either county or city governments evolved—councils of governments.

COUNCILS OF GOVERNMENTS   The first council of governments was formed with six counties in the Detroit metropolitan area in 1954 and is known as the Southeast Michigan Council of Governments. The idea to attack urban problems in this manner grew to 91 councils of governments (COGs) by 1969. They serve areas with populations ranging from 17,000 to 10 million persons.[3]

The principal function of COGs is planning, since they have no taxing or other

---

3. *1970 Municipal Year Book,* International City Management Assn., p. 40.

powers over the jurisdictions they serve. They may prove, nevertheless, the forerunner of future metropolitan governments. Federal funds became available for COGs in 1966. Usual fields of endeavor for COGs are land use planning, water and sewer planning, waste control planning, law enforcement planning, and coordination of planning activities within the COG area.

MORE COORDINATION   Counties are usually or should be bound with coordinating responsibility in comprehensive planning activities of the county, of municipalities within the county, of adjacent counties and the state, where the county in question is affected, or of COGs, if any, or similar superjurisdictional entities. This is an involved assignment for the easiest part of it lies in physical development planning and an intricately complicated and controversial part in such politically unpopular areas as education, welfare, race relations, and housing, particularly low- and moderate-income types (more thoroughly considered in Chapter 4). These same remarks about coordination apply as well to metropolitan governments and COGs, and to a more complicated degree.

State and Regional Governments

A natural conclusion to draw from metropolitan government planning and COGs is that county and state boundaries are a hindrance instead of a help in the planning determinations and decision-making required in solving current urban problems in a large metropolitan area or group of them—usually called a megalopolis. A metropolitan area is a logical basis upon which to plan many problem solutions. The industrial production and transportation system form the base for the economy of the metropolitan area with employment that in turn creates a demand for certain amounts of housing and commercial services of various types. To simplify, the land use plan accommodates this housing and these services and industry and community facilities are added. Then an implementation system is formulated. The simplification ends at this point, since the time has come to get the comprehensive plan approved. Several states may be involved and probably over a dozen counties as well as many towns of various sizes in the metropolitan area (see Chapter 12).

This is the course, notwithstanding, or some variation of it, that eventually will be pursued in planning metropolitan areas. Dissolving state lines is constitutionally taboo and the time to take such a proposal through Congress is not available, nor would there be much interest in it politically. Even if there were time, the passage would be likely to fail. There is a feeling of loyalty most people have for their state and a sense of competition between states that would be unfortunate to lose. Better still is the idea of greater coordination of activities common to two or more states. Most western states have their capitals or principal cities near the geographical center of the state and the metropolitan area entirely within the state. Smaller eastern states are less fortunate in this regard where metropolitan areas spill over into two or more states and interstate coordination is becoming more critical as growth continues (see Chapter 12).

THE STATE AND PLANNING   State planning offices recognize this need and this was one reason for their establishment in the first place. Another reason was the objective of coordinating county and municipal plans and planning between adjacent counties for orderly development, but an overriding reason was eligibility for federal Section 701 planning grants first available from the Housing Act of 1954. These funds are for towns, counties, states, and metropolitan areas or regional planning groups; state planning offices were set up to disperse the funds [see Figure 2-2]. The future availability of such funds is the key to orderly growth and development.

State planning has been progressing in many states with good results for years motivated by the above planning programs as well as federal highway systems, particularly interstate routes, airport and airways planning programs, and river basin planning encompassing several states in the interests of flood control, irrigation, harbors, hydroelectric power, water supply, barge traffic, and other similar functions between states.

One obstacle to progress at the state level is the state constitution in practically all states. If a state constitution is over 50 or 75 years old, it would, in all probability, be a difficult instrument to use in urban development control or dealing with individual social problems of people in modern cities. State constitutional amendments are not easy to come by for reasons of their protective provisions in the public interest and the fear of those in power losing some of that protection or power or both.

State legislatures have also been an obstacle in some states until the 1964 Supreme Court decision that state legislators shall represent a nearly equal number of voters in their state districts. This decision corrected the imbalance of rural area representatives governing the state at the expense and to the detriment of urban areas in many cases.

REGIONAL RESPONSIBILITIES   The federal planning programs usually are on a two-thirds or one-half grant basis with local participation coming from the town, county, or state. Regional planning agencies have similar funding arrangements with the local share from cities, counties, and states.

Regional planning is more completely described in Chapter 12 and only a few examples are included here. The Tennessee Valley Authority is an example of regional planning of a river basin completely within a country but covering several states. An international example is the St. Lawrence Seaway, of great benefit to Canada and the United States. A wide variety of types of regional planning groups are in operation and many of them have specific planning responsibilities to perform while others have comprehensive planning assignments. The importance of regional planning should increase, particularly if local government continues to resist or thwart alternatives to comprehensive problem-solving available in city-county governmental consolidation, metropolitan government, or councils of governments. Regional planning may be necessitated by federal legislation as an exigency and could even result in regional government as the last-ditch method (short of loss of a republican form of government) to solve problems covering extensive urban areas.

COMBINATIONS   One of the blind spots of those in positions of responsibility in planning, including some planners, is the absence of knowledge of the advantages to be gained by planning urban functions and works in combinations of related facilities or services. One-at-a-time way of planning and building, in total disregard of a similar facility alongside or across the street, both of which built together would cost little more than

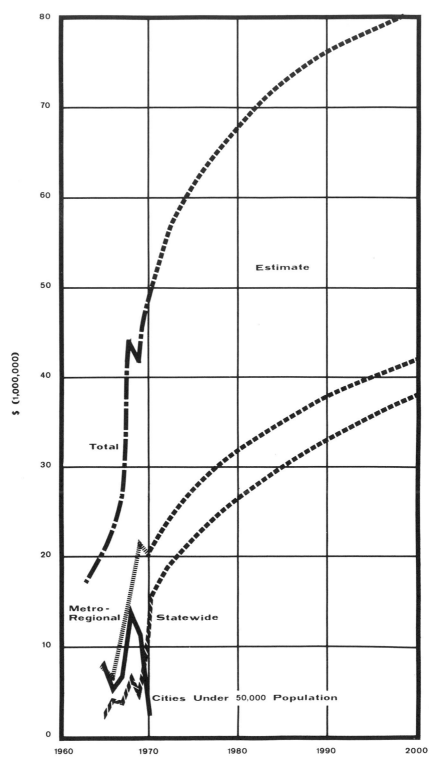

Figure 2-2 Planning funds to state and local governments 1960 to 2000.

half the cost of both, is a myopia, lack of cooperation, or stubborness that is too costly to tolerate longer. This could be the most important contribution a planner could make to planning, that is, to plan with more togetherness or comprehensiveness to realize the savings that combinations of uses or operations of facilities can produce. Regional as well as metropolitan planning help show the way to these combinations and savings by getting the whole picture of where programs can be interrelated and support each other. Yet, some regional planning organizations are single purpose or at least noncomprehensive and may concern themselves with a too limited list of goals. Nevertheless, examples of these combination economies are evident in many locations—Eisenhower Expressway in Chicago with mass rapid transit in a freeway right-of-way; cooperation between school boards and park departments in joint location and operation of their respective facilities resulting in savings in, not only first cost of land for schools and parks but operational budgets for maintenance of them; utilities in specially designed cells in urban highway bridges in Los Angeles; and many other examples.

These should lead toward other ideas or combinations that conserve resources and energies, such as freeway rights-of-way with underground high tension electrical distribution and power supply lines, instead of completely separate systems; more multi-use of land for related functions (living, shopping, recreation, working); greater flexibility in public-private combinations, such as electric sidewalks or ordinary public pedestrian routes through private structures on an easement arrangement. The potentials are virtually limitless. The chapters ahead point toward some of the possibilities.

Federal Government and Programs

Cities and counties under more and more dire financial pressure taxwise look to their state for relief and, little or no help available from that source, they have only the federal government to turn to [see Figure 2-3].

The assessed value of property subject to local general property taxation in 1966 was $498,962,000,000,[4] virtually one-half trillion dollars. As large as this is, local demands are not met for a simple political reason; the local politician who raises taxes is usually voted out of office when his term expires. The tax burden then shifts to the next higher government, state or federal, as the case may be. Revenue sharing legislation recently passed may alter this condition and should be closely watched by the planner.

Promises of politicians to get funds for this or that project into the community or state, if elected, and demand of the people for services started the proliferation of federal programs. This eventually, over a period of decades, built up an enormous bureaucracy in Washington. To reduce this to manageable size, a decentralization program, still in progress, is bringing the programs closer to the people. These programs are not intended as created solely by the politician, since many of them came about to meet pressing needs.

The planner, with little or no control over these political machinations, notwithstanding, has much to gain from being aware of them and their trends as they affect his

4. *1969 Statistical Abstract of the United States*, p. 427.

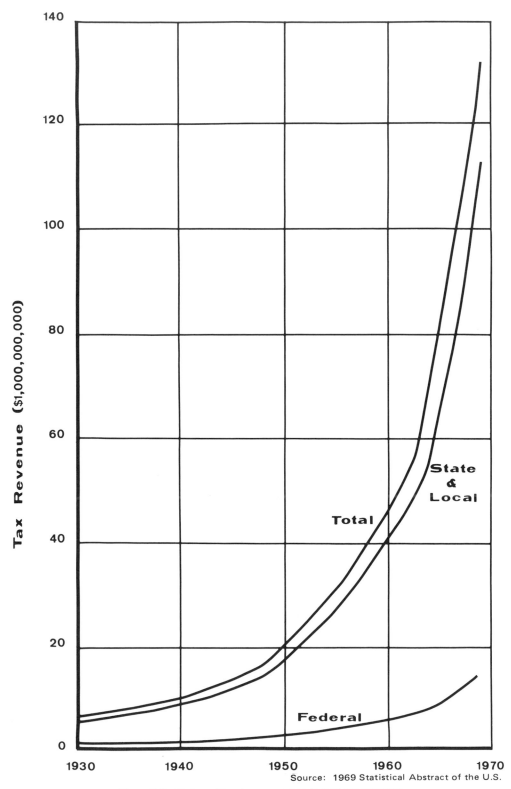

Figure 2-3 State and local compared to federal tax revenues.

objectives. Socioeconomic structures and their trends are another source of support for his endeavors.

PLANNING AND SOCIOECONOMIC STRUCTURES

Planners sensitive to the needs and desires of those for whom they plan would do well to investigate and analyze the social and economic structure of the community, as mentioned in the previous chapter. A more appropriate term is "socioeconomic," since few groups are purely social or purely economic, and this term will predominate.

This is usually the place where the planner finds the power structure, the power or powers behind the politicians, where decisions are made, where budgets are supported or not, where direction is determined for this or that program or project.

Socioeconomic structures should be studied or analyzed on a neighborhood basis, citywide, statewide, and nationally to be thoroughly appreciated and encouraged to help planning and orderly development.

Neighborhood Organizations

The neighborhood is the smallest complete geographical planning element the planner uses in formulating a general plan and it may be too small to generate the attention of most socioeconomic groups, most of which operate more effectively on a community-wide basis or even statewide. Groups interested in the neighborhood may include officialdom from a water, sanitary, or school district, an improvement district (set up for streetlights or sidewalks for example), a police precinct, or a fire district, for a variety of examples. They each have their spheres of responsibility and influence, usually single purpose. Private groups may have a broader outlook. The local PTA, the religious leader, a Homes Association (see Chapter 4), a PAC (Project Area Committee, described in Chapter 11), the union local, or a protective association are some of the multipurpose private groups that can "read" a neighborhood for a planner. The list is much longer and the key is to learn which have the more accurate information about the neighborhood. Often a visiting nurse, social worker, school principal, code enforcer, parole officer, or legal aid association attorney in poverty areas have more dependable information about the neighborhood and its people than most anyone else.

The neighborhood in the context here is an elementary school district of a quarter section of land more or less in a metropolis to a square mile or more in a small town (see Chapter 4). Two or more neighborhoods comprise a community and, in turn, two or more communities make up the city. The community or the city as a whole is the eventual entity that the planner should check out in putting together a list of objectives for the general plan of the city.

Community and City Groups

Both community (usually a high school district) and city groups are treated together here for brevity, but each has something for the planner to consider in his organization of land uses and areas and facts about them.

The city (or county) is a basic unit of political party organization, as well as affording many other elements of the socioeconomic structure, such as the chamber of commerce and other business groups, civic, social, religious, and professional societies, union chapters, service clubs, and many more. Somewhere in this maze are the string holders, the power structure, and this is not necessarily meant detrimentally. Often they are successful and wise leaders with much to gain from enlightened progress and a lot to lose without it. Sometimes they are selfish, introverted, fearful of change, and prejudiced. No two are alike and each has a part on the planning stage. They and the groups that represent segments of the population and the people as a whole should be sought after for opinions about and support of sound planning.

One quasi-public entity of fairly recent (past few decades) vintage is the Citizens Planning Advisory Committee, sometimes an ad hoc committee called together during the plan formulation period and more often a permanent planning support group. These citizen committees in larger cities relieve the overburdened planning commissioners of time-consuming community pulse reading and planning information dissemination. This kind of group can be useful in enlisting the support of otherwise recalcitrant persons in the power structure by appointing them or their representatives to the committee.

The metropolitan or state plan involves a different set of organizations for the planner to seek out and know.

State Groups

Many of the groups mentioned above have their state or regional counterparts that may offer support or data resources to the planner. The local chamber of commerce has a state chamber, the local Rotary Club has a state or regional headquarters, the Urban League has its regional counterpart, and so on. Valuable information is often found in the state municipal league, state bar association, or the state taxpayer alliance.

The political power structure is stronger at the state level than county or city one and decisions are often made at the state level by the political party in power on matters of policy or funds of far-reaching effect on the planner and planning. Professionalism is a must for the planner and his getting engulfed in politics is not intended nor intimated. However, a knowledge of the local and state political picture can help avoid misunderstandings, loss of support, and bad legislative bills. A good rapport with realistic politicians should generate respect by the politician for the planner's views and objectives and open more opportunities for each to see the others' problems and ideas for solving them.

There are many private groups, some without organization and others organized on a county, state, or national basis for the protection of minority groups and minority rights or to help in poverty situations in a variety of ways. Some of these groups are militant, some prone to violence, some action-oriented in a positive sense, and some quietly and effectively caring for the less fortunate where public welfare has missed them for one reason or another. They are part of a new power structure in the fields of community relations, action programs of several types, and person-to-person assistance. These generalizations about them are necessary in considering the whole of the United States, Canada, and other American countries; however, they are a factor to deal with in planning.

Naming some of them would be helpful in too few places and meaningless elsewhere. They may be imperceptibly organized or not at all. They can spell havoc or help in trying to get things done in a community or state, depending on the pace of improvement of the conditions to be corrected, how the general attitude is about these matters, and what the leaders, including planners, say publicly and do about these things.

National Groups

Literally thousands of nationwide groups have a hand in how urban development is planned or achieved and to sort them out in order of importance or influence, for lack of more space, may be accomplished by considering several of the more potent organizations. They are related to business, higher education, labor, politics, the press, professions, and religious organizations (in alphabetical order deliberatley).

Skipping over the extreme right and left groups with their fears, agitation, and concern manifested in violence, vituperation, marches, sit-ins, and other demonstrations and getting to the meatier sources of city-shapers, there are still quite the same set of motives mentioned in the previous chapter as the cause of development of the New World in the first place—adventure, opportunity, profit, security, freedom, respect, pleasure, dignity, recognition, and others. Frank Lloyd Wright in one of his unique oversimplifications pronounced cities as places for women to find men, and Carl Sandburg with all his gloriously delicious poetry on cities often refers to money as their main impetus. Sex and money—what else is there, some ask! Safety and quiet, others reply, and the proof is in the statistics of large urban areas that have lost population. This too is an oversimplification but the object is to pinpoit some motivations that form cities as they are.

BUSINESS   Dozens of dedicated groups deserve mention here as city builders directly or indirectly—the U.S. Chamber of Commerce, National Association of Real Estate Boards, the National Association of Home Builders, American Bankers Association, National Association of Manufacturers, and the Urban Land Institute. There are many more but those mentioned, as well as some not, are worth looking into for gradual policy shifts in recent years concerned more with quality than quantity. This is not to say profit is less a motive; on the contrary, it may be more so since it is harder to come by. When profit shrinks so does interest.

Real estate is singled out for a little more analysis than other business operations because of its impact on cities. The landholder who withholds his vacant property on the periphery of a city as the city builds up around him is in a position to realize enormous profit when he finally sells. The irony is, more often than not, that the less desirable the use for which the land is sold, the higher the profit. This ruthless game is played with expert promotional tactics, skillful avoidance of the controls of the land, if any, and unconcern for the public welfare. This is a large contributor to incongruity, blight, and disorder in a city and it can be mitigated by sound planning and straightforward plan implementation.

HIGHER EDUCATION   The hallowed halls of higher learning are chafing at the morphoses of giant proportions and through it all still contribute to the shape of urban things to come. These contributions come in several ways—through graduates, research, seminars, data, computer services, and consultation.

Both undergraduate and graduate curricula as well as continuing educational work are important to prepare the student for the world of urban realities. The key is the instructor, his experience and knowledge of his subject, his selection of the principal points to cover in the precious little time he has on his subject, and his ability to impart these points in a meaningful and inspiring manner. There are only a half-dozen or so undergraduate planning curricula in the United States and four dozen, more or less, graduate planning degrees. More are needed and coming along too slowly for the workload ahead in planning.

These remarks on higher education are not confined to planning, per se, but to the other disciplines at work on urban problems as well. Research in universities and colleges on urban planning, design, and economics is burgeoning in the fields of sociology, geriatrics, genetics, pollution control, housing, building construction, and a host of other support endeavors.

The proliferation of college seminars is making a large and often effective effort in dissemination of urban information, problems, techniques, and solutions. One resource improving these seminars is the accumulation of valuable data on cities that many universities are systematically collecting, codifying, and converting into easily retrievable form. Electrodata processing is of growing importance in this data work, and cities without their own computer services look to universities and elsewhere for this expertise.

Consulting by faculty members is a university service considered with varying points of view. Such services permit a faculty member to experience the realism of the rough and tumble world of city councils and planning commissions with potentially more experience to teach his subjects. Yet some complain this competes with private consulting firms unfairly and diverts time from teaching. Some consulting work by college professors has been useless theory while real, meaningful contributions have been made by others. This is a matter of experience, availability of or obtaining the right kinds of information and the knowledge of what to do with it. Accreditation of the school and the background of the faculty members to be selected is a worthwhile check to make in advance, if they are retained for consultation.

LABOR   The AFL-CIO with over 20 million members in the United States and more than 1.25 million in Canada is a powerful force in politics and can be for the urban environment. For example, the AFL-CIO set aside over a decade ago 6 of their 46 billion dollars of accumulated member dues for housing purposes, resulting in thousands of retirement homes in standard neighborhoods for their retirees and others. Labor union funds are the most active single source of nonprofit support for low- and moderate-income and elderly housing.

The labor part of the power structure should be encouraged and urged to increase its force and influence behind such policies as slum clearance, standard housing, pollution control, and the like, and sound planning to bring these goals into reality. Most labor members and leaders are solidly behind these programs and have been for years, with some of them instigated by unions. Straightening out these kinks in the lifeline of troubled cities could be of greater benefit to the average union member than a ten percent raise. Values and priorities need reassessment here as elsewhere.

POLITICS   The saying that the United States must be a country of great strength of character to have survived nearly two centuries of American politics still applies, but to a lesser extent with legal restraints put into action. The temptation to get into political office by promising voters handouts and the character required to raise taxes for needed services or facilities are dilemmas that the politician faces. The election of a President of one political party and a majority of the Congress in another party is a stalemate situation for many a good program or project. The authorization of a popular bill to gain votes at home and then purposely avoiding appropriating funds for it to avoid higher taxes and consequent loss of votes is another problem in national politics. The term of office of two years for a Representative in the Congress should be increased to four and the six-year one-term presidential idea may have equal merit, so that time spent stumping for reelection is reduced and sound operation of the government increased. (Some voters believe that the less time legislators have to pass bills, the better off the country will be—and this may not be entirely facetious.) Waste, inefficiency, extravagance, and favoritism result from these problems and indirectly plague urban areas.

The major political parties recognize the plight of cities and solutions are forming. The marshaling of all the forces, public and private, to attack urban problems is a political responsibility that should originate at the national level. This is in progress and demands massive amounts of money, management skills, and dedicated leadership.

THE PRESS   The mass media of communication (newspapers, newsmagazines, radio, and television) are unique in the socioeconomic structure, with their huge power to harm or help the urban situation. A subject is more readily printed if it is controversial. The written and spoken word have such impacts on votes, public decisions, projects, and programs that the responsibility in writing or speaking about them is awesome. This applies to the editor, reporter, commentator, and the public official, including the planner who issues a written press release or speaks publicly. Each has a certain knowledge of various urban subjects and is often called upon to expound on one he knows little about. With the complicated nature of city problems, the public can easily be confused to the point of frustration and lack of confidence by the wrong words. The planner should learn how to prepare an effective press release and to use the mass media positively. A reading must for the mass media and public officials should be the semantic classic of S. I. Hayakawa, *Language in Thought and Action*.[5]

PROFESSIONS   There are so many that only a few national professional societies closely related to planning can be touched on here. The largest in membership is the American Society of Planning Officials (ASPO) and one of the best in scattering useful planning information across the United States, Canada, and many other American countries. The Urban Planning and Development Division (with 8,200 members in 1970)

5. New York: Harcourt Brace Jovanovich, 2d ed., 1964.

of the American Society of Civil Engineers has been a champion of good planning since 1925. The American Institute of Planners, with nearly 7,000 members as of 1970, is the professional organization that should lead the way toward sound planning for the country and its cities. The American Institute of Architects has a community design function operating effectively and the National Association of Housing and Redevelopment Officials is a professional leader in the fields of planning, housing, and urban renewal (see Chapter 11). The American Municipal League is the parent body of similar state organizations fostering good municipal government. The policies and efforts of these organizations originate from some of the best minds in their respective professions and are valuable sources of reliable information for all who are interested in orderly urban development through sound planning.

RELIGIOUS ORGANIZATIONS   These are second only to labor unions as nonprofit sponsors of low- and moderate-income housing in the United States and this is representative of the many contributions they make toward a better life for all.

Appraising the socioeconomic role of religious organizations as they relate to the urban environment should include the effects of religion on human behavior. To ignore these influences as an unscientific approach to urban problems may be running the risk of missing the most important solution to them. The communist charge that the church is the opiate of capitalism was directed at a corrupt church at a certain point in time in a certain locality. On the contrary, religion in Canada, the United States, and other American nations is largely responsible for the keen sense of justice, tolerance, and the importance of personal dignity there. This deep and widespread concern for individual rights founded on religious beliefs may be the only route to take to eventually solve such tough problems as racial prejudice, slum elimination, more equitable educational advantages, and a standard home for every family. Churches champion these causes and even though some of the younger generation have strayed from organized religion, there is plenty of evidence that the seeds of truth are at work in their lives, a meaningful factor in solving urban and other problems.

The separation of church and state is necessary for freedom of religion, and the planner has a responsibility to keep the two separate in his work. However, his awareness of the role of religion in the socioeconomic structure may result in meaningful support of his plan.

PULLING IN THE SAME DIRECTION

There are many of the organizations mentioned in this chapter with the same basic goals for urban development and too often this advantage for a more united front to get a program under way is overlooked. The leaders of a community, the planner included, should check out these support groups and appeal to them for a statement at a public hearing or through a press release in favor of a project, for example, which the community may be uncertain about or split on. Surprising how often such support is overlooked. Those in charge of the group would normally respond if asked (unless they were afflicted with an internal split themselves) and normally would not respond if not asked.

At the national and state levels such support is continually urged to appear in favor or not, as the case may be, for this bill or program or that one, but here too, some of the support is overlooked.

There is no question but that many issues are determined in advance by the power structure, by favoritism in payment of a political debt, by trade-off (one politician or group of them supporting another in exchange for support of their issue), by avoiding a tax increase, by personal animosity, or by a number of other reasons not necessarily in the commonweal. Often these issues are marginally determined and, when the margin is sufficiently narrow, the right support at the right time could save the issue. Politicians want their records free of voting against motherhood or applie pie.

There may seem to be a thread of dissatisfaction with politicians running through this fabric of rhetoric but this should certainly not pertain to the many fine ones dedicating their time and energy in a selfless manner to their fellowman. These consecrated leaders are the great hope in urban problem-solving and the fulcrum about which the leverage of support pulling in the same direction rotates to the ultimate benefit of all.

3 BASIC DATA— SOURCES AND UTILIZATION

Russell H. Riley

A comprehensive plan includes so many important proposals and recommendations affecting the welfare and living conditions of all local citizens, that it must be based upon adequate, sound facts and data. The several phases or elements of the plan discussed in the following chapters emphasize the factors that must be considered in deciding upon the various recommendations. Several of these chapters, especially 4 to 8 inclusive, discuss the type or source of data needed for their particular analysis, as well as how they should be used. This chapter is concerned with types and sources of data of a general nature needed for other phases of the plan and, in several instances, will supplement the data discussed in the above-mentioned chapters.

The three major needs for basic data in preparing a comprehensive plan are (a) to indicate past trends, (b) to accurately determine and portray existing conditions, and (c) to prepare sound estimates of future needs. An analysis of past trends is especially essential in population and land use studies, but is also important in most phases such as housing, traffic and transportation, and community facilities. The following sections discuss the type of data needed, where normally available or how it might be compiled, and possible utilization.

The basic data discussed in this chapter is the information that should be used in preparing the comprehensive plan. Other types of data will be utilized in presenting the plan to the officials and citizens. The latter will normally include maps, charts, and statistical tables and their exact form can best be determined after the details of the plan have been decided upon.

BASE MAPS

The comprehensive plan should be presented in both graphical and verbal form. Since it primarily deals with the physical elements and facilities of the community, the type, location, and extent of such facilities, both existing and proposed, should be shown graphically. A verbal description would explain the conditions and proposals, including current defects and needs, as well as describing possible alternatives. Accurate base maps of the community and nearby areas are essential for graphical presentations.

Source

Most urban communities, especially the older and larger ones, have base maps that would be adequate for planning programs. In fact, in large communities, several of the administrative departments or agencies have base maps meeting their particular requirements. Among these would be the Engineering and Public Works Department, utilities (if operated by the city), the tax assessor, and Housing or Redevelopment Authority. The Planning Office should have copies of all available base maps or at least be familiar with the type and source of any that are available. Normally, the Planning Commission would also prepare additional base maps for its particular requirements.

In contrast, many smaller communities, especially in rural areas, have inadequate base maps and new ones must be developed for a comprehensive planning program. Among the several sources that should be checked to obtain information for new base maps are (a) county recorder, (b) county or township tax assessor, (c) county engineer or Highway Department, and (d) local public utilities, especially water, electric, and telephone companies. The Agricultural Stabilization and Conservation Service of the U.S. Department of Agriculture maintains aerial photographs of the states, except Alaska, which are reproduced at scales ranging from 1 inch to 330 feet to 1 inch to 1,667 feet. These are especially useful for county planning programs, but are also valuable for individual communities. To order such prints, the Department of Agriculture should be contacted to obtain the name and address of the photographic laboratory handling the distribution of the photography in the desired area.[1]

An alternate source of information for new base maps is to have private companies make aerial photographs of the subject area. If requested, such companies will also prepare the base maps to any desired scale. Such maps have a high degree of accuracy, but are much more expensive than those obtained from the Department of Agriculture. The companies will prepare these maps showing street rights-of-way and, at a higher cost, will also show lot lines, although the latter are not usually prepared. Neither rights-of-way nor

1. Attention: Coordinator, Photographic Work of the Department, U.S. Dept. of Agriculture, ASCS, Washington, D.C. 20250.

lot lines are shown upon the aerials prepared by the Department of Agriculture and will have to be developed locally.

The *Sandborn Insurance Atlas* contains useful information for the preparation of base maps. It contains maps showing streets, lot lines, and location and outline of buildings, including number of stories and type of construction. The data regarding buildings is also useful in preparing maps for checking of land uses in the field. They are also helpful in developing studies for housing and urban renewal projects as well as for street openings and improvements. Except in small, rural communities, a copy of the local atlas can usually be found in an insurance office. Otherwise, contact should be made with the Sandborn Map Company, Pelham, New York 10803.

Scale

A desirable scale for base maps will depend primarily upon the size of the area to be included and the uses to be made of the map. Normally, such maps should include the area extending beyond the corporate limits for a distance of approximately one-quarter mile. Further, a regional map should be available showing the relationship of the community to its surrounding areas for a distance of three to five miles. This regional map will be to a smaller scale and need show only dominant facilities, such as major streets and highways, railroads, lakes and rivers, and large public and semipublic areas—i.e., parks, universities, and airports.

For general planning purposes, the base map should be to a scale of not less than 1 inch to 600 feet in communities containing a population of 30,000 or less. They should show all street rights-of-way and lot lines with a separate delineation—usually stippling—for large permanent public and semipublic areas such as parks, cemeteries, and colleges or universities. Land use indications can be shown upon such maps. In smaller cities, the base map is usually prepared to scales of from 1 inch equals 100 feet to 1 inch equals 400 feet. In larger communities, the base map may be at a scale of 1 inch to 1,000 or 2,000 feet, or may be prepared in sections at a larger scale. These maps are frequently prepared so that a single line represents a street, rather than attempting to show the full right-of-way with two separate lines. Further, lot lines are not shown on such maps, and sectional base maps of a scale of not more than 1 inch to 400 feet will be needed for the lot lines. For detailed studies and plans of specific areas such as street intersections, parks, or other site improvements, enlarged maps to a scale of not less than 1 inch to 20 feet will be required. Base maps should be drawn—preferably with ink—upon a durable transparent material, usually linen, vellum, mylar, or acetate, so that full-size reproductions can be obtained therefrom. Some types of maps are also now being drafted by electronic computers, but this is seldom practical for community base maps.

STATISTICAL DATA

A large amount of statistical information should be compiled in the preparation of a sound comprehensive plan. Data regarding population, employment, housing conditions, traffic movements, school enrollments and similar conditions are especially essential. The following discussion indicates the more important sources for much of the needed information.

Population

A major objective of the comprehensive plan is the provision of adequate and convenient physical facilities, as well as improved living conditions, for existing and future citizens within the community. Since the plan is developed for the citizens, much information is needed regarding the population. Among the more important types of information needed are (a) amount and location of population, (b) age, (c) race, (d) sex, (e) marital status, (f) size of household, and (g) annual income.

Source

The most useful and comprehensive data regarding population is published by the Bureau of the Census,[2] which contains the data compiled in the census counts taken by the Bureau every ten years. The latest count was taken in 1970, and the first in 1790. The publications are available for each state and contain data for all political units within the state.

The census data regarding the amount of population during each of the past four or five census counts is a useful basis for estimating probable future growth. This information is usually shown in graphical form [Figure 3-1], but is also presented in tabular form. In addition to the amount of population for each decade, the tables usually show the numerical and percentage of increase or loss for each decade.

Amount

In estimating probable amount of future population, consideration must be given to several factors other than past growth. Among the other important factors that should be considered are (a) availability of vacant land that is adaptable for residential development, (b) possibility of encouraging a higher density of residential development, especially multiple dwellings, (c) opportunities for local increases in gainful employment, and (d) general characteristics of the community from the standpoint of desirable living conditions. Except in resort and retirement communities, opportunities for gainful employment are a major influence in encouraging future growth, but this need not be a dominant factor in suburban communities within a large urban region. Analysis of employment opportunities is discussed in Chapter 5. Further, in preparing estimates of future growth, consideration should be given to growth trends within the surrounding region and the entire country, as well as to those within the individual community.

In addition to the census data, there are usually other local sources for information regarding the amount of existing population. The public utilitiy companies—electric,

---

2. *U.S. Census of Population—General Population Characteristics,* Government Printing Office, Washington, D.C. 20402.

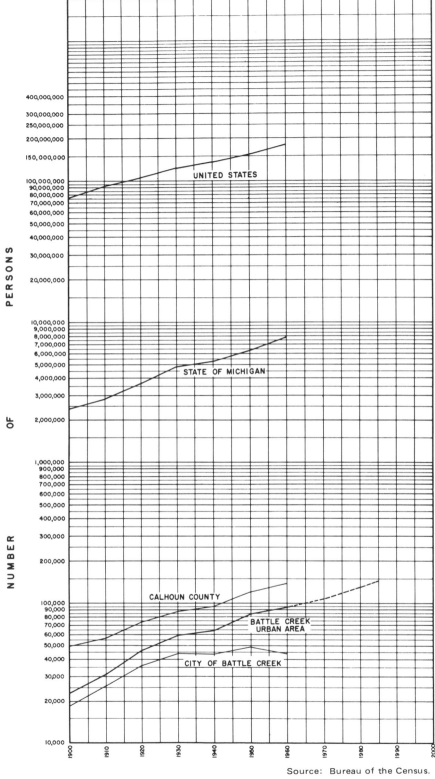

Source: Bureau of the Census.

Figure 3-1 Population growth—Battle Creek, Michigan.

telephone, gas and water—are among the more important. In many communities, the public school district makes annual counts of all families to determine the number of children that will enroll in the public school system during the next school year. The land use map, which graphically shows the use of all property (see Chapter 9), is another means of determining the amount of existing population, especially during years when the national census is not taken. Some cities, especially rapidly growing communities, finance the cost of making a special census of population. This is especially true in states where state refunds, such as gasoline tax, are related to population of cities and counties.

Age

Trends in the age groups of local population must be carefully considered in the preparation of the comprehensive plan. It is widely recognized that the number of older citizens is increasing substantially, and there has been some decrease in the birth rate during recent years, especially compared to the rapid rate that was experienced after World War II. The facilities proposed in the plan should be related to the several major age groups. For example, the number of rooms in public schools should be related to the probable number of children in age groups five to nineteen years, and different types of facilities, such as housing, passive recreation and community buildings for persons over sixty-five years of age. A graphic method of indicating past trends in age groups [Figure 3-2] is helpful as a basis for estimating the probable future number in each group.

Distribution

Data regarding the location of both existing and probable future population is also needed in the preparation of the comprehensive plan. It is particularly useful in determining the adequacy of existing physical facilities—schools, parks, public buildings and utilities—to the population that needs such service and in determining where such facilities should be located to serve future population. The data can best be shown in graphical form with dots or similar delineations representing units of population [see Figure 3-3].

The U.S. census data is compiled by tracts or census districts and in larger communities by blocks, so that the location of population can be readily determined. However, the most useful aid is a plan showing location and extent of existing land uses by major classifications [see Figure 9-2]. The land use map shows the location of all residential development by type, and when related to the number of persons per family as revealed by the U.S. census, accurate information is available for determining the location of the population. Another major advantage of the land use map is that it provides the most accurate information for periods between census counts. A plan showing the most practical and desirable location of future land use is also a most logical basis for determining the distribution of future population [see Figure 3-4].

Housing

During the past few decades, beginning in 1940, a substantial amount of information regarding housing conditions was compiled when the U.S. Census of Population was

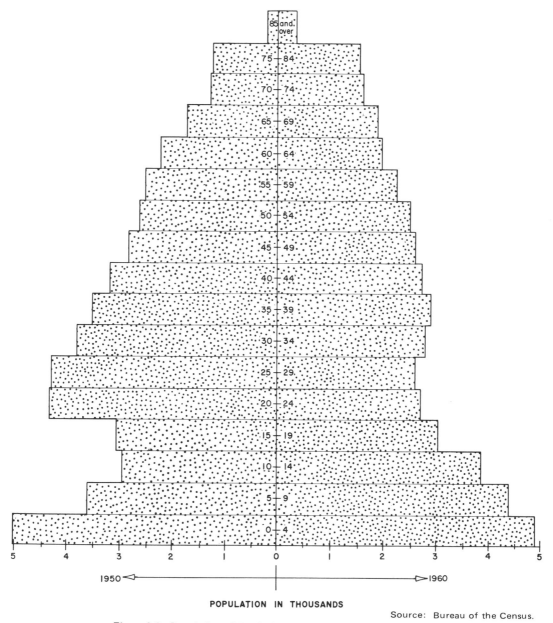

POPULATION IN THOUSANDS

Source: Bureau of the Census.
Figure 3-2 Population of Battle Creek by age groups 1950 and 1960.

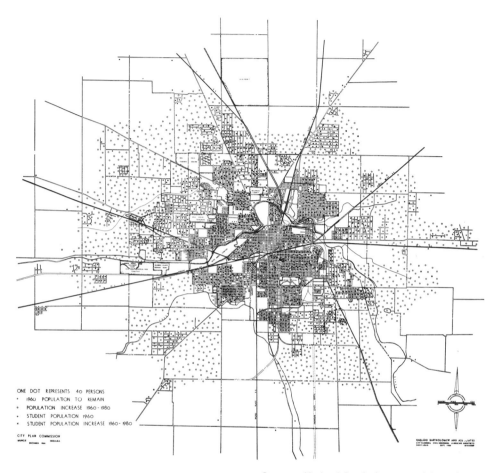

ONE DOT REPRESENTS 40 PERSONS
  •   1960 POPULATION TO REMAIN
  ◦   POPULATION INCREASE 1960 - 1980
  •   STUDENT POPULATION 1960
  •   STUDENT POPULATION INCREASE 1960 - 1980

CITY PLAN COMMISSION
MUNCIE   INDIANA

Source: Harland Bartholomew and Associates.

Figure 3-3 Population distribution—1980, Muncie, Indiana, and environs.

taken. Included was information regarding (a) housing structure, such as type, condition, and sanitary facilities, (b) occupancy, (c) amount of rent and several other factors that are useful in making an analysis of existing housing and in developing a program for improving local housing conditions and providing for future housing needs. This information is published for each state and for the District of Columbia and is available from the Government Printing Office.[3] Another useful source of information regarding housing is

3. *U.S. Census of Housing, States and Small Areas,* Government Printing Office, Washington, D.C. 20402.

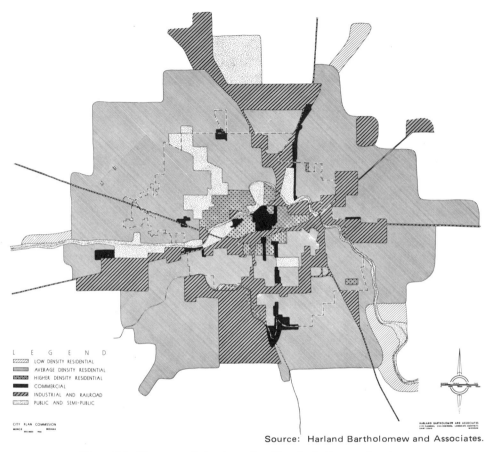

Source: Harland Bartholomew and Associates.

Figure 3-4   Diagrammatic land use plan, Muncie, Indiana, and environs.

the *Statistical Yearbook* prepared by the U.S. Department of Housing and Urban Development, and also available from the Government Printing Office. The first issue was for the year 1966.

Data regarding housing conditions should also be compiled from a field survey of the facilities. A visual inspection of each structure would enable a classification or rating such as good, fair, needing major repair, and dilapidated or substandard. This general inspection normally does not involve a detailed inspection of the interior. An interior inspection is necessary, however, in developing an urban renewal project and is usually made by the Building Department staff. Chapters 4 and 11 contain more detailed discussions of housing data.

It should be noted that in addition to the publications previously referred to, the 1970 census is available on electronic tapes which can be purchased for individual communities.

Economy

Useful information regarding the economy of local political areas is also compiled by the Bureau of the Census. This is the Census of Business and is compiled every five years,[4] with the last publication being for 1968. Separate publications are available for both retail and wholesale outlets, as well as for selected services, and are issued for each state. These contain information regarding the number of establishments by types, receipts, employees, and payrolls. Also the Census of Manufacturing is made every five years, the last being 1967.

Another publication by the Bureau of the Census that is helpful in planning programs in more rural areas is the Census of Agriculture.[5] It contains practically all the important information regarding farming activities, size and type of productive areas, income, and employment. The information is compiled every five years and a separate volume is published for each state.

The Census of Transportation is made every five years also and the latest one was taken in 1967. It should be noted that the Bureau of the Census publishes biannually a summary of various types of statistics for the entire country. This is the *Pocket Data Book*.

Another valuable source of information regarding nonagricultural employment is *Employment and Earnings Statistics for States and Areas, 1939-67*. This is compiled by the U.S. Department of Labor, Bureau of Labor Statistics and is also available from the Government Printing Office. The last publication was issued in 1968 and contains employment data for each state and for the larger cities therein, but not for the smaller or unincorporated communities. The data primarily indicates the number of employees in various work classifications. Another source of information regarding employment are the state employment offices, which normally have branches in all larger communities.

Of special assistance in compiling data regarding retail sales and employment is *Sales Management, the Marketing Magazine*.[6] It also contains data regarding estimated buying power and existing population. It is published bimonthly and thus contains current data. In the many states having a sales tax, data regarding volumes of retail sales within communities and counties can be obtained from the department collecting the tax and is thus quite current.

4. U.S. Bureau of the Census, *Census of Business*, Government Printing Office, Washington, D.C. 20402.

5. Available from the Government Printing Office, Washington, D.C. 20402.

6. Published by Sales Management, Inc., 630 Third Avenue, New York, New York 10017.

A detailed discussion of sources of data regarding the economy of local communities and how estimates can be developed regarding probable future economy is contained in Chapter 5.

Land Use

Accurate information regarding the location and extent of existing land uses according to major types is imperative in any planning program. It should be available both for the incorporated as well as the nearby adjoining area. The latter should extend approximately 1,000 feet beyond the city limits. The preparation and use of the land use map is discussed in the zoning section of Chapter 9.

A plan showing the location and extent of probable future land uses should also be prepared. This should be related to the existing land use pattern, but should also consider the amount of future population, areas that will be needed to accommodate the major types of future land use, and the adaptability of the area for the proposed type of land use. The latter includes topography, possibility of flooding, accessibility to transportation facilities—railroads, waterways, airports, and major highways—and feasibility of providing water, sanitary and storm water sewers, and other essential utilities and services. Data developed for industry and commerce, as discussed in Chapter 5, should be utilized in forecasting the area needed for commerce and industry, and the housing study should assist in determining the amount and type of residential areas.

If a map of existing land uses has been prepared for the study area in earlier years, a very useful plan can be developed to show the changes in type, location, and extent of land use during the intervening period. This would prove quite helpful in preparing the future land use plan.

Traffic

Much information should be available in developing the transportation systems to be proposed in the comprehensive plan. The source and use of such data is thoroughly discussed in Chapters 7 and 8 and need not be duplicated here.

Miscellaneous Types of Data

Several additional types of data are needed for the preparation of a comprehensive plan. The more important types and possible sources are discussed in the following subsections.

TOPOGRAPHY A topographical map should be available for the area in which the planning program is developed. The contour interval will depend upon the character of the topography. In level or gently sloping areas, intervals of 2 feet are desirable and should not be less than 5 feet. In rugged areas, an interval of not more than 10 feet is desirable; but in very rugged areas, intervals of 20 feet are frequently satisfactory.

The most frequently used source for topographical maps is the U.S. Geological Survey of the Department of the Interior.[7] Copies may be ordered directly, or there is normally a local office in each state (usually at the state capitol).

The majority of these maps have contour intervals of 10 feet, but a larger interval is used for steep slopes. They are usually drawn at a small scale, such as 1:62,500, but can be enlarged satisfactorily. In addition to contours, they show streams, lakes, streets, highways, and railroads. They also indicate the location of residences, school buildings, and cemeteries.

Currently, one of the most popular and efficient methods of preparing topographic data is aerial photogrammetry. These records can be obtained at any desired scale and contour interval and normally have a high degree of accuracy. If no satisfactory base maps are available, they can also be prepared by this method. There are several large companies throughout the country specializing in this type of mapping that are interested in submitting cost estimates on a proposed project. Smaller companies are also located in the majority of the larger cities.

Whenever accurate, detailed designs and plans are needed, such as for the improvement of a street intersection, the necessary information regarding existing conditions, including topography and spot grades, should be obtained by a field surveying party.

GEOLOGY   Data regarding soil and subsurface conditions within the subject area should be obtained for use during the planning program. Information regarding drainage characteristics, bearing or supporting qualities, and underlying rock formations are especially important. The first characteristic will influence the storm drainage system, as well as possible use of septic tanks and sewage lagoons for disposal of sewage and location of sanitary landfills for solid waste disposal. The second affects building construction, especially large structures which require firm support for foundations. Underlying rock also affects building construction where excavations for basements are needed and especially affects the construction of underground utilities.

It is also essential to be familiar with the location of minerals and raw materials with an economic value. Included would be ores of different types; coal, clay, sand, gravel, and limestone deposits are more frequently available and may be important in manufacturing processes as well as in the construction industry. In fewer instances, oil and gas may be encountered. Where such natural resources have a substantial economic use and value, they should be protected from normal urban development and construction which would interfere with their economical use.

The U.S. Geological Survey (USGS) has compiled data on geology in the major part of the country and is continually updating its information. Separate geology departments are found in most states and work closely with the USGS. Contact with the State Department should be the first step in attempting to obtain data on the geology in the planning area. Another potential source for information on geology and natural resources are the state universities. Several have Departments of Geography or Geology and may be able to provide much information upon the local planning area.

7. Washington, D.C. 20025.

FLOOD PLAINS   The control of urban development within areas subject to periodic flooding is of growing concern in urban areas, and many zoning ordinances now contain provisions for such control. The initial step is to obtain and chart data regarding the location and extent of the flood plain and the frequency of flooding. The district office of the U.S. Corps of Engineers is one of the best sources of such information. The office of the city engineer and the County Highway Department may also have data regarding height and extent of water during past floods. Sometimes, the memories of longtime residents within the flooded areas can prove helpful. Some of the larger planning commissions have undertaken comprehensive studies of flood plains. An example is the Northeastern Illinois Regional Planning Commission serving the Chicago Metropolitan Area.

WATER SUPPLY   An adequate source of potable water is essential for urban communities and the provision, as well as the protection, of such source is becoming a serious problem, particularly in the more arid sections of the country. The majority of inland communities rely upon deep wells or artificial lakes for their water supply. However, increasing demands are being placed upon underground supplies, and pollution, as well as soil erosion, is adversely affecting streams and lakes.

An integral portion of the planning program should include a thorough analysis of probable future water needs and possible sources of supply. The records of the local water department or company will indicate past trends and can be related to estimates of future population growth and especially to the needs of industries. County or state agencies may prove helpful in suggesting potential sources of water supply, and, frequently, experienced engineering firms are engaged to prepare reports and plans for a future supply of water.

The treatment of sewage is an equally pressing problem in many urban communities. While important in past years, it is rapidly becoming critical because of new standards and requirements recently established by federal and state agencies to prevent water pollution. Chapter 6 contains detailed discussion of these two important problems.

OTHER PUBLIC AND SEMIPUBLIC SOURCES   In addition to the sources discussed above, there are several other agencies and organizations that have compiled data that would be useful in developing the comprehensive plan. These should especially be available in larger urban areas.

The local chamber of commerce should have much information regarding community needs and problems. It is especially concerned with the attraction and expansion of commercial and industrial development, and thus should be conversant with the existing and possible future economy of the area. The chamber is also normally familiar with transportation facilities and problems, as well as with needed physical improvements.

Among the more important municipal, county or state agencies that normally have data useful for a planning program are the Health Department, assessor, city or county clerk, Housing or Renewal Authority, and Fire and Police Departments. The latter two departments can provide information regarding number and location of accidents, and crime and property damage.

Local social and welfare agencies should have knowledge and information regarding social conditions and problems. Much of their time is spent with unemployed or lower-income families and this is the group that experiences major social problems and difficulties.

Several organizations compile and publish data that is helpful in planning programs. These include the American Society of Planning Officials[8] and those professional organizations which all planners should be familiar with, including but not limited to the American Institute of Planners, the American Society of Civil Engineers (especially the Urban Planning and Development Division), the American Institute of Architects, the American Society of Landscape Architects, the Urban Land Institute, and others.

Early in the planning program, interviews should be conducted with the mayor, city manager, and members of the legislative body to obtain local opinions upon the community's needs and problems, as well as upon desirable future goals. The same persons should also be contacted during the program to secure views upon proposals that have been developed.

Finally, the staffs of Planning Commissions that have been established for several years, should have compiled, or be familiar with, much of the data discussed in this chapter. Since most planning legislation provides that the Planning Commission is responsible for the development of a comprehensive plan, it is essential that the planning consultant maintain a close relationship with the planning staff.

RECORDING OF DATA   Much of the data compiled during a planning program will be recorded in graphical form on maps or charts which should be preserved for future use. However, much of the statistical information will be in tabular form or in written notes. Whenever electronic computers are available for use by the Planning Commission staff or the consultant, much of the statistical data should be recorded upon tapes or cards for computer use. This is especially important for data regarding population, land use, and economy. This method affords convenient reference to the information in the future and also facilitates quick comparison of conditions and changes when similar data is compiled.

A new professional society concerned with collection, recording, and processing of urban data was established in 1966. This is the Urban and Regional Data Collection Systems Association. It publishes the proceedings of its annual meetings as well as a bimonthly newsletter.[9]

8. 1313 East Sixtieth Street, Chicago, Illinois 60637.
9. Frank J. Barone (ed.), Battelle Memorial Institute, Columbus, Ohio 43102.

4 | HOUSING IN PLANNING

Wm. H. Claire

Through the whole span of history man has spent much of his time, and it may be safe to say most of his time, creating adequate shelter for himself and his family. The process continued uninterrupted in the New World. Well over a half-million dwelling units were built when the United States was born and since then with many new techniques and improvements the total today exceeds an estimated 70 million housing units. At the same time there are over 5 million in Canada. Oh, that modern planning principles could have guided the siting, arrangement, location, density, and types of those millions of homes! If it seems unfortunate that they were built without the necessary degree of such guidance, what of the next 75 million? This is the opportunity of a lifetime to take advantage of the changes that lie ahead to set straight some of the aggravating paradoxes in housing today.

A significant American Institute of Planners publication[1] states "To provide new housing for our increasing population and replace dilapidated housing, we will need as much new housing by the year 2000 as we occupy now." Where and how we build 75 million housing units in the next three decades, more or less, in Canada and the United States, can spell the difference between utopia and chaos. Sound planning properly implemented can bring the result closer to the former. Since this is the first chapter in this handbook dealing with land planning for a specific land use—housing in this instance—a look at the vast area to be planned in the future may prove helpful.

1. *New Communities,* "Background Paper 2," (Washington, D.C.: American Institute of Planners, Oct. 1968), p. 3.

Land uses in the 50 states of the United States total 2.3 billion acres [Figure 4-1] only 3 percent of which is in urban and transportation use and something less than half of that is estimated to be in residential use. The 3 percent amounts to 69 million acres, an estimated 30 million of which are in residential use, an average of 6 2/3 acres per capita. A large majority of the 30 million acres contains standard housing with decades of useful life remaining, while the remainder is deteriorating and needs remedial action. This is the existing situation or one part of the planning responsibility; the other part involves the new growth and the rate that additional housing adds to the present supply.

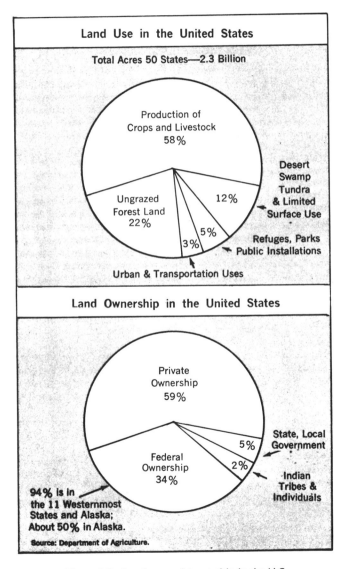

Figure 4-1 Land use and ownership in the U.S.

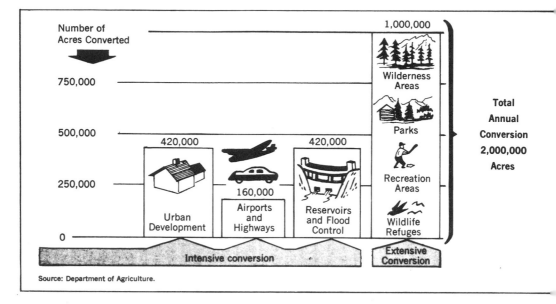

Figure 4-2 Annual conversion of rural land in U.S. to nonagricultural uses.

The rate of urbanization or conversion of rural land to nonagricultural uses in the United States [Figure 4-2] is approximately 2 million acres annually,[2] of which about half is for extensive conversions, such as for parks, recreation areas, and wildlife refuges. The other half is for intensive conversion for reservoirs and flood control, airports and highways, and urban development. The latter accounts for 420,000 acres per year, the area of land that needs the professional attention of the planner, and it will certainly increase through the years ahead.

Formulating a general plan for a community should start with the requirements indicated by an analysis of the economic base, which in turn should be interpreted in terms of the amount, types, and timing of housing in the planning process. The selection of the title for this chapter was deliberately aimed at the concept of the importance of both planning for housing and housing in planning.

Most people spend well over half their lives in their homes, and the home is the largest single investment most families ever make. Housing is an important part of the economy, with expenditures for new housing and alterations of over $30 billion annually in the United States, with an investment in 31.9 million owner-occupied housing of $544 billion as of 1970 and over $2 billion changing hands annually for rent in 22.3 million renter-occupied housing units.[3]

Residential land uses, including residential streets, occupy more land in a large

2. *Environmental Quality,* U.S. Council on Environmental Quality, Washington, D.C., Aug. 1970.

3. *General Housing Characteristics,* 1970 Census of Housing, U.S. Dept. of Commerce, Bureau of the Census, H C (VI)-1, Washington D.C., Feb. 1971.

majority of cities than any other single type, except possibly transportation in some cities, and, consequently, the best sites for housing should be relegated to that use and not for some other, wherever practicable. Some nonresidential land use types, such as for certain kinds of industry, have definite locational requirements and would not function as well or at all elsewhere. This could pose a conflict between those and residential land uses and should be decided, wherever feasible, in favor of housing [see Figure 4-3].

The ingredient that lifts the physical and economic plan for housing above impersonal statistics are the social aspects and more—the spirit of the end product. Does the plan result in housing areas that can be operated efficiently, protected readily, sold or rented easily, and lived in with dignity, joy, and inspiration? All this can be achieved and the planner can make it happen by appropriate planning for housing.

Housing is also an impersonal necessity to some urban dwellers, no more than a place to sleep. There are persons of any age, but mostly the young, who spend most of their time away from their place of residence and who derive no benefit of the spirit mentioned above from their "dormitory" dwelling. These too need recognition in urban housing planning even though they constitute a small minority, except in the largest cities.

Having accumulated all available and pertinent data, as described in the previous chapter, a general idea of land needs should result from analysis of the information. The needs should reveal the number of acres of industrial land in use now and required for the foreseeable future, the same reasoning being used for commercial and residential land.

One of the essential factors in forecasting housing needs is mobility of the popula-

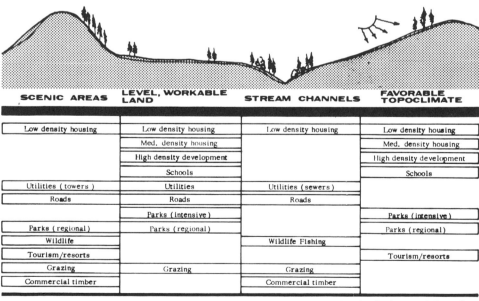

SCENIC AREAS	LEVEL, WORKABLE LAND	STREAM CHANNELS	FAVORABLE TOPOCLIMATE
Low density housing	Low density housing	Low density housing	Low density housing
	Med. density housing		Med. density housing
	High density development		High density development
	Schools		Schools
Utilities (towers)	Utilities	Utilities (sewers)	
Roads	Roads	Roads	
	Parks (intensive)		Parks (intensive)
Parks (regional)	Parks (regional)		Parks (regional)
Wildlife		Wildlife Fishing	
Tourism/resorts			Tourism/resorts
Grazing	Grazing	Grazing	
Commercial timber		Commercial timber	

Source: Charles Gathers and Associates.

Figure 4-3 Examples of site competition.

tion being studied. Trends of immigration or out-migration for a county or state may have a decisive bearing on housing forecasting accuracy. An appreciation of the movement of Americans [Figure 4-4] during the 1960 to 1970 decade should be considered, at least as a given state is affected, in estimating population or housing workloads for the future. Americans change their residence once every four years on the average and this could mean an acceleration of housing demand or deceleration in the years ahead, depending on the mobility and other factors.

As with other land uses, residential requirements are categorized into different types. For housing, the types are usually single family of several lot sizes or price ranges, duplexes and triplexes, and multifamily housing of four units or more. Each community will have its own policies as to how these types of housing are located and in what quantities, and the way to implement these policies is to formulate a list of objectives to guide the planner and anyone else who has a say in such matters, including other public officials, the architect, home builder, developer, housing investor, homeowner, and others.

RESIDENTIAL LAND PLANNING OBJECTIVES

No two cities normally would have the same objectives for housing and yet many of the goals usually found in such lists are common to most communities.

Objectives can be grouped logically into categories as to safety, economics, efficiency, ethnics, and aesthetics. Safety includes protection from man-made or natural dangers or catastrophes. Economics should include financial security for the home, supply of housing types and sizes in keeping with demands of all the people to be housed, and stability of housing investments. Efficiency consists of the facility of getting into and out of housing areas, ease of circulation of local traffic, and logical relationships between home sites, neighborhoods, necessary service facilities, and surrounding areas. Ethnics include preservation and enhancement of all the cultural advantages of each ethnic group and continuation of the better housing characteristics each group is accustomed to, as well as fostering a policy of fairness in housing regardless of race, creed, or national origin. Aesthetics covers the needs of the physical senses for a pleasant view, beauty, quiet, odor-free clean air, and protection from dust, vibration, glare, unsightliness, and the like.

One definite goal in planning for housing that falls into several of the above categories is the logic of locating it so that it stays put and is safe from subsidence. Too many homes built over coal or other mines have too often broken up from subsidence, resulting in too many headaches for all concerned—the owner, the miner, the insurance company, the judge, and others. The waste is not only in damaged houses but also in the loss of natural resources sealed off from further extraction because a simple principle was overlooked, objectives were not available to guide growth, or the objectives were ignored.

Another method of categorizing housing objectives is by type of community. The list of goals varies substantially depending upon whether the community in question is to be developed on vacant land or on that which is already built up. Still another approach is the type of city—single-center or multiple-center, radial or circumferential plan, and with or without satellite communities.

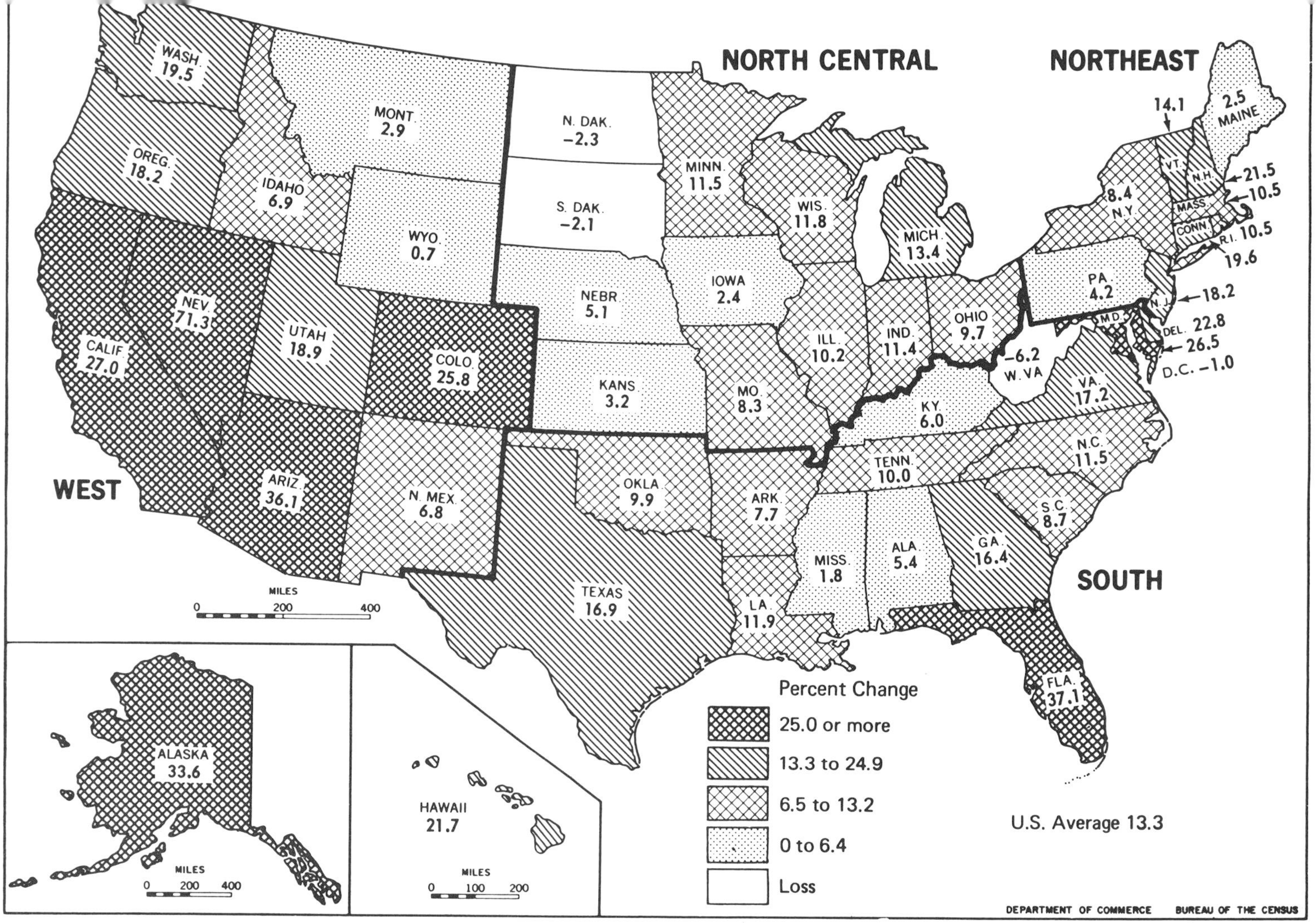

NORTHEAST

MAINE 2.5
VT. 14.1
N.H. 21.5
MASS. 10.5
CONN. 10.5
R.I. 19.6
N.Y. 8.4
PA. 4.2
N.J. –18.2
DEL. 22.8
MD. 26.5
D.C. –1.0

NORTH CENTRAL

MICH. 13.4
OHIO 9.7
W. VA. –6.2
IND. 11.4
KY. 6.0
WIS. 11.8
ILL. 10.2
TENN. 10.0
MINN. 11.5
IOWA 2.4
MO. 8.3
ARK. 7.7
N. DAK. –2.3
S. DAK. –2.1
NEBR. 5.1
KANS. 3.2
OKLA. 9.9
TEXAS 16.9

SOUTH

VA. 17.2
N.C. 11.5
S.C. 8.7
GA. 16.4
ALA. 5.4
MISS. 1.8
LA. 11.9
FLA. 37.1

WEST

MONT. 2.9
WYO. 0.7
COLO. 25.8
N. MEX. 6.8
UTAH 18.9
ARIZ. 36.1
IDAHO 6.9
NEV. 71.3
WASH. 19.5
OREG. 18.2
CALIF. 27.0

HAWAII 21.7
ALASKA 33.6

MILES 0 200 400
MILES 0 100 200
MILES 0 200 400

Percent Change

- 25.0 or more
- 13.3 to 24.9
- 6.5 to 13.2
- 0 to 6.4
- Loss

U.S. Average 13.3

DEPARTMENT OF COMMERCE   BUREAU OF THE CENSUS

Source: Bureau of the Census.

Figure 4-4 Percent change in population, by state: 1960 to 1970.

A unique set of circumstances, as an example of planning objectives, prevails at Shelby Farms adjacent to the east side of Memphis, Tennessee, a city developing on a multiple-center plan. Over 5000 acres was purchased years ago by Shelby County for a penal farm. This use is being phased out and consultants were retained to recommend what to do with the land, virtually vacant, in one ownership and public at that, and adjacent to a burgeoning city of 623,530 persons as of 1970. The detailed list of objectives[4] cover more than just housing but are shown here in their entirety to reveal the complete interrelationships espoused between land uses and especially the handling of residential proposals:

First Priority Goals
1. Implementability   The plan must be practical if it is to become reality.
2. Economic Feasibility   The plan must be one that private and public financial resources can accomplish within a reasonable time.
3. Improvement of the Physical Environment   The planned community should incorporate the best possible concepts in land use, street design, community facilities, and all other physical aspects of a community.
4. Improvement of the Social Environment   This goal recognizes the need for neighborhoods to promote the happiness and well being of their inhabitants as well as to provide efficient and functional surroundings. Monotony should be avoided. The need for privacy as well as the gregarious nature of human beings must be taken into account. A balance between the concept of separation and that of a lively mix of uses, things, and people is sought.
5. Provision of Homes for Low and Moderate Income Families   This is a necessity if total community needs are to be recognized. The private sector has been unable to provide housing for these families.
6. Enrich the Greater Community   Considered under this category were needs for more recreation and other open space lands, needs for more research facilities, more skilled industrial workers, and needs for a broader economic base for the community.
7. Improved Job Opportunities   Shelby Farms is already the site of the State Technical Institute which provides training to improve the job capabilities of area residents. The industrial, research and institutional areas at Shelby Farms should provide employment for a large number of Shelby Farms residents.

Second Priority Goals

1. Maximum Total Economic Return to the Public   Shelby Farms is a very valuable asset of the people of Shelby County and ought to be used in a way that will bring them the maximum dollar return consistent with first priority goals. Such return may include cash from immediate sale of property, appreciation of land value over a period of time, and tax return.
2. Achievement of a Balanced Community Concept   Shelby Farms should have a majority of the facilities needed for the residents of the community, including shopping areas, employment centers, and educational and recreational facilities. Such a balanced community would place a mini-

4. *Shelby Farms,* Harland Bartholomew and Assoc., 1970, p. 3.

mum strain upon existing transportation, employment, and industrial facilities of the Memphis area and provide a desirable living environment for its own residents.

3. Conformity with the Memphis and Shelby County Land Use and Transporation Plan The multiple centers plan adopted for the Memphis area anticipates a major center of commercial, residential, and cultural development in Shelby Farms. The recently completed Memphis Urban Area Transportation Study calls for one additional east-west major street and for three north-south major streets through Shelby Farms.

4. Provision of a Full Range of Housing Types Included in this goal was the concept of embracing many styles, densities, materials, and price ranges of housing.

5. Improvement of the Tax Base Selling the land to private developers would certainly improve the tax base. This option must be weighed against other possibilities such as leasing or retaining the land in public ownership for other reasons that might outweigh the tax benefits. Development of industrial, research, institutional and commercial installations at Shelby Farms was also an objective within this goal.

6. Conservation of Natural Resources The chief natural resource of the Shelby Farms area is the Wolf River and the trees and other vegetation along its floodplain. The rolling topography of the higher ground was also considered a resource to be preserved.

7. Provision of Industrial Opportunities A large sized industrial tract in single ownership within a major metropolitan area is a significant resource which may attract industries to the area that would not otherwise be attracted.

8. Provision of Cultural and Educational Opportunities Another institution of higher learning for the Memphis area is a distinct possibility. Research facilities of various kinds are also needed and would be a valuable asset to the new town.

9. Improve the Greater Region This is related to community deficiencies but with the emphasis shifted to facilities that would serve the Mississippi-Arkansas-Tennessee region and not just the people of Memphis and Shelby County.

10. Maximize Public Benefit from Land Value Appreciation Realization of this goal implies continued public ownership for whatever time is necessary for "maximum" appreciation to take place. This process, though not as easy and possibly not as acceptable politically as simply selling the entire tract as soon as the plan is completed, might in the long run be the most economically beneficial to the people of Shelby County.

11. Maximize Aesthetic Quality Human well being requires an environment that is pleasing to the sight as well as economical and functional. An adequate approach to aesthetics requires that it be considered as an integral part of the planning of a new community from the beginning and not something to be added in cosmetic fashion at the end of the development process.

Third Priority Goals

1. A Model for the Nation Many planners and other urban specialists believe that the development of new towns is one method by which some of the urgent problems of cities may be solved. Shelby Farms is unique among new towns in that it is publicly owned and can be developed by

public agencies. This, together with Memphis' recent designation as a prototype city for Operation Breakthrough, means that a national spotlight will be on Memphis. Procedures and policies may be developed and tested at Shelby Farms that will set precedents and serve as examples for many similar developments to come.

2. Development of Innovative Planning Techniques This goal is an expression of the hope that Shelby Farms will also serve as a laboratory for testing of new techniques for dealing with problems of housing, traffic, utilities, community facilities, and public administration.

3. Safer Environment Shelby Farms should have adequate separation between pedestrians and vehicles, a street pattern that directs heavy traffic away from residential areas, and schools and parks arranged to provide the greatest safety to children as they come and go.

4. More Healthful Environment Concern for the quality of life of Shelby Farms' residents requires a healthful as well as efficient environment. Purity of air to breathe and water to drink, recreation opportunities and medical care are just a few of the health matters that should be considered.

5. Improved Public Administration Shelby Farms is scheduled for annexation by the City of Memphis in 1973. The plan developed under county government will be implemented primarily under city government. Thus, Shelby Farms is a laboratory for city-county cooperation and the development of better methods for administering a major metropolitan area.

6. Improved Regulatory Measures Zoning and subdivision regulations, together with housing and building codes, have been the laws upon which the public chiefly depends for carrying out planning decisions. They have not been sufficiently effective. Public ownership at Shelby Farms may provide an opportunity to improve on these traditional codes or to devise new ones.

7. Continuing Planning Demonstrations Complete development of Shelby Farms with full realization of the goals described above will require many years and a continuous program of planning and implementation. It is hoped that Shelby Farms will be a permanent demonstration of the value of advance planning.

This is a fine example of the goals of a new community to be built on vacant land as one of seven subcenters in a metropolitan area. Most planning, however, is concerned with already built-up urban areas and San Jose, California has a comprehensive set of objectives as an example of a city working toward solutions through planning of its problems for the purpose of making it a better place to live.[5] The titles for the goals are shown without the detailed text of each part, as follows:

I. Provide a Total Environment for Maximum Human Development and Dignity.
II. Create a Sense of Identity, Pride and Responsibility in and for San Jose.
III. Preserve and Celebrate San Jose's Multi-National and Ethnic Heritages.
IV. Concentrate on Developing the Full Potential of Our Young People, Through a Wide Variety of Programs, Facilities and Other Incentives.

5. *Goals for San Jose,* San Jose Goals Committee and City of San Jose Planning Department, City Hall, San Jose, California, July 1969, p. 6.

    V. Require the Highest Standards of Quality and Appearance for All Future Development, Both Public and Private.

    VI. Encourage the Attraction, Retention and Expansion of a Sufficient Number and Variety of Industries and Businesses to Provide Jobs for all and a Healthy Tax Base.

    VII. Create and Maintain an Attractive Central Core, and Make It the Cultural, Financial, Commercial and Entertainment Center of the South Bay.

    VIII. Promote A High Level of Culture in San Jose, and Actively Encourage the Highest Artistic Vitality.

    IX. Develop San Jose's Full Potential as a Tourist, Sports and Convention Center.

    X. Require Public and Private Developments of All Types to Conform to a Complete and Periodically Reviewed and Up-Dated General Plan with Realistic, Clearly Defined Priorities.

    XI. Plan and Present a Capital Improvement Program as Contemplated by the City Charter.

    XII. Provide An Interrelated, Balanced Transportation System, Adequate to Meet the Needs of Everyone in the Community.

    XIII. Establish and Maintain a Consistent Housing Policy Providing for: Decent Housing Open to All Persons in the Community at Prices and Rents within Their Means; Vigorous Programs of Inspection, Maintenance and Renewal, with Encouragement of Self-Help and Neighborhood Action; Organized and Adequate Relocation of Persons Displaced by Public Activities; and Maximum Quality and Variety in Housing Types and Patterns.

    XIV. Develop Park and Recreation Facilities to Optimum Standards Based on Local Needs, Preserving as Many Sites of Natural and Historic Significance as Possible.

    XV. Encourage Broad, Continuing Citizen Participation in All Aspects of Government and Community Life.

    XVI. Support Educational Institutions and Actively Develop Closer Coordination Between Them and the City in Providing Quality Education.

    XVII. Insist That All City Personnel Have Qualifications Commensurate with the Position Involved and Have the Highest Integrity.

    XVIII. Provide Public Services and Facilities That Efficiently Meet and Anticipate the Needs of All Segments of the Public Not Adequately Provided for by Private Enterprise.

    XIX. Study All Sources of Income to Provide the Quality of Community Service Sought in These Goals.

    XX. Promote Maximum Cooperation Between Government Jurisdictions, Both County-Wide and Regionally, in Order to Provide Public Facilities and Services Which Are Advantageous and Economic, Through Joint Planning, Reciprocity and Consolidation.

    XXI. Establish a Strong, Permanent Program for (1) Continued Solicitation of Citizen Opinion on Community Goals, (2) Constant Review and Revision of Goals to Reflect Changing Citizen Consensus, (3) Realistic Analysis of Cost, Priority, and Timing, and , Most Important, (4) Implementation of Group Goals.

Noteworthy is the number of the above goals directly or indirectly related to housing. Number XIII is especially worth additional study for its thoroughness, and the detailed text is as follows:

A.   Assure that all persons, regardless of race, color or creed, have equal opportunity to secure housing of their choice, in the neighborhood they desire, within their financial means.

B.   Avoid the creation of ghettos, by establishing a healthy blend of economic levels in housing throughout the community, and avoid the introduction of higher residential densities into existing ghettos where they would tend to perpetuate or aggravate the ghetto problems.

C.   Develop a more complete program for meeting the housing needs of low-income families, using both private initiative and public programs to the fullest extent possible.

D.   Provide that all persons displaced as a result of public action be relocated in decent, safe and sanitary housing, within their ability to pay, and convenient to their needs.

E.   Encourage the development of neighborhoods as social and recreational units, and promote neighborhood organization and involvement in the improving of local services, facilities, transportation and living conditions.

F.   Continue the community-wide attack on existing blight, and the prevention of blight, using a balanced program of all private and public resources available, including code enforcement, neighborhood rehabilitation and redevelopment.

G.   Promote the development of a broader range of housing choice, including the encouragement of better urban design, the fostering of aesthetics, the provision of open space and the use of higher density planned unit development.

H.   Review all ordinances which affect development, subdivisions, zoning, housing, building and the use of structures, to insure that they incorporate the most modern and progressive means of achieving the other objectives stated in this section.

As comprehensive as the above goals are, they often, even in a long listing like this, do not cover every critical point. Geologic considerations is one of these. A place on Earth free of adjustments in its 30-mile thick crust is difficult or perhaps impossible to find. Hundreds of earthquakes occur daily all over the world and fortunately only a relatively few are destructive. The crust of the Earth has been and will be cooling for thousands of years, and in this process portions of it shrink and slip past other portions relieving stresses in the crust one place and building them up in another. These built-up stresses eventually give way and result in earthquakes, or sudden movements of the crust of the earth at the surface or below. The deeper the better usually, since the forces generated are absorbed more so than those that occur at or near the surface. More seismological data is available as more study is given to past earthquakes and especially since more analysis is being made of stresses building up in the crust. This is leading toward more accurate designation of earthquake-prone areas and a better understanding of structural design to resist seismic forces.

Urban planning should be enhanced by a broader knowledge on the part of planners of earthquakes and their frequency and intensity at locations with earthquake history [Figure 4-5]. Other locations, and particularly those with little or no earthquake experience since they were urbanized, may need more careful land planning. A case in point is the area in and north of Memphis in western Tennessee where probably the most intense earthquakes in the history of the United States took place. Fortunately, the time was 1811 and 1812, when population was sparse and several years before Memphis was founded. No serious damage has been caused by earthquakes in the area since, and this could mean adjustments in the crust of the Earth are due again. However, to overplan or overdesign for these possibilities is wasteful, while to underplan or underdesign is risky to life and property. The engineering geologist should have the best answer and should be consulted by the planner wherever a question of earthquake risk prevails.

Tornadoes by the hundreds annually in the United States are another factor affecting development and more the responsibility of the architect and engineer to provide for in building codes, but certainly not to be ignored by the planner in the general plan, zoning ordinance, or subdivision regulations. His study of these natural disasters, particularly in flat areas of the country, should influence his planning accordingly. Excellent records [Figure 4-6] are kept on tornadoes and full use should be made by the planner of protection against them afforded by hilly terrain or other physiographical features.

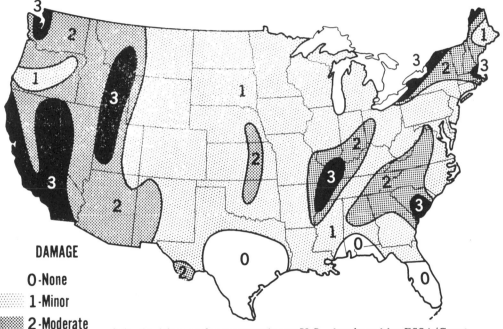

DAMAGE

0 - None

1 - Minor

2 - Moderate

3 - Major

Seismic risk map for conterminous U.S., developed by ESSA/Coast and Geodetic Survey and issued in January 1969. Subject to revision as continuing research warrants, it is an updated edition of the map first published in 1948 and revised in 1951. The map divides the U.S. into four zones: Zone 0, areas with no reasonable expectancy of earthquake damage; Zone 1, expected minor damage; Zone 2, expected moderate damage; and Zone 3, where major destructive earthquakes may occur.

Source: U.S. ESSA, Coast and Geodetic Survey 1969.

Figure 4-5   U.S. seismic risk.

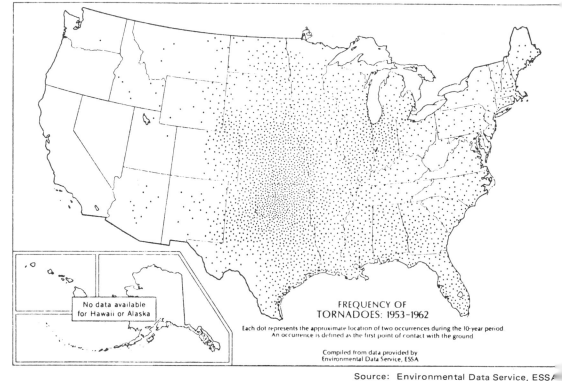

FREQUENCY OF
TORNADOES: 1953-1962

Each dot represents the approximate location of two occurrences during the 10-year period.
An occurrence is defined as the first point of contact with the ground.

Compiled from data provided by
Environmental Data Service, ESSA

No data available
for Hawaii or Alaska

Source: Environmental Data Service, ESSA

Figure 4-6 Frequency of tornadoes: 1953-1962.

Another factor of importance to a list of objectives is the protection of natural resources of benefit to the people as a whole from the location of housing, such that the resources are sealed up or encumbered by housing developments. Examples of this are sand and gravel deposits which have commercial value that too often are built upon with housing or other urban development, thereby locking in the deposits. This may have the unwanted effect of increasing the cost of these vital supplies by necessitating a longer haul from other deposits.

A corollary to this goal is housing built over former locations of natural resources which have already been extracted, such as coal or other minerals, as mentioned above. The risk here is subsidence, and a real one according to court cases in Illinois, Kentucky, and elsewhere where homes have split and sunk from cave-ins of old mines beneath the homes. The geologist or mining engineer may need to be consulted by the planner in such instances.

Natural resources used as described should also implicate the aesthetic qualities of an environment that have a value to humankind—void of the commercial, yet validly precious. More examples of this kind of lack of natural resource protection are extant than should be—streams converted to culverts, hilly areas leveled, views of mountains, rivers, or oceans interrupted, rock outcroppings covered over, woods chopped down, and creeks lined with concrete. How good to have these natural assets in their original condition close to a home!

The developer or his engineer or architect are often the guilty party here with their desire for ease of control of storm water runoff, the nuisance of building in and around trees, and contour control that levels the ground for easier building conditions. However there should be a balance between construction simplicity, maintenance costs, and preservation of natural amenities and resources [see Figure 4-7].

Based on the foregoing, a generic set of planning objectives may be formulated for residential development as follows:

1. Select land for residential use that is geologically safe, is easy to work, drains readily, is free of obnoxious influences, provides an inviting outlook, and is easily accessible.
2. Organize residential land into neighborhoods to provide the community facilities, including utilities, adequate for the population being provided for and necessary for a complete living environment on a logical geographic scale.
3. Relate residential neighborhoods appropriately to adjacent neighborhoods or other land uses.
4. Provide a residential street system that accommodates local neighborhood traffic readily without generating traffic through residential neighborhoods.
5. Supply housing to meet the total demand in keeping with required types, sizes, and ability to buy or rent.
6. Maintain standards of zoning, housing, and subdivision regulations compatible with the community generally.
7. Encourage widespread home ownership and pride in and care of home, neighborhood, and community.
8. Utilize the tools of renewal through code enforcement, rehabilitation, and redevelopment of blighted properties or areas, where necessary.
9. Protect valuable mineral resources from being built upon thereby inhibiting or preventing extraction of the minerals.
10. Preserve natural beauty features to enhance the residential environment.
11. Preserve historic and ethnic housing and other treasures to enrich the lives of present and future generations.
12. Foster ethnic and artistic features in homes and neighborhoods to preserve and extend culture and beauty.

There are many details implied in the wording selected for the twelve goals above. For instance, "obnoxious influences" in the first goal is intended to include unpleasant odors, air pollution, noise and vibration, and other adverse effects. "Community facilities" in the second goal should be considered as covering schools, parks, places of worship, public transit, police and fire protection, utilities (especially water and sanitary sewers), and neighborhood shopping outlets, among other appropriate facilities. In goal 5 "types and sizes" of housing includes private single and multifamily dwellings, as well as public housing or moderate-income units. The point here is that brevity is important but should

Source: Perry Park, Colorado—Charles Gathers and Associates.

Figure 4-7 Environmental considerations in site selections.

not govern understandability by the general public of a given set of goals. A good rule is to start brief and add wording where necessary to reach the comprehension level of a broad cross section of the people who should support the goals.

Some essential desiderata of goals are that they should be (a) comprehensive and complete, (b) formulated by, for, and with the people affected by them, (c) set forth before planning determinations that should be based upon them are made, and (d) changed as subsequent events indicate.

Having formulated a list of goals, given them widespread publicity and review, and having officially adopted them, the next step is to use them in guiding planning decisions. The selection of home sites would be the next step in the residential land planning process.

SITES FOR HOMES

All too often the critical process of choosing home sites is left to chance or, put another way, residual land is used for housing only after other land uses have been accommodated. Industrial and commercial sites have been selected in the past and housing grouped around them on the periphery. This is often the way a town develops and usually for good reason. The industrial sites may have been the only practicable ones to select—on the edge of a body of water, along the railroad, or at the mine or forest. Commercial sites are also important to locate properly and both commercial and industrial land planning and selection of sites are covered in Chapter 5. The essence of sound planning lies in selecting sites for all of these uses without violating or failing to observe the principles governing site selection for each. The essential principles of residential land planning are covered in the housing goals above generally by inference but need more detailed description. First a few definitions are in order at this point.

A neighborhood is the basic planning element in residential land and may be an elementary school district or equivalent in area or population. A site for housing may be a lot for a single family home, a tract of land for several of them, a parcel of land for multifamily housing, a whole neighborhood, or several of these. A community, in this chapter especially, is an urban area composed of two or more residential neighborhoods or the equivalent of a high school district. A small town may be a community by itself in this nomenclature. A city is an urban area of two or more communities and a metropolitan area consists of two or more cities. The region usually includes two or more metropolitan areas but is sometimes used for a single metro area. Finally, a megapolis is two or more regions, usually including several states or provinces, examples of which may be found between Boston and Washington, Milwaukee and South Bend, Ottawa and Quebec, or Santa Barbara and Tijuana. Chapter 12 treats the planning of metropolitan areas and regions.

Basing neighborhoods on the school system should recognize the difference in school systems from city to city and changes that occur in the system within a single city. Some school boards use the 6-3-3 system, that is, the six elementary grades in one school building, the next three grades in a separate junior high school building or plant, and the next three in a senior high layout. There are also 8-4 systems where the first eight elementary grades are together and the four years of high school in another plant.

Returning to principles common to new or built-up areas that should guide selection of residential land uses, they are as follows:

1. Areas should be large enough for at least one residential neighborhood arranged in a manageable shape.
2. Maximum acceptable walking distances should control location and spacing of schools, parks, convenience goods outlets, transit lines, and similar facilities in each community.
3. Densities of housing units should permit adequate ventilation, sunlight, privacy, quietness, and outlook or view.
4. Sites selected should be safe from subsidence, faults, or fracture zones near them, from floods, forest fires, mudslides, snowslides, falling aircraft, or other known natural or man-made dangers.
5. Housing should be built on land easily accessible from and to places of employment, business, and shopping and yet sufficiently separated from them to be spared fumes, ordors, noise, and similar adverse influences.
6. Housing should avoid areas considered unhealthful for reasons of dampness or swamps, insects, reptiles, rodents, or similar pests, or near waste dumps or objectionable manufacturing operations, such as oil refineries and chemical plants.
7. Housing sites should be on the highest safe ground in the community, on land which drains well, may easily be worked for roads, foundations, and utility trenches, and which affords both an inspirational outlook and natural landscaping or other original beauty.
8. A housing policy should be established regarding open tax-supported housing to all regardless of race, creed, or national origin.[6]
9. A relocation program should be established to assist families that need help in finding adequate housing and that are displaced by any governmental action.
10. Housing areas should be selected for ease and efficiency of providing urban services such as fire protection, waste pickup, meter reading, mail delivery, utilities, and other types.
11. Adequate codes should be adopted and enforced to control the safety and continuity of stability of housing investments and should include at least a zoning ordinance, subdivision regulations, a housing code, and a building code that includes provision for new materials and methods of construction as well as conventional ones.

What may seem to be an omission in the above list of principles is a corresponding list of parameters acceptable for walking distances in the second paragraph, for example, or for densities in the third. These are standards, not principles, and should be determined and observed in the planning process. Standards should be flexible to adjust to or

6. See Civil Rights Act of 1968, setting such a policy nationwide for the United States.

conform with local conditions. Principles, however, should be universally applied, and even though the above list may appear to result in an ideal living environment, this must remain the consistent objective of planning and planners. There are so many pitfalls between the ideal and what actually occurs that the planning function should assume an attitude of adhering to the ideal wherever possible to avoid missing the ideal target the least. What are some of these pitfalls?

Answers to a question like this are as numerous as cities but this is an appropriate place in the discussion of planning for residential land to touch on some of the more pertinent answers before the subject is split into new and built-up communities.

Private ownership of property is one of the key answers, at least in the United States. One reason the New World was so eagerly sought and developed was the desire to escape the tyrannical seizure of personal property in Europe up to the eighteenth century. This was one of the fundamental reasons for the American Revolution, the same tyranny having been attempted in the colonies here. Consequently, the ownership of private property has since been a near-sacred matter and persists to this day. This once-noble attitude has been twisted to cover up less-noble arbitrariness, selfishness, and greed. Meanwhile the rugged individualistic use of private property is necessarily being replaced by a more reasonable point of view compatible with the general welfare through zoning and other controls as the population explosion continues.

Diehard holdouts meantime are encouraged to retain their uncooperative ways by unscrupulous real estate promoters. Some of these promotional operators bring pressure on planning commissioners and other public officials in a series of deliberate steps leading toward approval of their schemes. The steps usually include wining and dining, threats to take their economic bonanza to a more receptive city, dealing with the public official in an indirect and unobtrusive manner, and, failing these methods, bribery or worse.

Fortunately, these tactics are on the wane as more enlightened public officials and more sophisticated legal controls protect the general public more effectively. Planning and zoning are relatively new, however, and many parts of North America have neither, and this applies to more urbanized areas than it should. This is another pitfall—the untutored public official in the smaller urban area where the glitter of added jobs from the new manufacturing plant blind him to the realities of appropriate development controls that should govern the plant and related urban development.

These are the political realities the planner faces, but now he has more company in his profession than previously, more comprehensive planning going for him, more zoning ordinances adopted, and more favorable court decisions on planning, zoning, and renewal as time passes.

New Communities

The people with the money back of most new communities (over 25,000 population) are usually knowledgeable in matters of planning and urban development to the degree that they will insist on the formulation of a thorough general plan and a complete set of plan implementation tools—zoning ordinance, subdivision regulations, housing code, building code, and others.

The United States Congress, recognizing the need for new communities and the opportunity they offer to study and develop new ways to build, operate, and live in modern urban areas free of the mistakes of the past, adopted, and the President signed, the Housing and Urban Development Act of 1968 with Title IV on new communities. The act limited loans to $50 million for any one community and up to 80 percent of the value of the property when land development is completed. Columbia, Maryland, and Reston, Virginia, re well-known new communities in progress years before this legislation was available and were outstanding pioneering achievements. Since the new communities bill became law, Jonathan, Minnesota, was the first new community to receive a HUD commitment.[7] The amount is $21 million as a guarantee for debt obligation for 5,000 acres to house an ultimate population of 50,000. Other communities followed, among which were Park Forest South, Illinois, with $30 million in bonds guaranteed by HUD[8] and to have an ultimate population of 110,000, and later Flower Mound between Dallas and Fort Worth with 100,000 population in 20 years on 6,155 acres, as well as several others.

There are relatively few examples of new communities in the hemisphere to date but dozens are in planning or being built. Most of them are privately owned and developed and this trend should continue. Shelby Farms mentioned earlier in this chapter is an exception to the private ownership rule [Figure 4-8]. The map shows how densities higher than average may be incorporated in an overall plan for a new community with optimum living amenities. A list of older communities built on vacant public land in the United States should include the pioneering greenbelt towns built in the thirties, a community development experiment of significant value. Most new communities eventually end up in public or municipal corporations when they are developed to the extent that a city government can be formed.

The ideal planning assignment, referred to in the profession as a planner's dream, would be planning a new community of an optimum size for a location the planner selects. More often a new community is built on land that developers have painstakingly assembled over a period of years. Nevertheless, a planner may materially enhance the site by adding adjacent sections previously overlooked or rejected as too steep, rocky, or densely vegetated, and which may enhance residential use, if not directly usable as such. There may be a gully with a small natural watercourse that would make many fine home sites, provided the drainage basin were not so large that flooding could result. There might be a small mesa with excellent views or a site might permit a good vista of sunrises or sunsets, an amenity that never becomes commonplace. Water is nearly always a major attraction in home site selection [see Figure 4-9]. A near or distant view of sea, lake, or river enhances a site, unless pollution causes odors or unsightliness. Mountains and hilly terrain and the changing lighting of them through the day and seasons is a consistent best seller for home sites. Additional capital outlay to realize some of these amenities in new communities could be justified by increased value of home sites by virtue of the amenities.

7. *HUD News,* No. HUD 70-79, Feb. 13, 1970, p. 1.
8. *HUD Newsletter,* Vol. 2 No. 9, March 29, 1971, p. 1.

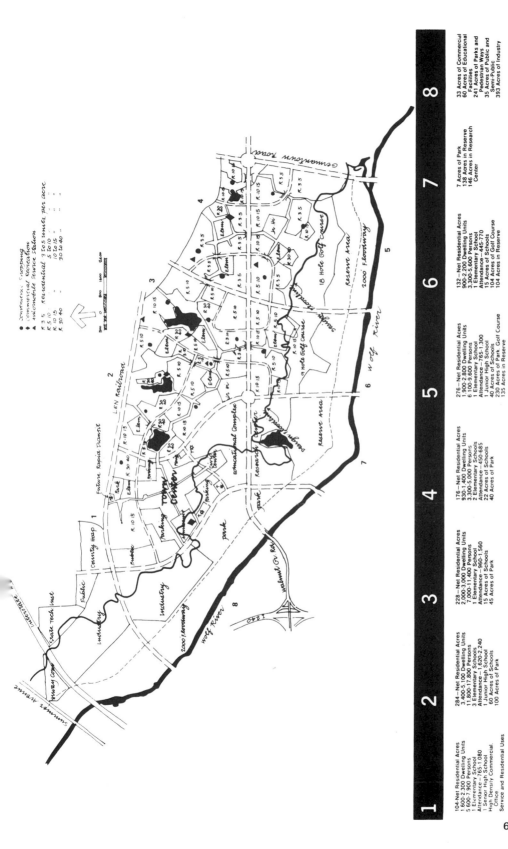

Figure 4-8 Shelby Farms proposed land use plan.

Source: Harland Bartholomew and Associates.

1

104-Net Residential Acres
1,600-2,300 Dwelling Units
5,600-7,900 Persons
1 Elementary School
Attendance—765-1,080
1 Senior High School
High Density Commercial.
Office
Service and Residential Uses

2

284—Net Residential Acres
3,400-5,100 Dwelling Units
11,800-17,800 Persons
3 Elementary Schools
Attendance—1,620-2,240
1 Junior High School
60 Acres of Schools
100 Acres of Park

3

228—Net Residential Acres
2,000-3,000 Dwelling Units
7,000-11,400 Persons
1 Elementary School
Attendance—960-1,560
15 Acres of Schools
45 Acres of Park

4

176—Net Residential Acres
930-1,400 Dwelling Units
3,300-5,000 Persons
2 Elementary Schools
Attendance—450-685
40 Acres of Schools
40 Acres of Park

MEMPHIS

5

276—Net Residential Acres
1,900-2,800 Dwelling Units
6,900-9,600 Persons
1 Elementary School
Attendance—765-1,300
1 Junior High School
40 Acres of Schools
230 Acres of Park, Golf Course
135 Acres in Reserve

JUNE 1970

6

132—Net Residential Acres
900-2,200 Dwelling Units
3,300-5,600 Persons
1 Elementary School
Attendance—445-770
15 Acres of Schools
104 Acres of Golf Course
104 Acres in Reserve

7

7 Acres of Park
138 Acres in Reserve
146 Acres in Research
Center

8

33 Acres of Commercial
60 Acres of Educational
Facilities
241 Acres of Parks and
Pedestrian Ways
35 Acres of Public and
Semi-Public
393 Acres of Industry

65

G CHARLES GATHERS & ASSOCIATES HIDDEN LAKE DEVELOPMENT
Architects and Planners Denver, Colorado

Source: Charles Gathers and Associates.

Figure 4-9 Example of a water-oriented community plan.

Much more flexibility in home site selection is available to the planner in new rather than in built-up communities. There is no excuse for not reserving the best housing sites for residential use with the practical consideration of working into the plan other necessary land uses—industrial, commercial, and public. Some new communities, retirement ones included, are without industry. This simplifies the planning process. Those with industry, however, should have certain industrial operations located according to their peculiar needs for flat space, utilities, and communications (road, rail, air, and water), and some of these requirements may necessarily mean industry will occupy good home sites. This is as it should be, but alternative sites for industry should be sought and investigated and a practical balance worked out for both (see Chapter 5).

The procedure for planning a new community starts with a list of objectives to achieve for the particular type of community—retirement, educational, industrial, governmental, recreational, suburban, a combination of two or more of these, or other types. The next step would be an economic analysis of the price range and types of residential accommodations—detached or semidetached (duplex) homes, row or town houses, walk-ups, or high-rise apartments, and the rental or sales range of each. A land use evaluation matrix was used in planning Shelby Farms and makes a convenient checklist [Figure 4-10] for these considerations.

Next an estimate is made of the number of each type and size of home or apartment the economy of the community could support. Then follow land studies to determine the location and size of buildable sites for housing; a contour map is used in this process to record areas with acceptable slopes for home and other sites (a slope map), and this will vary according to the cost of the land, the expense of grading to gain more sites, the geological conditions of the subsoil, and the ingenuity of the architect and engineer working with the planner to optimize each site.

Factors Affecting Land Use

Land Use Types	Compatible With Goals and Objectives	Helps Fulfill Area Needs	Easily Implemented	Highly Acceptable to Community	Efficient Use of Land	Efficient Provision of Utilities and Facilities	Compatible With Adjacent Land Uses	Maximum Fiscal Return	Aesthetically Valuable	Easily Constructed	Technologically Innovative	Convenient for Residents	Auto-Pedestrian Separation	Low Maintenance Factor	Others
RESIDENTIAL															
1. Estates															
2. Single-Family															
3. Low Rise-Multiple															
4. High Rise-Multiple															
5. Public Housing															
6. Elderly, Handicapped Housing															
7. Factory Built Units															
8. Hotels, Motels															
9. Condominiums															
10. Cluster Housing															
11. Others															

Source: Harland Bartholomew and Associates.

Figure 4-10 Land use evaluation matrix.

The next step consists of organizing the various land uses required into a logical harmonious relationship with one another. Acreage requirements for each use would be ascertained at this point and those with fixed needs (industry near water, warehousing near rail service, and the like) would be tentatively located with possible alternative locations noted. Simultaneously, the most desirable residential areas would be marked in on the slope map and would include the wooded valleys and ridges, the sites with interesting views, and similar areas. Then the next most desirable residential space would be indicated with yet a third category—if all housing space could not be accommodated in the first two—best and next best. Density may be an essential factor at this point in the planning process. Higher residential densities, unless overcrowding results, could be more desirable and economical than extending residential development onto the least acceptable land for housing—near marshes, too close to railroad lines, and the like.

At this point mention of microclimatology should be included and may benefit land use selections for housing. Microclimatology is as old as the art of providing shelter for human habitation but was known by this term relatively recently, in the 1930s. The term may be defined as the science of detailed effects of climate and weather on a given parcel of land. Less has been heard of the term since the advent of air conditioning, since the latter is capable of overcoming climatological shortcomings of heat, cold, humidity (too much or too little), and even air pollution in some air-conditioning systems. The tremendous urban development in the warmer climates of the United States started only as air conditioning became economically within reach of the middle- and low-middle-income range of families. Nevertheless, there is a housing trend started and a housing need to be met, both of which can use microclimatology. The trend is the desire, mostly by young adults, for a simpler and more natural way of life free of the complications and gadgets of modern society and the need, mostly by the elderly or middle-aged for fresh air and relief from stiffness and nasal congestion attributed to air conditioning. They can always turn off the air conditioning and open the windows but they do not for several reasons—heat, odors, lack of fresh air, security, and noise. Microclimatology would not help these people unless such objections were corrected; this is possible in a new community and, in fact, these are some of the reasons new communities are necessary and successful. Another segment of the housing market that could use microclimatology are in the sections of the continent where the need for air conditioning is negligible, in much of Canada, in Alaska, and in parts of the United States and Mexico above 6,000 or 7,000 feet elevation, for example.

Microclimatology recognizes the total effects of the angles of the sun's rays throughout the four seasons, the shadows cast by trees and hills during the day, the direction of prevailing winds and the dampness they may carry with them, the effects of nearby bodies of water on humidity, the accumulation of snow in a driveway or sidewalk, the rate and kinds of precipitation, and the effects of cloud shadows on a home site. These are small matters but, if ignored or misunderstood, could be a nuisance, a costly oversight, or even a disaster.

Returning to the planning process, the next step should be the arrangement of tentatively selected residential sites into organizations of neighborhoods and communities. A useful gauge many planners use for the amount of land for housing is persons per acre. Average family size would normally be determined between three and four persons, say 3.5, for example. A neighborhood with an elementary school of 400 pupils would need 400 such families, if one person were found as the average per family for elementary school age population. The junior and senior high school students would be, say, 0.5 students per family average. Thus, the neighborhood comprised of 1,400 persons would occupy 80 acres net area for housing at an average density of five housing units per acre. To this would be added a school site, a neighborhood park, and a neighborhood shopping center, bringing the net total to, say, 120 acres. Then add about 20 percent for streets and other public or semipublic uses, such as churches, for a neighborhood gross total of 144 acres. Five such neighborhoods would support a 1,000-student high school consisting of a site of, say, 30 acres. To this should be added a community shopping center of 40 acres, more or less, and space for other public and private functions, such as a branch library, a fire station or two, possibly a golf course, a cemetery, a branch post office, a private recreation center for bowling, dancing, and the like, and similar uses. The five-neighborhood community would cover between 800 and 900 acres gross area and house about 7,000 persons. Thus, a new town of 50,000 population would consist of seven such communities and cover 6,000 or 7,000 acres of land.

The foregoing example, for simplicity, excluded more sophisticated housing types, such as 10-acre or larger estates and high-rise or other types of apartments, all of which would have a substantial impact on density of housing and persons per acre. The housing lot in the example was selected in the 6,000 square foot minimum category with some larger lots bringing the average up to nearly 9,000 square feet, 8,712 to be exact.

The controls mentioned in the example would be included in a zoning ordinance (see Chapter 9). A sample of these and other controls [Figure 4-11] is shown for the residential portion of the City of Los Angeles Zoning Ordinance in a condensed form as a general idea of the key points covered in a zoning ordinance adopted to control urban growth in an orderly manner. Note that the smallest allowable single family lot is 5,000 square feet and the highest density for multifamily use is 217.8 units per net acre.

Density can be a key element in the financial success of a new community. The lower the density, the higher the cost per lot of public or common improvements—grading, streets, and utilities—and the higher the cost of land per home site, since more space would be used per lot. The other extreme can be as risky. The higher the density, the lower the cost of land and improvements per lot, but this can be carried to a point where the public would not buy as readily and would, instead, insist on more space and privacy elsewhere. The market is the answer and here the planner needs the advice of the real estate market analyst who can estimate the approximate number of buyers a given development will attract over a specified period of time within a certain price range. The plan should be tailored to that market and the density set accordingly, with variations in density to broaden the market. The owner or developer may bring pressure to cram more housing units into the area, but the planner should resist on the grounds that the development would not appeal to the same market, sales would not be as readily forthcoming, and the long-range stability of the development would suffer.

The next step is determining the shape of neighborhoods. Standard distances children walk to an elementary school or playground (half a mile is usual) are customarily established and used by planners and these and other standard spacing of community facilities are covered in Chapter 6. The ideal shape of a neighborhood adhering to such standards would be a circle with the school and park in the center; however, the circle would result in irregularly shaped pockets of land not associated with any particular neighborhood with major or collector streets as boundaries. A square or rectangular shape would work better with the street system, but care should be exercised by the planner to avoid a monotonous rectilinear street system in the neighborhood plan. His skill is called upon here to take advantage of the spatial benefits of the rectilinear system of land subdivision and at the same time avoid the disadvantage of a monotonous layout.

Another factor equally effective in shaping the neighborhood is the drainage system—sanitary sewers especially, but storm water drains also. The drainage problems in uneven terrain may be acute enough to govern—overriding streets, schools, and other considerations—the boundaries of neighborhoods. Gravity flow of sanitary and storm waste waters without pumping is an efficient and economical goal to work toward; it is given more in-depth consideration in Chapter 6 and should be worked in with related information on streets in Chapter 8. A broad overlook of the effect of these facilities on good planning and a knowledge of engineering design is necessary to select housing sites

SUMMARY OF ZONING REGULATIONS
CITY OF LOS ANGELES

Classification	Zone	Use	Maximum Height		Required Yards			Minimum Area		Minimum Lot Width	Parking Space	Eagle Prismacolor Pencil Chart
			Stories	Feet	Front	Side	Rear	Per Lot	Per dwelling Unit			
AGRICULTURAL	A1	AGRICULTURAL One-family dwelling—parks—playgrounds—community centers golf courses—truck gardening—extensive agricultural uses	3	45 ft.	25 ft.	25 ft. maximum 10 % lot width 3 ft. mimimum	25 ft.	5 acres	2½ acres	300 ft.	Two spaces per dwelling unit	909 Grass green
	A2	AGRICULTURAL A1 uses	3	45 ft.	25 ft.	25 ft. maximum 10 % lot width 3 ft. minimum	25 ft.	2 acres	1 acre	150 ft.	Two spaces per dwelling unit	912 Apple green
	RA	SUBURBAN Limited agricultural uses	3	45 ft.	25 ft.	10'-1 & 2 stories 11'-3 stories	25 ft.	* 17,500 sq.ft.	* 17,500 sq.ft.	* 70 ft.	Two garage spaces per dwelling unit	910 True green
ONE FAMILY RESIDENTIAL	RE40	RESIDENTIAL ESTATE One-family dwellings Parks Playgrounds Community centers Truck gardening	3	45 ft.	25 ft.	10 ft.	25 ft.	* 40,000 sq.ft.	* 40,000 sq.ft.	*	Two garage spaces per dwelling unit	950 Gold
	RE20				25 ft.	10 ft.	25 ft.	* 20,000 sq.ft.	* 20,000 sq.ft.	* 80 ft.		
	RE15				25 ft.†	10 ft. maximum 10 % lot width	25 ft.†	* 15,000 sq.ft.	* 15,000 sq.ft.	* 80 ft.		
	RE11				25 ft.	5'-1 & 2 stories 6'-3 stories	25 ft.	* 11,000 sq.ft.	* 11,000 sq.ft.	* 70 ft.		
	RS	SUBURBAN One-family dwellings—parks playgrounds—truck gardening	3	45 ft.	25 ft.	5'-1 & 2 stories 6'-3 stories	20 ft.	7,500 sq.ft.	7,500 sq.ft.	60 ft.	Two garage spaces per dwelling unit	911 Olive green
	R1 R1-H	ONE-FAMILY DWELLING RS uses	3	45 ft.	20 ft.	5'- 1 & 2 stories 6'-3 stories	15 ft.	5,000 sq.ft. ------------- 15,000 sq.ft.	5,000 sq.ft. * 15,000 sq.ft.	50 ft.	Two garage spaces per dwelling unit	916 Canary yellow
MULTIPLE RESIDENTIAL	R2	TWO-FAMILY DWELLING R1 uses Two-family dwellings	3	45 ft.	20 ft.	5'-1 & 2 stories 6'-3 stories	15 ft.	5,000 sq.ft.	2,500 sq.ft.	50 ft.	Two spaces one in a garage	917 Yellow orange
	RD2	RESTRICTED DENSITY MULTIPLE DWELLING ZONE Two family dwelling Apartment houses Multiple dwellings	Height district no. 1 3 stories 45 ft.		20 ft.	10 ft.	25 ft.	8,000 sq.ft.	2,000 sq.ft.	60 ft.	One space each dwelling unit of less than three rooms One and one half spaces each dwelling unit of three rooms Two spaces each dwelling unit of more than three rooms One space each guest room (first thirty)	940 Sand
	RD3							12,000 sq.ft.	3,000 sq.ft.	70 ft.		
	RD4								4,000 sq.ft.			
	RD5		Height district nos. 2, 3 or 4 6 stories 75 ft.						5,000 sq.ft.			
	RD6								6,000 sq.ft.			
	R3	MULTIPLE DWELLING R2 uses Apartment houses Multiple dwellings			15 ft.	5'-1 & 2 stories 6'-3 stories	15 ft.	5,000 sq.ft.	800 to 1,200 sq.ft.	50 ft.		918 Orange
	R4	MULTIPLE DWELLING R3 uses Churches Hotels—schools	☆ Unlimited		15 ft.	5' plus 1' each story above 2nd 16 ft. max.	15' plus 1' each story above 3rd 20 ft. max.	5,000 sq.ft.	400 to 800 sq.ft.	50 ft.		943 Burnt ochre
	R5	MULTIPLE DWELLING R4 uses Clubs—hospitals Lodges—sanitariums	☆ Unlimited		15 ft.	5' plus 1' each story above 2nd 16 ft. max.	15' plus 1' each story above 3rd 20 ft. max.	5,000 sq.ft.	200 to 400 sq.ft.	50 ft.		946 Dark brown

☆ See height districts at the bottom of page 2
† Same as R1-H (if lot recorded prior July 1, 1967)
* "H" hillside or mountainous area designation may alter these requirements in the RA-H, RE-H or R1-H zones. Subdivisions may be approved with smaller lots, providing larger lots are also included. Each lot may be used for only one single-family dwelling. See minimum width & area requirements below

Zone combination	Minimum to which net area may be reduced	Minimum to which lot width may be reduced
RA-H	14,000 sq.ft.	63 ft.
RE20-H	10,000 sq.ft.	60 ft.
RE15-H, RE11-H	7,500 sq.ft.	60 ft.
R1-H	7,500 sq.ft.	50 ft.
RE40-H	20,000 sq.ft.	No reduction

Sheet 1 of 2
Prepared By City Planning Department Aug. 1967

CP Form 10

Figure 4-11 Summary of zoning regulations, city of Los Angeles.

intelligently. The cost, for instance, of streets and sewers on ridges in rolling terrain should be compared with the cost of them in the valleys between ridges, or the cost of streets on the ridges and the sewers in the valleys. The size of home sites and space available on and between ridges may automatically make these determinations. Then the drainage pattern should be traced to a logical location for sanitary interceptor sewers leading to a sewage treatment plant and a suitable body of water to receive the treatment plant effluent.

Every effort within reason should be made to preserve natural beauty wherever practicable and especially trees that take scores of years to grow to maturity. Several areas which lend themselves better as neighborhood or community parks than home sites should be reserved for the general public. These may include wooded watercourses, with hiking, biking, and horse trails, or bodies of water, forests, or rocky overlooks. Small dams often simultaneously create flood protection, water supply, recreation facilities for boating, swimming, and fishing, and lake-view lots.

The size of lots has been mentioned but not their shapes. A minimum width of 60 feet for single family lots of the 6,000 square foot minimum size is a good norm, but 50 feet or even less should be allowed at cul-de-sacs or other special situations. A rectangular lot 60 by 100 feet with a 30-foot front setback and a house say, 40 or 50 feet long by 30 or 40 feet wide (6 or 7 rooms with 3 or 4 bedrooms) provides at least a 10-foot side yard (20 feet between houses), and a backyard 20 or 30 feet by 60, ample for numerous outdoor games, cookouts, clotheslines, gardens, and the like. Trapezoidal lots should be the exception rather than the rule; they waste land or saddle an owner with unusable parts of his lot. Terraced steep lots with masonry walls separating the levels is attractive to some and avoided by others and should be kept to a minimum; properly interpreting the slope map should obviate most of these difficulties.

The size of lots for multifamily housing varies from a minimum depth of 100 feet or so for town houses to many acres for large garden or high-rise apartment developments. Observing acceptable standards of density, setbacks, provision for light, air, and privacy, garden apartments may be built on 100-foot deep lots. A better arrangement where the lots backing up to each other are assembled for apartment development may result in a layout 200 feet deep without alleys with more privacy, easier parking, and more landscaping amenities.

A feature of security for the home, used in recent times to avoid crime, is a street system without alleys in residential areas. One disadvantage of this is front yard waste pickup and other services, but this is offset by eliminating the alley where crimes, usually against women, are often perpetrated.

High-rise apartments are usually feasible in larger cities only where high rentals necessitated by high cost of land and construction can be paid by enough tenants who desire this type of living accommodation. There are literally millions of Americans and Canadians who have this desire, even though they represent slightly over one percent of the population. The ease and simplicity of apartment living and especially the high-rise variety with exciting vistas of landscapes, cityscapes, sunrises, and sunsets provide a privacy and relief from the hubbub of city life seldom found in most urban living. There is much in favor of high-rise apartment living from the standpoint of the privacy and inspirational view of land and sky. The effect on the outlook on life and the spirit and joy of living should not be overlooked or scoffed at, since this type of living is the best for a growing segment of modern urban society. An example is Brooks Tower in downtown Denver [Figure 4-12].

With all the requirements to consider in planning new communities, the job is easy compared to planning for built-up urban areas. Yet nearly three-fourths of the people live in built-up areas and most of the additional population for the rest of this century will live there or near there. Consequently, built-up areas are increasingly important to plan properly.

Source: Photo courtesy Denver and Colorado Convention and Visitors Bureau.

Figure 4-12 Modern hirise apartment—Brooks Tower, Downtown Denver, with new Federal Reserve Building in foreground.

Built-up Communities

Most of the foregoing procedures and planning steps for new communities apply to built-up ones as well. One big difference is the influence of existing conditions and making an accurate record of them upon which planning decisions should be based. The attitude on the part of too many public officials including some planners is that the existing conditions present too many problems too costly to correct, and time would be spent more effectively on adding to the city, usually on the periphery. This point of view does not take full cognizance that cities are growing organisms changing daily through natural or man-made disasters, through growth and progress, and through urban planning and development, i.e., improvements made by man in his tireless efforts toward betterment or desire for profit or both.

First, however, in the planning process for built-up communities is the accumulation of pertinent data upon which a multitude of decisions may be intelligently based. A system of gathering the required information should be logically thought out and set forth in a procedures manual. This was accomplished in South Bend, Indiana, as a solid foundation for the city's future needs.[9] A step-by-step procedure guides the work of the planners, surveyors, and analysts without wasting time in the accumulation of necessary data, analyzing existing studies and reports, and forecasting needs for the future as a basis for a land use plan.

The same objectives for the most desirable sites for homes apply to built-up as well as new communities. A potentially desirable residential neighborhood in transition from residential to industrial should be carefully and unemotionally analyzed as to the cost and benefits to reverse the trend back to residential. Plenty of common sense and political know-how is useful in such an endeavor. The problem may mean renewing an old factory area, along a riverbank, for instance, into a new housing area with high-rise apartments near downtown as proposed in the Lafayette, Indiana, Central Renewal Area Plan [Figure 4-13]. Note how the industrial area along the river is retained and screened from the new residential with a buffer of trees, and how alternate streets or alleys are converted to a system of pedestrian ways connecting high-density residential development with the commercial core of the city.

Most older cities would usually not have their residential areas organized into neighborhoods and communities with bordering arterial streets as described above. As the street system is planned (see Chapter 8), the opportunity is there to form neighborhoods by selecting major streets in both directions such that residential areas between them will contain sufficient space or population to support an elementary school. Skeptics may decry that the school is already there, is nearly dilapidated, overpopulated with pupils, and located in the corner instead of near the center of the proposed neighborhood. This would indicate the timing is right for replacement of the old school with a different one that is modern, easier to heat and maintain, large enough and properly located; a new school site may use space formerly occupied by substandard housing, eliminate streets substandard in width, and provide a much-needed neighborhood park.

9. Procedure Manual P, Forecast of Land Use, South Bend (Indiana) Urban Area Transportation and Land Use Study by Harland Bartholomew & Assocs., Dec. 1970.

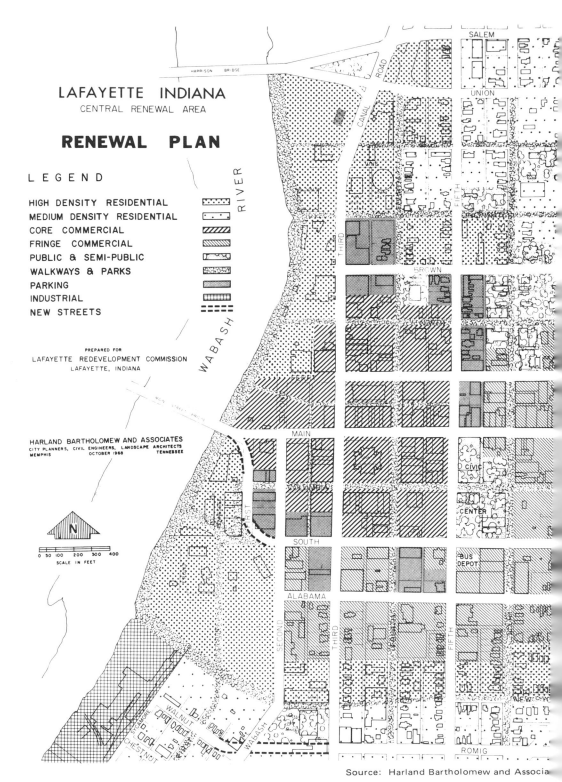

Figure 4-13 Lafayette, Indiana, central renewal area plan.

The same planning process of formulating an orderly arrangement of sanitary sewers, interceptors, and a sewage treatment plant applies to built-up areas. Advantages and costs of more than one sewage treatment plant should be compared with the cost of installing new or adding to existing sewage pumping stations and treatment plants.

The old street system may not lend itself to modern planning concepts of minor streets in a residential neighborhood serving the homesites without inviting large volumes of through traffic. A rectangular street system used in many cities with 8 blocks to the mile north and south and 16 east and west may appear too removed from a curvilinear street system to modernize the streets. However, one of the simpler street systems to convert to a modern one is the rectilinear system by looping two minor streets together near the major street, by use of cul-de-sacs, and with elbow turns [Figure 4-14]. The main purpose here is giving integrity and protection to the residential neighborhood and to replan the street system to discourage through traffic. Chapter 8 covers the internal transportation system, including street systems. The sketch [Figure 4-14] assumes 50- by 120-foot lot sizes, more or less, with 24 per block and with collector streets bordering two sides and major streets the other sides of the neighborhood; notice how a neighborhood shopping center is located at the opposite corner from the community shopping center. The high school or junior high site would occur only in every fourth neighborhood or so and not in each one. There could also be space devoted to places of worship at or near the shopping centers to take advantage of ample parking on Sundays or near intersections of major or collector streets for exposure to the public.

The size and shape of old lots may discourage conversion to more up-to-date standards. This usually is worse in the poorer districts where 20- and 30-foot wide lots are common. Most zoning ordinances and housing codes recognize this problem by permitting the substandard lots to remain as long as the structure thereon remains as is, without substantial additions. The structures are an equally important part of the lot size problem. Usually structures in old and especially poorer districts are of inadequate original construction, built without modern conveniences, and often without benefit of an adequate building code. Code enforcement of such structures to attempt to bring them up to an acceptable modern standard more often than not means a harsh financial burden on the owner and especially the homeowner-occupant. Demolition and rebuilding on a larger lot may be a better answer (see Chapter 11 on urban renewal) but this is difficult or impossible to do privately a structure at a time. A neighborhood-wide renewal program is usually the only plausible answer for many of these situations.

The changes affecting built-up communities, briefly mentioned above, amount to never-ending opportunities to improve on existing conditions and bring communities in line with a general plan—if there is one. Many of these opportunities may be lost without a plan. Take, for example, a new freeway or expressway proposed through an old area composed of a mixture of mostly housing and some light industry. Several routes for the freeway may be feasible and, if the general plan for the area calls for renewal of the area as a residential neighborhood, the freeway route selected should be on the edge instead of through the middle of the neighborhood. The expressway right-of-way requirement may be from 100 to 300 feet wide. This may require extensive demolition and should occur where as much residential and industrial blight can be eliminated as possible. The freeway

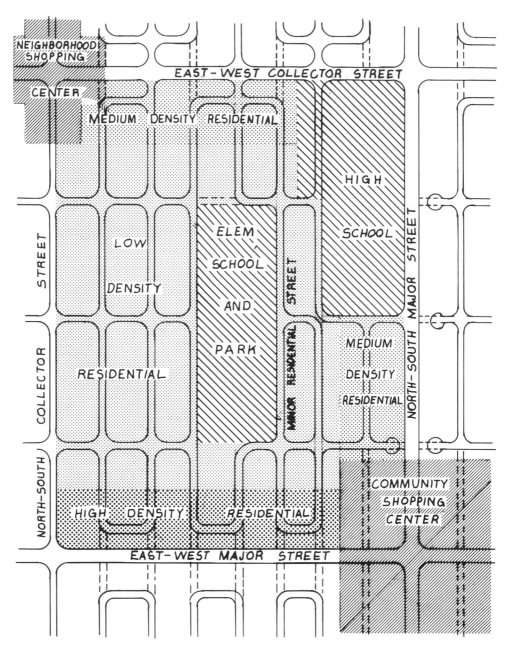

Figure 4-14 Enhancing neighborhood integrity by modernizing old rectilinear street systems.

route selection should be influenced by this consideration as well as by location peripheral to the neighborhood.

Another example is a need for a new school as a substitute for, say, the 80-year-old one that may be a death trap. The location for the new one need not be where the old one is unless the latter is near the middle of the ultimate neighborhood; but assuming, for an example, that it is not, the opportunity prevails to select a site for the new one that simultaneously solves other problems of the neighborhood through demolition of substandard housing, removal of industry, vacating a street with substandard conditions, or filling in an area that does not drain properly. Simultaneously, the old school site may be converted to a park, public housing, a fire station site, or one of a number of facilities the neighborhood needs. These objectives may seem to be urban renewal, but, on the contrary, they may be accomplished without the total process of renewal and still gain some of the benefits.

These benefits are maximized only if a general plan has been formulated, adopted, and recognized as the way the community is to be developed. This means in the case of residential land use that the most desirable living areas in the city have been designated for housing and that such areas are each large enough for at least a complete residential neighborhood. There are practical exceptions to this rule, of course, with smaller pockets of land, for example, in the hills or woods or near bodies of water; notwithstanding, the service demands of the modern urban inhabitant are such that organizing residential land into viable neighborhoods pays off in the long run. The neighborhood concept is, however, a controversial one among some planners.

THE NEIGHBORHOOD CONCEPT AND IMAGE

Each city during the plan formulation process should ask itself if the neighborhood concept is a logical one for its requirements. St. Petersburg, Florida, or Sun City, Arizona, both with high incidences of elderly population, have no need to organize all residential land on a neighborhood basis as far as elementary schools or children are concerned. The downtown apartment complexes in larger cities present another example of residential development that does not need to be arranged along conventional neighborhood lines. Still other examples are the skid rows, the communes, the hippy hangouts, the religious retreats, and other esoteric gatherings of people living together in unconventional ways. This is not to categorize them as alike or approve or disapprove of these trends but to recognize them as factors affecting planning of housing. They are in the minority as far as the bulk of the population goes but deserve a place in a comprehensive plan.

The vicissitudes of American family life are factors affecting housing planning that need more introspection and less exaggeration. There are family trends that materially complicate orderly neighborhood life—one marriage out of four ending in divorce in the United States, illegitimate births over 30 percent of the total in some cities, a move in residence every four years on the average, and now an additional complication, busing of schoolchildren. Nevertheless, broken-home families need a place to live and so do the restless who move every few years. Busing school children affects only about 20 percent of the total and these need a home to return to when school is out. Such aggravations to normal family and neighborhood life still apply to a minority of the people.

Probably the most concern some planners have about the neighborhood concept stems from the sociological metamorphoses the family is going through now. The generation gap, women's liberation, parental permissiveness, the new morality, greater affluence, trial marriages, and other vectors impinge on family integrity and the strength of filial ties. Families experience normal changes earlier than previously owing to a step-up in communications, and three generations in the same household, the rule up to the early part of the current century, is now the exception. The really long-range look at these trends, say a century hence, gives the futurist broad license to imagine types of urban living where the neighborhood of today could be an anachronism of history. The pill or other forms of birth control coupled with new attitudes of morality could spell an era of sexual freedom hardly conducive to family continuity as it is known today. Polygamy, polyandry, and monogamy could be a matter of choice under a new set of rules that would take most of the risk of incompatibility out of current haphazard mating practices. Child upbringing could start at birth under scientific controls that leave nothing to chance; the child would be spared the trauma of family dissension and instability in a government-controlled laboratory instead of being raised by parents with little or no experience in child rearing and some with small interest as well. Employment could be guaranteed by an educational system that would make the most of a person's talents and avoid placement where his shortcomings would be a hindrance to society. The personnel needs of commerce and industry could be planned by generations for exactly the number and types of employees required and coordinated with the educational system accordingly. Retirement at an earlier period in life could be free of the anxiety of rising costs of living, since complete facilities would be available in government retirement communities for all the aging.

The problem is how to come by the better parts of the preceding effects without loss of individual liberty and rights in a free society. The signs of the times indicate a desire for more freedom and less regimentation. Most of the results above require more regimentation and control. Assuming some of the points are attainable, the question is when—in a century or only half a century? Meantime, problems are crying for answers now, especially in large urban centers. The vast majority of people in the free world are not willing to rush into the type of society described and, instead, are much more conservative and willing to support a more gradual change with some guarantee of keeping the liberty they now enjoy. This means efforts to solve family problems will increase and family as well as neighborhood integrity will continue to be a valid means of solving many urban ills.

The impression may have been assumed that the neighborhood was conceived as a practical basis for planning an elementary school district. This is true, but by no means the only reason for a neighborhood. From the planner's point of view the neighborhood is a logical size for planning, building, and operating a host of public services the people need or demand—recreation, health services, fire and police protection, library service, a sanitary sewerage district, waste pickup service, street tree maintenance, transit service, and others. Many private endeavors also find the neighborhood a practical size for organizing such services as neighborhood shopping centers, taxi service, churches, and the like. The neighborhood concept is a pragmatic one and proof of its worthiness is its widespread use in organizing land for residential purposes. Whether elementary schools form the nucleus or not, the geographical size of a neighborhood lends itself to public and private service planning and management. One other feature of the neighborhood, its image, deserves exploration.

Man is a product of his heritage and environment. To correct the shortcomings of his heritage takes generations and the achievements already accomplished in reducing physiological and sociological flaws are noteworthy even though there is much left to be done. These are the responsibilities of the doctor, sociologist, and clergyman. Environment is the planner's responsibility and his opportunity. The problems of family instability and division mentioned above may in substantial measure be solved or mitigated by placing the family in an adequate environment or upgrading the environment to an acceptable residential neighborhood. The image of the neighborhood as a social problem-solver is the planner's opportunity. Admittedly, he can only set the stage; the rest is up to the people of the neighborhood and the social services and other forces for the good of the community. The image of the neighborhood that would benefit the resident should be one of dependability, continuity, attractiveness, security, pride, dignity, and inspiration. These require beauty in trees and other landscaping, quiet, safety, and orderliness. Much research has been done on establishing a definite relationship between crime, juvenile delinquency, and family disintegration and an environment of ugliness, noise, congestion, and confusion. A picture [Figure 4-15] tells the story better; once the environmental deficiencies have been corrected [Figure 4-16] and the improved image of the neighborhood is appreciated, the attitude of the residents toward the city, the neighborhood, the neighbors, and themselves should improve. Then the residential atmosphere is set for the more important improvements of the spirit and fulfillment of life of each individual.

CAPITALIZING ON PREVIOUS INVESTMENTS

One feature of planning or replanning built-up areas that planners should check out thoroughly is taking full advantage of or capitalizing on previous investments. As outmoded and worn out as some areas of cities appear, there is usually a large investment of public funds in them.

Every single lineal foot of underground utilities, public or private, has some monetary value. Every square yard of pavement and lineal foot of curb, gutter, and sidewalk was paid for by tax dollars and may have many years of useful life left in it. Every square foot of floor space of public buildings, regardless of their present use or lack of use, represents more public investment. Every acre of land in public ownership, whatever the use, has been acquired by means of the hard-to-come-by taxpayers' dollars, except for donated land, and it usually carries with it a trust to use it in a stipulated manner in the public interest.

The bustling cities in most American countries are still growing and building at a rapid pace, and the United States particularly has made many a costly mistake in its

Source: Photo by author, May 1971.

Figure 4-15 Typical southern U.S. substandard housing proposed for renewal.

development process. Lack of proper planning is the main reason for this unnecessary waste. A corollary reason is exigency development—single-purpose development to satisfy a pressing need as early as possible. Naturally, this is wasteful and costly and usually creates other problems that cry for solution. There are hopeful signs of looking this process squarely in the face, setting reasonable goals, making better plans to achieve them, using the tax dollar more wisely, and finally realizing there is a limit to available natural and human resources.

The material good things of life have been so widely distributed among the public generally in the United States, to a degree never equaled in the history of man, that the impression prevails that there is no end to this flow of good. This is true at least to the point that there is no limit to the good things that are needed—proper food, shelter, clothing, medical care, education, and the like. Yet there is a limitation to the amount of unnecessary luxuries every person or family may feasibly acquire. This thought process or philosophy is one that should be grasped by the planner in planning decisions for his city as a means of spreading available tax dollars to cover the essential needs of all the people in that city. Part of this process means capitalizing on previous investments of a public nature especially but not exclusively. This applies to private investments worth saving as well, such as utilities, housing, and others.

Source: Photo by author, May 1971.

Figure 4-16 Privately renewed housing in a Memphis renewal area.

Keeping all the facts in mind that a planner needs in formulating a plan thoroughly and carefully is no simple task and to appreciate the value of and use wisely available facilities in the planning process a detailed set of records of these improvements is essential. The existing land use inventory should contain the necessary data on size, location, capacity, and useful life left in all public lands, buildings, and facilities and those private ones that affect his decisions. For some of these decisions the planner may need the professional advice of the utilities engineer, the architect, the real estate market analyst, and others, and if they are not "in house" or part of the city government they should be sought in the consulting field.

The reference to making use of available housing in the private sector of the economy has certain merits of a limited nature where rehabilitation promotes capitalizing on previous investments, if a structure can be feasibly rehabilitated. This is covered in the following section.

One parting shot at the subject at hand for the planner is a paraphrasing of a popular prayer. Make the best use of the facilities that cannot be changed, change only those that must be changed, and develop the know-how or obtain from other sources the wisdom to know the difference.

BELOW-MARKET HOUSING

A paradox in a society as affluent as the United States is the need to subsidize with government funds or credit low- and moderate-income housing. Affluence may be the reason, though. Profit is usually less than 5 percent for a builder of this housing compared to the 10 percent or better he can realize in market housing. Yet, the United States is not unique in this. Most of the housing in Sweden, an affluent nation too, is publicly owned or backed and that is only one example of several countries in a like situation.

There were as of 1969 1,034,700 low-rent public housing units in the United States[10] housing better than an estimated 4 million persons. This does not include many privately owned low-rent housing units but does include 218,900 public units for the elderly. This is the supply of public housing [Table 4-1] and now for a look at the demand.

An encouraging sign is the gradual reduction in the number and percentage of substandard housing units in the United States during the last few decades. Only since 1950 has the Bureau of the Census collected data on the condition of structures but since 1940 related criteria regarding basic facilities for a home, such as plumbing or heating equipment, have furnished a common denominator of sorts for a comparison of condition of structures as well. For example, there was no piped water inside 25.8 percent of residential structures in 1940, 17.2 percent in 1950, and 7.1 percent in 1960 [Table 4-2].

One difficulty with such comparisons is the lack of agreement among housing experts on what is a definition of substandard. For this handbook a substandard housing unit is defined as one which is of original construction or deteriorated such that it is unsafe structurally or unhealthful sanitarily, or which is unable to protect occupants from cold weather or dampness, or which lacks basic plumbing, heating, or electrical facilities. Applying this definition to American or Canadian housing to arrive at a number of substandard units is difficult at best. However, an educated guess would give a rough idea of the workload ahead to eliminate or reduce substandard housing to a negligible amount. HUD Secretary Robert Weaver estimated in 1964 substandard housing units in the United States at 9 million. There are an estimated 6 million units as of 1970 in the United States in substandard condition housing over 20 million persons [Figure 4-17]. This is the low- and moderate-income housing workload to concentrate on now and in the future. The subject is considered further in Chapter 11 regarding urban renewal.

A significant report[11] estimates 24 million persons (12.2 percent) had incomes below the poverty level as of 1969 and this tends to corroborate the above estimate. More significant, however, is the statement in the report (page 1) that the 24 million represents "a decrease of 15.2 million over the past decade." So the overall picture continues to improve even though much is left to be done.

Note in Figure 4-17 that three valid measurements (not estimates) of substandardness were used in arriving at an estimate of number of units substandard through the

10. *1970 Statistical Abstract of the United States,* U.S. Dept. of Commerce, Bureau of the Census, Washington, D.C., p. 682.

11. *Consumer Income,* Series P-60 No. 76, U.S. Dept. of Commerce, Bureau of the Census, Washington, D.C., Dec. 16, 1970.

TABLE 4-1

Low-Rent Public Housing Units, by Progress Stage: 1950 to 1969

(In thousands. As of December 31. Includes Puerto Rico and Virgin Islands. Covers units subsidized by Department of Housing and Urban Development (HUD) under annual contributions contracts).

Year and Program	Total	Under management[1]	Under construction	Not under construction[2]	Year and Program	Total	Under management[1]	Under construction	Not under construction[2]
1950[3]	302.1	201.7	31.5	68.9	1960-Continued				
					New construction	888.0	742.5	75.6	69.9
1955[3]	489.7	413.6	21.1	55.1	Conventional[5]	819.5	720.4	46.3	52.9
					Turnkey[6]	68.5	22.2	29.3	17.0
1960	593.3	478.2	36.4	78.8	Acquisition	38.7	25.7	2.3	10.7
Elderly[4]	18.9	1.1	4.1	13.7	Rehabilitation:				
					With[7]	28.9	17.6	2.3	9.0
1965	735.7	604.9	42.4	88.4	Conventional	19.5	13.3	.7	5.5
Elderly[4]	97.7	36.2	21.6	40.0	Turnkey	9.4	4.2	1.6	3.5
					Without	9.9	8.2	(x)	1.7
1968	923.7	744.5	73.5	105.7	Leased housing[8]	108.0	54.3	6.9	46.8
Elderly[4]	183.7	97.2	42.8	43.7	New	29.2	5.6	3.9	19.6
					Rehabilitation:				
1969	1,034.7	822.6	84.8	127.4	With[7]	23.7	12.4	2.9	8.4
Elderly[4]	218.9	110.4	59.9	48.6	Without	55.1	36.3	(x)	18.8

X Not applicable.

[1] Occupied or available for occupancy.

[2] Comprises units to be constructed and units that will go directly into "under management" category because they need no rehabilitation.

[3] Excludes units which have been sold to mutual housing associations, limited dividend corporations (PWA), and homestead associations on which HUD has mortgages for collection.

[4] Covers units designed specifically for persons 62 years old or over, disabled, or handicapped.

[5] New housing constructed on the Local Housing Authority (LHA) site pursuant to a contract let by the LHA.

[6] New housing purchased by the LHA from a private developer upon completion of construction pursuant to an earlier agreement.

[7] Existing housing acquired by the LHA, requiring substantial rehabilitation which can be done either by the LHA (conventional) or by the seller (turnkey).

[8] Existing housing leased by the LHA from an owner under a contract permitting the LHA to sub-lease the units.

Source: 1970 Statistical Abstract of the United States, U.S. Dept. of Commerce, Bureau of the Census, Washington, D.C., p. 682, Table 1090.

years. These measurements are (a) "no piped water inside structure," available as such in the 1940, 1950, and 1960 censuses but not in the 1970 one, (b) "over one person per room" (literally in the census "more than 1.01 persons per room"), available in 1960 and 1970 only, and (c) "dilapidated," available in 1950 and 1960 only. Consequently, all three of these measurements are plotted in Figure 4-14 to fortify reasons for the estimate of substandard units for all four censuses. There is a correlation between the measurements and the estimates, since the measurements deal with structural conditions, facil-

TABLE 4-2
Housing Units—Selected Characteristics: 1940 to 1960

(Number in thousands. All 1940 data and 1950 data for heating equipment and cooking fuel exclude Alaska and Hawaii. Data for 1940 represent a complete census count; 1950 data for water supply, toilet facilities and bathing facilities represent a complete census count; data for all other 1950 items and all 1960 items are based on a 5-, 20-, or 25-percent sample of housing units. For a measure of the sampling variability, see source).

Item	1940 Number	1940 Percent	1950 Number	1950 Percent	1960 Number	1960 Percent
Total housing units	37,325	100.0	46,137	100.0	58,468	100.0
Not dilapidated	(NA)	(NA)	41,634	90.2	54,466	93.2
Dilapidated	(NA)	(NA)	4,503	9.8	4,002	6.8
All units with water supply	37,325	100.0	46,137	100.0	58,318	100.0
Hot and cold piped water inside structure	27,708	74.2	32,344	70.1	50,870	87.2
Only cold piped water inside structure			5,875	12.7	3,321	5.7
No piped water inside structure	9,617	25.8	7,918	17.2	4,128	7.1
All units with toilet facilities	37,325	100.0	46,137	100.0	58,318	100.0
Flush toilet, exclusive use	22,299	59.7	32,963	71.4	50,609	86.8
Flush toilet, shared	1,855	5.0	1,872	4.1	1,731	3.0
Other toilet facilities or none	13,172	35.3	11,302	24.5	5,978	10.3
All units with or without bathing facilities	37,325	100.0	46,137	100.0	58,318	100.0
Bathtub or shower, exclusive use	20,986	56.2	31,973	69.3	49,706	85.2
Bathtub or shower, shared	1,754	4.7	1,784	3.9	1,699	2.9
No bathtub or shower	14,585	39.1	12,379	26.8	6,922	11.9
All units with or without heating equipment	[1] 34,855	100.0	[1] 42,826	100.0	58,318	100.0
Steam and hot water	7,581	21.8	10,071	23.5	12,694	21.8
Warm air furnace, with ducts	5,844	16.8	11,508	26.9	18,355	31.5
Floor, wall, or pipeless furnace	1,218	3.5			6,528	11.2
Built in electric units	(NA)	(NA)	([2])	([2])	745	1.3
Other means with flue	[3] 16,257	46.6	15,399	36.0	13,152	22.6
Other means without flue	3,954	11.3	[2] 5,268	[2] 12.3	5,825	10.0
Not heated			581	1.4	1,020	1.7
Occupied housing units	34,855	100.0	42,969	100.0	52,955	100.0
Not dilapidated	(NA)	(NA)	39,066	90.9	49,871	94.2
With all plumbing facilities	(NA)	(NA)	27,713	64.5	43,949	83.0
Lacking or sharing 1 or more plumbing facilities	(NA)	(NA)	11,353	26.4	5,922	11.2
Dilapidated	(NA)	(NA)	3,903	9.1	3,084	5.8
With all plumbing facilities	(NA)	(NA)	609	1.4	947	1.8
Lacking or sharing 1 or more plumbing facilities	(NA)	(NA)	3,294	7.7	2,137	4.0
Occupied units with cooking fuel	34,855	100.0	42,826	100.0	53,022	100.0
Utility gas	17,026	48.8	22,085	51.6	27,296	51.5
Bottled, tank, or LP gas			3,417	8.0	6,491	12.2
Electricity	1,865	5.4	6,404	15.0	16,351	30.8
Other	15,963	45.8	10,921	25.5	2,884	5.4

NA Not available

[1] Represents all occupied units.

[2] Built-in electric units included with "Other means without flue."

[3] Heating stove. Source: U.S. Dept. of Commerce, Bureau of the Census; Sixteenth Census Reports, 1940, Vol. I *U.S. Census of Housing: 1950,* Vol. I, *U.S. Census of Housing: 1960,* final report, HC (4) Part 1A-1, *Components of Inventory Change,* and Working Paper No. 25, *Measuring the Quality of Housing.*

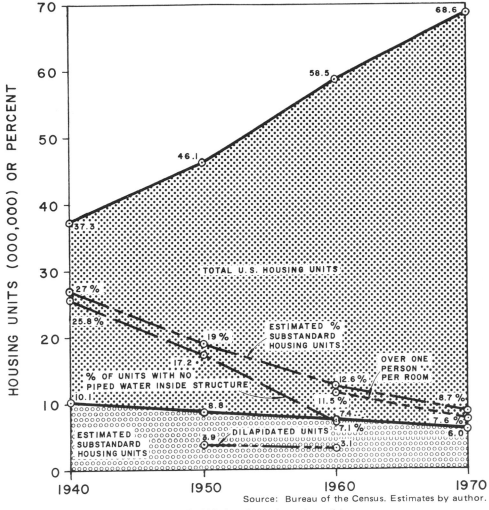

Figure 4-17 U.S. housing units and condition.

ities, and overcrowding, three important criteria of substandardness. The estimate was intentionally set slightly higher for each census than the highest of the measurements to avoid understating the problem. However, the exact number is academic since various public and private programs are whittling away at the substandard units daily while new and standard ones are abuilding to reduce the percent of substandard housing units further.

Therefore, six million, more or less, is the number of substandard housing units as of 1970, some of which will be brought up to standard by code enforcement, conservation, or rehabilitation. Also, these six million substandard units do not automatically signal a need for that many public housing units; far from it. Most of them are in the moderate-income category and only those are considered public housing candidates whose income is below public housing admission levels. An analysis of family income ranges should give an estimate of the approximate number.

Those 7,343,000 individuals and 4,775,000 families with incomes below $3,000 annually in 1970 would normally be considered public housing candidates, but many of them are content living with relatives or friends or making it on their own. There are 5,457,000 families making between $3,000 and $5,000 per year, some of whom may also qualify for public housing. Many of these are on farms or in moderate-income housing in urban or rural areas. Another two million or more public housing units could certainly be used for those in the worst of substandard housing and this may be a small fraction of current need. The answer lies in surveying and analyzing the need in the urban area being planned and including in the plan enough of all types of housing required to eliminate substandard living conditions completely.

A general plan for an urban area usually indicates generally the land to be devoted to residential purposes and, even though various types or densities of residential land use are identified, such as low, medium, or high density, there are no indications in the general plan of where low- or moderate-income housing should be developed.

Low-Income Housing

There are advantages to the planner in having an appreciation of how public housing is generally funded, located, and implemented. There are three basic types of public housing in the United States—conventional, turnkey, and leased. Conventional is designed and built under supervision of the local housing authority (LHA), and turnkey is not only designed and built by a developer but also the site is selected with LHA and HUD approval. Leasing is the quickest way to realize public housing and consists of the LHA leasing privately owned housing units at the market rental and then, in turn, they are rented to low-income families at rents not in excess of 20 percent of their income. Most public housing is of one, two, or three stories and only the elderly may occupy high-rise public housing, except in special cases.

Location of low-rent public housing is controversial for a variety of reasons—higher juvenile delinquency rates in some public housing projects, adverse effects on nearby property values, overloading of schools, and increase in traffic volumes on neighboring streets, to mention some of the usual objections. So controversial is the issue of location of public housing sites in some cities that several states are considering or have adopted legislation enabling a municipality to leave it up to the voters in a referendum whether this or that public housing site should be used for that purpose.

Further complicating the picture are HUD regulations urging public housing in other than ghetto areas or locations of racial minority concentrations. In fact, HUD regional offices, in setting priorities for approval of public housing applications, use a set of evaluation criteria that lean hard on the subject of location of sites, as follows:

EVALUATION OF APPLICATIONS FOR LOW-RENT PUBLIC HOUSING

1. Community Need for Low-Income Housing
   (a) Relative need for Housing by Low Income Families in the Neighborhood and Market Area to be served.
   (b) Proposed Unit Types
       Conform with the Composition of the Low Income Housing need in the Neighborhood and Market Area to be served.
   (c) Housing will serve as a Relocation Resource for families displaced by Governmental Action.
   (d) Waiting List for public housing.
2. Efficient Production
   (a) Time expected to be required from date of application approval to construction start, acquisition, or lease.
   (b) Cost of housing relative to prototype costs.
3. Nondiscriminatory Location
   (a) Outside an area of minority concentration.
   (b) Area substantially racially mixed.
   (c) In area of minority concentration but project will be part of major comprehensive development providing housing at various income levels and expected to be racially inclusive.
   (d) In area of minority concentration but responsive to overriding need for housing which cannot feasibly be met by other new or existing housing.
4. Improved Environmental Location for Low-Income Families
   The opportunity for Low Income Families to live in Neighborhoods which are:
   (a) Outside areas which have an excessive concentration of subsidized housing.
   (b) Accessible to Job Opportunities.
   (c) Provided with good transportation at reasonable cost.
   (d) Accessible to good Educational, Commercial and Recreational Facilities.
5. Effect of Proposed Housing Upon Neighborhood Environment
   (a) Compatibility of the land use concept and Architectural design of the proposed housing with the existing Neighborhood.
   (b) Use of scattered sites.
   (c) Compatibility of Density Levels of the proposed housing with existing and projected plans for the Neighborhood.
6. Relationship to Orderly Growth and Development
   (a) Neighborhood is undergoing Comprehensive Improvement via Urban Renewal, Model Cities or Rehabilitation—either Federal, State or Locally Assisted.
   (b) Proposed housing is compatible with A-95 area-wide planning and/or other established local planning.
   (c) Project will contribute to orderly and economical community growth.
7. Employment and Utilization of Employees and Business in Project Area
   Project will provide an opportunity for training and employment of Lower Income Persons residing in the area and/or opportunity for work to be performed by business concerns located in or owned in substantial part by Persons residing in the area.
8. Provision for Sound Housing Management
   (a) Administrative capacity.
   (b) Financial position.
   (c) Maintenance.

(d)   Crime prevention encouragement.
(e)   Provision of community services.
(f)   Administration of tenant selection plan and good faith efforts to achieve integration.
(g)   Management-tenant relations.
   9.   Homeownership
(a)   Homeownership opportunities of the proposed project.
(b)   LHA has other homeownership projects existing or under development.

The increase in housing starts in recent years in the United States in the moderate-income bracket has lessened the pressing need for low-rent units. The trend toward home ownership in subsidized housing is behind this change with the theory that a family will take better care of its own home than a rented one. Eligibility of families for these various types of subsidized housing is directly proportional to family income and size [Table 4-3]. The maximum income allowable for initial entry into low-rent housing may be increased after entry up to the limits shown under the heading of continued occupancy before the family must move out of public housing and up into moderate-income housing (between low-rent and market housing). The column identified as "special" applies to the blind, disabled, or otherwise handicapped.

Public housing has always been since its inception in 1937 considered as a temporary stopover for families unable to afford adequate housing until they get their affairs in order, learn a trade, obtain gainful employment, and move on into the housing rental or sales market. This should not imply more public housing is not needed. More is definitely needed and will be until the bulk of the substandard housing units are corrected and sufficient numbers of moderate-income housing is available to fill the gap between public and market housing.

Often the planning director and his department, as well as the Planning Commission, wishing to avoid controversy wherever they can and treading on thin ice on so many

TABLE 4-3
Allowable Annual Income Ranges for Subsidized Housing in Memphis

Number of Persons	Low Income (Public Housing)		Continued Occupancy	Rent Supplement	FHA 235,236 221d3 BMIR	FHA 220 231 (Elderly)
	Regular	Special				
1	$3,000	$3,750	$3,750	$3,100	$4,185	$4,450
2	3,600	4,500	4,500	4,200	5.670	5,400
3	3,800	4.750	4,750	4,400	5.940	6,350
4	4,000	5,000	5,000	4,600	6,210	6,350
5	4,200	5,250	5,250	4.800	6,480	7,300
6	4,400	5,500	5,500	4,900	6,615	7,300
7	4,500	5,625	5,625	5,000	6,750	8,250
8	4,600	5,750	5,750	5,000	6,885	8,250
9	4,700	5,875	5,875	5,000	7,020	8,250
10 or more	4,800	6,000	6,000	5,000	7,155	8,250

Source: Memphis Housing Authority and Federal Housing Administration, 1971.

subjects they are involved in, sidestep the issue of location of public housing sites. Thus, the housing authority or similar local public agency has sole responsibility of determining their location. True, the housing agency is obligated to refer the public housing site plan to the Planning Commission for approval but this procedure often ends with disapproval instead of approval with all the wasted motion involved. A better process involves the formation of a united front on the issue of public housing site locations with the Planning Commission and housing agency backed up by the mayor, council, and other organizations, public and private. The general plan could include general (not specific) locations for public housing sites needed years in the future, thereby putting all on notice years in advance and affording plenty of opportunity and time to adjust to the idea.

Much depends, too, on how the public housing units are planned, designed, and operated. Density looms large here as a critical factor. HUD has set a maximum of 100 units in any one housing project and densities below 15 units per net acre (25 was the custom in the early days of public housing) down to 10 or even 8 in special situations can mean mitigating much of the main objection to public housing. Excellent results have been achieved with one-story brick duplexes on a 6,000 square foot lot with a density of 14 units per net acre. These can be planned unobtrusively into a residential neighborhood in small clusters of 10 to 40 (20 to 80 units) without the depressing "project" appearance and the stark institutional architecture that too often results from the two-story barracks type of public housing. Another useful design is a combination of one- and two-story town houses in several groups of 8 or 10 units each offering an opportunity to use less land for each unit and make more common open space available for recreational and appearance purposes as a cluster or planned unit development. The cost per unit here would be less than for the duplexes. HUD sets a budget allowance for public housing units related to the cost of construction and land in the city. Savings on either may be used for essential facilities or necessary landscaping, both of which could help the development harmonize better with adjacent private housing. Recreational facilities in public housing or nearby in a neighborhood park are important to a well-run project.

How public housing is operated has much to do with its acceptance in a community. Training in the "dos" and "don't dos" of urban living is a must, especially for those who have lived most of their lives in the wide-open spaces of rural areas or in the confines of the urban slum; they both usually have living habits to change and new ones to assume regarding respect for others' property and privacy. These matters are not the responsibility of the planner but leaving them to chance could complicate residential land planning, especially the public housing parts of it. The planner could persuade the housing agency officials to adopt a better-disciplined policy of management of public housing and thereby reduce the objectionable features, resulting in broader acceptance in the community.

Rent supplement is a form of privately owned housing which fills a public housing type of low-income need whereby the difference between the rent the owner could realize in the open market and what the low-income family can pay (one-fourth of the family income) is subsidized by the government. This is similar to leased, as contrasted to conventional or turnkey, public housing.

One other point of interest to keep in mind in planning for low-income housing is the sale of the housing development to the occupants as a cooperative with a homes association to operate the venture. This transforms the development from the low to the moderate income category usually. A HUD publication[12] recently reported on this trend:

> The HUD-developed Turnkey III program . . . first tested in Gulfport, Mississippi in a project sponsored by the National Council of Negro Women . . . has attracted considerable attention throughout the country. Built by private builders under contract with the local housing authority . . . 200 homes were sold under lease-purchase agreements . . . which gave the families financial incentives for maintenance and repair work they did. The Council has been advising housing authorities in other localities . . . 36 communities in 10 States . . . on undertaking similar projects. A Ford Foundation grant of $315,000 has been given to the NCNW to make possible the continuation and expansion of its advisory services . . . to explore new techniques of self-help housing programs . . . and develop training programs for home-buyer associations which will take over the management and maintenance of future projects.

Moderate-Income Housing

The vast majority of the six million substandard housing units in the United States are being and will be replaced by moderate-income housing. A variety of programs, most of which are administered by the Federal Housing Administration (FHA), provide housing for moderate-income families, those whose income is too high for admittance to public housing and too low for market housing [Table 4-3, referred to previously]. The formula for subsidization of moderate-income families varies according to the size and income of the family and usually benefits the family by rent or mortgage supplements amounting to an interest rate on the mortgage of as low as one percent up to three percent or more.

Moderate-income housing in the United States includes the following programs:

1. Financial assistance to nonprofit sponsors (FHA Section 106).
2. Interest supplements on home mortgages (FHA Section 235).
3. Rental and cooperative housing mortgages (FHA Section 236).
4. Mortgage credit assistance for prospective homeowners (FHA Section 237).
5. Rehabilitated homes for low-income buyers (FHA Section 221h).
6. Individual homes for moderate-income families (FHA Section 221d2) for as little as $200 down payment.
7. Housing in declining neighborhoods (FHA Section 223e).
8. Nonprofit and limited dividend multifamily housing (FHA 221d3).
9. Rent supplements under Title 1 of the Housing and Urban Development Act of 1965.
10. Senior citizen housing (FHA Sections 202 and 231).

These government programs, as well as low-rent public housing, come under the provisions of equal opportunity in housing, or Title VIII (Fair Housing) of the Civil

12. *HUD Newsletter,* Vol. 2, No. 6, March 8, 1971, p. 3.

Rights Act of 1968 and the Civil Rights Act of 1866. This open housing provision has provoked opposition to some of these housing programs for racial reasons, to prevent potential reduction in property values, to resist overloading community facilities, or a combination of these factors, real or imaginary, as the case may be. Of interest here is the fact that a majority of states have adopted open housing legislation as of 1970.

These programs have been used for literally millions of dwelling units since their inception and millions more are sure to be built and occupied by moderate-income as well as many low-income families. The programs mentioned above are useful or not depending upon availability of funds in the locality at the time and should be checked with the nearest HUD office.

Perhaps more FHA detail is included above than is actually useful to the planner in a technical sense; however, his knowledge of the availability and understanding of the requirements in applying these housing types to his low- and moderate-income family housing needs places him in a position of being able to inform the power structure of his community of the advantages each type affords to the families involved. The planner, then, can more intelligently formulate a plan for residential land or analyze a developer's or builder's request for approval of a subdivision or other housing development and simultaneously expect support by the community for his decisions.

Two other types of moderate-income housing assuming larger shares of the housing supply as the years pass are industrialized housing and mobile homes, both of which resulted from high costs and short supplies of standard conventional housing. Standards are being adopted by the states to guide building installation and occupancy of these units. Mobile homes in urban areas are usually confined by zoning requirements to mobile home parks but industrialized housing (also referred to as manufactured or prefabricated) has a much wider acceptance, depending upon standards adopted and their degree of comprehensiveness. Industrialized housing is burgeoning and avoids the long delay in conventional housing between start and completion of construction with taxes and interest eating up profits. A complete three-bedroom house set up ready for occupancy in eight hours is demonstrated for publicity purposes, but the regular service takes something longer in time. Nevertheless, the assembly at the site of large portable sections of a home or apartments fabricated with modern assembly-line techniques is a boon to housing and a promise of greater things to come from this method in the future. More is included below on industrialized housing in this chapter as well as in Chapter 11 on urban renewal.

Mobile homes fulfill a variety of needs and desires from the temporary shelter at a construction site or beach resort trailer court to the seasonal sojourner seeking a more benign climate for the winter and on to the young or retired couple in a more permanent placement, usually a mobile home park. The latter group may be considered more or less as continuing residents and certainly the space they occupy as a residential land use for planning purposes.

The number of mobile homes and travel trailers sold [Table 4-4] exceeded half a million for the first time in 1969, evidence that the planner should include them in space considerations as well as work toward adoption of acceptable standards for their use in urban areas.

TABLE 4 - 4

Mobile Homes and Travel Trailers - Manufacturers' Shipments:
1960 to 1970

(A mobile home or housing-type trailer is a vehicular portable structure built on a chassis and designed to be used without a permanent foundation as a year-round dwelling when connected to utilities. Mobile homes are defined as units 29 feet or longer and weighing over 4,500 pounds; travel trailers, as units less than 29 feet long, regardless of weight, or weighing less than 4,500 pounds, regardless of length. Excludes units designed for commercial uses, pickup cabs, folding campers, and amphibious units.)

Year	Mobile homes	Travel trailers	Year and Quarter	Mobile homes	Travel trailers
1960	103,700	40,300	1966	217,300	122,700
1961	90,200	40,500	1967	240,360	130,420
1962	118,000	57,000	1968	317,950	[1] 115,200
1963	150,840	72,170	1969	412,690	[1] 144,000
1964	191,320	90,370	1970, Jan.-Apr.	116,430	(NA)
1965	216,470	107,580			

NA Not available. [1] Data not comparable with earlier years due to change in methodology. Source: Dept. of Commerce, Business and Defense Services Administration; *Construction Review,* and unpublished data.

The differentiation between mobile homes and travel trailers in the definitions in Table 4-4 distinguish between the vacation or recreational use of the travel trailer and the more or less permanent place of residence characteristic of the mobile home. The millions of each of them in Canada and the United States, as well as Mexico, and the flexibility in living they provide, involves the planner and other public officials in their location and occupancy. The travel trailer is inadequate as a permanent living unit and was not designed for this purpose, nor should it be permitted to be used as such. Travel trailers belong to a group of vehicles, together with pleasure boats, snowmobiles, campers, and the like, which have created a nuisance in some neighborhoods by cluttering driveways, streets, yards, and vacant lots to the extent that some zoning ordinances require them to be under cover just as a car is required to be stored inside a garage.

Mobile homes, on the other hand, often have their wheels removed and a permanent foundation built in their place. The mobile home has graduated from a luxury or novelty to a continuing segment of the housing supply. Mobile home parks are no longer the tawdry or seamy collection of contraptions down by the vinegar works but many are located in carefully chosen sites, planned, landscaped, and equipped to attract increasingly selective clientele, usually with mobile homes valued in excess of $10,000. The mobile home park equipment often includes laundries, utilities, swimming pools, party lounges, and other popular recreational facilities.

This is the easy part of the mobile home problem for the planner, since higher-income families are involved who demand quality and are willing to pay for it. The tough part of the problem is the smaller towns and urbanizing areas with ten years or more of mobile home use with inadequate or no controls over such use. The mobile home here may represent the choice between an old substandard house or a modern mobile one. The cost of a standard conventional house, even with FHA mortgage insurance, is beyond the owners' pocketbook. Some urban areas with no zoning ordinances have mobile homes located on lots adjacent to middle- and high-priced homes, the owners of which object to the incongruity. Some mobile homes are parked in the rear, side, or front yard of a home owned by a relative, friend, or landlord; the neighbors object in this case too.

Where a general plan is being formulated for the first time in an urban area, the zoning ordinance should provide for all subsequent mobile homes to be located in mobile home parks under specified conditions of density, use of utilities, number of units permitted, and the like. Meantime, existing mobile home owners should be given a moratorium period, usually five years, to relocate to a park, sell the home, or convert it to a dwelling compatible with zoning requirements for the neighborhood.

THE HOUSING ELEMENT OF THE GENERAL PLAN

The principal elements of a general plan have customarily been the land use, transportation system, and community facilities elements and only in comparatively recent years have general plans included a housing element. One impetus was the HUD requirement that general plans include a housing element when Operation Breakthrough was generating data for the nationwide aggregated market for housing in the late 1960s. Years before, however, several state planning enabling statutes required, or at least permitted, a housing element in the general plans of the communities in those states.

The *HUD Handbook* contains an Initial Housing Element[13] consisting of an appraisal of current housing problems and obstacles and formulation of a program of planning and development to correct housing deficiencies over a given period of time. The HUD outline or set of requirements is a comprehensive checklist to guide the preparation of a housing element and consists of five basic components or statements, as follows:

1. Statement of Problems This statement identifies and lists in order of importance, housing and related problems. Examples are the number and percentage of substandard housing units in the community compared to the state or nation, minority or other families without the means to afford private standard rental or sales housing, lack of public transportation from acceptable housing areas to employment centers, absence of a coordinated relocation program, and the like.

2. Statement of Obstacles   This statement lists in order of importance obstacles to solving housing problems listed in the previous statement. Examples here are inadequate information about the supply and demand for housing, absence of a state policy regarding solution of housing problems, inadequate planning funds for housing, lack of local governmental agencies such as a housing authority to deal with the problem, high land and construction costs, inadequate local resources for financing housing, absence of a Workable Program for Community Improvement, an unrealistically restrictive zoning ordinance or lack of one at all, and the like.

13. *HUD Handbook* MD 6041.1 Appendix 2-A, Washington D.C., Feb. 1969.

3. Statement of Objectives A set of goals are described here to be achieved each year for a period of three to five years and are related to the housing problems. Examples are preparation of needed state enabling legislation regarding housing, adoption of a Workable Program for Community Improvement, drawing up and adopting a local housing code, organization of a Fair Housing Council to help implement an open housing ordinance, or formulation of a comprehensive housing plan for the community, and others.

4. Statement of Planning Activities This includes an identification of previous planning work related to housing and future planning activities necessary to cope with housing problems during the ensuing three to five years. For instance, collection of housing data may be included, or a housing market analysis should be made, a study of available sponsors or housing sites for low- or moderate-income families, or a survey may need to be made of substandard housing.

5. Statement of Implementing Actions This should be broken down into previous actions taken to implement a housing program and the program of action proposed for a three-to-five-year period into the future. Some examples here are adoption of required state enabling legislation, provision for sewers in an area that needs them, instigation of a code enforcement or urban renewal program, creation of a housing authority, enacting an open housing ordinance, or building a certain number of moderate-income housing units.

Following the five basic statements, the housing element, according to the HUD regulations, should be coordinated with other elements of the general plan and, in this connection, they suggest indirect solutions to housing problems such as raising incomes, improving transportation, changing tax policies, and the like, as well as planning and programing for construction of housing. A reminder is also made that the housing element should take into account and supplement current and past planning endeavors, such as a Community Renewal Program, (covered in Chapter 11), urban renewal project plans, or a neighborhood development program.

Finally, HUD recommends that the local planning agency (city or county or other) take the responsibility to ascertain that the housing element or plan be forwarded to interested planning organizations for coordinating purposes, such as the state Planning Commission, interagency planning clearinghouses, district coordinating offices, or regional planning agencies (see Chapter 12). Then one last word of advice from the HUD directive points out the necessity of endorsement of the housing element or plan by the authorities responsible for housing policy and implementation. All the work on the housing element is for naught unless it is adopted and used in guiding growth and development of the community.

The directives prepared by HUD are necessarily intended for any community in the United States, and the one described above may have sections that are inapplicable to some communites. On the other hand, there could be special conditions not covered by such directives that should be included in a housing element of a general plan.

Purpose

The basic purpose of the housing element is to correct housing deficiencies so that every family and individual is housed adequately. The rapid pace of development in

Canada and the United States has left housing for many a catch-as-catch-can matter and only when the United States was well over a century old was serious attention given to the plight of millions of persons in abject slums. Gradually through a long period of studies and wars and a worldwide depression in the 1930s, a public housing program was finally begun with the Housing Act of 1937. The pioneering efforts then eventually pointed the way to the pressing need to broaden the base of understanding and identification of housing problems as a more pragmatic approach to their solution.

Consequently, the housing element as a section of a general plan for a community is set forth as the comprehensive attack on housing inadequacies. This very word *comprehensive* as it relates to housing symbolizes the key purpose behind coordinating the housing element with all public and private agencies involved, up and down the whole line, from HUD to the hamlet or separate neighborhood where housing is a problem.

Value and Use

Too many people take substandard housing too much for granted as a condition as certain as death or taxes. This thinking (or absence of it) was used not long ago regarding smallpox and polio. The housing element would be a more valuable action lever if it described the progress in the reduction of substandard housing nationally, statewide, or locally, if figures are available. This would be convincing evidence t hat somewhere something is being done about this untidy municipal "housekeeping" and that more can be done locally.

The public bodies that have responsibilities for decision-making may or may not be in a position to do something about correcting substandard housing directly, but with a housing element as part of their background data, they should appreciate the problem and foster and support corrective measures. For instance, a regional planning body, such as a council of governments, as yet has little or no responsibility or authority regarding residential land planning within its jurisdiction. Nevertheless, if each municipality or county within the jurisdiction consistently made available to the councils of governments their housing elements and updates thereof, an overview of housing deficiencies and obstacles to overcoming them could lead toward needed state enabling legislation, more uniform housing codes, concerted relocation efforts, and other benefits. Many decisions public bodies are called upon to make could be more intelligently made with a foreknow-ledge of the housing situation in the region, county, or community, as the case may be. Condensing such information into an easily readable graph may help; this technique was used in the Hopkins County, Kentucky, Housing Element,[14] where dilapidated, deterio-rating, and sound housing from 1950 to 1990 is shown and estimated [Figure 4-18] . Here the 4,916 housing units in the county in 1950 increase to an estimated 19,000 in 1990. The 1950 units with deficiencies were 2,362 and estimated to be 5,100 in 1970 and reduce to virtually zero between 1970 and 1990, on the assumption that adequate public and private action is brought to bear on the housing problem. Noteworthy is the public housing supply building up to a maximum need of 1,000 housing units by 1980 and then,

14. Housing Element, Hopkins County, Kentucky, for Joint Planning Commission, by Harland Bartholomew Assocs., May 1970, fol. p. 13.

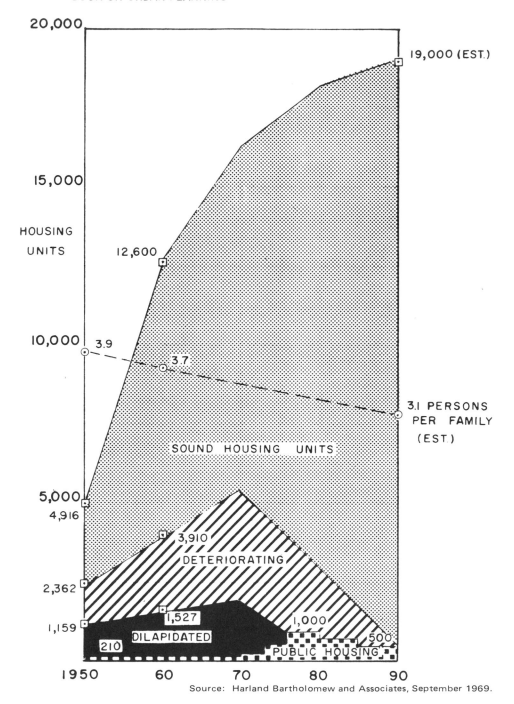

Source: Harland Bartholomew and Associates, September 1969.

Figure 4-18 Possible housing program for Hopkins County, Kentucky.

taking a positive approach, tapering off to 500 units by 1990 through sales to tenants. Such ideas as spring from the overall picture of all housing in the minds of public officials should alert them to the scope of the problem, help overcome the fixed belief that nothing much can be done about it, and aim their programs at an ultimate solution.

Local public agencies, such as housing authorities or urban renewal agencies, should find a housing element one of the key documents in a general plan in guiding their programs and efforts in the fields of public housing and urban renewal where these efforts would be more efficaciously directed. The Planning Commission should have the responsibility of scheduling, locating, and generally determining the type of effort these agencies should be involved in and the housing element should be the instrument to guide these responsibilities.

The housing element can also be a valuable tool to the private sector of the housing industry.

Private Enterprise

One of the principal risks in the home-building field is the ever-changing market and its sensitivity to supply and demand of housing and the condition of the economy generally. The housing element, if properly prepared, should indicate generally the demand for different types of housing and locations where the need is greatest. This applies not only to profit-motivated segments of the housing industry but as well to private nonprofit or limited dividend sponsors of housing for low- and moderate-income families.

Relationship to Public and Private Enterprises

The housing element of a general plan should be a joint effort of public bodies, particularly the Planning Commission, and private enterprise to formulate *and* implement the program. By private enterprise is meant especially the home-building industry, including related professionals in the fields of planning, architecture, and engineering.

An easy assumption to make is that the home-builder knows all about all facets of home-building and that his lack of interest in low- and moderate-income housing is entirely a matter of profit. Even though this may be true for some builders, there also may be others who want to get at this less attractive side of the housing field but have many blocks in their path to prevent their doing so. The planner should know about these blocks and do something about removing them. They may be the frustrations a builder or developer encounters due to lack of planning or absence of an adopted general plan that all can rely on as the way things are going to be done. The unions may be resisting new methods of construction or substitute materials which save enough on costs to make low- and moderate-income housing profitable and feasible. There may be an attitude in the community that the poor should live in used housing rather than new, and there are two positions a planner may take here: agreements, or disagreements. If he agrees, he should first ascertain that the used housing supply equals the demand in the size, location, and price range for standard units or that a rehabilitation program can bring this about. If, on the other hand, he disagrees, he should have ample factual reasons for his position and recommend how to come by the new housing through a convincing housing plan. Ordinarily, a combination of these two positions prevails, since good housing is in short supply in the lower price ranges in most communities the world over.

The search for acceptable nonprofit sponsors for low- and moderate-income housing is often a time-consuming activity but a necessary one for a well-rounded housing program. This is normally not the planner's chore but accomplishment should be, and if a little foresight will help a church, union, employees' pension fund, or utility company organize the required nonprofit group sponsor a year or two in advance of need, accomplishment will be more likely.

Another aspect of private enterprise in low- and moderate-income housing often overlooked is the need for private counseling of families in substandard housing. There are not enough taxpayers dollars to hire the thousands of people required to help these bewildered people through the maze of red tape and regulations they are confronted with to get the housing they need. Too often their bewilderment is mixed with suspicion, especially on the part of blacks, and the first task in these cases is to gain their trust and confidence. The right approach succeeds in this and comes often from church groups. Family advisory services, Volunteers of America, Salvation Army, Vista, YM/WCA, and many others have accomplished much in this area and, yet, much more needs to be done with 24 million customers.

RESIDENTIAL IN RELATION TO OTHER LAND PLANNING

A sound general plan is one that coordinates all land uses in an efficient and harmonious relationship with one another. The demands and characteristics of each type of land use necessitate compromise, and weighing the merits and demerits of these demands and the more desirable of the characteristics of each in the plan formulation process is an essential planning function. The main land uses that residential planning should meld with are commercial, industrial, and public or semipublic ones. Several examples were given earlier in this chapter regarding commercial and industrial land uses and more on the subject may be found in the next chapter.

Commercial Uses

There has been a divisiveness on the part of some planners on the subject of separation of residential and other land uses. The less desirable aspects of home and store together were considered by a school of thought in the planning profession a few decades ago as reason to separate residential and commercial land uses completely. The same thinking, but more vehement, prevailed to keep industry apart from homes. Lately, some of the more onerous objections to commercial and industrial land uses have been cleaned up or eliminated, with the result that both land uses now are finding ways to exist compatibly with housing.

The excellent advantages of many European postwar developments of shopping plazas built with apartments on top of them were copied by both Canadian and American planners and architects with considerable success and enjoyment of the occupants. The advantages of this arrangement include simplicity of shopping, especially for the elderly or mothers with small children, ease of commuting for residents who work in the stores or shops, the availability of baby-sitters at the shopping location, the added security of being able to look after one's shop in off hours or for any resident to call the police or fire station in an emergency, the interesting outlook with people around, particularly for the older residents, and the benefit to the stores in having captive customers. Some of these advantages apply equally well in mixtures of certain light industrial operations with stores and apartments.

Now zoning ordinances reflect the common sense that gets these land uses together again in a mutually helpful arrangement. The apartment-shop provisions of the Memphis Zoning Ordinance is a good example:[15]

SEC. 1911 EXCEPTIONS AND MODIFICATIONS (MEMPHIS AND SHELBY COUNTY ZONING ORDINANCE)

F.   Apartment-Shop Plan: (Ordinance Nos. 558 and 1516)

> The owner or lessee of a tract of land upon which it is proposed to erect a multi-story building of not less than twenty-five (25) living units, with shops located on the ground floors, mezzanine or basement, may submit to the Board of Commissioners of the City of Memphis a plan for the use and development of a tract of land for such purposes. The development plan shall be referred to the Memphis and Shelby County Planning Commission for study and report and for public hearings. Notice and publication of such public hearings shall conform to the procedure in Section 1918 for hearings on Changes and Amendments. If the Commission approves the plans, these shall then be submitted to the Board of Commissioners for consideration and action. The approval and recommendations of the Planning Commission shall be accompanied by a report stating the reasons for approval of the application and specific evidence and facts showing that the proposed apartment-shop plan meets with the following conditions:
>
> 1.   The property adjacent to the area included in the plan will not be adversely affected.
> 2.   The plan is consistent with the intent and purposes of this Ordinance to promote public health, safety, morals and general welfare.
> 3.   That the building or buildings shall be used only for residential purposes, except the ground floor, mezzanine and basement may be used for such of the uses authorized in the "C-1" Neighborhood Shopping District as the Planning Commission may deem justifiable under the two preceding paragraphs.
> 4.   That the parking and loading regulations shall be those provided in the "C-1" Neighborhood Shopping District.
> 5.   In considering the lot area per family contained in the site, exclusive of

15. Memphis and Shelby County Zoning Ordinance, Sec. 1911, Memphis, Tenn., p. 81.

the area occupied by streets, the application shall comply with the lot area per family required in the district in which the proposed development is located; provided, however, upon presentation of cogent evidence that a different lot area per family would be required or desirable to meet the above requirements, the plan may be approved with lot areas per family more or less than that required in the zone in which the tract is located.

6.   In addition to all data required in ordinary zoning change applications, each application shall contain a plot plan, showing all proposed land use; building lines, setbacks, parking areas, driveways, walkways, recreation areas, service areas, and other uses proposed on said tract; ground floor area of the portion proposed for commercial use and a list of uses limited to those authorized in "C-1" Neighborhood Shopping District, indicating any which will be excluded from this tract, but may not include any not authorized therein; number of living units and floor area of each, together with floor plan on each floor; and elevation of the complete structure or structures, as proposed.

If approval is recommended by the Planning Commission of all or part of the proposed plan, either with or without shops on the ground floor, mezzanine or basement, and further approved by resolution of the Board of Commissioners, the applicant shall file a final plat of such approved uses within such time or extension thereof as the Commission shall specify, suitable for recording, listing thereon the uses, if any, authorized in "C-1" Neighborhood Shopping District which shall be excluded from the ground floor, mezzanine or basement commercial occupancy, if such occupancy is authorized, together with architectural elevations, as approved. Thereafter, no occupancy permit shall be issued for any such excluded commercial use, unless application for variation therefrom is made and appoved as provided for the original application herein.

If the Board of Commissioners approves the plans and elevations, building permits and certificates of occupancy may be issued even though the use of land and the location and height of buildings to be erected in the area, the lot area per family, and the yards and open space contemplated by the plan do not conform in all respects to the district regulations of the district in which it is located. If more than one structure is contained in the approved plan, separate building permits may be taken out; provided, however, no permit shall be taken out for the store portion of a structure only, unless the residential portion is constructed simultaneously. Any portion of the approved plan, construction of which shall not have commenced within one (1) year from date of approval thereof, shall be considered as having expired, but application for renewal on the original or an amended basis may be made under the original procedures set out herein.

All things shown on the plan and elevations or in the regulations shall, upon final approval of the governing body, become part of the Zoning Regulations of the district and nothing in conflict therewith shall be done on the premises shown on the plat. Enforcement and penalties for violation shall be as provided for in any other zoning regulations.

Some noteworthy points in the provisions of the foregoing ordinance are (a) no less than 25 housing units are permitted, (b) protection of adjacent property is included, (c) neighborhood or convenience shopping (C1 zone) is the only applicable commercial type of development, and (d) the residential portion is to be built simultaneously with the commercial. These points protect not only the integrity and soundness of the development but the surrounding area, particularly housing, as well.

Strip commercial development is often the result of proceeding without benefit of planning and zoning and occurs for several reasons: land for commercial use is cheaper, plenty of street frontage or exposure is available, the individual entrepreneur enjoys less traffic congestion, and other reasons. However, the deleterious effect on nearby residential development lies in the hubbub of adjacent commercial enterprises, traffic hazards, unsightly rearside of commercial properties, and others. Chapter 5 treats the organization of land for commercial uses into neighborhood, community, and regional shopping centers to avoid haphazard shoestring commercial development.

One excuse, valid to a point, for commercial uses to border a major thoroughfare is that they act as a buffer between high volumes of traffic on the arterial route and the residential uses. Much of the buffering is offset by the objectionable characteristics of the commercial development. A better answer is bordering arterials with multifamily housing oriented more toward the quieter minor streets of the neighborhood with buffering achieved by walls, landscaping, recreational space, or fencing. Access to such apartment development should be off the minor rather than the major streets, thereby channeling more local traffic to controlled intersections and reducing friction between local and through traffic.

Certain commercial uses should be carefully buffered from residential ones and include such heavy commerce as certain wholesale operations, highway enterprises, and recreation types, such as bowling alleys, drive-in theaters, dance halls, and skating rinks.

The opposite is true of another commercial type, the golf course, which is often a key element in a residential development around which homes and apartments are located. The clubhouse with the traffic it usually generates should be located near, if not adjacent to, an arterial street or highway to avoid high volumes of traffic through minor residential streets.

One other relatively recent combination of commercial and residential development meeting with considerable success is referred to as the vertical mix. High land values in larger cities and delay in getting from place to place have resulted in a "neighborhood" within a skyscraper for retired persons, the nest-free, and young adults, all usually without school-age children. Arrangements often include parking facilities, convenience stores and service shops, private recreation clubs, restaurants, entertainment, and buildings are usually topped with many floors of apartments. The planner's concern with these developments is that they have ample parking, access is plentiful, and densities in the vicinity can be adequately accommodated.

Industrial Uses

Performance standards have been established for various industries, with the result that many of them are now compatible with certain types of residential land uses. The electronics industry can be a welcome neighbor, not only due to its prestigious jobs, but also for the appearance of the plant with landscaping and impressive buildings. If traffic, parking, waste control, and shipping are planned and designed well and operated accordingly, housing, at least multifamily, could locate adjacently or across the street with little or no difficulty or adverse effects from one to the other.

One way to reduce time wasted in commuting is to shorten the distance between work and home, and recent developments in the field of ecology, particularly with regard to air pollution, point toward shorter trips or less use of the automobile.

There are still many industrial activities that necessarily should be separated completely from housing, such as oil refineries, chemical plants, steel mills, slaughterhouses, and ore refineries, to mention a few. Air pollution control measures already in operation in some of these plants indicate eventual compatibility is possible; even though they may never be acceptable next-door neighbors, at least separation of a few blocks is preferable concerning commuting than several miles as is presently necessary.

Railroad yards and lines have their own peculiar breed of nuisances to residential land uses. These are dirt, noise, delay, and danger, often in that order but not always. The smoke and dust agitated near fast-moving trains leaves much to be desired residentially. The noise of the train engines and cars, as loud as they are, seem inaudible when whistles blow at crossings. The moral here is to eliminate as many grade crossings as possible and simultaneously reduce noise, delay, and danger. However, there is another danger, unassociated with crossings: derailment of toxic, inflammable, or explosive cargo—a good reason to keep residential development at least several hundred feet away from railroad tracks. This poses a question for the planner; what to do with that much space—a swath through town a thousand feet wide, more or less. This may be much more industrial space than the urban area needs or wants. There are numerous uses for this better than housing, such as for water or sewage treatment plants, airports, utility yards, parks, and certain other commercial land uses where the railraod nuisances would not be detrimental.

There is at least one case of railroads and housing existing in proximity with compatibility and that is in a vertical mix. This requires several floors of parking or other nonresidential uses between the trains and apartments above, and it is only fair to add that this is feasible only if the added cost of apartments using air rights over the railroad property can be justified by demand.

Public and Semipublic Uses

There is a logical way (and also not so logical) to locate housing with respect to public and semipublic land uses. Several instances of this described earlier relate to schools and parks or neighborhood shopping mostly. There are several others and Chapter 6 goes into more detail than this one; nevertheless, a few random examples will bring out some principles the planner should observe. Fire stations need to be near residential areas to respond as quickly as possible to a fire alarm and should be located on a major street near, but not necessarily at the intersection with, another arterial. The fire station acts as a buffer between the arterial traffic and residential properties.

Churches should be near homes and yet have exposure on major streets, not only to attract persons to their services and activities but as a reminder of what they stand for. Churches also make good buffers between traffic and housing.

Cemeteries present one of those thin-ice problems the planner often skates around.

The law prohibits burying a person in the ground in England and many other countries where land is scarce. The argument may be raised that land is plentiful in Canada and the United States. Yet how plentiful it is in built-up urban areas is more to the point. Crypts or vaults with or without cremation makes wiser use of space and still offers a respectful means of caring for remains. Housing near a cemetery is harder to sell or rent than farther away, everything else being equal.

Airports have an adverse effect on housing, causing noise, air pollution, danger, and interference with television reception. Approach zoning has mitigated the problem but too often after much housing is already in place—the wrong place. A solution in several localities has been buying up older housing for industrial or commercial development, but this is sometimes infeasible with newer homes. The point is to get restrictions on building more housing in an area where airport nuisances are or will stem from airport expansion plans.

Hospitals and health clinics are growing in size to keep up with Medicare and Medicaid demands and to concentrate on special problems of heart disease, cancer, and surgery. While hospitals on the one hand get more sophisticated and concentrated as technology expands, health clinics on the other are decentralizing to be nearer the daily health needs in housing areas, especially of low- and middle-income categories. The clinics should be located on major streets in the neighborhoods and the larger hospital plants near the center of the city, with an ample supply of apartments of a variety of prices and sizes within walking distance.

The measurement in acres of future needs of all of these land uses—residential, commercial, industrial, and public-semipublic—is a function of amount of each use at present and an estimate of what future population expectations are. A safe assumption is that density will increase in proportion to population and usually much more space is used or zoned for commercial development than can profitably be supported. Another assumption that should be checked before using it in land-need forecasts is that too little area is set aside for parks or open space.

Making land forecasts on a regional or at least countywide basis for future urban or rural use involves more factors and is more complicated, but the end result is better than estimating a town at a time. An example of four towns in a growing county [Table 4-5] shows both the urban and rural land uses and population in 1968 and forecasted to 1990 for Hopkins County, Kentucky. The big changes anticipated are the reduction in strip mining by several thousands of acres in the county over the next 20 years, since state legislation recently passed requires costly reclamation of areas so mined, and the opportunity now of reserving beautiful wooded and hilly terrain for public open space amounting to more than 10,000 acres, or about 500 acres per year average.

RESIDENTIAL LAND PLANNING AND URBAN RENEWAL

The urban renewal chapter, 11, covers in more detail some subjects closely related to residential land planning that should also be brought out here—conversion of slums to viable neighborhoods, the Community Renewal Program (CRP), the Neighborhood Development Program (NDP), Operation Breakthrough, and effect of decentralization of

TABLE 4-5
Estimated Land Area Requirements for 1968 and 1990
Hopkins County, Kentucky
(000)

| | Dawson Springs | | | | Earlington | | | | Madisonville | | | |
| | 1968 | | 1990 | | 1968 | | 1990 | | 1968 | | 1990 | |
Land Use	Acres	%	Acres	%	Acres	%	Acres	%	Acres	%	Acres	
Residential	206.8	11.6	458.0	25.7	200.5	16.4	240.0	19.7	982.1	14.5	1,630.0	2
Trailers	3.0	0.2	7.0	0.0	2.0	0.2	2.6	0.2	20.2	0.3	30.0	
Commercial	19.5	1.1	44.0	2.5	7.1	0.6	40.0	3.3	186.2	2.6	320.0	
Public	19.3	1.1	120.0	6.8	42.4	3.5	140.0	11.4	403.4	0.6	1,200.0	1
Semipublic	23.3	1.3	50.0	2.8	26.0	2.1	40.0	3.3	79.5	1.2	160.0	
Light industry	3.2	0.2	80.0	4.5	5.0	0.4	160.0	13.2	33.1	0.5	500.0	
Heavy industry	132.5	7.4	300.0	16.8	13.7	1.1	16.0	1.3	100.2	1.6	600.0	
Streets and railroads	123.9	6.9	275.0	15.5	143.8	11.8	280.0	22.8	693.2	10.3	1,760.0	
Agricultural and open space	1,249.4	70.2	447.7	25.4	782.9	63.9	304.8	24.8	4,257.7	63.0	555.6	
Nonparticipating cities	--	--	--	--	--	--	--	--	--	--	--	
Total	1,780.9	100.0	1,780.9	100.0	1,223.4	100.0	1,223.4	100.0	6,755.6	100.0	6,755.6	1
Population and %	3,914		9.6 10,500	18.4	2,655	6.5	3,800	6.7	16,000		39.2 31,800	

* Includes strip mining.

Source: 1968 data by State Division of Planning and forecasts by Harland Bartholomew and Assoc.

industry on housing. The planner in general planning or in residential land planning, even though he does not get closely involved in renewal, should have a general knowledge of the programs mentioned in this paragraph.

The general planning process should by law[16] precede urban renewal programs or projects, and the residential land uses in the general plan should define those areas to continue as or become residential neighborhoods. A great part of existing residential land use normally fits into one neighborhood or another, but the difficult areas to decide on are the blighted ones. There are towns where most residential areas are blighted but these are the exception rather than the rule. Often blighted areas are in a state of transition

16. U.S. Housing Act of 1949 as amended in 1954.

TABLE 4-5 cont'd

| Nortonville | | | | County Rural | | | | County Total | | | |
| 1968 | | 1990 | | 1968 | | 1990 | | 1968 | | 1990 | |
Acres	%	Acres	%	Acres	%	Acres	%	Acres	%	Acres	%
83.3	11.9	254.0	36.0	1,540.2	0.5	2,000.0	0.6	3,012.9	0.8	4,582.0	1.3
3.6	0.6	7.0	1.0	8.9	0.0	20.0	0.0	37.7	0.0	66.6	0.0
10.5	1.5	40.0	5.7	55.0	0.0	80.0	0.0	278.3	0.1	236.0	0.0
6.7	0.9	60.0	8.5	513.5	0.2	10,000.0	2.9	985.3	0.3	11,520.0	3.3
15.6	2.3	40.0	5.7	413.2	0.1	600.0	0.2	557.6	0.2	890.0	0.3
0.6	0.1	60.0	8.5	5.1	0.0	l00.0	0.0	47.0	0.0	900.0	0.3
1.4	0.3	40.0	5.7	13,500.0*	3.9	8,000.0*	2.3	13,747.8	3.9	8,956.0	2.5
80.0	11.4	180.0	25.5	8,043.9	2.4	9,000.0	2.6	9,084.8	2.6	11,495.0	3.3
503.4	71.0	24.1	3.4	317,928.8	92.5	313,435.0	90.8	326.085.4	91.8	314,767.2	88.6
--	--	--	--	1,363.2	0.4	1,500.0	0.4	1,363.2	0.4		
705.1	100.0	705.1	100.0	343,371.8	100.0	344,735.0	100.0	355,200.0	100.0	355,200.0	100.0
1,264		3.2 4,700	8.0	17,022	41.5	5,200	9.0	40,855	100.0	56,900	100.0

from outmoded residential to modern industrial or commercial use and knowing what to do about the housing in these areas poses a real problem for the planner.

At least two urban renewal programs have been of decisive help in this dilemma, the feasibility survey and the Community Renewal Program (CRP). Each is discussed more in detail in Chapter 11 but for residential considerations it should be pointed out that the feasibility survey gives an overview and rough estimate in a predetermined blighted area within the survey of the conditions of blight (buildings, streets, mixed land use, flooding, and the like) and an approximate cost of city and federal funds to eliminate or correct the substandard conditions. Housing is usually involved in such surveys and a rough idea of numbers and types of housing required is determined in the feasibility survey. The practicality of continuing this or that housing area as a residential neighborhood may also be a result of the survey and provide the planner with a basis for his decisions.

The CRP, even though a broader look at blight, is a community-wide assessment of all areas good and bad for the purpose of formulating a program of renewal. This may mean a light touch of conservation in most neighborhoods and many will need no attention in some cities. Another group will require more conservation in the form of correcting street deficiencies, providing a park, or changing incompatible land uses (junkyard near homes, for example). The next category down the blight scale would involve code enforcement of housing and other buildings and finally, if the area is too deteriorated (over 50 percent of the buildings faulty), clearance and redevelopment is the only sensible course. As of June 30, 1970, 221 communities (cities and counties) had contracted with HUD in the amount of $51,953,000 for CRP work.[17]

The CRP should settle another perplexing question the planner is confronted with—where to start all the renewal work needed. A sound general plan with its short- and long-range capital improvements program plus the CRP findings should pinpoint several areas needing attention. A wise balance would involve starting where life and property are in jeopardy, where available funds cover the local share of costs, where adequate community support will be forthcoming, and certainly where the action would conform with the CRP and the general plan.

If a blighted residential area is proposed for nonresidential redevelopment, the planner has an obligation to ascertain the relocation resources available and their adequacy for meeting the rate of renewal proposed.

A relative newcomer in urban renewal is the Neighborhood Development Program (NDP), a provision of the Housing Act of 1968. The name of this program has been a source of misunderstanding, especially for the layman. Community Development Program would be more accurate but would conflict with CRP. NDP usually encompasses more than a single neighborhood and this is where much of the confusion stems; some cities with a fairly general spread of blight in varying degrees have declared all the area within the city limits in NDP boundaries. The main thrust of NDP is to expedite the lagging, cumbersome renewal process that usually takes at least two years of surveys, planning, and approvals before the work of development starts. NDP requires development to start the first year or approval of funds is withheld. This is one way to expedite fulfilling the residential neighborhood requirements and realizing the living amenities, such as street changes, parks, utilities, and the like sooner. More on the funding, administration, and planning requirements under NDP are included in Chapter 11.

Operation Breakthrough, also an offspring of the Housing Act of 1968, is proposed as an experiment in housing and urban living to achieve breakthroughs in a number of housing or housing related fields that have clung tenaciously to a modus operandi traditionally costly and ponderous, and to reduce the cost and complications of urban life. A large order! Eight prototype sites are in construction and deserve close scrutiny of new methods of modular and manufactured construction of housing, new zoning techniques, new combinations of land uses, new operating procedures, new financing

---

17. *Urban Renewal Directory,* June 30, 1970, HUD, Washington D.C., p. i.

methods, new ownership and rental agreements, new labor union relationships, new utilities services arrangements, and new living habits of the occupants.

The aggregated housing market mentioned earlier in this chapter will be the basis for 26 million housing units during the next 10 years under this program. Two of the original ten years have already transpired, but adding two more or another one or two additionally is expected so as to get the clinical results from the eight prototype sites after they have been occupied and observed for at least a year. They were scheduled for occupancy in June of 1971 but may miss this mark by a year or so. The prototype sites are in Indianapolis, Jersey City, Kalamazoo, Macon, Memphis, Sacramento, St. Louis, and Seattle. Two other cities, Houston and Wilmington pulled out of the program. Kalamazoo is the first site with housing units for sale or rent (as of November 1971). The effect of Operation Breakthrough on mass production of housing and the impact it will have on not only the 26 million housing units in the present decade but also the 100 million additional Americans and how they are housed by the end of this century is a phenomenon housing specialists the world over are watching.

The effect of decentralization of industry on housing is a subject perhaps oddly located here under the heading Residential Land Planning and Urban Renewal. Yet, the reason is that renewal usually plays an important role in the problems remaining as industry moves out. The next chapter treats this trend from the point of view of industry while the housing aspects are related here.

There are several reasons for industry to move—taxes, high land cost, unwillingness of adjacent property owners to sell at a reasonable price, high labor wages, pilferage, the high cost of doing business in the congested city, management dislike of the blighted neighborhood where the plant is located, and other reasons. Individually or collectively these reasons have caused industries to move out of crowded cities to peripheral or rural locations, leaving those nearby unemployed and often in substandard housing. This worsens the renewal process financially but should expedite renewal to avoid higher future costs—reduction in tax revenue, increased demand for public housing, higher proportionate cost of municipal services in a deteriorating area, and the like.

The general plan and the CRP should indicate whether such an area should be cleared of its remaining substandard housing for industrial expansion or, conversely, cleared of a few rundown industrial plants, having the housing upgraded, and bringing about a viable residential neighborhood. The industrial decentralization trend presents either opportunity or a combination of the two courses in some cases where both remaining industry and housing benefit as incompatibly mixed land uses are unmixed by means of the renewal process.

CARING ENOUGH FOR ALL TO LIVE IN STANDARD HOUSING

This title may seem to have an altruistic and even moralistic connotation; yet there is more implied. The only way substandard housing will be eliminated or converted to standard is for someone or some group to care enough for it to happen. The props are ready, the cast is selected, and the play has at least a modicum of financial backing but the stage is not set. This parable interpreted is that the tools of renewal and standard housing are available, the actors (planner, engineer, politician, and others) chosen, and there is some financial assistance in FHA 235i, 221d2, and limited renewal funds, admittedly; yet the tough job of where to start and how to do it often is delayed and delayed.

The words of a Great Man are often used as a crutch for more delay, "The poor you always have with you . . . "[18] He did not add that we should do nothing about the poor. There is an Old Testament answer. "If there is among you a poor man, one of your brethren, in any of your towns within your land which the Lord your God gives you, you shall not harden your heart or shut your hand against your poor brother, but you shall open your hand to him, and lend him sufficient for his need, whatever it may be."[19] The next question may be "Who is a brother?" and to avoid interminable debate on this subject, at the risk of further delay of standard housing for all, some practical aspects of the subject are in order.

Substandard housing is a tax liability in any community. The tax revenue from blighted areas nowhere near pays for city and other services, public and private; these areas are subsidized by the taxpayer and the more affluent segment of the populace through charitable contributions. So, to care enough for all to live in standard housing is more than an ideal or a moral issue; it is a pragmatic necessity.

There is another practical aspect to this subject touched on above and reemphasized here to employ one of the psychological factors of memory, repetition. The planner and other professionals involved in the housing field, and more particularly the layman on the fringes of the problem, often have a fixation about families in substandard housing being rehoused in new housing, public or private. A straight look at this situation is worth a few words.

The familiar stories of coal stored in the bathtub and garbage clogging the toilet usually apply to an uneducated minority from unsophisticated areas and are a reminder that modern urban living is an experience that requires instruction and understanding to be fully appreciated and for appropriate adjustments to be made in the process of living closely together.

A large majority of benefactors in the process of reduction of substandard housing have moved into used housing and rarely into new housing. Even public housing, though it is new the first time it is occupied, has a turnover of something in excess of four percent of its units annually. Pertinent too, is the fact that only those eligible for public housing are admitted, considerably less than half of substandard housing occupants on the average. Where do the remainder go? Into private sales and rental housing, most of which is used.

Lately, FHA 235 and 236, sales and rental programs, respectively, have produced private housing in competition with public in a progressive program there will likely be much more of. The numbers and percentages of the total are small, but the effect is encouraging. A pride of ownership in the 235 category has overcome many of the earlier objections critics have had of the poor in an ownership situation.

18. John 12:8 (RSV).
19. Lev. 15:7,8 (RSV).

The flight of the more affluent to the suburbs since World War II, leaving behind housing in the city, some of which is not too bad and with plenty of useful economic life remaining, has resulted in a housing supply for those who are unable to afford the suburbs yet desire better than their substandard homes. This trend has been a blessing to many moving up the housing economic ladder into standard, if old, shelter.

Elimination of substandard housing happens only if a concerted program is formulated, each participant knows his responsibility, and a continuing hammering away at the job proceeds relentlessly through the years. The planner is a key person in this process.

FUTURE IMPORTANCE OF HOUSING

The timeworn phrase "A man's home is his castle" with all the nostalgia, pride, and security implied is as true now as in the past and, in spite of recent American housing trends and, perhaps to a lesser extent, Canadian too, housing has an important future. The trends that may seem to refute this are not universal and include such activities as travel away from home, the home as principally a dormitory, the instability of housing associated with mobile home living, the younger generation leaving home at an earlier age, and just plain restlessness.

There is no doubt that housing is in for vast changes, and ways of living, especially in urban areas, are going to be altered by ecological, environmental, and technological influences not meant here as survival scares but as a practical need for more order and tranquillity.

The industrialization of housing will further reduce costs as manufacturing and field-assembly techniques improve and mass production increases. Condominium apartments will reach a broader market, including more middle-income and some low-income families. These units will not be in the luxury category but in the smaller size units such families can afford. This trend will enhance home ownership.

The future importance of housing embraces three general categories—economic stability, social progress, and peace of mind.

Economic Stability

The forces that have been eroding the solid state of continuity of a neighborhood for decades have been analyzed, finally, and categorized as obsolescence, shifting land uses, structural deterioration, neglect, economic decline, and others. The viable neighborhood with informed inhabitants and plenty of economic life left in its facilities and structures knows now how to defend itself against these inroads of time and fortune. There are too many families with large personal investments in their homes to let their property and their neighborhood slide into decay.

Consequently, neighborhood improvement associations and similar organizations have come into being to supplement and energize officials responsible for neighborhood conservation. The home, the largest investment of a lifetime for many, is getting some of the recognition it deserves from the point of view of economic stability.

This privately originated form of economic safeguard is catching on in other than higher-income neighborhoods also. Blacks who have worked hard to save for a home and who usually have looked longer than whites for one in an adequate neighborhood are guarding their investment with zeal. Moderate-income whites are showing concern for neighborhood conditions and bringing about corrective action where necessary to protect their investments.

With the percentage of homeowners on the increase [Figure 4-19], the economic stability of the home has a better likelihood than ever before. The percentages were derived from total white homeowners as a percentage of total white renters and white owners and the same for nonwhite percentages. Personal interest in care of property generally follows with home ownership. Figure 4-19 shows an even faster rate of climb from 19.0 in 1890 to 41.5 in 1970 for percent of nonwhite ownership, an encouraging sign for economic strength and continuity and broadening distribution of wealth. Noteworthy is the drop in white ownership during the Great Depression of the thirties of 4.5 percent while the nonwhite drop was only 1.6 percent. Homewonership is at the foundation of the free enterprise system and its steady growth connotes not only economic stability but social progress as well.

Social Progress

Measurement of social progress may be accomplished in numerous ways and the home, the condition of housing, and the degree of homeownership should be considered essential gauges of progress. Some may quarrel with the position that social progress is being made or that society is progressing. The facts speak for themselves in the social advances in health and medicine, distribution of wealth, less illiteracy, increased communications, a more knowledgeable populace, more leisure time, greater educational and

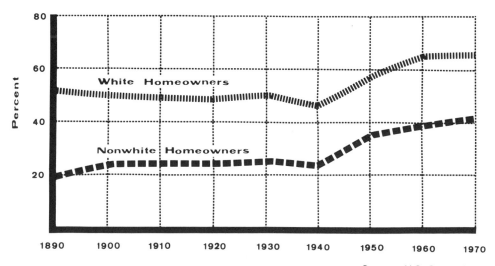

Source: U.S. Census Bureau.

Figure 4-19   U.S. homeowners.

recreational opportunities, more travel by more people, more cultural activities, and many other signs.

Problems should not, however, be ignored; crime, suicide, illegitimacy, drugs, and other evils are real deterrents to social progress. These problems are more constantly and more vehemently brought to the attention of more people than ever before. The incidences of these problems are impossible to compare within only a few decades, or years back in some cases, since records were not kept on these subjects in the detail they are now. The rise in numbers killed annually on highways is staggering until a comparison is made with the increase in number of drivers, the many more miles they drive, and the enormous increase in manhours behind the wheel.

The refreshing signs of better ways of life in new communities across the land is a bellweather of social progress tied to modern housing in modern neighborhoods that get better each year new ones are built and new ideas make life more pleasant [Figure 4-20]. These ideas are spreading. More and more people want the good life they see and hear about on television and in magazines and a whole new market is opening up to satisfy these wants for a broader base of the population. Housing is one of the most wanted of these commodities and the future looks good for more and more people to enjoy standard housing in standard neighborhoods in communities void of substandard housing and other conditions of blight. A good start is already made!

Peace of Mind

This is the end result—to know that economic stability is established, that social

ECHO   RIDGE   LOOKING WEST
Source: Perry Park, Colorado, by Charles Gathers and Associates.
Figure 4-20   Example of a new planning technique on a hillside.

progress is a reality, and that each person has a place to call home where peace can be found, where the mind, as well as the body, can rest easy, where anxiety is overcome, and the joy of living is a daily experience of more and more people.

This is not universal but an illusive goal achieved spasmodically for some and not at all for others. But it is there to grasp and enjoy. The right kind of environment helps set the stage and an adequate home helps substantially to complete the picture. Peace of mind regarding relationships with neighbors, with fellow workers, and with one's self is so rewarding and it takes so little from each individual for it to happen, that it's a wonder there isn't more of it. But the secret is that it comes from within. The stage can be set in the environment, in the neighborhood, in the home, and these stand for the least that should be done, but the answer in the last analysis is in the heart and spirit of each individual.

BIBLIOGRAPHY

1. Harland Bartholomew, *Land Uses in American Cities,* Harvard Univ. Press, Cambridge, Mass., 1965.
2. FHA Economic and Market Analysis Division, *FHA Techniques of Housing Market Analysis,* Washington, D.C., 1970.
3. William H. Claire (ed.), *Urban Planning Guide,* American Society of Civil Engineers Manual on Engineering Practice 49, New York, 1969; especially Chap. 3, "Residential Land Planning," by George C. Bestor.
4. Technical Committee on Industrial Classification Office of Statistical Standards, *Standard Industrial Classification Manual,* Government Printing Office, Washington, D.C., 1957.
5. President's Committee on Urban Housing, *A Decent Home,* Government Printing Office, Washington, D.C., 1969.
6. F. Stuart Chapin, Jr., *Urban Land Use Planning,* 2d ed., Univ. of Illinois Press, Urbana, Ill., 1965.
7. Francis C. Murphy, *Regulating Flood Plain Development,* Univ. of Chicago Press, Chicago, 1958.
8. Institute of Traffic Engineers, *Traffic Engineering Handbook,* Washington, D.C. (latest issue).
9. John S. Shelton, *Geology Illustrated,* W. H. Freeman & Co., San Francisco, 1966.
10. Urban Land Institute, *Community Builders Handbook,* Washington, D.C.
11. W. I. Goodman and E. C. Freund (eds.), *Principles and Process of Urban Planning,* International City Management Assoc., Chicago.
12. "Population Growth and America's Future" by Commission on Population Growth and the American Future, March 16, 1971, U.S. Government Printing Office, Washington, D.C., 20402.
13. "Urban Growth and Land Development—The Land Conversion Process" by the Land Use Subcommittee of the Advisory Committee to the Department of Housing and Urban Development, National Acadamy of Sciences and National Academy of Engineering, Washington, D.C., 1972.

5 | PLANNING FOR INDUSTRY AND COMMERCE

Harold M. Mayer

Cities exist because people find increased satisfaction of their social and economic needs by mutual proximity, which facilitates interaction. Concentrations of people and facilities in limited areas at relatively high densities is an inherent characteristic of cities and urban regions. Since all activities which benefit from mutual proximity cannot occupy the same space, there is a sorting out of such activities with respect to the most accessible portions of the urban complex, partly by "natural" forces of centralization and decentralization in accordance with the relative ability of each activity to benefit from, and hence pay for, centrality, and partly as the result of intervention in the public interest. The latter constitutes the essence of planning, insofar as physical patterns of land use and spatial interaction are concerned.

Most urban activities are either essentially economic in character, or they have important economic ramifications; they are concerned with making a living or of enjoying the fruits of economic success. They take place on specific sites; therefore it is the concern of the planner to facilitate the provision of adequate sites, in adequate amounts and at efficient locations, for the performance of urban economic functions, while at the same time securing to the extent possible the noneconomic effects, such as visual pleasure, of a successful economic base. Urban land is a scarce resource, and its allocation among the many competing uses for it is a major concern of the city, metropolitan, and regional planner, who must, at times, recommend various forms of intervention into the "natural" evolution of the urban form and pattern.

The classical economists developed the idea that there are three major types of inputs into an economic system: land, labor, and capital. Since labor and capital are relatively mobile in location and land is the only element which has a fixed one, the location of sites for specific activities is the major determinant of their value which, in turn, is a function of their accessibility to the sites of other functions with which interaction takes place. In other words, the principal determinant of the value of urban land, which is a scarce resource, is its accessibility, or convenience of location. In this it differs from nonurban land, in which the inherent characteristics, such as soil fertility, also constitute necessary, but not always sufficient, elements of value. It is among the principal functions of the urban planner, therefore, to facilitate the process of allocation of land among the various functions that can take place upon it, to secure maximum economic efficiency from the resultant pattern of land uses and mutual interactions, while at the same time maximizing, wherever possible, the noneconomic satisfactions, such as visual pleasure, attendant upon satisfactory patterns of land use. The planner should determine the most efficient and satisfactory patterns of land use, and assess the relative feasibilities of, and methods of achieving, the physical, economic, and social goals, in which physical arrangements of land uses play a major role. In other words, planning should be concerned with the relative efficiencies of alternative patterns of land uses.

Since having an income is indispensible to everyone, the economic base of cities and regions is the first concern, after determination of the community goals, and is an indispensable part of the determination of prospective patterns of spatial arrangements for the land uses, many of which are involved in the processes of making a living. The totality of such processes, and the establishments involved in them, is called the "economic base" of the city, metropolitan area, region, or nation. These establishments include those involved in production, distribution, and consumption of goods and services, and the ultimate establishment is the consuming unit: the individual or household. Studies of the economic base, present and prospective, therefore, constitute essential parts of the planning process. Economic base studies are vital parts of the process of economic and social planning; they are equally necessary parts of the process of land use and transportation planning, because of the need to provide for adequate, but not superfluous, amounts of land in the proper places for all of the multitude of activities, establishments, and facilities involved in the economic processes of the city.

URBAN ECONOMIC FUNCTIONS

Economists, geographers, and others customarily divide economic activities into several categories, which they term primary, secondary, tertiary, and quaternary. These categories are useful in investigations of the economic base of cities and urban regions; certain categories are essentially urban, and others are not.

Primary Functions

The primary functions are those involved in the extraction of natural resources. They must be carried on where the resources are found. Except for mining, fishing, forestry, and similar activities, which give impetus to specialized cities, relatively little urban development involves primary resource extraction; on the other hand, certain resources such as rock, sand, and gravel must be available to support urban growth. But resource-oriented urban communities generally have only one dominant and basic function, and their continued existence is dependent not only upon the continued availability of the resource at or near the community, but also upon market conditions which favor continued extraction of the resource at the given location, unless substitute sources of support can be found. Even though many urban communities directly depend upon primary resources, they actually function as service centers or manufacturing towns. The resources themselves, such as the products of agriculture, sustained-yield forestry, fisheries, or hydroelectric power, may be replaceable, or they may be irreplaceable, such as is the case with the mining of metals or the extraction of fossil fuels, such as coal or petroleum. In the case of irreplaceable resources, if one becomes depleted or market conditions make continued extraction submarginal, the community must find alternative sources of economic base or it will die.

Secondary and Tertiary Functions

Secondary economic activities are those involving handling of goods, either as to changing the form or changing the location; the principal types of secondary activity are manufacturing and transportation. Because both involve intensive utilization of labor and concentrations of investment in plant, they are characteristic urban functions.

Tertiary activities, in turn, are those involved with the performance of services or the transfer of ownership of goods, including wholesale and retail trade; all urban places have a multiplicity of tertiary activities, and for many towns and cities such activities constitute the major portion of the economic base. Some authorities include under "tertiary" activities the keeping of records and communication; others set up a separate category, the quaternary, for such activities; in any event, such activities are characteristically urban. Like secondary and other tertiary activities, they take place where there are concentrations of people and facilities; thus there is a cause-and-effect reciprocal relationship between economic base and population concentration.

Thus, primary activities—the extractive industries—are of necessity resource-oriented as to location. Secondary activities, such as manufacturing, may be resource-oriented, market-oriented, or "footloose," depending upon whether the goods are heavy, bulky, of low value, and hence not easily and cheaply transported, or, on the other hand, compact and of high value in proportion to weight or bulk. With improvements in the efficiency of transportation systems, secondary industries are increasingly market-oriented or footloose; in the latter case the availability of skilled or low-cost labor may be a major determinant of location.

As more and more activities become market-oriented or footloose, due to increased efficiency in transportation and communication, they tend to be attracted to those locations which offer maximum "external economies," or specialized services and amenities. Thus there is a "multiplier effect," stimulating location in or near the larger urban concentrations—although, in many instances, at or near their edges in order to avoid the inconveniences, including congestion, and the high land values near the urban centers. Manufacturing establishments, therefore, seek locations which represent acceptable compromises between central and peripheral sites, but in any event, since they require a labor force and external services, they must be in or near urban concentrations.

Wholesale activities represent a transitional category, with some of the characteristics of secondary type, since goods are handled and stored, but others are of tertiary type, since transfer of ownership takes place. The goods are stored in warehouses, which in some respects resemble the buildings occupied by manufacturing establishments. On the other hand, wholesaling involves commercial transactions, which may take place in office-type facilities, with or without storage on the site, and with or without display of samples. Thus, wholesaling is either "industrial," resembling secondary types of activities, or "commercial," resembling tertiary and quaternary activities, in their physical requirements. Competition for centrally located land in cities generally forces wholesale establishments, such as those involving warehousing, to the peripheries of the cities, while the office types of wholesale establishments, depending upon comparison displays for the buyers or upon rapid communication, in the case of fashion goods, may tend to locate closer to the urban centers. Generally, the land requirements for wholesale establishments are decreasing, because of improvements in transportation and changes in marketing, including an increase in chain stores and centralized purchasing, which combine to reduce the need for extensive inventories.

All goods and services ultimately are for the consumer—the individual or family—and the tertiary activities, which represent the final links in the chain from origin of the resources to final delivery of goods and services at the destination, whether or not change in form is involved en route, are, of course, market-oriented, which means that the location of tertiary establishments is correlated with the locations of the people they serve. Thus, retailing and service establishments are less concentrated in location than are manufacturing or wholesaling establishments.

In the location of retail and service establishments, however, there are noteworthy patterns of concentration. Food retailing, for example, tends to be more ubiquitous, with more and smaller establishments, than specialized types of retail and service activities, such as fashion goods retailing, or highly specialized medical services. In general, the more specialized the goods and services, the less ubiquitous are the establishments dispensing them, and the greater the tendency for them to concentrate in larger centers, where they are accessible to a larger population, with a larger "disposable income," and hence a larger and more extensive market. Larger centers, spaced farther apart than smaller ones, have more specialized establishments, as well as more numerous establishments, for they draw upon a larger economic base of support. Nevertheless, the larger centers, or "higher-order" centers, may also include establishments characteristic of smaller or lower-order centers; such establishments serve less extensive trade or service areas than do the larger and more specialized ones within the same center. Thus there is a "nested hierarchy" of central places, or clusters of establishments, each with its own trade or service area. Each successively higher central place in the hierarchy tends to include within it the functions and establishments of the lower order of central places, in addition to the less ubiquitous and more specialized functions and establishments characteristic of the higher order, constrained only by the competition for sites, which, in some of the highest-order central places, may force out those functions or establishments which cannot afford the high-value sites and are outbid for them by the higher-order establishments. The "ma and pa" local grocery store cannot afford to be in the central business district of a large city, where the land, in scarce supply, is needed by those functions and establishments which serve more extensive areas and populations, characteristically the entire city or metropolitan area.

The hierarchial arrangement is not confined to commercial establishments and services; public service establishments and their associated service areas commonly also involve nested hierarchies. Thus, there are several neighborhood elementary schools for each community high school, and several high schools for each college or university; local municipalities and unincorporated areas are grouped into counties which, in turn, are parts of states. The states together constitute the nation; each has its own set of governmental establishments and facilities appropriate to its particular level in the hierarchy. In order to determine the extent of need for particular functions at various locations, as an important aspect of land use planning and zoning, the planner should determine the appropriate extent and location of the requisite support, in terms of population and purchasing power or need for establishments, commercial and otherwise, providing various combinations of goods and services at various locations.

The numbers, relative sizes, and spacings among "central places" are functions of the nature of the population served, including its density, demographic and occupational structure, and its income, as well as of the transportation pattern which provides accessibility between the various establishments and their respective service areas. These variables, and the patterns which are associated with them, constitute one of the most generally accepted concepts in urban geography, and there is an extensive body of empirical as well as theoretical literature on the subject, much of which has direct planning application.[1] Central Place Theory is generally accepted by urban geographers and regional scientists, and its application in planning for land use controls and in location of commercial and other establishments has been generally useful. The basic idea of the central place hierarchy, the association of related establishments and their respective service areas each with its distinctive "range" or extent, and the role of transportation in providing access between the establishments and those served, should be generally familiar to planners. These concepts are applicable at any scale from the national or regional to the local clusters of enterprises within a community or neighborhood.

Closely related to the concept of central places are the gravity and potential models,

1. Brian J. L. Berry, and Allen Pred, *Central Place Studies: A Bibliography of Theory and Applications* (Philadelphia: Regional Science Research Institute, reprinted 1965, with supplement), contains an annotated listing of over 1,000 items dealing with the subject. Central Place Theory is treated extensively in virtually all textbooks on urban geography.

discussed in Chapter 7. The basic idea is that accessibility varies in proportion to the size or pulling power of a center—which, in turn, is related to the numbers and kinds of services and the sizes of the establishments providing them within the center—and inversely in proportion to an exponetial function of distance. Thus, the attraction of a center decreases with increasing distance, but at a decreasing rate. The result is an imaginary surface of attraction, with a peak at the center, and with negative slopes in every direction, much like the shape of a volcano. With respect to any given function or type of establishment the slopes from "nearest neighbors," such as competing shopping centers or cities, may overlap, creating a boundary zone within which the attraction may be in either of several directions, depending upon the number of centers or businesses whose service areas overlap, in contrast to sharp lines of demarkation where defined boundaries, such as those of administrative units, or major topographic features such as coastlines, cut off the respective service areas. Thus, studies of the economic base of a city or region may be unrealistic and misleading unless the complementary service area, trade area, or "hinterland" is taken into consideration. Bounded units, such as those of a municipal area, or even of an SMSA (Standard Metropolitan Statistical Area) rarely coincide with the boundaries of service areas unless, as in the case of governmental units, such service areas are arbitrarily defined. The planner must be constantly aware that, in terms of many of the urban functions, the area for which he is doing the planning is an arbitrarily bounded one, and that many of the urban functions, particularly economic ones, may cover more or less area than his planning unit.

ECONOMIC ACTIVITIES AND TRAFFIC FLOWS

Because cities are agglomerations of people and facilities resulting from the necessity for mutual proximity in the performance of certain functions which, generally, do not include the extraction of raw materials, foodstuffs, or fuels, it follows that such necessities must be brought into the urban areas, and must be paid for by the supplying of goods and services not only to those within the city, but also to persons and establishments outside, the latter constituting the city's hinterland, which may vary in areal extent; for some functions of large cities some of the specialized hinterlands may be worldwide.[2] One may, therefore, differentiate between those functions which exclusively or predominantly serve the urban area itself and those which produce goods and services in substantial proportion for consumption outside that area, or for which people travel to the city. Flows of people and goods—traffic—and the facilities for such flows are essential components of the urban economy.

The planner, therefore, should be vitally concerned with efficient transportation, not only within the urban area, but also between that area and the various hinterlands which the city serves. The latter concern is the subject of Chapter 7. Along the transportation routes, interchange of people and goods between city and hinterland takes place. It follows, therefore, that an excellent method of study of a city's commerce and

2. Harold M. Mayer, "Urban Nodality and the Economic Base", *Journal of the American Institute of Planners,* Vol. 20, No. 3 (Summer 1954), pp. 117-121.

industry—its economic relations with its service areas—would be to study the flows of people and goods to and from the urban area. Because not all physical flows of people and goods are balanced in direction, the imbalance is compensated for by flows of money and credit. The terms "import" and "export" are commonly used to describe these flows of people, goods, money, and credit into and out of a city or urban area, respectively, not necessarily in their international context, but as a concept relating to the nodal or focal character of the city in relation to its various nested hinterlands. These flows indicate the nature of the urban functions which give rise to them.

In the study of flows, especially goods movements to, from, and within cities, the principal difficulty—and it is an important one—is the general lack of adequate data. The reasons for such lack are several: (a) the high cost of data collection and processing, (b) commercial competition in the United States and Canada, where much of the movement is by private-enterprise common and contract carriers, (c) the use of private vehicles, the operators of which cannot supply detailed data with reasonable effort and cost, (d) military security, and (e) in some instances, lack of adequate determination of appropriate area boundaries for such studies. Some of these problems are discussed in Chapter 7. Thus, studies of flows in and out of cities and urban regions, although hypothetically forming an excellent method of study of the urban economy are, in fact, usually impracticable in sufficient detail to be useful specifically for economic studies. Nevertheless, economists, geographers, and regional scientists utilize several surrogate methods of analysis of the economic base of cities and regions.

METHODS OF ECONOMIC BASE STUDY

Planners are concerned with the studies of urban and regional economic base because they need to know the present and prospective employment (which is reciprocally related to population size and characteristics), income, transportation, and space requirements for the various economic functions. The cliché that people do not live by taking in each other's washing is a simple way of expressing the fact that the economic base of a community essentially is that which involves the specialized supplying of goods and services to the external areas. Therefore, studies of the urban economic base generally concentrate on those activities which serve the external areas: the "city building" rather than "city serving" activities, or those that are sporadic or unique, rather than those which are ubiquitous. In recent years, the service functions have been growing much more rapidly than have the activities involving goods, and with increasing emphasis upon the quality of urban life, the internal side of the urban economic base has been receiving increased attention.[3] In any case, all of the methods of economic base study involve the concept of flow or movement.

The methods which have been most developed for studies of the urban and regional

3. Hans Blumenfeld, "The Economic Base of the Metropolis: Critical Remarks on the 'Basic-Nonbasic' Concept," *Journal of the American Institute of Planners,* Vol. 21, No. 4 (Fall 1955), pp. 114-132.

economic base are: (a) the basic-nonbasic method, (b) the balance-of-payments approach, (c) input-output analysis, and (d) the minimum- or average-requirements method.

Basic-Nonbasic

The basic-nonbasic approach to the study of a city or region's economic support is relatively crude, and can be used only for a rough approximation of the nature of a city's economic base. Determination of the essential nature of a city's specialization, however, can be made in a general way by use of the method, as a first step toward ultimate determination of the strengths and deficiencies, which are indicative of the direction in which economic development activities may most effectively be carried out. Essentially, the method consists of ascertaining the proportion of each category of economic activity which is devoted to meeting the needs for goods and services on the part of the city or region's own population—residential and labor force—and the proportion which is devoted to supplying goods and services externally, the "export" sector of the economy. The former is "nonbasic" and the latter is "basic," for it produces an exchange, in the form of "imports" into the city or region, in return for the "exports" of the specialized goods or services of the city.

There are several criteria by which the extent of specialization of the economic base may be measured. For each category of activity, the ratio between basic and nonbasic components—the so-called B/N ratio—represents the extent to which the given category exceeds the activity in the same category in a larger region, such as the nation, within which the given city or region is located. These relationships may be expressed in terms of employment, income, or other items which may be relevant to the particular problem. Thus, if a given activity produces, in a city or metropolitan area, a proportion of the total employment in the area three times as great as the proportion of employment in the same activity bears to total employment in the nation or larger region, three-fourths of the local urban or metropolitan employment in that activity is said to be "basic" or "city-forming," presumably producing for "export" out of the area, the remaining one-fourth of the employment in that activity being for production of goods or services for the city or metropolitan area itself.

The basic-nonbasic dichotomy is a simple concept, but its practical application involves many difficulties. One is the difficulty of obtaining adequate data; aggregated statistics may be for geographic areas other than those for which the planner is working, and statistics for individual establishments may be unavailable, or may not justify the time and cost involved in obtaining, compiling, and processing them; in many instances competitive relationships preclude their availability. Another difficulty lies in the selection of the measures to be used: whether employment, payrolls, income, space, or physical volume of production. If employment is used as the measure, allowance must be made for part-time, overtime, and seasonal employment, marginal workers such as married women and young people who may enter and leave the labor force depending upon fluctuating economic and other conditions, and many other variables. Physical production is not always usable, because many components of the urban economic base consist of services, and even where goods are involved, various measures apply to different kinds of goods. Furthermore, the B/N ratio will vary with the extent of the area and the location of its boundaries; a planner concerned with a "central city" or municipality will come up with a very different economic base pattern than will a planner for that city's metropolitan area if—as is common—a significant proportion of the economic activity is within the metropolitan area but outside the central city. Generally, the larger the area and population, the greater the variety of components of the economic base (diversity), and the lower the proportion of basic to nonbasic activity.

The basic-nonbasic dichotomy has been subjected to many criticisms. It is crude: the selection of measures and of area boundaries may be subjective, the nonbasic component increases in importance relative to the basic as the quality of urban life improves, and projection of the individual component trends, as well as the aggregate B/N ratio for a city or region, is subject to many variables which cannot be anticipated, such as the direction and rate of technological and social change and externally influenced in-migration.[4]

Balance of Payments

The balance-of-payments approach to the study of urban economic base is, in theory, quite simple, but experience has demonstrated that it is virtually impossible to apply. Furthermore, it measures only one among the many economic variables with which the urban planner must be concerned, and there is no possibility of converting the method so as to apply to estimates of population, employment, or land requirements. It is, simply, the measurement of the flow of money and credit in and out of a region or city. It has long been used in economic studies of nations, where adequate statistics are available relative to the financial transactions across national borders. Since cities and urban regions are much more interdependent with their external hinterlands and most statistical series are not available, and many cannot be compiled for geographically meaningful areas, such as individual cities and metropolitan complexes, the method is of very doubtful utility for the urban planner.

Input-Output

Input-output analysis, like the balance-of-payments approach, is concerned with the flows into and out of an area.[5] The technique has been developed mainly for the study of national economies, but has also been applied, in a few instances, to subnational areas. Unlike the balance-of-payments approach, it can be utilized in studies of employment and

4. For a general review of the basic-nonbasic concept see: John W. Alexander, "The Basic-Non Basic Concept of Urban Economic Functions," *Economic Geography*, Vol. 30, No. 3 (July 1954), pp. 246-261. A more detailed discussion of the method is in a series of articles by Richard B. Andrews in *Land Economics*, 1953-56, most of which were reprinted in Ralph W. Pfouts (ed.), *The Techniques of Urban Economic Analysis* (Chandler-Davis Publ. Co., 1960).

5. Walter Isard and Robert Kavesh, "Economic Structural Interrelations of Metropolitan Regions," *American Journal of Sociology*, Vol. 60 (Sept. 1964), pp. 152-162; also: Walter Isard, *Methods of Regional Analysis* (Cambridge, Mass.: M.I.T. Press, and New York: Wiley and Sons, 1960), especially pp. 309-363.

physical goods and services, as well as of money and credit flows. It shares, however, with the balance-of-payments studies, the limitations inherent in the difficulties, and commonly, the impossibility, of obtaining adequate data for areas smaller than nations.

Inputs consist of all items whether payments, goods, services, or investments, which make possible economic activity in a nation, region, city, or individual establishment, including households—the ultimate consuming units. Similarly, outputs consist of the total flows of goods, services, and payments from an area to the rest of the world. The input-output analysis, in essence, involves investigation of the effects of changes, individually and collectively, in any sector of activity or any category of establishment, upon all the others. Some of the effects may be confined to within the area being studied; others may involve external areas, from the immediate vicinity to worldwide. It is obvious that tremendous masses of data must be assembled, collated, interpreted, and processed. The modern electronic computer has made possible the handling of such data, although there are capacity limitations in even the largest of such machines. The method consists of compiling, in a matrix of rows and columns, with each row or column representing one category of activity, the effects of changes in any given activity or set of activities upon each of the others. The matrix, because of the complexity of economic activities in even a relatively simple urban area, would have hundreds of rows and columns, and the number of cells would be, of course, equal to the square of the number of activities or categories represented. In working the matrix, information is entered into a given cell on the input requirements proportional to the outputs for each item—such as labor, raw materials, components, fuels, and so on—in each kind of activity required for given levels of output from each category of activity. The input requirements change with changes in technology in the particular industry, or in other related industries, in labor productivity, in response to regulatory or other stimuli or constraints, and with many other variables. As an example, a ton of finished steel, given the present stage of technology and the present institutional organization of the processes of assembly of material inputs, labor, transportation, distribution, and so forth, requires a certain set of inputs of iron ore, scrap, limestone, coke, labor, transportation, etc. The ore, in turn, must be mined, concentrated, transported, and stored, as must the limestone and coal, the latter in turn requiring inputs in order to be processed into coke. At each stage, from the extraction of the raw materials to the delivery of the final consumer products, and, indeed, the subsequent disposal of the wastes, there are input components: land, labor, and capital, the classical economic components, plus fuels, raw materials, sub-assemblies, etc., and, in addition, transportation, which gives the other inputs "place utility." Supposedly, each of the inputs can be quantified, and each stage in the process produces outputs, most of which—except for wastes—constitute inputs into the next stage in the chain. A change in the input requirements at any stage will produce changes in the output at that stage, and at antecedent and subsequent stages as well. In addition, there are secondary effects: production workers must be supplied with the goods and services which they consume, and these requirements will also affect a variety of other activities. Additional inputs into one process or stage, such as an increased demand for steel—which, of course, is in turn due to changes in other activities—will produce increased requirements for inputs at all stages of steelmaking and distribution. Thus more workers will be required, and their demands for food, clothing, shelter, transportation, education, recreation, and so on, will affect many other aspects of the economy. Each change sets in motion a complex chain of inputs and outputs, through many successive stages, until at last the effects are subsumed in the total economy many stages removed from the original impetus or stimulus. Some of the effects will be felt in the local community; others may affect distant places, as, for example, a change in Chicago's or Pittsburgh's steel industry with relation to the mining of ore in Minnesota, Labrador, or Liberia; these, in turn, may be reflected in changes in shipyards in Japan, or mining machinery manufacturing in Germany.

In one sense, the input-output approach is a refinement of both the basic-nonbasic and the balance-of-payments approaches.

All three approaches to an economic base study are concerned with flows, as shown diagrammatically [in Figure 5-1]. The circular portion of the diagram, in the center,

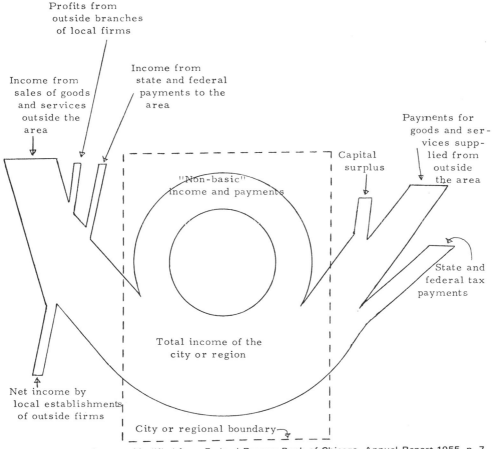

Source: Modified from Federal Reserve Bank of Chicago, Annual Report 1955, p. 7.

Figure 5-1 Schematic diagram showing basic-nonbasic dichotomy and balance of payments for a city or urban region.

represents the "nonbasic" or internal circulation of people, goods, money, and credit, and, as indicated earlier, this portion of the dichotomy is becoming increasingly important. However, because cities and urban regions, by their very nature, generally do not produce sufficient foodstuffs, primary natural resources, or other basic necessities, such commodities and items must be "imported," and they constitute the inputs represented on the left side of the diagram. In return, the city or urban region must provide services and manufactured goods for external areas, both rural and urban, as the products of its specialized activities; these are represented as outputs on the right side of the diagram.

Minimum or Average Requirements

The minimum- or average-requirements method of studying the urban economic base involves comparison of the city or region with other cities and/or regions which are analogous with respect to relevant qualities such as location, size, and age.[6] The attributes involved in the comparisons may be employment, land areas devoted to particular categories of uses, income generated by the various forms of activity, or demographic characteristics. Depending upon the attributes involved in the particular study, the minimum, or the average, requirements, measured quantitatively, for the particular attribute or set of attributes, are used, taking the quantities in the analogous cities or regions as guides. Allowances are then made for special circumstances, since no two cities or regions are completely analogous. Thus, for example, in estimating the amount of land area or floor space for certain types of commercial activity in a given city, the set of analogous cities is studied to determine either the minimum space for such activities in the city having the smallest amount of space, or the average amount of space in the analogous set of cities is considered.

Reasoning by analogy must always be employed with caution, and the minimum- or average-requirements approach to study of the urban economic base has certain inherent dangers, in spite of its utility. Once can never be quite sure that the set of cities or regions are really analogous with respect to all of the relevant attributes; there may be major differences, perhaps due to the time interval since the last available statistics, in technological, economic, social, or other characteristics of the respective cities or regions.

In order to maximize the validity of comparisons, it is highly desirable to consider as many independent variables as possible, for any one or combination of them may be significant. Modern electronic data processing has made possible the handling of a large number of attributes for each city, region, or set of cities and regions; we can classify them as to their economic functions as well as many other attributes. Many students of cities have, in the past, classified cities and regions according to single attributes or combinations of a limited number of these, but now it is possible to consider a large number of characteristics simultaneously, limited by the time and cost of data gathering and the capacity of the computer. Thus, the dangers of analogy are greatly reduced, and

6. Edward L. Ullman and Michael F. Dacey, "The Minimum Requirements Approach to the Urban Economic Base," *Papers and Proceedings, The Regional Science Association,* Vol. 6 (1960), pp. 175-194.

useful multivariate classifications of cities and urban regions are possible. The method is known as factor analysis or principal component analysis. A large number of characteristics, obtained from a variety of sources, are grouped by a standard computer program into a small number of groups of related variables, and the degree of interrelationship determined. Cities may be grouped in accordance with the extent to which they resemble each other or differ in accordance with given attributes. Thus an economic classification of cities may be obtained. Transfer of the results of planning experience from one city to another can be made with a greater degree of confidence if it is objectively determined that the respective cities are, indeed, analogous.

Although there is no completely satisfactory method of determining the urban economic base, an understanding of the economy of the city or region is indispensable in the early stages of planning, and a continuing evaluation of the extent, character, and direction of change must be made. The planning agency, in this process, should work with other civic agencies, including the Chamber of Commerce, local universities, and others. In some cities, such collaboration is more or less formally arranged through a "research clearing house" or other organization, representing the producers and consumers of statistical data on the urban and regional economy. Since most urban functions are primarily economic, and virtually all urban activities have important economic ramifications, the economic base studies constitute vital tools which are essential to the planning process. They form the basis for estimates of prospective population, income, and land requirements, and for the scaling of public capital improvements and operations to the anticipated fiscal resources of the city, which in turn are largely the result of the state of the local, regional, and national economy.[7]

INDUSTRIAL AND COMMERCIAL LAND USE

The economic base studies, described in the preceding section of this chapter, can assist the planner in determining the strengths and deficiencies of the particular complex of economic activities which characterize the city or metropolitan area with which he is concerned. Knowing the relative contributions to the economic support of the city or region which are made by each category of commerce or industry, and comparing the particular "mix" of activities with those of analogous cities and regions, however, are far from sufficient as a basis for determination of the direction in which promotional efforts should move.

Each urban area is characterized by a special set of assets and liabilities, and an inventory of them is an indispensable prerequisite and an integral part of the planning process. The major inputs into an economy, land, labor, capital, and transportation, constituting the principal resources, vary both quantitatively and qualitatively from place to place; they are spatially nonubiquitous. Transportation is discussed in Chapters 7 and 8. Labor and capital are relatively mobile, although labor having special experience or

7. For a more detailed discussion of urban economic base studies see: Charles M. Tiebout, *The Community Economic Base Study* (New York: Committee for Economic Development, 1962), and Wilbur R. Thompson, *A Preface to Urban Economics* (Baltimore: The Johns Hopkins Press, 1965).

talent may be concentrated in certain areas as the result of past activity, such as the concentration of scientific skills associated with major clusters of universities in the Boston, Chicago, and San Francisco Bay areas, or specialized industrial skills and external economies such as those associated with the automobile industry in southeastern Michigan and nearby Ohio, the rubber industry in Akron, the aerospace industry in Southern California, and so forth. Nevertheless, labor may migrate in response to economic opportunity in the long run; in the short run, however, the presence of "pools" of special types of labor may be a major consideration in the selection by industry of locations in one as compared with another region. Capital, although concentrated in certain major cities, is quite mobile within national areas, but subject to certain impedences internationally, such as currency controls and other regulations. Land, on the other hand, is the only resource input which is fixed in location. It, however, is not a uniform resource, for the presence or absence of certain attributes, such as degree of slope, climatic conditions, mineral resources, and drainage, may encourage, or may discourage, or in extreme instances, prevent, certain types of activities. Geographers are especially qualified to study, inventory, and recommend actions relative to the unevenly distributed—nonubiquitous—characteristics of land; therefore geographers are increasingly among the specialists found on planning staffs. It is not possible, within the space of this book, to discuss in detail the many attributes of land which are related to its prospective development.

Nonurban land, with relation to the extraction of primary resources, or other nonurban uses, including agriculture, forestry, grazing, recreation, or conservation, has value as the result of two sets of attributes: inherent characteristics, and location, the latter relative to the locations of other land uses, and especially to the people who utilize the resources of the land. Urban land, on the other hand, generally owes its value especially to its location, for the very nature of the city consists of its concentration of nonubiquitous activities. Therefore, the planner, in considering prospective urban land uses, and subject to the constraints of unfavorable physical conditions, such as susceptibility to natural hazards of slides, earthquakes, climatic impediments, etc. is primarily concerned with location. The site of an urban activity, existing or prospective, is related to the sites, existing and prospective, of all other urban activities. The total of all the sites and the activities located on them is what is termed the urban "structure" or "pattern" and the interactions among all of the urban sites produces the physical city. In this chapter, we are concerned with the economic activities and the reciprocal relations of such activities with each other, and with the other activities which take place in urban areas, and which together constitute the demand for urban land.

Industrial Land Use

Industrial activity, like commercial, is characterized by concentration on limited land areas. Because many types of industrial activities, unlike residential land use, require locations with specialized characteristics, and because industrial land use requires much more extensive area than does commercial, the designation of those areas which are recommended for industrial development are among the earliest tangible steps in the preparation of a comprehensive land use plan for an urban area.

Industry—involving the physical processing, storage, and handling of goods—has certain characteristics which must be recognized at the outset. In many cities, industry constitutes the largest component of the economic base; its locational requirements may be specialized and consequently only a limited supply of properly located land may be available. Industrial establishments, furthermore, have complex sets of linkages with each other and with other activities and establishments, which must be considered in the determination of industrial locations. Industrial establishments, also, are major contributors to the tax base of many, if not most, cities, and they exert a significant "multiplier effect" upon the entire economy of city and region. They also constitute major focuses for transportation, both within the urban area and externally (Chapters 7 and 8), and the concentrations of industrial employment are symbiotically related to virtually all other urban land uses.

The amount of land devoted to industry will vary widely from city to city, in accordance with the nature of the city's economic base, and, of course, the extent to which the city boundary embraces the built-up area. Also, the definition of "industrial land use" may differ among cities and regions, so that strict comparability is difficult. Some studies, for example, include all land devoted to wholesale use, including establishments with and without inventory stock, and some studies include such transportational uses as railroad terminals and airports, while others set up a separate category for such uses. Because of the great diversity of physical and other characteristics among the various kinds of industrial land uses, any generalization relative to the total amounts, or the proportions of total urban areas, devoted to industrial use, is of very limited utility to the planner. Nevertheless, the percentage of the total metropolitan area, or built-up (urbanized) area, or municipal area is frequently tabulated. One study, embracing 53 "central city" municipalities prior to 1955, found that industrial land, including railroads, constituted from 9.6 to 12.8 percent of the total "developed" area, with an overall average of 11.3 percent. The percentage did not vary significantly with the size of the city, and the range of industrial (including railroad) acreage per 100 persons in the residential population was generally within the range of 0.6 to slightly over 1.0.[8] A later study, including 48 cities, found that industrial land, including railroads and airports, constituted a mean of 8.6 percent of the total land area within the municipal limits, and 10.9 percent of the developed area.[9]

The planner is concerned with the location of industry on two different scales: (a) at the regional or interregional scale, and (b) at the intraurban or intrametropolitan scale. The former involves consideration of the nature and amount of industry which is desirable for a region, metropolitan area, or city to have in light of its economic base strengths and deficiencies and the potentialities of the resources available to it. The latter involves the process of site selection, in which the planners, the industrial real estate developers, and the industrial firms themselves should collaborate, in order to assure that industry is properly located with reference not only to its own requirements but also in

8. Harland Bartholomew, *Land Uses in American Cities* (Cambridge, Mass.: Harvard Univ. Press, 1955), p. 59.

9. John H. Niedercorn and Edward F. R. Hearle, *Recent Land-Use Trends in Forty-Eight Large American Cities* (Santa Monica, Calif.: The Rand Corporation, 1963).

relation to the other elements of the city and region's economic, physical, and functional patterns. Since industrial establishments are important generators of traffic as well as major sources of environmental concern, their locations constitute very important nodes in the entire urban pattern.

Considerations of the amount and kinds of industrial activity which a city or metropolitan area should contain involve the results of studies of the economic base, considered earlier in this chapter, and essential portions of such studies, in turn, involve inventory, mapping, and evaluation of the resources which the area can draw upon in attracting and retaining industries of each type. Such resources include the labor force —qualitatively as well as quantitatively—water, fuels, bulk raw materials, and manufactured components, all brought together by the area's systems of transportation and utility lines. These are factors which relate the city or metropolitan area to the external areas with which it has interaction, and there is a considerable body of theoretical and empirical knowledge—"location theory" and its application—which is beyond the scope of this chapter. Once it has been determined that an industry should locate within a metropolitan area or a city, selection of an appropriate site should be considered.

As for most land uses, there is generally no ideal site for an industry, and site selection involves a series of compromises. In some instances, an industry may wish to locate on a site which may appear to be well suited for its operations, but other considerations, relating to the situation of other elements of the city or metropolitan pattern, including environmental relationships, may make the location undesirable from the viewpoint of the public; in other instances sites which may appear to be well suited in terms of external considerations, such as access and environmental relationships, may not have certain attributes which the industries may consider essential. One of the most important compromises is that between central and peripheral location, between central convenience and low local transport costs on the one hand, and lower land costs but higher external costs in peripheral locations on the other hand.

Three classes of factors work together in the determination of the best locations for industrial establishments. They are (a) accessibility, (b) site availability, including size, shape, relief, drainage, and other characteristics of the parcels of land which may be possible locations, and (c) relations of the site, and of the prospective industrial activities, to the vicinity, including linkages to other activities and land uses nearby, and possible adverse environmental effects to both the industry and its incompatible neighbors.

It is very difficult to generalize relative to industrial site and location requirements, because the term "industry" includes a tremendously varied assortment of operations and establishments, with differing physical and other characteristics. Employment density, for example, may vary from one or two persons per acre in a highly automated petroleum refinery or petrochemical plant, to hundreds or even thousands per city block in a cluster of multistory, multiestablishment loft buildings in central city locations, containing such labor-intensive activities as clothing manufacture. Such diversity of industrial establishments affects not only such characteristics as employment density but also the volumes of traffic movement, both of people and goods, which they generate, in the amount of air and water pollution which they produce and which, in the future, must be controlled, in the numbers and kinds of utilities and public services which they require, and in their linkages with other establishments, including the "external economies" and "agglomeration economies." Some types of industrial concerns have considerable flexibility in choosing among many types of locations; others are very restricted in the number of options available. A shipbuilding or repair yard, for example, must be on a shoreline with suitably deep water and must be insulated from residential areas; a "light" manufacturing plant may have a much wider choice of locations.

The urban planner, in carrying out his responsibilities to guide industry into suitable locations from the standpoint of both industry and the public, has several legal and other instruments at his disposal, but he can utilize them only after consideration of the vast complex of variables subsumed under the term "industry." At the outset, it is necessary to classify industries into a number of categories, based primarily upon those physical characteristics which affect the relations between them and the rest of the urban area.

Economists and others find considerable utility in classifying establishments in accordance with the nature of their product or service. The *Standard Industrial Classification* (SIC), published and revised at intervals by the Bureau of the Budget, Executive Office of the President, in the United States—with somewhat similar counterpart classifications for other industrialized nations including Canada and the United Kingdom— provides a useful classification for some purposes, but it is not primarily concerned with those physical characteristics of industrial establishments and their operations which the planner must be aware of in the determination of land allocation for industry, or in the encouragement or prevention, as the case may be, of particular types of industrial plants in particular areas. The SIC is a widely used classification of types of industrial—and commercial—establishments, using a four digit code, the first two digits indicating the general category (for example, in the United States SIC digits from 20 through 39 indicate manufacturing, 40 through 49 are transportation utilities, and 50 through 59 wholesale and retail trade, etc.), while the third and fourth digits indicate in increasing detail the nature of the goods or services produced by each category of establishment. However, the operational characteristics of individual firms and plants within each category—even in four-digit detail—may differ widely, and consequently the SIC has serious limitations for physical planning.

The conventional zoning ordinance, characteristically in force until recently, and still surviving in many cities, designated a number of different categories of industrial or manufacturing districts, within each of which certain types of establishments were permitted or excluded, as the case may be, in one or more locations within the city. The establishment types which were permitted, restricted, or prohibited were generally based upon more-or-less subjective judgment as to the characteristic amount of noise, odor, vibration, or other "nuisance" characteristics which were presumed to result from the operation of typical plants of each type. Thus, some industrial districts permitted "light" industries, which were presumed to produce minimal "nuisance" emissions; other districts permitted industries with presumed greater emissions, and, in many cities, "unrestricted" industrial districts would permit any kind of activity which was otherwise legally permitted, regardless of its operational characteristics. For all but the unrestricted industrial districts, the typical ordinance listed, usually alphabetically, those kinds of industries which were permitted or restricted. Many difficulties arose in the formulation and administration of such ordinances. For example, it was difficult and in many instances impossible to anticipate the technological changes within a given type of industry which would decrease—or increase—the undesired characteristics, nor was it possible to anticipate the proliferation of new types of industries; for the latter, provision was commonly made for "special" use permits or other administrative actions. Of course, the text of the ordinance could be amended, but there was almost inevitably a lag between the need for change and the actual change in the ordinance.

These difficulties have to a large extent been mitigated or eliminated by "performance standard" industrial zoning provisions, in which any type of industrial establishment or activity is permitted in any industrial district, providing that the establishment does not produce an undesirable amount or intensity of emission or result beyond a given distance from the origin or beyond the boundaries of the respective industrial district. Thresholds are established which are subject to quantitative measurement, and industrial operations are not permitted to exceed these. For example, noise in a given industrial district cannot exceed a certain decibel level at a certain distance from the origin, and particulate matter (smoke) must not exceed a stated threshold on the Rigelmann scale, which is visually measured.

Many municipalities have amended or replaced their older industrial zoning provisions by performance standards in regulating the types of operations permitted in their various industrial districts.[10] Basing the location of industry upon inherent characteristics rather than upon an arbitrary listing of types of activities is a much more logical method. Nevertheless, performance standard industrial zoning is not without its own set of difficulties. Administration of a performance standard zoning ordinance requires, for some of the criteria, a level of technical competence in enforcement which small and medium-sized municipalities may not possess or cannot afford; in such instances joint arrangements for personnel among a number of municipalities may be possible. Abuses in enforcement of an ordinance with complex technical provisions may occur, but the administration of any regulations is, in any event, apt to be no better nor worse than the general administration of the city. In instances where an industrial district adjoins the municipal boundary, enforcement on the leeward side of the district, within the adjacent municipality, may be difficult or impossible. In many instances, performance standard industrial zoning is supplemented by the recent inauguration of federal standards for air and water pollution control; ecological considerations loom increasingly important in the location of industries in any event.

Designation of industrial districts is, in many instances, complicated by, and very commonly distorted by, the existence of a multiplicity of local governmental areas, each of which may enact its own set of zoning regulations and designate its own industrial districts, with little if any regard for the balance of supply and demand for industrial sites in the region as a whole. Fortunately, the trends and devices relative to regional and

10. Much of the popularity of industrial standard zoning follows the presentation of a brief paper by Dennis O'Harrow, "Performance Standards in Industrial Zoning," in *Planning 1951* (Chicago: American Society of Planning Officials, 1951), pp. 42-55.

metropolitan planning, involving cooperation and coordination among the many local governments, and described in Chapter 12, have greatly reduced the deviations from reasonable metropolitan-wide patterns of industrial location, although progress in that direction is slow in most instances. Municipalities still, in many cases, seek industries to enhance their tax base even where, from a metropolitan or regional viewpoint, less industry or no industry would be more appropriate; on the other hand, some suburban municipalities and unincorporated areas may exclude industry, seeking to develop or maintain their status as dormitory communities within the commuting orbit of the larger cities. Typically, land is designated for industry far in excess of the demand for industrial locations in the forseeable future, while in other localities the development of industry may encounter considerable local resistance.

Accessibility of industrial sites is of great importance; not only must the industrial establishment be able to assemble raw material, component, and fuel inputs economically, as well as its labor force, but it must also distribute its products. On the broad regional and interregional scale, industries, as previously indicated, may be resource-oriented, locating at or near the source of those inputs which are most costly to transport, in order to change their form into lower-cost transport units. They may be market-oriented, or they may be "footloose," locating at any of the many possible sites between their sources of inputs and their markets. Transportation access costs generally govern at that scale, and those costs, in turn, depend upon the weight-value ratios of the inputs and product outputs, modified by such considerations as vulnerability of inputs and outputs to loss or damage en route. On the metropolitan and local scale, many of the same considerations are relevant, but others also assume importance, such as the time, convenience, and cost of local access to the labor force, which, of course, is a function of the residential pattern of the area and the effectiveness of the local highway and mass transportation systems. External transportation considerations in urban areas are treated in Chapter 7, and internal circulation in Chapter 8, but there are some additional considerations, of importance to the planner, relative to the role of transportation access, in connection with industrial land use planning at the local scale.

Transportation costs can be minimized by reducing the volume of goods and/or people to be transported, and this can be accomplished by maximizing "agglomeration economies" or "external economies." This means that establishments which are related or "linked" tend to locate in mutual proximity, producing, thereby, nucleations or clusters. This is one of the reasons why industrial districts, whether developed in response to organized planning or otherwise, tend to form, and it is also the reason why industrial activities tend to gravitate toward each other at the regional scale. The planner can, to some extent, anticipate the linkages and estimate the "multiplier" effect in a given area of the advent of a particular kind of industrial establishment. Among the more obvious kinds of linkages are those in which the output of one plant becomes the input of another at the next stage in the chain of industrial production. For example, a steel plant using the basic oxygen process may produce its own oxygen, but it may also be supplied with oxygen from a plant operated by a different firm located nearby. Components may find their principal, or exclusive, market in an adjacent or nearby plant. Similarly, symbiotic relationships may exist among establishments of like type, which rely upon a common set of external services, such as communication, legal, or utility services of specialized character, or which share the necessity of good access to buyers, research facilities, universities, or other establishments. The aerospace industry concentrations in San Diego, Wichita, and Seattle, the several rubber plants in Akron, the automobile industry in the Detroit-Toledo-Cleveland area, the concentration of steel plants in Chicago-Gary-Burns Harbor and in the Cleveland-Youngstown-Pittsburgh area are similar examples of linkages and industrial symbiosis. Once significant linkages are broken, as for example by the out-migration of major plants, others of similar or complementary character tend to follow until new sets of linkages are established. The rapid migration of the textile industry southward from New England and the very quick decline of meat-packing in Chicago demonstrate that industrial site linkages cannot be taken for granted, but must be maintained at one location or another. In the determination of location for a prospective industrial district, the planner and the developer should consider the existence or enhancement of linkages among complimentary or competitive establishments likely to locate in the district, as well as nonindustrial facilities that may be required to service the prospective industries. If mutual proximity is not possible, local urban transportation, both for people and goods, must be efficient if the linkages—the industrial complementarity—are to be created or maintained.

Industrial plants which receive or ship large volumes of bulk commodities, such as ores, grains, oil, coal, lumber, or manufactured goods like heavy machinery, industrial chemicals, newsprint paper, or transportation vehicles are generally relatively specialized in their site requirements insofar as bulk transportation facilities are concerned. The same industries commonly also have other requirements which normally indicate the need for extensive sites; bulk commodities require storage stockpiles or elaborate handling equipment, and their processing may involve extensive by-products or effluents which may, if not fully controlled, cause adverse environmental effects. Because of the weight of the commodities, fuels, or products, or their bulky dimensions, they may require production facilities, either structural or nonstructural, at ground level. Such industries may, in many instances, be capital-intensive, rather than labor-intensive, and therefore may have a low density of employment relative to the areas of the sites. For these reasons, extensive land areas may be required, and such areas are, of course, scarce in the central portions of cities and metropolitan areas. Industries of such type have formerly been termed "heavy," and they were relegated to the least restricted industrial districts in most zoning ordinances. Typically, such industries were located closer to the city centers, but found that their former locations were circumscribed with urban development which prevented expansion or made it very costly. Consequently, they tended to move to sites on the peripheries of the metropolitan area, or to such sites in other parts of the country, leaving behind an area of discard, where renewal, involving more modern, and often less dense, industrial redevelopment, or renewal for nonindustrial use, became imperative, if the city were not to lose important tax base and population. From the industrial viewpoint, such areas provide opportunities, because the "infrastructure," including streets, utilities, public services such as police and fire protection, and, often, an available and underemployed labor force remain, whereas all of these would have to be introduced, frequently at great cost, at peripheral locations.

One of the major advantages that industry finds in locating in large cities and metropolitan areas is the broad choice of transportation modes and carriers for assembling their inputs and in reaching their markets, whether within the city or region, or outside. Gateway cities, including ports, major railroad centers, nodes on the interstate highway network, and vicinities of hub airports are particularly advantageous; in such cities and metropolitan areas the industry finds that transport competition produces better and more frequent service, and, in many instances, lower transport costs. Most large cities have several or all of these advantages, in addition to internal agglomeration and scale economies, and therefore the gravitative attraction of such cities produces a multiplier effect in attracting industrial growth. If sites are not available in the "inner" portions of the cities—and often times they can be made available for all except "heavy" industries by urban renewal—the manufacturers will locate on or just beyond the urban periphery. In any event, the flexibility of the motor truck and the automobile, the development of intermodal, unitized goods-handling, including containerization and railroad piggyback, and the scale economies of barge-carrying ships and container ships, together with development of pipelines and air cargo, all are mutually reinforcing in making locational decisions for many types of industry less dependent than formerly upon direct access to navigable waterfrontages and to railroad sidings and private switch tracks.

Nevertheless, there are still many bulk-using and bulk-shipping industries which receive and ship in shipload, bargeload, and railroad carload quantities; for them, access to navigable waterways or to railroads remains important. Such industries, however, tend to be those which not only require extensive tracts of land, but also produce the greatest difficulties in the control of adverse environmental effects. Rarely can they find suitable locations close to the centers of cities, unless on land previously utilized by industries, which, because of obsolescence or for other reasons, terminated operations or moved to other and more peripheral locations. Heavy industry not only may be incompatible with the general present and prospective future character of much central city development but, because of its inherent physical characteristics, cannot afford the high price of centrally located city land. Fortunately, in many instances, the flexibility of modern transportation permits peripheral location of many such industries with respect to the urban centers.

Access to waterfronts is important to some industries for many reasons, in addition to transportation. The principal advantage that such concerns derive from waterfront locations are (a) transportation by ship or barge with direct transfer of cargoes, (b) use of water bodies for disposal of liquid and solid wastes, (c) use of water for cooling, (d) use of water as raw material inputs in the plant processes, or as components of the product, (e) plant protection, and (f) prestige.

Waterfront land is scarce, and not every waterfront location is suitable for industry; even where it is, often other uses of waterfronts are more desirable, and industrial development may be in conflict with other existing or prospective plans. The planner should determine, as a basic element in the structure of city and region, which waterfront areas may be devoted to industry and which to residential, park, conservation, or other functions.

Water transportation access, as previously mentioned, is important only to those industries which regularly ship or receive bulk commodities, including fuels, in bargeload or shipload quantities. All other industries, even though they make extensive use of water transportation, need not have direct access to navigable waterways, since intermodal transportation to and from marine terminals, in the same or different cities, is available by highway and railroad, and the trend toward larger and more sophisticated ships, discussed in Chapter 7, is paralleled by the concentration of waterborne traffic at fewer, but larger and more sophisticated, terminals. In most large port cities, such terminals tend, as do many industries, to be located in peripheral areas—providing good rail and highway access is available—rather than in the centrally located waterfront sections which were formerly devoted to marine terminals. The obsolescence of such older terminals furnishes an opportunity to develop the older central waterfronts to new uses which may or may not be industrial, and commonly are not.

On the other hand, those industries which can substantially benefit from direct access to water transportation should be sited where channels of sufficient depth and width can be provided, and where access from open water, in the case of ocean and Great Lakes shipping, is convenient and safe. In the United States, the federal government provides the access channels, free from tolls, if the benefit-cost ratio is considered favorable, but the local interests, whether public or private, must provide the terminal facilities as well as the appropriate depths for vessels alongside. As indicated in Chapter 7, the total cost may not be reflected in the individual project, for the local port authority or industry need not consider, in its own accounting, the cost of providing the access channel.

In many instances, access to frontage along navigable harbors and waterways cannot be effectively utilized, partly because of the trend toward increasing concentration of waterborne commerce at fewer terminals, with less berthage for vessels required, and partly because of inadequate physical characteristics of the channel or immediate access. Recent studies have indicated that sometimes a high value not justified by prospective transportation use is assigned to waterfront sites which are relatively centrally located but which remain underutilized in comparison with sites at similar distances from the city center but not on waterfronts.[11] In such instances, continued designation, by zoning and otherwise, of such areas as industrial should be justified only on the basis of other attributes than direct access to water transportation.

Access to bodies of water for disposal of solid and liquid wastes is important to many industries. In some instances, of course, the public sewage collection and treatment facilities should be used for liquid wastes, and even for those solids which can be carried in suspension, but in many instances, particularly for industries which create heavy volumes of chemical wastes, disposal must be more direct. In recent years the increasing concern for mitigation of water pollution, and the enforcement of standards for waste disposal, have compelled industries to treat their liquid wastes before discharge into nearby bodies of water, or before final treatment in a public disposal system. Neverthe-

11. For example: David M. Solzman, *Waterway Industrial Sites: A Chicago Case Study* (Chicago: Univ. of Chicago Dept. of Geography, Research Paper No. 107, 1967).

less, disposal of liquid effluent into nearby water bodies, after suitable treatment, may be an important localizing force for the siting of many industries. Similarly, disposal of solid wastes may advantageously occur in water bodies, but in such instances, it is important that impervious bulkheads be provided wherever the possibility of contamination exists, or where currents may create the possibility of movement and subsequent deposition of the waste fill at undesired locations. In many instances landfill, comprised of industrial solid wastes, can be placed to furnish sites for industrial expansion, or other uses such as offshore islands for industrial, marine terminal, airport, recreational, or residential use. The many steel companies along southern Lake Michigan, for example, have expanded their plants on fill composed of slag and other waste materials. Often such extension of plant sites into the water is more convenient and economical than the commonly traumatic and disruptive operations associated with land acquisition on the inland side of the plants.

Some industries require vast amounts of water for cooling. Among them are electric generating plants, many chemical industries, iron and steel plants, and others. Boiler water, and other inputs of water, must be available in sufficient quantities, but also of adequate quality. After use for cooling, the water is discharged back into the source, and, of course, it is usually at a much higher temperature. Thermal pollution is generally disadvantageous to the ecology of the water bodies and the biotic environment, and therefore the water, after use in industrial cooling, may itself need to be cooled before discharge. In some instances, however, the higher temperatures of the effluent water may be advantageous, as, for example, in preventing or retarding ice formation in navigable waterways, or in preventing or breaking up ice jams in rivers which may otherwise constitute flood hazards. Heated effluent water discharged from electric and other industrial plants in the Chicago area has facilitated winter navigation on the Illinois River, and there is considerable interest in the location of electric plants and other water-using industries on the Great Lakes and along the St. Lawrence Seaway where the heated water may result in extension of the navigation season, particularly in the vicinity of the locks, which are especially vulnerable to ice.

Of course, surface waters do not constitute the only sources for industrial use, whether for cooling or as inputs into industrial processing; groundwater supplies many industries. Generally, access to groundwater is more ubiquitous than is access to frontage on large water bodies.

The value of water frontage for plant protection is obvious. Like the moats surrounding the castles of an earlier era, the modern industrial plant may be provided with protection across bodies of water, due to the reduced necessity for fencing, and the visibility across the water. With the increased vulnerability of many industries to vandalism and pilferage, as well as the possibility of arson, surveillance across water may, in some instances, reduce the costs of plant protection. Fire protection, furthermore, is enhanced by proximity of large bodies of nearby surface water.

Prestige of an industry may be enhanced by proximity to a body of open water, due to the increased visibility of the plant. The planner, however, should develop methods by which the potential prestige of waterfront locations for industry are not negated by unattractive development, and the industrialist must be made aware of the value of an attractive shoreline bordering his plant.

Access to railroad routes, like access to navigable waterways, need be direct only for those industries which receive or ship large volumes of bulk commodities, or which ship bulky products which cannot be transported to and from rail terminals by highway. Modern TOFC (piggyback) and COFC (container) transportation make every industrial site accessible to railroad transportation. The industrial development departments of the railroads seek to attract industries to their lines in part to realize a return from the use of the land, which, often they own, and to derive revenue from the freight movements which the industries generate. As discussed in Chapter 7, in the larger railroad gateway areas, which include most of the major metropolitan areas of the United States and Canada, an industry has a choice of trackside locations on any of several railroads, including belt and switching lines which, within certain circumscribed areas, make all radiating intercity lines accessible on a neutral basis. The choice of industrial site with direct railroad access, therefore, is generally a broad one. However, many industries occupying land along rail routes do not make extensive use of the railroad directly, even though, in some instances, they may have direct switch tracks or sidings. Such industries, when their plants become amortized, are ripe prospects for relocation into the newer industrial areas on the urban periphery, or, less commonly, in renewal areas of the central city. Commonly, railroads have themselves been, and continue to be, major developers, either directly or through subsidiary organizations, of industrial sites, often in the form of industrial "parks," or organized industrial districts, discussed later in this chapter.

Accessibility to a labor force is important to most industries, even those which are capital-intensive and highly automated. As a matter of fact, the more sophisticated the industry, the more automated, the more necessary it is that highly qualified service and technical personnel be available to install, maintain, repair, and modify the equipment. [12] At the other end of the scale, labor-intensive industries obviously must be located with regard to convenient access by the labor force. As discussed in Chapter 8, the vast majority of workers commute to and from their jobs by automobile, except in the central portions and a few major outlying nodes in the very largest metropolitan areas. Except in such situations, highway access is extremely important, and adequate terminal facilities, in the form of parking areas, must be provided, either on the plant site or nearby. On high-value land in central locations in the larger cities, provision of adequate parking is prohibitively expensive, and mass transportation becomes essential. In smaller cities, mass transportation cannot economically be provided because the demand falls below the minimum threshold, and industries there must either provide for extensive parking at central locations, or locate peripherally where such provision can more economically be made. Urban renewal for industry may provide sites where the transportation and other infrastructure already exists and can be improved, but in cities where such sites are scarce, industries generally prefer to locate at outlying sites where highway access, preferably by expressways, is good. The newer peripherally located industrial districts, for the most part, are located at or near outlying nodes in the highway network, not only so as to maximize access to the labor force, but also to provide fast and convenient truck access.

With the virtual ubiquity of automobile transportation, the commuting areas for

12. David G. Osborn, *Geographical Features of the Automation of Industry,* (Chicago: Univ. of Chicago Dept. of Geography, Research Paper No. 30, 1953).

two or more cities may overlap, and the worker has, within the limitations of his skills and qualifications, a wider choice of establishments and locations than if such overlaps did not occur. With modern express highways, commuting for as much as fifty or sixty miles, or up to an hour's time in each direction, is not unusual. With wider access to a labor force, industrial locations in relatively undeveloped open areas, commonly in rural environments, become increasingly attractive. Lower land costs and the ability to acquire extensive sites with few of the traumas associated with locations within urban areas, combined with good transportation and access to a labor force from several or many cities and metropolitan areas, makes limited deconcentration of industry very attractive, in locations between the established urban concentrations. On the other hand, the opportunities for the broader choices of work locations made possible because of the presence of several nearby cities make such locations equally attractive for residence, and in many instances industrial, residential, and concomitantly commercial, development at some distance from, but convenient to, established urban areas expedites the coalescence of urban agglomerations into multinucleated "conurbations" with cross-commuting in many directions. The multicity "corridor" or the "dispersed city" is growing up in many parts of the United States and Canada and is making the concept of the metropolitan area itself obsolete.

The newer outlying, or multinucleated, complexes of industrial development, drawing upon a commuting labor force from several nearby cities, very quickly tend to precipitate development of residential communities in the formerly open country nearby. Since industrial linkages become significant in most instances, location of one industry in an area tends to be followed quickly by location of others which are symbiotically related, and a nucleus for a new city—although generally at lower density than the older cities—is formed. The planning of such an industrial development, therefore, must include adequate provision for all of the facilities and amenities that are required not only by the industry, but also eventually, by adjacent and surrounding developments, including mutual access. Reciprocal relations between industrial areas and their environs are discussed later in this chapter; here we are considering only those involving access to the industrial labor force.

A complementary situation to that of the industry or cluster of industries located outside the relatively high-density areas of the city is the industry or industrial cluster located within the "inner city." It is well known that, in the majority of cities, industrial activity has been declining in recent decades, due to the constraints and diseconomies of congestion, pollution, high taxes, high land costs, and other costs and inconveniences. This contrasts with the attraction of the urban periphery, where larger sites can be assembled more easily and at less cost, and where diseconomies, except those involving distances, are minimized. In spite of the costs of duplicating much of the infrastructure of facilities and services which remain in the inner cities, peripheral locations continue to attract industries from the central cities. Except in the very largest cities, the central location is much less significant than formerly in attracting and holding industry because of accessibility to the local labor force. With the loss of employment opportunities and tax base because of the decline, or at least the faster relative growth, of industrial activity at and beyond the urban periphery, the central cities are turning increasingly to the task of not only attracting new industry to sites vacated by earlier ones but still having an adequate infrastructure of facilities and service, but also of holding those already present, or at least of arresting the out-migration, thus providing work opportunities for the population resident within the borders of the central city; hence the many programs of urban industrial renewal, model cities, and others.

The problem is basically that the population of many of the inner city areas does not possess the knowledge or skills increasingly demanded by industry, and, restricted thereby in the range of employment opportunities, does not possess the financial ability or knowledge of alternate opportunities to take advantage of the increasing job market in suburban and peripheral industrial areas. Access to automobile transportation, or, in larger metropolitan areas, to suburban railroad commuting, requires at least a minimum income, and many prospective workers do not possess such minimum until the cycle is broken. In spite of "open housing" and "equal opportunity" a very large proportion of the prospective labor force resident in central cities consists of blacks, Puerto Ricans, and other members of minority groups who are "disadvantaged" and cannot participate fully in the labor force. The difficulties of transportation between residence and industrial employment areas in Los Angeles has been established as a major factor in the Watts riots, and similarly in many subsequent disturbances in a number of cities the separation—and hence added cost, time, and inconvenience—of transportation from work, has seriously restricted the job market and thus contributed toward the "urban problem" of the disadvantaged. It is quite possible too, that many industries shun central city areas because of the increasing pressures to employ the nearby population, whereas in the peripheral locations, because of distance, such pressures would be lessened, and the available labor force would, at least in the short run, possess a higher level of education and skills, with consequent greater mobility and access to job opportunities.

In spite of these trends toward the urban periphery, certain types of industrial activity—and commercial as well—continue to demand central city locations, at least in part because of access to the metropolitan labor force with its diversity, especially in the larger urban areas where mass transportation exists. The central core areas and their immediate surroundings, generally, are the only areas which can generate sufficient traffic to justify concentrations of mass transportation; consequently nearly all of the transit systems have a radial pattern focusing upon the central core of the city. While, in general, commercial establishments can outbid industrial establishments for the most central locations, many types of industrial activity continue on the "fringes" of the central business district, taking advantage not only of lower costs of older building space, but of good access to the metropolitan labor force, a large part of which must depend upon mass transportation. In spite of the general trend toward a decrease of industrial activity in the inner cities, some types of labor-intensive industries, as well as those depending primarily upon local and metropolitan markets, favor relatively central locations, and the planner should be aware of the necessity of preserving and enhancing the infrastructure of utilities, facilities, services, and amenities which can mitigate the peripheral movement, particularly of labor-intensive industries which can take advantage of accessibility not only to the general metropolitan labor force, due to the convergence of transportation in the inner city, but particularly of the available underemployed labor force represented by the minority groups in proximity to the inner industrial areas.

Access is of no value to a prospective industry unless sites are available. In addition to accessibility, industry seeks sites which are sufficiently extensive to permit assembly-line production, in most cases with a minimum of vertical movement, with adequate off-street truck facilities and automobile parking—or, in some cases, mass transit—with adequate subsurface foundation conditions, an attractive local environment including relative freedom from constraints imposed by incompatible surrounding land uses and activities, and with adequate public and utility services. All of these requisites are usually demanded at locations involving minimal land costs, and with minimal problems of site assembly.

Some of these requirements are mutually incompatible, and the planner and industrialist should explore the extent to which departures from optimal conditions are tolerable by each particular establishment. "Trade-offs" are almost always necessary.

One of the most basic compromises is that between central and peripheral locations, which is tantamount to saying between high land costs (called by the economists "site rentals") and high costs of transportation, communication, and other "distance inputs" associated with peripheral or low-density locations. Some aspects of this dichotomy are discussed in Chapter 7.

High land costs result from the competition of many prospective users for urban, centrally located land, which is a scarce commodity. The more prospective users, the higher the cost. Central locations are most in demand, and there tends to be, in the typical city, a negative exponential curve of demand, and hence of land cost, declining from the center in every direction, most rapidly in directions with the poorest access, but at a declining rate in each direction with increase in distance. Thus each type of industrial and commercial establishment tends to locate in theory in accordance with its own requirements for land versus proximity; there is a "trade-off" between site costs and distance costs, and a consequent sorting out of activities and establishments in accordance with their relative ability to benefit from, and hence pay for, centrality. There are of course constraints, for the public interest is not necessarily the same as the interest of the individual establishment; hence we have zoning, subdivision controls, building codes, condemnation of land for public purposes, and other forms of intervention by public authorities. But these are essentially modifications of a free-enterprise real estate market, and any deviation from the characteristic negative exponential curve of land costs, reflecting accessibility and density, is at some social and private cost. The question in any individual public decision is whether the benefits, which may not always be quantifiable, are greater than the costs, while a related issue is who benefits and who should pay the costs, and in what proportions.

The modern urban complex represents a significant modification of the classic model described in the preceding paragraph, in that, although in many instances one center—the central business district—may dominate, there are typically many other nuclei or centers, around each of which a negative exponential curve of land values, density, building coverage, and other attributes, may be observed. While typically the central business district may be surrounded by a zone or belt of industry—most usually labor-intensive, and occupying older buildings, often of multistory construction—the major outlying nuclei may be primarily or exclusively, in many instances, individual industrial plants or clusters of plants. Such plants may be manufacturing establishments, or they may be wholesale and warehouse facilities, or some combination of the two. In any event, the plant or cluster represents a particular compromise between central and peripheral location. Because of the gravitative force exerted by the industry or industries with the consequent employment opportunities, the weights change due to the mere existence of the industry, so that locational obsolescence, like physical and functional obsolescence, is an inevitable attribute of every location. One of the objectives of the planner is to anticipate changing conditions in order to either slow up the rate of locational obsolescence or accommodate to it.

Central locations almost invariably are ones in which the parcels of land tend to be too small for modern industry. The need for additional area in which to expand is very commonly given by industries in many studies as the prime reason for abandoning central city locations. Parcels are not only small, but the grid of city streets typically interrupts the continuity of adjacent areas that might be otherwise available; modification of the street pattern, including vacation of streets and alleys where necessary, and not incompatible with the requirements for general circulation, can often remedy such constraint. Buildings, typically, have reached the end of their economic lives, and have been amortized, but often marginal industries requiring low rents—sometimes below the level of adequate return for the building owner—occupy them. Commonly, such buildings house a number of individual establishments; should one fail, the owner can rent to another, and should it succeed, it may tend to move to more adequate quarters, usually in a lower-density area farther from the city center. The old buildings typically have inadequate floor-loading capacity for modern manufacturing and storage operations, although labor-intensive industries without heavy machinery may find them relatively satisfactory. They may not be sufficiently fire resistant, they are typically inadequately provided with off-street truck-handling facilities and inadequate or no parking, and very often the adjacent neighborhoods, as well as the industrial areas themselves, are unattractive, and sometimes hazardous. Industrial workers, with increasing sophistication, tend to resist employment in such unattractive environments, in spite of convenient location. Many industries in such locations find difficulty in recruiting and retaining female workers, particularly if public transportation is not in immediate proximity. Insurance costs are high, and, in spite of the fact that public services may be numerous and adequate, taxes are also typically high. Almost inevitably, at some point, an industry decides to abandon such location, and, in recent years, the number of establishments available to replace them has been declining in most cities.

Some cities have had a moderate degree of success in retaining centrally located industries, but usually at the cost of substantially modifying and improving the environment and the level of services, and often with more-or-less extensive change in the pattern of physical layout of the area. The planner should be aware of the constraints imposed in many cities by obsolete zoning, building codes, street layouts, and institutionalized procedures which inhibit industrial renewal. In spite of these difficulties, some cities have successfully renewed obsolete industrial areas. The Morgan Industrial District has attracted many diversified manufacturing and wholesale establishments on the site of the abandoned Union Stock Yards in Chicago; a private company is building supertankers in a portion of the former Brooklyn Navy Yard; and inner portions of a number of other cities are being renewed for industry. In most such instances, however, the employment density after renewal is substantially less than that within the same area prior to renewal. This is to be expected, for a typical industry requires single-story rather than multiple-story buildings, more space for access, parking, truck-loading facilities, and external facilities and services. In order to meet these requirements, the Floor Area Ratio (FAR: the ratio of floor area within structures to the land area of the sites which they occupy) is of necessity less after renewal than before. There is simply no room for the former high density of activity.

In taking advantage of the existence of facilities and services, as well as of the organizational structures to operate and provide them, in inner city areas, as an inducement for industry to remain or new industry to locate, cities must generally be aware of the necessity for maintaining a high quality not only of public services, but also of improving the quality of the environment, both within and surrounding, these older industrial sections. Air and water pollution controls must be applied to the incoming industries, and, where possible, retroactively to existing industries, but not at such a rate or intensity as to discourage them from remaining unless they are conspicuously undesirable. Streets can be modified to improve access, and parking facilities may be provided collectively. External services, where the size of the industrial concentration justifies, should be anticipated in the land use plan for the area, whether the services are publicly or privately provided; thus, an industrial area may support restaurants, shops, banks, a post office, and other nonindustrial accessory and service activities in immediate proximity.

The development of the express highway system typically offers opportunity for the provision of industrial sites, both in older centrally located and renewable industrial areas, and in areas for redevelopment as industrial areas which prior to such redevelopment were occupied by deteriorated and largely evacuated housing—providing, of course, that adequate allowance is made for relocation of both the residential and business occupants of the sites. The expressways typically converge upon an inner distributor loop highway, outside of but conveniently located with relation to the central business district. Bordering such highway loop is typically located a complex of parking lots and garages serving primarily the central business district, but such facilities can also serve industrial areas nearby; such areas may often be located just across the loop highway from the central business district, and at locations attractive to those industries primarily serving the establishments within that district, as well as some requiring rapid access from a central location to all parts of the metropolitan area. The "wholesale-light manufacturing district" of the classic urban model of the 1920s, sometimes called the "core-frame" is undergoing a metamorphosis, but in some cities its resurgence offers attractive possibilities.

While accessibility and existing infrastructure, including relations to the city and metropolitan area as a whole, are the dominant considerations which make centrally located sites amenable to industrial utilization, site conditions themselves are of some significance. In peripheral and open areas subject to prospective industrial development for the first time, however, many more site conditions and attributes must be considered.

Assuming that the site for a prospective industrial plant or industrial district is located with adequate access to inputs, markets, and labor force, the specific attributes of the site must then be evaluated before a determination relative to either kind of utilization or site plan can be made.

Subsurface factors at the site, which are of possible significance in industrial location, include foundation conditions. The bedrock must be stable. If it is not too deep, foundations such as piles can be laid directly; on the other hand, there may be sites where the bedrock outcrops or is so close to the surface that excavation of hard rock may be necessary to provide a basement, or to provide a level ground floor. In some regions, it may be necessary to ascertain the extent of earthquake hazard. Stability of the mantle, the material above the bedrock surface, may be a relevant consideration. Foundations may involve spread footings, or an apron or mattress to support the structures, and in that case, the bearing capacity underground must be sufficient to support the weights of the structures, as well as any impact loads that may be imposed as the result of industrial operations. If groundwater is to be utilized, the quantity and quality of the water, including its chemical composition, pressure, volume, depth, and the character of the aquifer as well as of the material above it, must be known and evaluated. Also, it is important to have knowledge of the existence of any subterranean flows which may affect building construction. In some instances, availability of construction materials on or near the site may have considerable relevance for costs of construction at alternative locations.

The characteristics of the surface at the site may be significant. Most industrial operations are best carried out on level locales, which permit maximum flexibility in site planning and in the layout of buildings and utilities, including roads within the industrial districts. Straight-line assembly is typically favored by level sites, permitting single-story buildings for continuous flow. Some industries, however, require multistory buildings, or vertical movement. Grain elevators are characteristically vertical, as are sugar refineries, and some labor-intensive activities, such as administrative offices, may find multistory buildings preferable, because of the shorter distances involved as compared with a single-story building of the same floor area.

On the other hand, some slope may be desirable in order to permit drainage of the site. Flood plains are generally to be avoided, and most zoning ordinances now prohibit permanent new buildings on sites with high flood frequencies. It is possible, however, at additional expense, to flood-proof buildings, or to lay out an industrial plant so that machinery and materials can be moved easily to locations within or without the building which are less vulnerable to floods; but the probability of interruption, nevertheless, remains. Slope, also, may be utilized in landscaping of the site, and in placement of the buildings to maximize or minimize, as desired, visibility.

Other surface site characteristics which may be relevant include vulnerability to landslides, erosion, avalanches, heavy snow accumulations, and other adverse natural conditions. In some locations, vulnerability to forest and brush fires in the adjacent areas must be considered.

Weather and climate also present a set of conditions which may be relevant to evaluation of a prospective industrial location. Some industries seek general areas where climate permits year-round operation; this is particularly important to outdoor industrial activities, such as aerospace companies where airport operation is involved, shipyards, and other firms which may include extensive outdoor storage. Within the buildings, air conditioning and heating, depending upon the general climate, may be indispensable, but the costs of these may have bearing on the choice of location, not only as to general region, but also on the local scale. Orientation with respect to sunlight, particularly in hilly areas, may be of significance to some industries.

Local climatic and meteorological conditions may affect choice of industrial location within regions; for example, the frequency of rain and snowfall, as well as its intensity, may vary widely within a given metropolitan area, particularly where hills or major water bodies exist. In some instances, air circulation may be significant, particularly in situations in which stagnant air and temperature inversions produce concentrations of pollutants which may constitute health hazards, as, for example, in the industrial valleys of western Pennsylvania. Even though major advances have been made in the control of pollutants, the planner must take into consideration the patterns of air circulation in the siting of industrial plants, particularly in relation to residential areas, present and prospective.

No planner can have all of the specialized knowledge necessary in the process of determining the suitability of a site for major industrial development. Specialists are available on geology, soils, drainage, flood hazards, surface and ground water supply, air and water pollution, meteorology, and many other significant and relevant disciplines, and the planner should be aware of the necessity to employ or consult them appropriately.

Relatively few industries are in a position to develop individual plants of sufficient size to be completely self-contained; the Garys, Pullmans, Burns Harbors, and Oak Ridges represent very rare circumstances in which an industry can develop virtually all of the facilities and amenities, including housing, which it requires. More commonly, industrial location involves reliance upon external and linked establishments not only to supply inputs and nearby markets, but also to supply the needs of the industrial operations themselves, and the daily requirements of the plant personnel. Small and medium-sized industrial establishments increasingly have tended to locate in planned, organized industrial districts, or "industrial parks." These are large-scale developments intended for industries which can share certain facilities or external economies, and which therefore may benefit from mutual proximity. Such developments require large initial capital investments in land acquisition, site preparation, and the provision of utilities. Industrial parks, or organized industrial districts, very often are comparable to "new towns" in size, location, and extent, and, indeed, they may constitute major elements of new towns. In some instances, however, they may be developed in or near central cities, on land cleared as the result of urban renewal. Wherever they are located, they have the common attributes of large-scale, comprehensive planning, including financing, land acquisition, site preparation, and the provision of certain facilities and services which the industries within the district or park share. Since World War II such developments have proliferated, but the prototypes, some of which have maintained their viability through the years, date back to the 1890s and the early twentieth century.[13] The Central Manufacturing District and Clearing Industrial District in Chicago, the Central Manufacturing District in Los Angeles, and the Bush Terminal District in Brooklyn, New York, represent outstanding examples of early concentrations of industrial establishments located as the result of comprehensive large-scale planning, in which "spin-off" organizations of transportation facilities, typically railroads, developed areas for industry where land adjacent to the railroad yards and piers was available, and where, in the "horse and buggy" days, proximity to the carrier terminals for general freight was more significant than it is now. Most such organizations have continued actively to develop industrial tracts; the Central and Clearing District organizations in Chicago, for example, have developed and are developing a succession of "tracts." Whereas the earlier ones typically were developed with multiple-story, multiple-establishment structures at high densities, the newer tracts, generally on the periphery of the city or in suburban and exurban areas beyond, are developed with single-story structures at much lower densities, with relatively low land coverage, thereby leaving space for adequate truck facilities, on-site parking, and, in many instances, employee amenities such as athletic facilities, and attractive landscaped areas, constituting, in a real sense, "parks."

In the organized industrial districts, the developer provides the industry with an immediately available site, with or without structures. In some instances, the structures are of standardized design, with standard modules, permitting flexibility; if an industry needs more room, it can expand on the site or within the district, rather than moving elsewhere, and if it fails or requires a new location, the building, or space within the building, is available for a successor establishment. The developer and the management organization—they may be the same or different—offer the industry a "package" arrangement, with either purchase or rental of land and/or buildings, relieving the firm of the burden of arranging for financing, utilities, protective services, and even design services, as well as the complex of legal arrangements, including extensive negotiations, zoning, and other details. The industry is assured of compatible neighbors, both within and adjacent to the district, and selection of industries by the developer commonly involves a complex of external linkages, including scale economies of shared facilities. In many instances, leasing and long-term financing reduce the amount of capital which the industry requires to be tied up in its facilities. Scale economies in site development further reduce costs to the plants established within the district. The community, on the other hand, receives many benefits from industrial development in the organized district or park format: the sites are developed in an orderly manner, preferably within a limited span of time; the pleasant and efficient environment and site plan augment the attractiveness of the community for new and expanding industry; and the concentration, both in area and in time, of industrial development facilitates the planning, installation, and operation of public facilities and services. The location, extent, and character of the industrial district must, of course, conform to a comprehensive plan for city and region. Formerly, industrial districts which located outside municipal boundaries could often do so without

---

13. For a brief history and discussion of the early examples of organized industrial districts see: Robert L. Wrigley, Jr., "Organized Industrial Districts, with Special Reference to the Chicago Area," *Journal of Land and Public Utility Economics*, Vol. 23, No. 2 (May 1947), pp. 180-198.

reference to a comprehensive plan by a public authority, but the spread of county, metropolitan, and regional planning in recent years has all but eliminated such independence; now most such plans provide directly for, or have the flexibility to accommodate, planned industrial district developments.

Since World War II, several hundred industrial districts, with from one to several distinct "tracts" or areas, have been active, and they have had a major effect in transforming the industrial landscape of many areas. An increasing proportion of small and medium-sized industrial establishments, including manufacturing plants, wholesale warehouses and distribution facilities, and service establishments, have located within the tracts developed by organized districts.[14]

Organized industrial districts or parks have much in common with large-scale planned commercial developments, including shopping centers and office parks, which have developed in many cities and suburban areas in recent years. Such developments are characterized generally by adequate provision for parking, location at or near major highway interchanges, selection of establishments which are mutually supplementary or complementary, provision of attractive environment, and location with regard to accessibility to clients and labor force. Since such developments constitute integral parts of the total pattern of commercial land use and activity within urban regions, planning for that activity is discussed extensively in the following section.

Commercial Land Use

Commercial land use refers to the use of land for activities involving trade, administration, and record-keeping, the so-called tertiary and quaternary activities. Trade, in turn, involves the transfer of ownership of goods and the provision of services. Administration—office functions—also is generally included in the commercial category, although governmental administration is sometimes included as a separate land use category: public and institutional. Governmental functions are somewhat ambiguous in terms of land use, because many of them are essentially similar in space and location requirements to other commercial office activities, and some of them may occupy parts or all of commercial office buildings. However, care must be used in intercity comparisons because of differences in definition; commercial activities and establishments occupy relatively small areas of land in contrast to their importance. Some commercial activities occur in virtually every urban place, however small, but in many cities they constitute the major portion of the economic base. The locations, extent, and patterns of commercial activities, as expressed in the patterns of commercial land use, therefore, are of great importance to the urban planner.

14. For further discussion of organized industrial districts and industrial parks see: Marshall Bennett, "Industrial Parks: Big Business in the Suburbs," *Britannica Book of the Year 1964* (Chicago: Encyclopaedia Britannica, 1964), pp. 433-434; Robert E. Boley, "Rx for Successful Industrial Park Development," *Urban Land,* Vol. 26, No. 6 (June 1967), pp. 3-11; Ross McKeever (ed.), "The Community Builders Handbook," Section 4, "Industrial Parks", (Urban Land Institute, Washington, D.C., 1968), pp. 449-467.

Commercial areas generally constitute the sections of cities and metropolitan regions which have the tallest buildings, the highest density of land coverage by structures, the highest daytime—as distinguished from nighttime or residential—concentrations of people, the heaviest volumes of traffic and largest number of origins and destinations, and the highest land values. In addition, the locations, as well as in many instances the profiles, of commercial centers constitute major points of orientation and of visual identification in city and region. In spite of the proliferation of commercial activity in outlying areas and the development of multiple nodes with the increasing availability and flexibility of individual transportation by automobile and truck, the nodal character of commercial activity remains. The pattern of commercial nodes largely conditions the internal network of urban transportation, which, in turn, constitutes the major skeletal elements upon which the city and metropolitan pattern is developed. In most modern cities, the Central Business District (CBD) continues to be located at or near the point at which the urban settlement began (some geographers call it the "point of attachment"), and the radial lines of transportation, initially focusing upon that node, continue to be major axes of urban development. Since the CBD in most instances remains as the principal transportation focus, reinforced by the radial-circumferential pattern of express highways, it continues to be the dominant commercial nucleus, even while changing its functions and competing to a great extent with the newer outlying commercial areas and nodes. In this chapter we consider first the general pattern of commercial activity and land uses within cities and metropolitan areas, and then devote special attention to the central business district.

Since commercial activities are highly concentrated, the amount of land devoted to commercial use is relatively small. Although definitions of "commercial" vary, and intercity comparisons must be made with caution, there are some studies which indicate that the amount of commercial land in proportion to the urban area and the built-up areas of cities is remarkably consistent, and in every instance is less than 5 percent of the developed area. A study of 53 cities prior to 1955 showed that the average proportion of the total developed areas of the central cities varied from under 3, to slightly over 4 percent, with no consistent trend with changes in city size, while in eleven urban areas, including city and suburbs, the average proportion of total developed area devoted to commercial uses was 2.65 percent, with a range of from 1.15 to 4.64 percent.[15] Since the proportion for the urban areas as a whole was consistently less than for the developed areas of the central cities, it is clear that there is a trend, though not a prominent one, for the lower proportion of the developed area to be devoted to commercial use in the outlying portions of the cities and metropolitan areas. Another study, more recently, of 48 cities, embracing only the central cities of the metropolitan areas, found that 3.7 percent of the total land area of such cities was devoted to commercial use, but 4.8 percent of the developed land area within the city limits.[16]

The patterns of commercial land use constitute, in most regions, and within most large and medium-sized cities, a hierarchy of "central places" or nodes, interconnected by

15. Bartholomew, *op. cit.*
16. The RAND Corp., *op. cit.*, p. 4.

a network of transportation, principally by highways and streets, with certain types and intensities of commercial activities characteristic of each level of hierarchy. As explained earlier in this chapter, the association of functions and establishments in a cluster represents a gravitative pull, generating traffic in a reasonably predictable volume with decreasing intensity as the distance increases, in accordance with the "gravity model," with high peak volumes at the node, and with overlapping patterns of movement between nodes. Each type of activity or establishment has a particular complementary service or trade area, the extent of which is a function of the population, with its purchasing power or demand for goods or services, and the level in the hierarchy represented by the nature of the function and the establishments performing it. Thus there are several levels or orders, and each central place, whether a shopping center or other commercial node, tends to contain most or all of the functions and types of establishments which are characteristic of the lower orders of central places or nodes, as well as the more specialized and hence less ubiquitous functions of the higher order. The trade areas or service areas of the lower-order functions, however, are less extensive than those of the higher-order ones in the same center or node, since the establishments offering the particular lower-order goods or services require a lower threshold of population and purchasing power for their support. Thus, food retailing is virtually ubiquitous and of a lower order, but specialized or gourmet food shops are of a higher order, while major department stores are of a still higher one, typically located in or adjacent to large shopping centers. The central-place hierarchy is as characteristic of the internal structure of retailing and service within cities as it is among cities and towns.[17]

The hierarchical arrangement of retail and service centers is characteristic of almost all "advanced" countries and regions, to the extent that this seems to be a "natural" configuration. Any deviation from it which may be desired within a city or urban area can be achieved only at some cost, and, in general, city and metropolitan planners have adopted and applied the concept.

The locational pattern of commercial land uses within the urban areas of the United States and Canada represents a combination of two somewhat different sets of forces, reflecting the technological, social, and marketing conditions of two eras. On one hand, many of the commercial establishments, whether nucleated into clusters or arrayed in long ribbons along the principal arterial streets, within the central city areas and older suburbs, represent locational patterns which developed during, and survive from, the era of dominance of mass transit, at first characterized by the horse-drawn omnibus, later by the street railway horsecar, supplanted by the cable car and then the electric street railway car, and eventually replaced by the motor bus. In and near the larger cities, these modes of local transportation were supplemented by rapid transit lines, elevated, surface, and subway, and by railroads with suburban commuter service, around the outlying stations of which business nucleations developed. The typical pattern of retail and service establishments outside the central business districts, of the mass transit period, which ended approximately during the time of World War II, was that of nucleations at the

17. For a concise introduction to the structure of retail and service functions at both the intercity and intracity scale see: Brian J. L. Berry, *Geography of Market Centers and Retail Distribution* (Englewood Cliffs, N.J.: Prentice-Hall, 1967).

intersections of the major streets, upon which the street railway cars and buses operated, and with long narrow tentacles, usually only one lot deep, along the major arterials, with most intense development at the important intersections—the transfer corners—and with the density, and hence also the land values, declining in all directions away from such intersections. Where the street pattern was rectangular—the most common situation—the adjacent intersections marked the nodes of a grid of commercial ribbons, marked by business frontages which were more or less continuous, corresponding to ridges of high land values along the streetcar and bus routes. The familiar negative exponential pattern of land values, centering on each node or transfer intersection, correlates with density of commercial development along the ridges. The pattern, in another sense, may be viewed as a series of interlocked cruciform-shaped nucleations, with the arms extended outward along the arterials from each nearest-neighbor node coalescing as the influence of each of the respective nucleations or nodes extended outward along the main streets. Such was the typical pattern in most cities until after World War II, and it is important for the planner to recognize that a very substantial portion of the retail and service activities in most cities is still carried on in establishments which are located either in the intersectional nucleations or along the street-oriented ribbons in accordance with the pattern inherited from an earlier era. The key to the pattern was, of course, access, and the most accessible locations were those at the intersections, where transportation was available from the greatest number of directions, and hence the largest market. Impulse buying took place at the transfer corners, and hence exposure to the maximum number of prospective buyers maintained the peak land values at the intersections. Establishments which could not sustain as high a turnover per square foot of floor area tended to locate along the ribbons at greater or lesser distances from the intersections, and consequently, as in many other aspects of the urban structure, a sorting out, or stratification of business establishments took place in accordance with their ability to benefit from the maximum "exposure" at the intersections.[18]

The advent and spread of zoning, during the period between the two world wars, reinforced the pattern of intersectional-oriented retail and service business and the ribbons connecting the nodes. The intersections, being the points of maximum access and hence of highest land values, were generally zoned for 100 percent land coverage, and for multiple-story commercial buildings. Subsequently, it became evident that such nodes could accommodate most, and in some instances, all of the business requirements of most parts of a city, and that the long ribbons or strips, except for specialized types of establishments such as automobile salesrooms, service stations, and used car lots, or of tradesmen such as plumbers, represented a very substantial overestimate of the amount of land required to meet the needs of the residential population for commercial goods and services. The typical zoning ordinances of the 'twenties and 'thirties, however, provided, in many instances, for miles of uninterrupted ribbons of commercial use on both sides of

18. For a description of a typical city pattern of retail and service areas at the end of the mass transportation era, see: Harold M. Mayer, "Patterns and Recent Trends of Chicago's Outlying Business Centers," *Journal of Land and Public Utility Economics,* Vol. 18, No. 1 (Feb. 1942), pp. 4-16. The evolution of the pattern is featured in: Homer Hoyt, *One Hundred Years of Land Values in Chicago* (Chicago: Univ. of Chicago Press, 1933).

each of the major arterial streets, most of which constituted the routes of streetcar or bus lines. It was inevitable, in retrospect, that most portions of such ribbons would atrophy, if, indeed, they ever developed. The result is that today a very large proportion of the middle-aged and older portions of cities are interlaced with aborted or atrophied ribbons, literally constituting avenues of blight intruding upon otherwise moderately salvageable "conservation" areas, and contributing to their decline. During the 1930s, when such "strip" zoning was at the height of its popularity, and when rigid segregation of commercial from residential land uses was the rule, the automobile began to supplant mass transit in many cities, and contributed to the decline of the older commercial pattern. At the same time the Great Depression and the slowing up of in-migration to the cities further accelerated the vacation, and evacuation, of many of the commercial ribbons, leaving in their wake the surplus, unsightly, deteriorated vacant storefront buildings which were intended to be, and sometimes were, occupied by retail and service establishments. In many places, also, the intended commercial ribbons, not being needed, failed to develop, but the strip commercial zoning, when large-scale building resumed after World War II, inhibited the development of residential uses on the frontages along the commercially zoned streets. Many portions of the ribbons, not developed with buildings, contained vacant lots. The high-density developments at and near the intersections, furthermore, became less accessible when the automobile produced the need for parking, and these buildings, too, atrophied in many instances, the upper stories generally being the first to be vacated. The outward movement of purchasing power, with the succession of lower-income population, characteristic of the older areas of most cities, further reduced the need for extensive commercial land use in many instances; this was further accelerated by the absolute declines in population with the outward movement of the population wave.

In some of the inner city areas, the planner is offered the opportunity to redevelop along the superfluous commercial ribbons, for residential and other uses, and with a more rational pattern of commercial land use. In many areas, however, the prospective extent of urban redevelopment and renewal resources does not permit, in the forseeable future, complete replacement of the obsolete elements of the commercial pattern, particularly where even intermittent, and economically marginal, establishments serve the nearby residents. The problem is especially difficult where ethnicity—the presence of especially identifiable population groups with special preferences relative to kinds of goods and services—creates specialized but limited demands. In some places, some of the commercial frontage can be converted, although generally not very satisfactorily, to noncommercial use, with a minimum of structural change. Such uses commonly involve small industries, storage, and storefront churches; more recently public and quasi-public agencies and institutions serving the needs of disadvantaged and low-income populations and able to utilize only facilities with very low rentals, have found quarters, in old, obsolete, and deteriorated, formerly commercial structures, but such uses are, hopefully, ephemeral.

Also characteristic of the older inner portions of cities, and in some instances of older suburbs, is the individual small store or store cluster; the "ma and pa" establishment, most often dispensing "convenience" goods and services, the corner grocery store, the shoe repair shop, or the tavern. Very often such establishments occupied the ground-floor portions of buildings originally designed as single- or multiple-family residential structures, but which were converted to commercial use as the neighborhood acquired ethnic characteristics, or as it generally faced a declining demand for residential use. Such establishments, however, met a real need. They were—and where they survive, they are—oriented to pedestrian access; their trade area seldom extends more than a block or two from the site. In many instances, they serve the specialized demands of an ethnic population, which the larger commercial establishments cannot afford to serve. They also often were, and are, centers for "neighboring," for social interaction. Zoning, with its emphasis upon rigid segregation of land uses in its early years, commonly did not provide for such needed commercial establishments, or, if it did, it provided only for continuation of the existing ones as "legal nonconforming" uses. The insensitivity of early urban renewal efforts in many places resulted in elimination of the remaining small neighborhood stores and store clusters, and much of the backlash against urban renewal has been focused upon the demise of the neighborhood store. Often it is doubtful whether many such establishments could have survived the postwar competition of the newer merchandising and service establishments, with their economies of scale, in any event. But there are still thousands of older neighborhoods where such establishments survive, and even though many of them are economically marginal, they continue to serve the specialized needs of the nearby population. Recently, planners have become increasingly aware of the necessity of preserving, and where necessary, of re-creating, the small shop and the local neighborhood pedestrian-oriented store cluster, whether in older areas subjected to renewal, or in newer peripheral developments, particularly those occupied by lower-income groups and ethnic populations.

In short, one of the major challenges to the planner with regard to commercial land use is that of integrating the remnants of the older pre-automobile pattern of retail and service functions and establishments, which continue to have significance in some portions of the cities, with the newer patterns which are introduced. In zoning, no longer is rigid separation of land uses desirable in every case; convenience establishments may be desirable, and even necessary, in some instances. The long commercial ribbons, too, are not undesirable in every instance, providing that some nucleation can be introduced, and providing that portions of the ribbons can be converted into automobile-oriented types of use, with more adequate provision for parking, and for unloading and loading of trucks.

When extensive urban building was resumed, after the long interruption of the Great Depression of the 1930s followed by World War II, the atrophy of public transit was very rapid, and the automobile quickly resumed its interrupted role as the dominant intracity as well as intercity mover of people. Developers were not long in evolving new commercial patterns in response to the automobile and the increasing affluence which it, in part, represented. At first, parking spaces were provided behind store buildings at the intersections and along the commercial ribbons, but often such provisions proved to be improvisations, very inadequate for the numbers of vehicles which sought access. The comprehensively planned shopping center was not long in coming, and within the following two decades it rapidly became the dominant form of commercial land use in all portions of the cities except the central business districts, and in some cities even there. It is basically an island of shops and service establishments, sometimes also including offices, surrounded by a sea of parking.

Both the unplanned pattern of commercial land use inherited from the earlier era and the postwar pattern of planned shopping centers are mutually complementary, in that they tend to conform to a hierarchy of several levels, each level characterized by certain associations of types of activities and establishments, and each with a set of trade areas representing the range or extent of distribution of the goods and services of the particular order or level which the center represents, as well as the more areally limited ranges of the lower-order activities which are also contained in the center. In addition the store frontage ribbons of the mass transit era have their counterparts in the more recently developed portions of the urban regions in the form of highway-oriented ribbons, extending into the suburbs and the countryside beyond. The hierarchy of centers, or nucleations, is so widespread, not only in the United States and Canada, but also in most other urbanized and industrial regions of the world, that the planner can deviate from it only with difficulty, and at unknown cost. Virtually all of the successful postwar developments of any size conform to the pattern, which was established long before the present era of planned commercial centers.

At the top of the hierarchy of commercial nucleations is the central business district (CBD) which is discussed later in this chapter. In descending order are: (a) the major regional centers, (b) the community centers, (c) the neighborhood centers, and (d) the small local clusters and the individual convenience stores and service establishments. Overlapping the hierarchy is the network of strip or ribbon commercial developments, including both the earlier store-frontage type along the mass transportation streets and the later highway-oriented ribbons, with their more adequate facilities for automobile access and parking. In many instances, the spatial boundaries between nucleations (centers) and the ribbons are indeterminate, with gradual transition, in the older developments, between the high-density nucleations and the long ribbons which radiate from them along the principal streets. The newer areas are characterized by somewhat sharper divisions between the nucleations or centers, which are surrounded by extensive parking areas separating them from adjacent noncommercial developments, although in many instances parasitic commercial uses tend to locate just beyond the center's parking area, across the bounding peripheral streets. The planner and developer should anticipate the need for expansion of the centers, and also should be prepared for the development of nearby commercial establishments outside the center, which share the "agglomeration" economies of the center, including use of its parking areas for overflow.

The retail and service centers (nucleations) are separated by distances proportional to the population and the purchasing power in their respective service areas, since the range of each type of good and service depends upon these variables. The planner and developer, therefore, must precede any decision relative to the location, size, and character of a nucleation by careful estimates of the existing and prospective demand for the goods and services which are to be offered by the establishments to be located in the center. The demand in turn is a function of the density and purchasing power of the existing and prospective population within range—within the trading area—and these, in turn, result from the demographic age, family composition, income, occupations, and ethnic characteristics of the prospective population. All of these variables, and many others, affect the success of the center, and there is a considerable body of empirical experience, resulting from many thousands of centers which have been built, with respect to the weights to be assigned to each of the variables. Planning of retail and service centers is both a science and an art. It is beyond the scope of this book to review the process of trade area analysis and projection in detail, but there is extensive literature on the subject.

At the lowest level in the hierarchy of retail and service centers, the local convenience store or shop serves essentially the residents within walking distance. Some such establishments are typically located in the older commercial ribbons along the arterial streets, but they also are located, in older communities, on the corners of intersecting local streets, and even in otherwise residential blocks. Commonly, they are on the ground floor of residential buildings which have been partially or completely converted for commercial use. Because such establishments cannot generally compete with the more efficient and larger units, such as supermarkets and other large-scale establishments, they have been rapidly declining in numbers, and they survive as discrete focuses or nuclei principally in areas of specialized demand, such as those containing ethnic populations who require specialized types of food, or where individualized personal service is characteristic. In addition to food retailing, typical convenience establishments may include barbershops, hairdressing establishments, shoe repair shops, local laundries, dry cleaning pickup establishments, and small taverns. Urban redevelopment and renewal projects in many older portions of cities have accelerated the demise of such establishments as isolated businesses or small nuclei, but recently, in many instances, there has been a reaction against indiscriminate elimination of such small clusters or individual business establishments, particularly in ethnic areas, and in low-income locations where a substantial proportion of the population does not have access to transportation, or finds it inconvenient to walk to the larger clusters, which, of necessity, must be farther apart. There is a counter trend to facilitate the retention, or provision, of small sub-neighborhood convenience clusters, both in inner city areas subjected to renewal, and in outlying newly developing locales, where subdivision design and zoning can make adequate provision.

Neighborhood Shopping Centers

On another level from the individual small local retail or service establishment and the small convenience cluster is the neighborhood shopping center. In the older portions of the urban areas such centers are typically located at the intersections of arterial or local collector streets, and commonly they are simply more intensive concentrations along the typical street-frontage ribbons. The land-value pattern at such points is characterized by a minor peak along the ridge which represents the commercial ribbon. In many cities such as Chicago, where the pattern has been studied intensively, the rectangular grid pattern of major streets produces a tendency toward fragmentation of such neighborhood centers, with one-fourth of each center located at each of the four corners of the intersection, and with each neighborhood thus served by one-fourth of each of four neighborhood concentrations, at each of the four corners of the neighborhood. The concentration of traffic moving on the streets which intersect in the center constitutes a serious impediment to orderly development, and a hazard to the shoppers. Intersectional delays, furthermore, are augmented by additional traffic of a local nature generated by the shopping concentration, and compounded by the maneuvering in and out of the parking spaces, which are generally confined to the curb areas, and are typically inadequate. In urban renewal, modifications of such patterns may often be desirable, and the neighborhood shopping and service facilities may be located within the neighborhood, rather than at its borders, thereby facilitating internal access, and reducing the distances between residence and neighborhood shopping. Such relocation, furthermore, would facilitate separation of the local short-distance street traffic from longer-distance movements, and thereby would speed up circulation on the major streets, which form the borders of the neighborhoods.

The more recent neighborhood shopping centers typically have more adequate provision for parking, although vehicular access from the nearby streets may be inadequate. One of the objectives of the planner in the location of a neighborhood shopping center, provision for which can be made in the neighborhood plan and location affected by subdivision design and land use zoning provisions, is to reduce the proportion of the patronage which arrives by automobile, particularly where convenience shopping is involved. Perhaps this is futile, because in the United States and Canada the use of the automobile for even convenience shopping is almost universal.

The typical newer neighborhood shopping center developed as a continuous row of establishments set back from the street with parking areas in front, and commonly also in the rear, preferably with access to the parking areas from the street at a limited number of points [Figure 5-2].

Types of establishments in neighborhood shopping centers are similar to those in the small local cluster, which may be regarded, in a sense, as a small neighborhood center, except that the characteristic principal establishment in a neighborhood center is a supermarket. While many supermarkets are located independently of shopping centers, and therefore may be regarded as a form of shopping center containing only one establishment, the typical neighborhood center is built around the supermarket as the essential element. The neighborhood center serves a trading area with a population of between 5,000 and 40,000 or 50,000 population, and, of course, the sizes, numbers, and distances apart of the neighborhood centers, as of centers of any type, are dependent upon the characteristics of the population to be served, especially its residential density and its per-capita purchasing power. Experience has demonstrated that the preponderant mode of access is by automobile—in contrast to the convenience goods store or small cluster— and that five or six minutes driving time is about the maximum from the periphery of the center's trading area. Typically, the area of rentable commercial space in the center is about 50,000 square feet, although it may be as much as double that size. With the adjacent parking areas, which are integral parts of the center, the total land area required is from three to ten acres, the equivalent of one or two typical city blocks.

Community Shopping Centers

The community center is intermediate in size, and in the number and variety of its retail and service functions and establishments, falls between the neighborhood center and the regional center [Figure 5-3]. It typically contains the same types of establishments as does the neighborhood center, but such businesses have a low-order trading area

Source: Interstate General Corp. (Borinquen Towers), San Juan, Puerto Rico.

Figure 5-2   Modern neighborhood shopping center built integrally with hirise apartments.

of limited extent, so that, in a sense, a neighborhood center is contained within, and constitutes a part of, a community center, serving a smaller area than do the establishments more typical of and specific to the community center. The latter provide a much greater variety of goods and services than do those of the neighborhood centers, and their trading areas are much more extensive, usually embracing several neighborhoods nested within the "community." The principal establishment within a community shopping center is typically a "junior" department store, which may be independent or a branch of a downtown store or of a regional or national department store chain, or a variety store. More recently, community shopping centers have been built around, contain, or, in many instances consist entirely of, a discount department store which carries a large variety of merchandise. Clothing stores and appliance stores are typically present in community shopping centers. At the lower end of the size range, small community shopping centers may overlap the neighborhood centers, containing under 100,000 square feet of rentable space, and with correspondingly small trading areas; at the upper end of the range such centers may have many of the characteristics of the regional center, with over 300,000 square feet of space, and one may have, including parking area, over 25 acres of land. Its

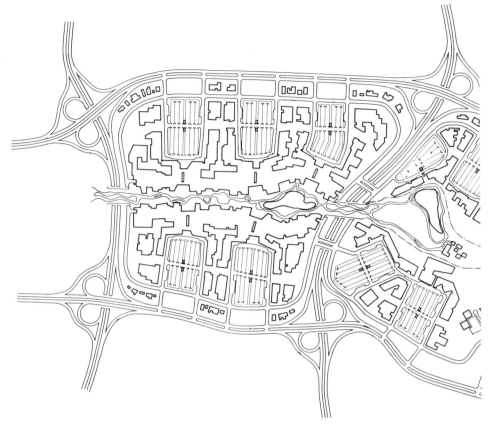

Source: Charles Gathers and Associates.

Figure 5-3 Example of a planned community shopping center in a new city, Perry Park, Colorado.

supporting population may exceed 100,000. In most medium-sized and larger cities, two or more community shopping centers may be in competition, with their respective trading areas overlapping. The shopper thus has a choice of shops, enlarging the variety and range of the goods and services which are available. "Shoppers' goods," involving comparisons among alternatives, are typical in community shopping centers, in contrast to neighborhood centers, where comparison shopping is rare, and goods and services are more standardized.

Regional Shopping Centers

The largest and least ubiquitous type of retail and service center, other than the central business district, is the regional center. Several regional centers may be developed within the larger metropolitan areas, and each may have a volume of business and variety of establishments resembling the central retail and service area of a medium-sized city.

The population within the trading area predominantly served by a regional center typically ranges from about 100,000 to over one-half million.

The older regional centers, like many neighborhood and most community centers prior to World War II, were generally located at the intersections of major arterial routes which carried transit lines—streetcars or buses—and at or near major suburban stops of the railroads having commuter train service. In cities with rapid transit elevated or subway lines, the regional centers were often characteristic of developments adjacent to, or surrounding, important stations, including the outer terminals, where the establishments could draw upon extensive peripheral urban and suburban areas in an outward direction for their customers. The characteristic shape of the trading area for such centers, as well as for their more modern counterparts, tends to be hyperbolic, with the shopping center near the inner end, because of competition from the central business district and other commercial concentrations in the inner city, and the lesser frequency of intercepting centers outward.

As in the case of neighborhood, and more especially community, centers of the earlier era, the older regional centers tended to be cruciform in shape, focusing upon a major intersection, and with arms or tentacles extending outward along the arterial highway. As in the case of the smaller-type centers, land values, land coverage, building densities, and vehicular and pedestrian traffic were highly concentrated at and near the intersections, with all of these characteristics decreasing in accordance with a negative exponential curve—at a decreasing rate—with distance from the main intersection, merging outwardly with the ribbon developments. As in the instances of the smaller types of older commercial nucleations, the centers of access in the mass transportation era became disadvantageous with the automobile, because of congestion and relative unavailability of parking. In the major portions of many cities, urban renewal and conservation efforts in recent years have included provision for replacing, insofar as possible, some of the access advantages of the newer planned centers—whether neighborhood, community, or regional size—by provision of parking around their perimeters, commonly involving land acquisition and demolition of nearby residential and other structures. In addition, some such centers have received extensive treatment in the form of elimination of vehicular traffic on one or more of the intersecting streets, with bypass routes being provided around them. In such instances, pedestrian malls with attractive landscaping have been provided where formerly the arterial streets were located. This duplicates some of the physical character of the newer shopping centers, but has not in every case arrested the decline of the older ones. The population density in the trading areas has declined, along with per-capita purchasing power, with the succession of waves of outward-migration as the expansion of the urban areas has taken place. Nevertheless, some of the older regional centers compete with central business districts for retail and service trade, and in some instances they are physically and functionally scarcely distinguishable from central business districts. For example, the central business district of Newark, New Jersey, is also a regional center for a portion of the New York region, and downtown Evanston, Illinois, is also a regional shopping center for a portion of metropolitan Chicago. As nearby urban agglomerations expand and coalesce to form multinucleated conurbations and corridors, the central business districts of some of the older cities take on many of the characteristics, and the functions, of regional centers within the emerging larger urban complex, but, in such instances, they must modernize if they are to compete effectively with the newer planned regional centers.

Whether of the older or newer type, the regional center is characterized by one or more "full-line" department stores, usually with floor area of 150,000 to 500,000 square feet each. These are, most commonly, units in regional or national chains, or major branches of downtown department stores; in a few instances the downtown store has been terminated, to be replaced by those of the same organization in the regional centers. In the regional centers, the department stores usually occupy up to half of the total floor area, which ranges from nearly one-half million to one and one-half million square feet. In developing a regional center, the developer first secures rental agreements from the major department stores, and then uses them as inducement for the other establishments to locate in the center. The larger regional centers may contain as many as a hundred specialty establishments, and in a few instances the annual sales volume of a regional center may approach one hundred million dollars. Such centers may have parking areas, either surrounding the center proper or in multilevel structures designed as integral parts of the center, for as many as 10,000 cars, and many have underground facilities for truck deliveries and shipments. Some of the largest and newest regional centers have two or three levels of shops, while the individual department stores may also be multiple-storied, the different levels being connected by escalators or continuous belt "people-movers."

The earlier examples of regional centers constructed in the 1950s and early '60s typically consisted of an elongated open mall, with attractive landscaping and with major department stores at each end. In a few instances, the malls were triangular, with department stores at each apex. The mall was open to the sky, but with overhangs along the store frontages to provide protection against the weather. Later in the 1960s and early '70s, the newer regional centers were constructed with enclosed malls, which were heated and cooled to provide weather-free pedestrian movement. Such regional centers are essentially single structures of enormous size.

The planner should provide, in any comprehensive plan, whether for a neighborhood, a community, a sector of a city, a suburban area, or a metropolitan region, for a complex of commercial nucleations, hierarchially arranged as to size, character, and spacing, related to the anticipated population density and the pattern of access routes [Table 5-1 and Figure 5-4]. Through the use of the gravity model and other experience, the traffic volumes can be estimated, and there is an extensive body of experience which can be drawn upon to estimate the numbers and types of functions and establishments that can be supported in centers of various types and sizes. The total sales volume, by type of establishment, can be fairly closely determined on the basis of experience elsewhere, and estimates of the volume per square foot of floor area can be made. From this, the frequency of customer turnover can be estimated and the requisite parking areas and capacities of the access routes estimated. This field is highly specialized, and the planner is advised to consult with specialists in connection with shopping center planning, or to employ such specialists, where the size and budget of his organization permit. The main point is that residential areas must be "blanketed" by the nested trade areas of centers at each level in the hierarchy and specialized centers should be provided as well.

TABLE 5 - 1
Size and Population Served by Shopping Center by Type

Type of Center	Typical Land Area (acres)	Typical Floor Area (sq. ft.)	Typical Population size of Trading Area	Characteristic Major Establishments
Neighborhood center	3-10	40-100,000	5,000-50,000	Supermarket, drugstore, barber, beauty shop
Community center	8-25	80-350,000	25,000-150,000	Variety, discount or small department store; movie theater, bank
Regional center	20-60	350,000-1,500,000	100,000 plus	Large department stores, specialty shopper's goods stores
Central Business District				

MERIBEL   COMMERCIAL   CENTER

Source: Perry Park, Colorado—Charles Gathers and Associat

Figure 5-4 Example of a community shopping center planned integrally with multifamily housing.

On the other hand, repetition of the errors of the 1920s and 1930s, when zoning provision for commercial land use far in excess of any possible demand created incipient blight, must be avoided.

The Central Business District

The central business district is, in most instances, the core of the city. In addition to containing the greatest concentration of retail and service establishments, and hence constituting the top of the central-place hierarchy within a given urban complex, the CBD also characteristically is the locale of other types of establishments, including both business and public administrative offices, theaters and other entertainment facilities, wholesale establishments and warehouses, hotels, convention halls, and light manufacturing establishments. Such is the traditional set of roles; in recent years, however, with the virtual omnipresence of the automobile and the flexibility of movement which it has made possible, and with the concomitant deconcentration of most urban areas and the changing demand for access, these roles have been rapidly shifting in both relative and absolute significance. In planning for the future of CBDs, several types of opportunities and constraints should be taken into consideration. What are the prospective roles of such districts; which should be encouraged and facilitated, and which should be discouraged? The problems are quite different in many major respects from those associated with planning for commercial centers in outlying portions of the urbanized areas and beyond, for they invoke building upon a matrix of structures, streets, utilities, services, institutions, establishments, diffuse ownerships, leases, and traditional organizations and attitudes which already exist, and which may prove to be both advantageous and disadvantageous, but which must be recognized and either utilized, modified, or eliminated. At the same time new patterns of structures and new organizational formats need to be developed. CBD planning, in nearly every instance, is urban renewal planning in the broad sense.

Just as outlying nucleations, as explained in the preceding section, contain functions and establishments serving several "orders" or levels of trade areas nested within one another, so CBDs commonly contain a variety of businesses serving a hierarchical level of trade areas of varying extent.

In a large city, some of the establishments may have nationwide or worldwide significance, with extensive hinterlands. At another level, establishments within the CBD may supply goods or services for an extensive area, well beyond the limits of the city's own metropolitan region, overlapping the service areas of other cities of comparable size and of a comparable level in the hierarchy of cities. The area served in common constituting a competitive service area or hinterland. A lower order of establishment within the CBD serves essentially the city's own metropolitan area; such concerns include major department stores, including the downtown operations of regional and national chains, and branch offices of large service firms such as insurance companies. These are the establishments, in most instances, which utilize the advertising pages of the metropolitan daily newspapers and which supply the local "commercials" for the city's radio and television stations. The dominant circulation areas of the newspapers, and the daytime listening and viewing areas of the local broadcasting stations, therefore, are indicative of the areal extent of the service or trade area which constitutes the market for the goods and services of the CBD establishments at that level in the hierarchy.

Finally, there are establishments within the CBD which serve less than the metropolitan area; these in many ways resemble the comparable establishments in the neighborhood, community and regional shopping and business centers described in the preceding section. Such establishments depend in part upon the purchases made by the employees of firms having offices, shops, or other operations nearby within the CBD, and also, in many instances, by residents within the central area of the city. The maintenance of purchasing power for the lower order of retail and service establishments within the CBD, and the socioeconomic upgrading of actual and prospective residential areas close to the city's core have been prime objectives of much of the urban redevelopment of the late 1940s and the 1950s. It has been severely criticized for its placing of economic values above human values in stimulating waves of population pressure which, moving outward, contributed to the acceleration of decline in other parts of the cities. It is a fact, of course, that the local establishment, such as a grocery store, cannot afford the high rents of the CBD, and therefore cannot survive in such locations unless it develops a highly specialized trade; gourmet food retailers may have a chance in such spots, but the ordinary supermarket is out of place there.

Much of the planning activity in the typical city is, in part at least, based upon the desire to continue the dominance of the CBD. The core of the city furnishes a much higher financial return to it than does any other part, principally through real estate taxes, but also, commonly, in the form of municipal income or wage taxes upon the earnings of businesses and workers in the urban core. The desire to arrest the deconcentration of economic activities from the central core of the city is almost irresistible; as long as the boundaries of the municipality do not include the entire urbanized area, the forces of deconcentration work against the fiscal solvency of the central municipality and create the necessity for planning, zoning, and other instrumentalities for maintaining and, if possible, enhancing the dominance of the CBD, or, failing that, at least arresting its decline.

Among the most important reasons for justifying the attempts to maintain the primacy of the CBD is the existence there of an intensive infrastructure of facilities and services; the economists call these "externalities" or "external economies." Specialized services which require a high threshold of demand can best be located centrally, where their market is most concentrated; this, in turn, facilitates further specialization. Thus, the CBD contains the greatest variety of establishments, offers the greatest variety of goods and services, and this, in turn, tends to produce a momentum which, at least to some extent, helps to maintain the area's primacy. Few outlying department stores offer the shopper the variety of choice offered by downtown stores; specialized professional practitioners tend to locate centrally; conventions tend to assemble in proximity to the variety of downtown attractions; and, of great importance, commercial endeavors and their establishments find it easiest to recruit and retain employees in downtown locations, where externalities such as eating places, retail shops, clubs, and other facilities are most accessible, but also where maximum accessibility by urban and metropolitan transporta-tion—both highways and mass transit—is available.

Although the internal transportation of cities and metropolitan areas is discussed in Chapter 8, it is significant to point out here that in virtually every city, the maximum access to residents, and hence consumer markets, is in the CBD, for it is there that the major transportation routes converge. Practically all urban and metropolitan rapid transit and commuter railroad services—both of which exist only in the largest cities—converge upon the CBD, with little or no rush-hour service oriented to other parts of the city, while even in medium-sized cities, as well as many small ones, the express highway system is radial, focusing upon the CBD, which then tends to be confined within an inner distributor belt highway. Thus, not only is access maximized in the CBD, but also the latter's functions are "anchored" by the infrastructure—particularly transportation and other utilities and externalities—but any change in relative importance of the various functions in the CBD and elsewhere is not so much a matter of gradual growth in one direction and atrophy in another, causing slow migration as in an earlier period, but rather a matter of relative rates of growth and decline in the CBD and elsewhere in the respective metropolitan areas.

In spite of the relative permanence of the infrastructures of facilities, services, and institutional organizations which tend to perpetuate the primacy of the CBD in most cities, the character and functions of the district are undergoing rapid change. In attempting to preserve the CBD, many strategies are attempted, and many others have been suggested. These are political, economic, and physical in nature.

Among the political strategies, one of the most superficially attractive is the extension of the boundaries of the central municipality to take in more of the suburban territory, where many of the former CBD functions and establishments have relocated, migrated, or have experienced more rapid growth. By embracing a more extensive area, the central city can reap the benefits of a wider tax base, including revenues from real estate in the outlying areas, as well as sales and income taxes from the establishments in those areas. The difficulties of this approach, of course, are many, and few cities have in recent years successfully annexed extensive suburban areas or consolidated with county or other governments on a metropolitan or sub-metropolitan scale; this problem is discussed in greater detail in Chapter 12. Proposals for revenue sharing, in which state and federal revenues are rebated to the cities without being specifically earmarked for particular purposes, offer some promise of giving the cities a more adequate share of public finances; at present few cities receive federal or state financial aid in proportion to the revenues which they produce in spite of the deconcentration trend. Many of the CBD functions which cities perform, furthermore, benefit the entire metropolitan region, while in turn, the region does not, in many instances, share the costs of such services proportionately. In some cases, user charges have been proposed, as for instance, tolls on the streets and highways serving the CBD, particularly during peak hours, or licenses for the use of the streets in the central areas of cities, particularly for vehicles registered outside the city. This, however, might be self-defeating, for it would tend to divert additional business away from the central area. In most cities, there is an optimal balance between the "agglomeration economies" and "externalities" of high density, and the diseconomies of congestion. While in many cities the relative importance, and in some cities the absolute importance, of the CBD has been declining, the number of vehicles entering the area has substantially increased, even in the face of a decline in the number of persons in the district, because of the shift from mass transportation to the automobile.

Economic strategies for preserving and enhancing CBDs include promotional activities, provision of more modern externalities and infrastructure, reduction of congestion, air pollution, noise and other concomitants of high density. Urban renewal strategies are also mainly economic. Before considering the economic and physical measures for preserving or enhancing the primacy of CBDs, it is necessary to consider the nature of the changes in central city functions which have occurred in recent years, and the prospects for their continuation.

The principal and traditional CBD functions include administrative offices for business, public offices, retailing, wholesaling, light manufacturing, entertainment including conventions, theaters, public events, and transient hotel accommodations.

Business offices in American cities represent a dominant function, both economically and physically, of CBDs. The skyscraper is the epitome of high density, and is the visual focus, giving symbolic unity to the central areas of many cities. The urban profile centers on the skyscraper, which developed partly in response to the need for mutual proximity of related activities—the "linkages" among the specialized functions, other than large-scale manufacturing and physical distribution—and in turn, the high land values which are expressions of the concentration of demand for space in the CBD.[19] High land values and high concentrations of activity are, of course, mutually reinforcing.

Recent developments in communication and in information processing, storage, and retrieval are having significant effects upon the office functions of CBDs. Much of the necessity for mutual proximity of the decision-making and record functions has been reduced by the availability of efficient computerized data systems and by instantaneous communication, including high-speed data transmission systems. Record-keeping does not normally necessitate extensive space, as it did in the pre-electronic era, nor is the space necessarily located centrally. The result is reflected in a relative decline in the demand for CBD space for those purposes, and, concommitantly, in the location of many of the former CBD record-keeping functions in outlying portions of cities and metropolitan areas.

On the other hand, the increasing trend toward scale economies in business operations, as reflected in corporate mergers and the growth of conglomerates, has produced a demand for a limited number of very large headquarter office locations. In New York, Chicago, Los Angeles, San Francisco, Houston, and a few other very large cities, tall skyscrapers were still under construction in the early 1970s, although a temporary glut of office buildings began to appear even in New York City. In many instances, individual large organizations, such as the Port of New York Authority and Sears Roebuck and Company, in New York and Chicago respectively, occupied the major portions of very

19. Jean Gottmann, "Why the Skyscrapers?" *Geographical Review*, Vol. 56, No. 2, (April 1966), pp. 190-212.

large, tall skyscrapers, with a variety of office tenants in the remaining space. In many such instances, as well as in the case of smaller firms, the prestige of location within the CBD continues to represent a significant attractive force.[20] In general, however, the business office function has experienced a relative decline in recent years in all but the largest cities; there appears to be a "critical mass" of the city size below which prestige and economies of scale are insufficient to retain many business offices in the CBDs. Large corporate headquarters, with few exceptions, continue to concentrate in the largest metropolitan areas, although not in the central city in every instance.[21]

As in the case of many other types of land use, the office function is subject to the forces of centripetal and centrifugal attraction, and each establishment must weight the balance between the advantages of mutual proximity in central locations and of peripheral locations which offer more space at lower cost, but with reduced accessibility to the urban center. In even the largest cities, many business as well as professional service offices have located in outlying areas. For the former, the "office park" as well as individual office buildings and clusters, replicate in peripheral portions of the cities and in suburban areas many of the external economies and advantages which, in an earlier period, were available only in the CBDs. Office parks, like industrial ones, offer services to their tenants, such as communal parking facilities, protective services, local shopping, and in some instances, specialized professional and business services like job printing, branch banks, repair services, and many others. In some instances, such outlying clusters, whether planned as a whole or not, generate sufficient travel to justify introducing public transit, most commonly by bus, but in a few instances involving either the provision of, or the construction of office buildings adjacent to or over, suburban railroad or rapid transit stations. In large cities, creating such transportation may be vital in providing access to the metropolitan labor force, in competition with the CBD, where the principal in outlying modes transportation node is normally located. Some types of offices, including principally those providing personal and professional services—physicians, dentists, lawyers, and related establishments—are located in office buildings within or in proximity to planned shopping centers, in which case the center itself may provide parking and other externalities.

Finally, many firms prefer to locate their office operations, including the record-keeping functions, the decision-making functions, or both, adjacent to or within their plants; such establishments include manufacturing wholesale distribution. Public contact is necessary for only a small proportion of the employees in many businesses; for those who do not meet the public, central location may be less necessary and a separation of the office functions of a firm may result.

Large concentrations of office buildings have grown up in the vicinities of major airports in some instances; Chicago's O'Hare and Los Angeles' International airports both have adjacent office concentrations employing many thousands of people; these form, by

20. For a discussion of the role of prestige in central area location, see Walter Firey, *Land Use in Central Boston* (Cambridge, Mass.: Harvard Univ. Press 1947).

21. Concentration of the business administration function in the largest metropolitan areas is discussed in: William Goodwin, "The Management Center in the United States," *Geographical Review,* Vol. 55, No. 1 (Jan. 1965), pp. 1-16.

themselves, major nodes in the commercial land use patterns of their respective metropolitan areas. The airport is the principal point of external transportation contact of the metropolitan areas, replacing the railroad depot of an earlier era, and many office functions which depend upon access to and from other cities have locational linkages with air terminals.

In other instances, outlying concentrations of offices, not initially linked to external transportation, but conveniently located with respect to major traffic arteries within the metropolitan area, are approaching the respective CBDs in magnitude; such clusters are typified by Rosslyn, Virginia, across the Potomac River from Washington, D.C., the General Motors Center several miles north of Detroit's downtown area, and Clayton, Missouri, in a western suburb of St. Louis. In each of these instances, the newer outlying office clusters resemble, to some extent, in their relationships to the older nearby CBDs, the multinucleated character of Newark, New Jersey, in the metropolitan New York complex, and Oakland, California, in relation to San Francisco. With the growth of a more flexible automobile-oriented metropolitan transportation network and the concomitant decline of mass transportation, it cannot be assumed that a CBD district will forever retain its primacy as the dominant office center of its metropolitan area. Conversely, probably, the principal justification for the current interest in the development of new mass transportation facilities, particularly rapid transit in cities which heretofore were not so provided, and the extension of transit systems in places which already have them, is to reinforce the vested interests of such cities in their CBDs; in nearly every instance no other traffic-generating node has sufficient magnitude, at present or prospectively, to justify the tremendous capital investments represented by new rapid transit construction.

Even with mass transportation, only a very few of the largest cities—New York, Chicago, Philadelphia, and Boston in the United States, and Toronto and Montreal in Canada—have sufficient density of CBD traffic to justify rapid transit, although a few additional cities have recently been or soon will be provided with such facilities. Only in a half-dozen cities does a significant proportion of the CBD employees use mass transportation to a greater degree than the automobile. Parking, therefore, is a major CBD land use, and not uncommonly half or more of the city's central area is devoted to the storage of the automobile. It is especially difficult to provide employee parking, which involves occupancy of the parking space for the full working day, in contrast with shipper parking and other types involving short-term turnover, and hence the possibility of higher revenues through multiple and successive use of the same space. The high expense of parking works hand-in-hand with traffic congestion to discourage access to CBD employment and hence it contributes to the outward movement of the office function.

Public administrative offices have somewhat the same requirements as business offices: They may or may not require direct access by the public, but in any event, they must be accessible to the employees. In addition, the city hall, county buildings, or both, and in some instances state office buildings as well, represent their respective governments as symbols, so there has traditionally been an emphasis upon monumentality, both in their architecture and their sites. The most impressive and dominating site may or may not be the most practicable or accessible one. In the past, there has been a confusion of functions in the planning of public office locations between the symbolic and the practical. A monumentally symbolic public building may be principally a ceremonial one; it must be visible and impressive. An office building for routine public functions, however, must be efficient both in location and in design. In many instances, public office functions are not unlike the business office ones, and the former may be more closely linked functionally to the business type than they are to other public functions. A public office which involves keeping of extensive records, like a similar business operation, needs no longer to be centrally located; many public office functions can be efficiently deconcentrated into the local neighborhoods and communities, particularly where there are specialized requirements, as, for example, in areas undergoing redevelopment, or those characterized by specialized ethnic groups with unique demands upon the facilities of public agencies. Many government offices can be located in outlying clusters, including rented space in commercial office buildings, thereby reducing the necessity for the respective governments to pay high interest charges on construction of public buildings, and at the same time provides proximity to commercial offices with which the public ones may be functionally linked; lawyers' offices in proximity to a court constitutes an obvious example. The monumental civic center may have certain ceremonial, psychological, and practical functions, but many of the governmental office functions are more effective in connection with related nonpublic office functions, and for such functions the locational and other physical requirements are not essentially different than those for commercial offices. As for the latter, public offices may in some instances require CBD locations, but in many other instances they can be effectively located at outlying points.

Since the end of World War II, *retailing* in the CBD has generally been declining. In many cities, major department stores have closed, and the firms have been establishing suburban branches, which, in some instances, have exceeded the original downtown stores in size and sales volume. The planned shopping centers, with their parking facilities, attractive malls, climate control, and planned phalanx of establishments geared to the market, have almost irresistible appeal to the shopper, who can conveniently reach the centers on major highways relatively free from traffic congestion, and often after much shorter travel distances than those involved in reaching downtown retail facilities. The discount department stores and specialty shops also compete effectively with CBD establishments; few discount emporiums can maintain their low prices with the high land costs involved in downtown locations. On the other hand, in a few instances, as in New York City and Chicago, department store and discount chains which originally had only suburban locations established major downtown operations more-or-less successfully. On the whole, however, retailing in the CBDs of most cities has suffered a long-range decline as the population, and hence the purchasing power, has deconcentrated within the respective metropolitan areas, and as the ubiquity of the automobile has reduced or eliminated the dependence upon mass transportation, which, in turn, is practicable only with highly concentrated nodes to generate its traffic. The demand for retail space downtown, furthermore, has tended to decline because of reduction of the necessity to maintain extensive inventories at the point of sale, and with the growth of extensive delivery systems. Warehousing is no longer a major CBD function in most cities; the retail establishments maintain inventories at peripheral locations where low land costs, horizontal rather than vertical buildings, and good highway and rail access produce great economies. Many retailers bypass inventories on many items, shipping on direct orders from factories to customers.

In attempting to arrest or reverse the decline of retailing in the CBD, many cities have resorted to extensive programs of rebuilding or remodeling of their retail cores. Access, of course, can be improved, although at great expense, by provision of mass transit, and, as previously mentioned, in many instances the radial pattern of such transit is designed to reinforce the primacy of the CBD, in retailing as in other functions. Many devices are used to speed up mass transit by bus, where rail transit is supplemented, or where traffic density does not justify elaborate provision of such facilities. Reserved lanes for buses, preferential traffic signaling, sheltered stops, express buses to and from the retail center—these and many other devices can be utilized to improve access for the shopper. On the other hand, prohibition of on-street parking, provision of parking garages, both within and on the periphery of the shopping area, shuttle buses between the retail center and fringe parking areas, and other devices improve access for both mass transit and automotive shoppers. In some cities deliveries of merchandise by truck is regulated or prohibited during business hours, in order to expedite the movement of street traffic, including both automobiles and buses, and in a few instances trucks and other traffic are separated by means of multilevel streets, as in the case of Wacker Drive in Chicago.

Pedestrian malls, which are becoming increasingly common in central retail areas, are essentially attempts to replicate downtown some of the advantages of the newer planned outlying shopping centers. They feature separation of vehicular and pedestrian traffic, an attractive, restful environment, facilitation of pedestrian movement between major traffic-generating department stores and the specialty shops between them, and the provision of a festive atmosphere which, in itself, is intended to promote pedestrian movement and "window shopping." Among the cities which have provided pedestrian malls from which vehicular traffic is excluded are Minneapolis, Providence, Miami Beach, Fresno, and many others. In each such instance, however, it is essential that provision be made for parking peripherally, and also for the through movement of traffic which formerly used the malled streets. In some instances, as in Englewood, on Chicago's South Side, declining major outlying shopping areas, like CBD retail centers, have been provided with malls, peripheral parking, and traffic bypasses.

Roofing of the malls in some CBDs may be practicable, although as of 1973 no major downtown retail street had been so treated. However, some cities have, in the course of extensive redevelopment of their retail and other CBD areas, provided either underground pedestrian shopping arcades, or platforms above the street level for pedestrian movement, with vehicular traffic underneath. Examples of the former include the Penn Center development in downtown Philadelphia and the Ville Marie development in Montreal. Samples of the latter include the Constitution Plaza development in Hartford and a portion of Charles Center in Baltimore, both of which provide office and hotel functions in addition to some downtown retailing.

The typical CBD retail pattern consists of one or more department stores, interspersed with specialty shops, thus encouraging pedestrian movement between the larger stores, which constitute the principal nodes; if these nodes are separated by moderate distances instead of being located immediately adjacent to one another, the pedestrian shopper, in theory, will be attracted by the intermediate specialty shops. This pattern, characteristic of downtown retail areas, has been duplicated in the planning of a significant proportion of the newer outlying shopping malls, which also characteristically have separation between the major department stores. In the older downtown areas, however, the provision of adequate and attractive routes for pedestrian movement may involve significant cooperative effort and substantial capital expenditures.

Regardless of the extent to which physical remodeling or rebuilding of downtown retail areas may take place, there is little prospect, in general, of reversing the long-term downward trend in CBD retail sales. In a few of the largest cities—essentially the regional economic capitals, such as New York, Chicago, and San Francisco—or cities with large tourist and convention trade, department and specialty stores of extra-regional or national importance may survive, and discount department stores with extremely high turnover may prosper, but with rare exceptions the future role of the CBD in retailing appears to be one of declining relative, if not absolute, importance. The population density close to downtown continues to decline, and the per-capita purchasing power also lessens, in spite of the activities in many cities designed to "upgrade" the inner city residential areas closest to the CBD. Intervening opportunities in the urban periphery will continue to siphon off much of the retail business from the central city areas; while physical improvement may slow up the decline downtown, most, if not all, of the growth in retail trade will take place elsewhere. In most cities, what remains of retail activity downtown will consist, on the one hand, of highly specialized goods and services with a metropolitan or extra-metropolitan market, and on the other hand, mostly on the fringes of the retail core, establishments providing lower orders of goods for the residential population of the inner city, essentially neighborhood or community types of activities. In some of the larger cities, these two types of retailing will be supplemented and reinforced by provision of goods and services for the tourists and conventioneers attracted to the central city by its convention halls, hotels, and entertainment facilities. In most cities, however, in spite of the decline, the CBD continues to constitute the largest single center of retail sales.

Wholesaling and light manufacturing are activities which have been declining in CBDs for several decades, and there is every prospect that these will continue to decline. We have previously discussed industrial activities and land uses; wholesaling involving inventories of goods (warehousing) may be regarded as essentially an industrial activity, along with light manufacturing, while wholesaling without stocks of goods on the premises, aside from samples, is essentially a commercial activity, differing but slightly in physical requirements from other office activities.

Characteristically, these activities are located on the fringes of the CBDs. They were outbid by other commercial functions for prime locations within the core of the CBD; on the other hand, before the era of highway transportation, access by mass transit to a metropolitan labor force in the case of light manufacturing, and access to inbound goods and to the metropolitan market in the case of wholesale distribution required presence of freight transportation facilities became significant. In many cities, waterfronts furnished access to ship and barge transportation in central locations, and in most cities railroad transportation was provided on the fringes of the CBD, where the warehouses could have rail sidings and switch tracks, and where "team tracks" and freight stations were within easy horse-and-wagon ("teaming") distance of the many wholesale and light manufacturing establishments in the immediate fringes of the urban core. This gave rise, in the nineteenth century, to what Burgess, in his classic model of urban structure, called the "wholesale and light manufacturing" belt and which later urbanists have sometimes designated as the "core fringe" or "core frame." In general, this area is discussed in an earlier section of this chapter; here we are concerned with the opportunities which such obsolete areas provide for replanning.

The wholesale and light manufacturing areas of most American and Canadian cities are characterized by a multitude of multiple-story loft buildings, mainly dating from the nineteenth and early twentieth centuries; many, if not most, have reached or soon will reach the end of their economically useful lives. They represented intensive forms of land use, and with the advent of modern trucking and automobile transportation, such areas developed extreme street congestion. Few such structures provide adequately for off-street truck-loading docks; the streets are too narrow for the volumes of traffic which such areas generate, the buildings are deficient in floor-loading capacity for modern operations, commonly lack adequate fire resistance and hence command high insurance costs, and employee amenities are generally deficient or lacking. The areas are frequently unattractive, and in many instances, they border deteriorated residential areas with high crime rates, making employee recruitment and retention a major problem. Modern transportation and communication, as pointed out earlier, make it advantageous for many of the wholesale and light manufacturing establishments to locate on and beyond the edge of the city, and the inner wholesale and light manufacturing zones are characterized by extensive vacant areas from which buildings have been demolished; those older multistory industrial-type buildings which remain are, for the most part, largely vacant, or they can be rented only at such low rents that adequate maintenance becomes economically unfeasible. Compounding the decline of many such areas is the obsolescence of adjacent and nearby railroad freight yards, team tracks, and terminals, and some of the older complexes of truck terminals. Waterfronts adjoining such areas are characterized by declining use for transportation. On the other hand, proximity to the CBD offers opportunities for significant renewal for those uses which are advantageously located centrally.

Such core fringe areas, if properly redeveloped, can be important complements to the nearby CBDs. Typically, the high proportion of their land and buildings which are vacant, together with proximity to the CBD, are advantages which are utilized in the provision of rights-of-way for inner distributor loop highways, including expressways, and for fringe parking facilities, conveniently located to the expressways, and accessible from the central core either by short walks—compensated for by lower parking fees than those within the central district—or by shuttle buses, sometimes subsidized by the downtown businesses.

Thus, the locational pattern of wholesale establishments has changed with changes in transportation technology, and particularly the shift in modes from water and rail to the motortruck. One geographer, who has studied wholesaling extensively, classifies wholesale areas, in addition to the traditional "core fringe" or "core frame" wholesale and light manufacturing districts, into produce districts, product comparison districts, will-call delivery districts, manufacturing stock districts, and office wholesaling districts.[22]

Produce districts were originally located within or close to the city's central business district; they were places where farmers would bring their produce for sale directly to consumers, or to commission merchants. Such districts shared with the traditional warehouse districts the disadvantages of obsolescence, including congestion, when the motortruck replaced the horse-drawn dray, and when large-scale merchandising, including the supermarket chains, replaced the "ma and pa" local store. The newer produce markets, like the newer industrial districts, are generally located on lower-cost land, with convenient access to both radial and circumferential express highways and to railroads, close to or beyond the urban periphery, with extensive single-story buildings and with ample room for truck movements. The Washington Market in New York City, the Dock Street Market in Philadelphia, and the South Water Street Market in Chicago are examples of older centrally located produce markets which have been or are being replaced by newer facilities in outlying locations, leaving on their sites opportunities for renewal for modern industrial districts with single-story plants, including wholesale distribution facilities at lower densities than the typical older ones, or for nonindustrial uses. In Philadelphia, for example, the Dock Street Market site has been transformed into the prestigious Society Hill residential area.

The "product comparison" district is a common phenomenon in many cities. It consists of an agglomeration of competitive and linked establishments sharing common customers, and located at points with convenient access to those facilities used by out-of-town buyers, particularly hotels and convention halls. In the past, such districts tended to consist of a multitude of individual buildings, commonly of the multiple-story loft types, located in mutual proximity. New York's West Side garment district is an outstanding example, but hundreds of clusters existed, and many continue to exist, in American and Canadian cities. More recently, product comparison centers have tended to concentrate in large individual buildings, or planned groups of buildings. An early example was Chicago's Union Stock Yards, founded in 1865; more recent examples are the Merchandise Mart and the American Furniture Mart in Chicago, Peachtree Center in Atlanta, the World Trade Center in New Orleans, and—more spectacularly—the massive World Trade Center in New York, where many organizations involved in international trade benefit from mutual proximity. Planners may look toward such product comparison centers as furnishing opportunities to provide appropriate redevelopment for portions of the declining "core fringe" or "core frame" areas—the older wholesale and light manufacturing zones—which surround the CBDs of many cities.

Certain types of wholesale distribution facilities cluster in "will-call" districts. These are typically groups of establishments which maintain inventories for rapid delivery to retailers. They may consist of firms selling to individual retailers, or central distribution facilities for chain merchandisers, thereby eliminating the necessity for maintenance of

22. James E. Vance, Jr., *The Merchant's World: The Geography of Wholesaling* (Englewood Cliffs, N.J.: Prentice Hall, 1970), especially pp. 129-137.

large inventories at the points of retail sale. For such wholesale distribution points, access to the metropolitan highway system is important, although a central location may not be justified.

Another type of wholesale concentration, however, the "manufacturing stocks" district, supplies relatively standardized items to light manufacturing establishments, such as job printers, who require quantities of paper, inks, and other supplies, and garment manufacturers who require textiles, buttons, and other supplies. Establishments of this type tend to cluster in proximity to their markets, which in turn are characteristically on the fringes of the CBD.

Finally, there is the office wholesaling district, which may frequently be indistinguishable from, and coterminous with or overlapping, the general office concentrations within the CBD. In other instances, outlying or suburban locations, including office park areas, may be the sites of such activities.

A significant event in many cities is the *trade show* or the *trade fair;* this is a periodic—usually annual—event which brings together buyers and sellers of specialized goods and services; the fairs or shows may promote exchanges between manufacturers and wholesalers, wholesalers and retailers, or, in some instances, the ultimate consumers. These events may be local, regional, national, or international; some are of worldwide significance. Many cities have annual automobile shows and boat shows, at which new models are displayed to the dealers and consumers; the International Livestock Exposition in Chicago is still held annually in a large hall although the adjacent Union Stock Yards have disappeared. Such fairs or trade shows, in some instances, may be permanent, as mentioned above, or on the other hand, facilities may be provided for a succession of events; in a few instances large structures have been provided, either through public or private financing, wherein major trade shows or fairs may be held concurrently.

Convention halls or exhibition halls for such activities can be major economic assets by attracting thousands of visitors whose expenditures constitute significant portions of the economic base of the respective cities, and who set in a motion a "multiplier" effect as manifested in the provision of hotels, restaurants, entertainment, and other facilities associated with convention visits. In many instances, the convention and exhibition halls may be self-liquidating, but in others some form of public subsidy may be justified by the economic multiplier effects. Convention and exhibition halls may be located close to the core of the CBD, but most commonly on its fringes, where land costs are not so high as to preclude adequate provision of extensive parking areas; in a few instances where the location is not in immediate proximity to the CBD, hotels and other related facilities are adjacent to these halls. The New York Coliseum, Detroit's Cobo Hall, and Cleveland's Public Hall are examples of centrally located downtown facilities. On the other hand, some such facilities have recently been constructed at substantial distances from the CBD, as in the case of Chicago's McCormick Place, the facilities near Houston's Astrodome, San Francisco's Cow Palace, and others. In such instances, distance from the CBD necessitates good access to local transportation, by highway, transit, or both, and the location of the hall may stimulate growth of a hotel and motel complex in proximity. Since the decline of railroad passenger service and the deconcentration of many entertainment facilities, and with the growth of the rental car business, major trade shows and conventions need not necessarily be located downtown. Thus, there are two divergent trends in location of convention and trade show facilities, and in some cities, the CBD continues to be the major locus. On the other hand, some large hub airports are the catalysts for phalanxes of convention halls, hotels, motels, restaurants, and associated facilities, as on the borders of Chicago's O'Hare International Airport and the Los Angeles International Airport; in each of these instances, thousands of transient rooms and dozens of large convention and meeting rooms have been constructed in the hotels and motels, eliminating the need for any but the largest conventions from using the downtown facilities. As with many CBD functions, downtown is meeting a serious competition from outlying locations, and the planner, as an adviser to the decision-makers, must weight the advantages and disadvantages of central versus peripheral locations for such activities, and these may vary from city to city.

Hotels and motels constitute important CBD functions in most cities. In the largest cities, the downtown hotels depend upon a combination of convention and tourist business, and are symbiotically related to the convention and trade show facilities mentioned in the preceding paragraphs. With the decline of railroad passenger service, such hotels and motels are free from the necessity to locate near railroad depots, and, indeed, in most cities those so located have been adversely affected by the general shifting of the CBD from the terminals to which they had previously been "anchored." Many of the hotels built in the 1920s and earlier have been replaced by other types of facilities; a hotel immediately adjacent to New York's Pennsylvania Station has been converted to a hospital, while several close to Grand Central Terminal have been replaced by large office buildings, as has, also, Chicago's tall Morrison Hotel, which formerly stood in the geometric center of the Loop.

Motels, of course, are oriented to the automobile, but in recent years there has ceased to be a clear-cut distinction between hotels and motels; the term "motor hotel" typifies the difficulty in making any distinction. The growth of intercity automobile transportation, and the development of car rentals in combination with intercity air transportation, has made the hotel-motel relatively "footloose," although there tend to be several types of clusters: (a) hotels within the core of the CBD and motor hotels and motels in the core-fringe, at and near the major metropolitan nodes, (b) ribbons of motels along the principal highways, and adjacent to access-egress points and interchanges along the limited-access express highways, and (c) adjacent to, or within convenient access to, major airports. Thus whereas the CBD formerly had a virtual monopoly on the transient hotel-restaurant-entertainment industries, it must now compete with many alternate locations within the respective metropolitan areas. A common complaint in many cities is that the downtown area "dies at night"; in some instances a series of convention-hotel-entertainment facilities may at least partially remedy the situation, though some cities have so far exceeded their market for such types that overbuilding has created serious financial problems.

One aspect of CBD development and redevelopment which has attracted attention in recent years is the economic potential of the *"nostalgia industry."* Some cities have made conscious efforts, either with private capital or public funds, or a combination of both, to develop an atmosphere reminiscent of earlier periods, either by historic preservation and reconstruction, or by the introduction of an artificial physical atmosphere resembling that of an earlier time. The effect of Disneyland in California and Disney World in Florida upon urban development is obvious, but many cities capitalize upon nostalgia closer to their central cores. The Vieux Carré in New Orleans is a classic example of a historic preservation district close to the city's central business district, in spite of insensitivity to its value as represented by attempts to place an express highway adjacent to it, along the waterfront. Greenwich Village in New York City, with its "Bohemian" atmosphere, has served as prototype for artificial creation, in many cities, of entertainment districts with "atmosphere"; among the outstanding examples are Old Town in Chicago, Underground Atlanta, Gaslight Square in St. Louis, Larimer Square in Denver, and many others. Some of these have been successful; others, either because of inadequate concept, poor financing, or insufficient size, have been less so. In virtually every instance, however, they have been located on the fringes of, or within a relatively short distance of, the CBD.

Another form of nostalgia of considerable commercial importance to some cities is in the preservation, reconstruction, or creation of more-or-less authentic historic "urbanscapes," or in the maintenance and stimulation of concentrations of establishments with ethnic or historic interest. Authentic historic landmarks have commercial value in stimulating tourism, but perhaps, more important economically, the preservation of historic districts or their reconstruction, not as museums, but as vital commercial developments, has received attention in recent years, and the planner should survey such possibilities in his own city. Williamsburg, Virginia, Mystic, Connecticut, and Sturbridge, Massachusetts, are similar historic areas which attract tourists, but they are primarily museum pieces; more vital commercially are such districts as the German Village in Columbus, Ohio; San Francisco's Chinatown; Georgetown in Washington, D.C.; and the picturesque and historic old residential areas adjacent to the CBDs of Charleston, S.C., and Savannah, Georgia.

All of the CBD functions described in the preceding pages are undergoing rapid change in response to the changes in the technology of transportation, methods of distribution of goods and services, and an evolving way of life. The traditional roles of the urban core are being challenged, and there is little doubt that, in the future, the core will be much less dominant as the commercial center of the city than it has been. Some planners question whether a core is necessary. They point to its disadvantages, which include congestion, air pollution, noise, high taxes associated with high densities, and a disproportionate share of responsibility and financial burden placed upon the core of the city in supporting many facilities and services which should be shared by other portions of the respective metropolitan areas. Modern transportation and communication, changes in the aspirations of the public, and greater sensitivity to the adverse environmental conditions generated by high densities lead to a questioning of the value of maintaining an urban core.

Zoning, for example, began in the United States as a response to the need to control densities in the most congested portions of cities in the early years of the twentieth century, but it later became misused as an instrument of segregation in residential areas. Many innovations in zoning, such as the use of the floor area ratio (FAR), discussed elsewhere in this book, apply particularly to CBDs, and the use of height and bulk bonuses for projects in which certain open space is provided represents a desire to achieve density controls while at the same time increasing the flexibility available to developers; a similar objective lies behind the use of the Planned Unit Development (PUD) concept, which provides large-scale developers, within certain stated density limits, with opportunities to build innovative projects transcending the rigid constraints of typical zoning. Renewal of areas surrounding the CBD represents, in some instances, an attempt to arrest, and if possible reverse, the downtrend in retail sales within the central core.

SUMMARY AND CONCLUSION

Since cities exist in order that certain activities may be effectively carried on, and since the greatest proportion of urban activities are involved in making a living—the economic function—it follows that the economic base constitutes the starting point in the development of the process of urban planning. In order to accommodate economic activities, land, which is a scarce resource, must be designated in appropriate amounts and in appropriate locations for each of the prospective activities. An understanding, therefore, of the forces, both "natural" and fortuitous, which affect the physical patterns of those land uses involved in the urban economic base is indispensibly prerequisite to planning. In this chapter, we have examined, insofar as the limitations of space permit, the major forces and trends which condition the patterns of industrial and commercial land use, starting with general aspects of the urban economic base, and proceeding through each of the principal economic functions, both industrial and commercial.

As with all land uses, there are general tendencies for sorting out, or stratification, of locations by type of activity and establishment, in accordance with certain general models, or arrangements, which are well known to all urbanists, regardless of their specific discipline. These models are of great utility to the planner as a starting point in his considerations of the special conditions, or anomalies, which affect particular land uses and particular commercial and industrial establishments. To conform to the models means reinforcing the status quo, and intensifying the trends, good and bad. To deviate implies a willingness to pay the price of innovation, with the goal of improving upon the quality of life, economic and otherwise, of those who live or work within the city or urban region. The planner is faced with a set of alternatives; his choice from among them must inevitably involve a comprehensive knowledge and understanding of the nature of the available alternatives and of the probable consequences flowing from selection of each of them. Only by the planner's presentation of such alternatives and their probable consequences to the decision-makers to whom he is responsible can he adequately fulfill his professional obligations. In such presentations, his efforts cannot be circumscribed by preconceptions—either his own or those of his clientele—relative to the form, structure, or potentialities of his urban area. He must be relatively uninhibited; he must have vision without being visionary; he must be "down-to-earth" but not unduly constrained. He must understand existing conditions and trends without necessarily being bound to them.

Since the urban economic base is tantamount to the resources available, the planner must consider industry and commerce at all stages in the planning process. Goals, the determination of which is part and parcel of planning, must be economically feasible;

they must be within the range of the possibilities and subject to the constraints of the resources available, but at the same time the resources must be effectively utilized for maximum advantage. The advantages must be long-term in preserving and enhancing the quality of life and the environment within which it functions; yet at the same time advantage must be taken of short-term opportunities. Planning basically consists in maximizing the use of resources through the analysis of alternative policies and actions, while minimizing the use of them through analysis of alternative policies and actions, while minimizing detrimental results of the recommended choices. Nowhere is this more important than in the choices among alternative policies and actions relative to those activities which involve the use of an especially scarce resource: the land available for commerce and industry, the economic base of city and region.

6 | COMMUNITY FACILITIES PLANNING

Herbert A. Goetsch

Every urban community requires certain facilities which are designed to serve the general public. "Community" as used here denotes an area under a specific political jurisdiction as described in Chapter 2. These facilities and the lands on which they are located are usually in public ownership. They are planned, constructed, and operated by a governmental entity or by a private organization under government franchise or regulation. Such public or semipublic facilities serve either the entire population of an area or a particular political or geographic subdivision of it. In some instances their service areas extend beyond the boundaries of political jurisdiction. These concepts will become clear as the variety of community facilities is described.

Community facilities include the following: (a) a variety of buildings to house administrative, educational, religious, cultural, health, safety, recreational, and service needs; (b) public works and utilities to provide water, power, heat, light, communications, sewage treatment, flood control, solid waste disposal, and transportation; and (c) public lands to accommodate the buildings and public works facilities and to provide open space for parks, playgrounds, malls, landscaping, and beautification. Of the foregoing, transportation is covered in Chapters 7 and 8 and will not be specifically considered here.

PARTIAL LISTING OF COMMUNITY FACILITIES

ADMINISTRATION

Courthouses
City Halls
Office Buildings
Polling Places
State Office Buildings
Federal Office Buildings
Post Offices

COMMUNICATION

Telephone Systems
Telegraph Systems
Radio and Television Stations
Alarm Systems

CULTURAL

Libraries
Museums
Art Centers
Music Halls
Auditoriums
Conservatories
Planetariums
Historic Landmarks and Areas

EDUCATION

Nursery Schools
Elementary Schools
Secondary Schools
Technical or Vocational Schools
Colleges or Universities
Special Schools
Private and Parochial Schools

HEALTH

Hospitals
Health Centers
Clinics

HOUSING

Public Housing Projects

POWER SUPPLY

Electric
Gas
Steam

RECREATION

Parks
Playgrounds
Totlots
Stadiums
Sports Arenas
Zoos
Golf Courses
Picnic Sites
Swimming Pools
Natatoriums
Beaches

SAFETY

Police Stations
Penal and Correctional
    Institutions
Fire Stations
Civil Defense Centers
Emergency Shelters

SERVICE CENTERS

Public Works Yards
Garages
Repair Shops

SEWERAGE

Sanitary Sewers
Storm Sewers
Combined Sewers
Drainage Channels
Sewage Treatment Plants

SOLID WASTE DISPOSAL

Incinerators
Transfer Stations
Recycling Facilities
Disposal Sites

SPECIAL

   Industrial Land Banks
   Environmental Corridors
   Cemeteries
   Civic Centers
   Neighborhood Centers
   Places of Worship
   Convention Centers

TRANSPORTATION

   Airports
   Harbors and Port Terminals
   Marinas
   Freeways
   Highways
   Local Streets

   Alleys
   Pedestrian Walks
   Parking Lots and Structures
   Bridges
   Mass Transit Facilities
   Bicycle Paths
   Bridle Trails
   Railroad Tracks and Terminals
   Bus Terminals
   Heliports
   Ferry Terminals

WATER SUPPLY

   Filtration Plants
   Pumping Stations
   Storage Facilities
   Mains and Distribution Facilities

Community facilities should be planned and developed so that they will enhance the community's objectives. They should serve the residential, commercial and industrial activities within the community. They must not conflict with adjacent land uses or be a blighting influence, but on the contrary they should stimulate other desirable land uses and improve the physical appearance of the community.

MEASURING NEEDS FOR COMMUNITY FACILITIES

Every area is unique and possesses its own characteristics which determine its special needs for community facilities. Such physical factors as climate, topography, drainage, soil, and natural resources have a direct and continuing effect on the needs for community facilities, while other factors such as age, size, economy, density, political attitudes, social attitudes and institutional arrangements of the populace are subject to change and their effects vary.

While there are some examples in recent years of new towns, most community facilities planning activities will take place within established urban areas. Isolated political jurisdictions surrounded by unurbanized land must develop their own amenities while those within a metropolitan region may very well share many community facilities with others.

The real need for community facilities should be established through the will of the people to be served, but the expression of the public will must be based on a realistic presentation of all of the relevant facts. The objectives and goals of the political jurisdiction, the priority of facilities to satisfy those objectives, and the ability to produce the facilities based on financial, legal, spatial, and political considerations must be carefully presented to the public. The activities of pressure groups, the sudden availability of funds, and misguided civic pride may result in improper choices.

Determining Requirements

Every political jurisdiction should have a general plan as a guide to achieving its community objectives. One of the major elements of the general plan is the community facilities plan. In such a plan are listed the various public facilities to be developed and constructed to meet the requirements of the community. These requirements are based on such factors as population, area, type of land use to be served, regulatory measures, future projected changes in these factors, relationship with adjacent communities and other units of government, present condition and life expectancy of existing facilities, and financing capabilities.

Selecting Standards

Each political jurisdiction should determine the level of service it desires and can afford. It should establish standards of performance or service to be achieved by the operation of its community facilities. This can best be illustrated by giving several examples of standards as follows: The number of pupils per teacher in the elementary school, the frequency of solid waste collection, the quality of the effluent from the sewage treatment plant, the spacing of fire hydrants, or the intensity of street lighting. For facilities involving health and safety minimum standards are generally determined by law and are enforced by regulatory agencies. Since many types of community facilities involve permanent structures of considerable cost, their design should consider not only future needs but possible future changes in standards. Where feasible, flexibility and expansion possibilities should be included in the design.

COMMUNITY FACILITIES OBJECTIVES

The public can best provide for certain of its needs by using publicly planned, constructed, and operated facilities. In some instances private companies provide public utility services to the public with the service area, type and quantity of service, and user charges regulated by the public. The objectives which these facilities should attain are to satisfy the educational, health, safety, and public works needs of the community. These facilities are publicly owned or regulated and their operation is noncompetitive, nonprofit, and public supported either by taxes or user charges. The description of four major systems of community facilities will illustrate the objectives involved.

Educational System

State and local laws prescribe the minimum educational requirements of citizens by specifying either the grade level to be attained or the minimum age at which a student can terminate his formal ecuation. Local units of government provide the facilities for elementary, secondary, and junior college education. States provide college and university facilities, while the federal government provides financial assistance to both local and state educational plants. Federal aid is generally granted only if certain federal standards are met, in an attempt to assure greater equality in curricula as well as schools and equipment. Private educational facilities are affected not only by local regulations such as zoning but also by federal standards as they seek federal financial assistance. The objectives of the educational system include the development of a responsible, well-informed citizenry, a productive society, and an improved social and cultural climate within the community.

Recreational System

The public has long recognized the desirability of providing for the recreational needs of a community by furnishing the necessary facilities not only by procuring lands for parks and open space, but also by constructing the necessary grounds, buildings, and accessory equipment. Among the objectives of a recreational system are better physical and mental health, enhancement of property values, prevention of crime and delinquency, and promotion of safety.

Utilities

Certain essential needs or services directly affecting the public health and welfare are provided by public utilities. These utilities may be publicly owned and operated or may be privately owned, with their operation regulated by various governmental entities. Included here are water, sewer, electric, gas, telephone, and transportation services. The objectives of a utility system in a community are to provide a reliable, safe, regulated, coordinated, and economical system of essential services. Local regulations provide for the controlled location of the facilities, while state and federal regulatory authorities provide for standards of service and safety and an equitable rate structure.

Other Public and Institutional Types

Public and semipublic buildings and grounds include city halls, courthouses, post offices, fire and police stations, hospitals, health centers, libraries, museums, art centers, auditoriums, and municipal yards and shops. The objectives for these are to provide for the orderly and dignified conduct of governmental activities and to provide for the convenient and economical furnishing of public services which are institutional in character. It is generally accepted that in addition to the main objectives, these installations should enhance the appearance of the community by means of good aesthetic design [Figure 6-1].

Source: Photo courtesy of the City and County of Milwaukee.

Figure 6-1   Milwaukee Civic Center Plaza—an excellent design and source of community pride.

SCHOOLS AND THE NEIGHBORHOOD CONCEPT

Despite certain trends to the contrary, the elementary school still provides the nucleus of the neighborhood in many urban areas. Good land use planning provides land for the construction of an elementary school near the center of the residential area to be served by the school. This applies in newly developing areas as well as in older ones undergoing change, although there are other factors encroaching upon the scene to determine what will constitute the basic residential neighborhood.

School Planning and Residential Land Planning

The types and density of residential land use should be carefully planned so that sufficient land at the proper location may be set aside for school purposes as an area develops (see Chapter 4). Population characteristics and projected changes must be considered. Land developers and subdividers should be required to dedicate lands to the public to be used for school construction, or to contribute financially to the cost of land acquisition in proportion to the area if the area being developed is too small to require a school.

School Planning and Transportation

Elementary schools should be so located that children can walk to school without crossing a major traffic artery. If this cannot be accomplished it may be necessary to construct special pedestrian facilities or provide crossing guards. The walking distance for the elementary schoolchild is recommended to be one-fourth to one-half mile. Public transportation is generally not required for elementary schoolchildren in average or higher-density urban areas but may be required in outlying areas.

School Planning—Integration—Private Schools

Changing land uses cause an imbalance in elementary school population and may require transporting pupils to prevent overcrowding or excess of school capacity in declining neighborhoods. In addition, legislation may require transporting pupils to schools outside the neighborhood to achieve racial integration. The effect of private and parochial schools on school planning should be carefully evaluated. As private schools are abandoned, often for financial reasons, the public school may become overloaded. Conversely, objection to racial integration in some areas has caused the establishment of private schools, with a resulting decline in the enrollment of the public school.

THE EDUCATIONAL SYSTEM AND THE GENERAL PLAN

Increasing emphasis on formal education, modifications in educational philosophies, changes in land use, and population shifts combine to make the planning of educational facilities difficult. School authorities and other public officials should determine and specify educational needs for future land requirements so that the space may be reserved for school construction. Specifically the following basic items of information must be known; (a) population characteristics and growth projections; (b) land use projections; (c) inventory of present facilities with regard to capacity, condition, and location; (d) standards of design, space, and location; (e) and nature of organization of the educational system.

Space Requirements

Elementary schools serve a neighborhood which is generally less than one square mile in area. This, of course, will vary, depending on land use, population characteristics including density, and the presence of private or parochial schools. The minimum land area for an elementary school according to most authorities is 5 acres, with an additional acre for each 100 pupils. Land availability and cost may affect decisions regarding the amount of land to be used. There appears to be a trend toward abandoning the neighborhood concept, since some educators feel that the neighborhood school does not result in quality education. The planner has the responsibility to demonstrate the advantages, including the neighborhood school (if properly managed), of the many amenities of the residential neighborhood concept.

In most instances the location of schools and parks should be coordinated. By locating them adjacent to each other, parklands provide the outdoor recreation space for pupils, whereas the school buildings may provide shelter and comfort facilities for users of the park.

High schools serve a number of neighborhoods or an entire community and consequently are larger and more elaborate. Again such factors as land use, population density, and cost will influence the size. While standards are constantly undergoing change, past practice indicates that a junior high school may have an enrollment of about 1,500 and occupy a site of about 20 acres, while a senior high school may have an enrollment of 2,000 or more and be located on a site of about 30 acres. High schools should preferably be located on mass transit routes. These secondary schools normally provide athletic fields, auditoriums, and gymnasiums for athletic and cultural events. The large crowds attracted to these events dictate that adequate parking and transportation be planned. These facilities are required also for the adult evening classes frequently held in secondary schools. Some cities provide one or more comprehensive high schools offering a variety of curricula including vocational and general adult education. A recent concept is the school park or campus plan, which provides one campus for all levels of education.

Junior colleges and specialty schools fulfill special educational needs in an urban community by preparing students for technical or semiprofessional careers, by providing college credits transferable to a higher institution, and by affording adult and continuing education programs. Business colleges and vocational schools are included in this classification. Facilities for these educational institutions are generally modest and compact since the major emphasis is on academic work and vocational training with only limited attention being given to extracurricular activities. They should be carefully located within a community to give maximum service with the least disruption.

Universities cover substantial land areas. Many universities were established before rapid urbanization took place and now are surrounded by other land uses which frequently are not compatible with the activities and requirements of the university. However, the area may very well serve as an urban laboratory for several courses normally taught at city universities. Expansion of facilities should be carefully planned. If adjacent lands cannot be obtained, the university may have to resort to a more comprehensive use of its existing land including the construction of high-rise buildings. These facilities should be carefully coordinated with the transportation and public utility services available. The campus itself is usually a definite area with many of the requirements of a self-contained community, including circulation, communication, safety, utilities, and open space [Figure 6-2].

Scheduling Land Availability

Educational establishments usually require large tracts of land which should be available when the community finds it necessary to build such facilities. These sites should be incorporated into the long-range general plan of the community and usually

Source: Photo by Denver Planning Department.

Figure 6-2   Amphitheater, University of Denver.

must be purchased by the public to preserve them for their intended use. They should be compatible with projected adjacent land uses, should be capable of being served by transportation and utilities, and must have suitable soil and topography.

THE RECREATIONAL SYSTEM AND THE GENERAL PLAN

The most important element of any recreational system in urban areas is the land, the open or green spaces. As urbanization has increased, municipal governments have come to a greater realization of the importance of acquiring, developing, maintaining, and operating park or open space facilities. State and federal agencies too have aided in the development of open space for recreation both by providing financial grants to local governments and by developing recreational facilities under their own jurisdiction. The concern for the environment which became a popular cause in the late 1960s has stimulated governmental regulations to preserve parks and open space.

The acquisition and development of lands for parks and recreation should be carefully planned to ensure that the people will receive maximum benefits both at the outset as well as in the future. The planning phase must be the first step in the development of a recreational system and should be undertaken carefully and deliberately. Inappropriate planning, hasty or expedient acquisition, and indiscriminate modification of plans have resulted in inadequate or undesirable recreational areas. At times limited financial resources may cause a political jurisdiction to delay or neglect the development of these vitally needed facilities. It should be recognized therefore that regardless of the specific needs of a particular municipality, certain general benefits from park and recreational layouts will result. These include better physical and mental health of the citizens, increase in property values, reduction in crime and delinquency, and the promotion of safety [Figure 6-3].

Community recreational programs and goals must be understood and defined so that a plan or basic guideline to provide adequate facilities at proper locations can be developed and adopted. Included should be a land use policy covering the classification of park areas by purpose, a set of design standards, procedures for developing and adopting detailed plans for each park area, and a projection of future demands.

Many factors determine recreational space requirements. Among these are the density, age distribution, economic levels, ethnic backgrounds, and projected trends of the population; the physical layout of the area with special emphasis given to residential areas, educational institutions, and the traffic system; climate and topography; the proximity of recreational facilities owned by private interests or other units of government; the availability and cost of land; and the financial resources available.

Source: Photo by Denver Planning Department.

Figure 6-3 Park Hill Golf Course, Denver, a buffer between residential and industrial land uses.

Certain recreational space standards have been developed and generally subscribed to by recreational authorities. These include (a) a minimum of one acre of public park or recreation land for every hundred persons, (b) a minimum of 10 percent of the total land area of a municipality devoted to recreation, and (c) one-half of any municipality's park and recreation area reserved for active recreation and the other half for larger parks. These yardsticks should be applied with discretion since each local situation is unique.

No uniform terminology exists which can be readily applied to the various parks and recreational areas. It becomes necessary therefore to carefully describe any facility with regard to size, service area, and purpose or activity. From a planning standpoint, a convenient classification is one based upon the area which a facility is designed to serve. This leads to several general classifications, as shown in Table 6-1.

Play or Totlots

Playlots or totlots are facilities for smaller children located in high population density areas where private yard play space is lacking. They are equipped with sandboxes and other apparatus for small children and seats or benches for adults who bring the children to the lot.

Neighborhood Parks

Neighborhood parks, frequently called playgrounds, are designed to serve the recreational needs of the immediately surrounding neighborhood. They should serve people of all ages and therefore include both active and passive areas. These parks are rather

TABLE 6 - 1
Suggested Standards for Parks

Type of Park	Area of Facility	Service Radius	Population Served
Play or totlot	2500 sq. ft. minimum	1/8 mile	25-75 children
Neighborhood	8-15 acres	1/4 mile-high density 3/8 mile-low density	2,000-5,000
District	15-40 acres	1/2 to 1 mile average	15,000-35,000
Community	100-500 acres	1½ to 2½ miles	1000 per 1/4 acre
Special area	35-175	1 to 1½ miles	———
Park-school			
Elementary	8-15 acres	1/4 to 3/8 miles	———
Junior high	10-25 acres	3/8 to 1 mile	———
Senior high	25-50 acres	½ mile minimum	———

Source: Adapted from *Suggested Standards for Parks and Recreation*, National Recreation and Park Association.

intensively developed, with lesser emphasis on plantings and green space. They should preferably be located adjoining an elementary school, since they provide the necessary outdoor recreation space for pupils, while the school buildings provide shelter and comfort facilities for the users of the park, resulting in a reduction in the amount of land and equipment required for these facilities. Playgrounds should be lighted to provide for evening use, should not have streets except at the boundaries, and should contain adequate signs and traffic control facilities to protect pedestrians going to and from the park. Apparatus should be provided for such active sports as softball, basketball, volleyball, tennis, and ice skating. Also for passive recreation such items as tables, benches, grass, shade, shuffleboard, and lawn bowling may be provided.

District Parks

District parks, sometimes called playfields, are planned to serve several neighborhoods but not the entire municipality. They are designed for rather intensive use for baseball, football, softball, track, tennis, skiing, coasting, and similar active athletic activities. They should provide seating and parking for spectators, and be lighted for evening use. They may contain a fieldhouse, a community center, and a swimming pool. Substantial areas of open green space and landscaping should be designed into district parks, not only for the relaxation of park users, but also to screen the activities from the surrounding areas. Special benefits may accrue from locating district parks adjacent to high school campuses.

Community Parks

Community parks, sometimes referred to as metropolitan parks, may also have the designation large parks. They give greater emphasis to natural, open green space. Some of the more active recreational facilities may be provided but only where they are compatible with the natural features. Major emphasis should be given to such activities as picnicking, hiking, nature study, boating, golf, archery, fishing, and similar outdoor activities. Pavilions with rest rooms and refreshment stands are required. Where possible, existing rugged terrain, wooded areas, streams, and similar topographic features should be incorporated into and preserved within community parks. Because of the large number of people served and the size of the service area a substantial amount of off-street parking should be provided. Through streets should be avoided, and where this is not possible streets should be planned as parkway drives with meandering alignment and minimum traffic lanes to discourage speeding [Figure 6-4].

Special Recreational Areas

Many urban areas provide special parks and recreation areas. These facilities may be for a special purpose such as a zoo, marina, open air theater or band shell, golf course, stadium, athletic field, arena, or auditorium. Private interests frequently provide such

Source: Photo by Denver Planning Department.

Figure 6-4 A community park, Denver, Colorado.

facilities as amusement parks, outdoor theaters, and bowling alleys. A municipality may provide some of these to attract visitors and tourists.

Careful planning and research should be undertaken to discover, preserve, and develop any historical or terrain features which have geological, hydrological, archaeological, botanical, zoological or landmark values [Figure 6-5]. Where possible these should be acquired by the public so that they may be protected.

The regions along streams should be preserved through zoning and public ownership. They can frequently serve a dual role as flood plains and recreational areas. Scenic drives in the form of parkways with meandering roadways having restricted traffic should be considered for development along streams.

UTILITY SYSTEMS

Utility systems provide essential services and commodities to the people of an area on a noncompetitive basis. Since space in urban areas is limited, it is desirable that there not be duplicate utilities. This condition results in a monopoly which the public interest dictates must be either publicly owned and operated or be regulated by some government agency.

Source: Photo by Colorado Visitors Bureau.

Figure 6-5 Central City Opera House preserved for public performances of opera and drama.

These utility systems must be carefully planned in connection with the development of an urban area. The availability and cost of utilities will frequently govern the type and rate of development.

Water and sewerage systems are most commonly publicly owned, while gas, electric, and telephone systems are privately owned. Both federal and state commissions exist for the purpose of regulation. Various phases of utility operations including the granting of franchises, prescribing service levels, and setting rates are subject to regulations. Certain transportation systems which are covered in Chapters 7 and 8 fall into this classification.

Water Systems

Water is among the most basic of human needs and a safe, adequate, and economical water supply is a basic requirement of any city. Water is required for human consumption, sanitary sewer system operation, fire fighting, street cleaning, lawn and garden sprinkling, air conditioning, manufacturing, and recreation. Most water systems are publicly owned and their planning is an essential element of any municipal development plan.

The components of a water system are the source of supply, treatment plants, distribution system, and storage facilities. Technology is rather well developed and these systems are relatively simple in design and construction but represent a substantial capital investment. Future water needs involving quantities, rate of use, and locations of service must be carefully projected.

Water treatment plants should be located on adequately sized, well-landscaped sites so that they will be an aesthetic asset. Reservoirs and elevated tanks are required in the system to provide additional storage and equalize pressures. Consequently their location is based on technical rather than zoning considerations. Good planning and design will assure sites for these facilities before an area develops and will cause them to be in harmony with surrounding land uses. Water mains are most generally located within the street right-of-way.

Sewerage Systems

Sewerage systems consist of drains, sewers, pumps and treatment plants. Sanitary sewers carry sewage from plumbing systems of buildings to a sewage treatment plant. Storm sewers carry the rain water and surface runoff to a natural watercourse or body of water. Some older cities have combined sewers which carry both sanitary sewage and storm water in the same conduit.

The rapid urbanization since World War II has greatly taxed the capacity of existing sewerage systems, while the growing public concern for water quality in the 1960s required that new and improved sewerage facilities be constructed. Substantial capital investments are required for these systems and, while some state and federal financial assistance has been made available, urban development has been slowed or halted in certain areas because sewerage systems construction has not proceeded fast enough to meet the needs.

Since it is generally desirable to have sewerage systems operate by gravity flow, sewer mains follow the topography and drainage patterns of the area. The treatment plant therefore must be located near the low or outlet end of the drainage system. Because of public prejudices against facilities of this type, the planning of their location must be carefully done. Sufficient area must be acquired to provide for plant expansion, buffer zones and plantings, and possibly sludge disposal.

Since sewerage systems should follow the drainage pattern, they will cover a geographical area rather than following a political boundary. Planning, development, and operation of these systems is best done on a metropolitan or regional basis, with individual local municipalities responsible only for their local sewers and the regional authority handling the large sewers and treatment facilities.

Local sewers are located in streets for convenience since they serve the abutting properties. Because they flow by gravity they have a substantial effect on the street configuration and have priority of location over other utilities located in the street. In order that these sewers be built to the proper size, future land use and density must be considered. The redevelopment of any urban area must consider the location, condition, and capacity of its sewerage system.

The storm sewer system may involve both closed sewers and open channels. The latter should be preserved and protected by zoning or public acquisition. This should include enough width of land on the banks to prevent flooding of private property. The type of development, especially the amount of building and paving, determines the intensity of runoff and consequently the size and cost of storm sewer facilities.

Other Utility Systems

Electric, gas, and telephone utilities provide for the vital light, heat, power, and communication needs of a city. They are most often privately owned and therefore require planning coordination between the municipality, the developer, and the utility. Private utility companies provide their own plants and offices, on their own property, but normally use streets, alleys, or private easements for their distribution facilities. Electric and telephone lines have in the past been constructed overhead on poles except in the downtown areas of cities. With the concern for the environment and aesthetics of the late 1960s came the public demand to place these facilities underground.

PUBLIC BUILDINGS AND GROUNDS

Every incorporated urban area requires certain public buildings and grounds to house government offices and service centers. In addition to those mentioned earlier in this chapter this could include city halls, court houses, state and federal office buildings, post offices, fire and police stations, libraries, museums, art galleries, botanical gardens [Figure 6-6], performing arts centers, hospitals, health centers, convention centers, auditoriums, and municipal yards and shops. Since government has direct control over the location, size, and aesthetic quality of most of these, the municipality can plan to enhance the appearance of the area in addition to satisfying the functional and utilitarian needs. Since the location and character of these facilities not only create a civic image but also affect the development of private facilities, the urban planner is here afforded a unique opportunity to advance the goals and objectives of the municipality. Several of the major facilities are discussed in somewhat greater detail.

Source: Photo by Denver Planning Department.

Figure 6-6   Denver Botanical Gardens.

Civic Centers

A grouping of public buildings into a planned civic center can result in a number of advantages. Among these are (a) greater convenience to the citizenry, (b) more efficient coordination among public officials, (c) opportunity for aesthetic design coordination, and (d) the creation of a civic symbol. The inclusion of such cultural and recreational facilities as a library, museum, auditorium, art center, and similar buildings and the landscaping of the entire civic center will further enhance the civic image.

The civic center, where possible, should be located adjacent to the central business district. This proximity can enhance the relationship between government agencies and such downtown entities as banks, private utilities, and major business, professional, and civic offices. The presence of the governmental center is a stabilizing influence in the surrounding area.

Branch Administrative Centers

Smaller cities may be able to centralize all of their public and semipublic buildings in one location, but larger ones will require public buildings throughout their area. Decentralization of public buildings has a number of advantages including (a) accessibility to the citizens, (b) smaller land areas required, (c) less congestion, and (d) each branch center or building being planned separately for its own best advantage as to location, design, and construction.

Some facilities must be decentralized so that they may best serve the public. These include fire and police stations, health centers, branch libraries, and public works yards and shops. Their placement depends on the specific population and area to be served. For emergency services such as fire protection certain standards related to travel time and distance must be considered. All should be located not only for efficiency of service, but with the objective of enhancing the area. Again, there are advantages to grouping these into branch centers where possible. This is especially true of public works yards and shops.

Solid Waste Facilities

Disposal of solid waste has emerged in the late 1960s as a major urban problem. In the past the city incinerator or town dump has been tolerated. However, growing affluence and changing technology have increased the volume of solid wastes and changed its character. With increasing public awareness and concern for the environment came demands for air and water pollution abatement, the improvement of the landscape, and the conservation of resources.

The major methods of solid waste disposal have traditionally been by landfill and by burning, and technology exists to carry on both in a manner which will meet health and environmental standards. Increased solid waste research was undertaken in the United States in the late 1960s by government agencies, industry, and research agencies, some with federal financial assistance.

Planners must give careful study to the location of solid waste facilities. Public prejudice, frequently due to improper operations in the past, will make site acquisition difficult; changing technology increases the difficulty of selecting a particular type of disposal; and many factors such as climate, topography, geology, zoning, and transportation facilities have their influence. If properly planned, engineered, and operated, a sanitary landfill can be used to reclaim ravines, low-lying areas, strip mines, quarries, and similar lands for beneficial municipal uses such as parks and recreation areas. Incinerators and recycling facilities should be located in industrially zoned areas, should be attractively landscaped where possible, and should be carefully related to the transportation system.

Other Public and Semipublic Facilities

Certain special public and semipublic facilities, such as churches and synagogues, cemeteries, hospitals, convention centers, and amusement parks may occupy only a small portion of the land area of a municipality, but they nevertheless have a very great effect on community life and on the land area surrounding them. Most of these undertakings are permitted under "special exceptions" in the local zoning ordinances. Many are objected to by the public because of the traffic congestion they create. Others, like hospitals and cemeteries, have a depressing effect on certain people. Some of these objections can be partially overcome by giving special attention to the designing of attractive structures and the provision of adequate parking and elaborate landscaping.

Since World War II most larger cities of the United States have been building new convention and exposition centers to attract tourists and visitors to their area and to enhance their economy. This "smokeless industry" requires special planning, since a large building area is involved and traffic and parking facilities must be provided. It must be related to locations of hotels and motels, restaurants and commercial districts, and the entire development must enhance the image of the city.

BALANCING DEMAND WITH FEASIBILITY

The provision of community facilities must keep pace with other facets of urban growth. This indicates that in addition to the community facilities plan, a municipality must have a parallel financial plan. The converting of the community facilities plan into construction projects which result in completed installations is accomplished by a capital improvements program described in Chapter 10. The urban planner should see to it that the plan reflects the goals, objectives, and priorities of the community. Economic research and feasibility studies should be available and kept current. Alternatives should be clearly defined so that the decision-makers, the public or their elected representatives, can make decisions which will provide community facilities at the optimum time, considering both need and ability to finance.

FUTURE CHANGES

Community facilities planning in the predepression era was characterized by great emphasis on aesthetics, land use and orderliness. The depression, with its economic and social problems, brought more concern that community facilities plans contribute to the achievement of the municipalities' goals. Planners of community facilities will be challenged in the future to translate what may appear at times to be conflicting goals into tangible, vitally needed facilities. There will be additional disciplines and a vast array of technology and information to be considered. Greater emphasis will be placed on research, data collection, systems analysis, opinion surveys, and simulation.

Future governmental and institutional arrangements will have a direct effect on community facilities planning. It appears that the numbers and complexity of governments will continue to increase with increasing emphasis on state and federal financial assistance and consequent control over plans.

Because the population has become more mobile, future needs for, and locations of, facilities become more difficult to forecast. Demands for services will continue to increase both because population will continue to burgeon and because of its mobility.

There will continue to be a concern for the environment and the problem of preservation of the land, air, water, and natural resources. Community facilities will be critically evaluated by the public to determine their impact on the environment.

BIBLIOGRAPHY

1.   ASCE, *Urban Planning Guide,* Manuals and Reports on Engineering Practice, No. 49 (1969), pp. 163-194.
2.   International City Management Association *Managing the Modern City,* 1971.
3.   Abel Wolman, "The Metabolism of Cities," and Kevin Lynch, "The City As Environment," *Scientific American,* Sept. 1965, pp. 179-190, 209-219.

7 | TRANSPORTATION FACILITIES PLANNING— EXTERNAL

Harold M. Mayer

Transportation—the transfer of people and goods from one place to another—is what makes possible the differences in land use, economic activities, and other attributes which characterize every place on earth which is occupied by man. It is the dominant form of what some people call "spatial interaction"; other forms involve communication or the diffusion of ideas. Just as the various functional areas within cities and metropolitan regions are specialized because of their transportation interconnections, so cities and metropolitan areas themselves are functionally differentiated by being interconnected, not only with each other, but also with the nonurban areas from which they receive raw materials, foodstuffs, fuels, and other indispensible inputs into the urban economy. This chapter is concerned with those transportation modes and facilities which interconnect cities with one another and with their external complementary regions, while Chapter 8 is concerned with the facilities for transportation within cities and metropolitan areas. At the outset, it is important to recognize that the two are in most instances inseparable. The same highways that lead traffic in and out of cities also constitute important arteries of internal circulation, the airplane trip from one city to another involves access to the airport via the city's internal transportation routes, and the freight which is moved via railroads, ships, barges, airplanes, and pipelines must be collected and distributed within the urban areas. Nevertheless, it is convenient, if not entirely logical, to consider some of the major problems of planning for the routes and terminals of a city or metropolitan area's external transportation.

PRINCIPLES OF SPATIAL INTERACTION

It is important that the planner be aware of certain general principles relative to transportation systems and the movements of goods and people which they handle. Most of these principles are applicable at any scale, from the local movement within a neighborhood to the intercontinental and transcontinental movements which constitute the main ties making this, in theory if not in actuality, one world. Transportation facilities are, indeed, facilitative; they are not created in response to satisfactions which they furnish themselves. Economists term the demand for transportation a "derived demand"; that is, the desires and needs which transport answer are not for transportation as such but, rather, for the utility of delivering a resource, whether it be a "natural" resource, a service, or man himself, where it can be utilized for some purpose. The result is "place utility" at the destination. There are a very few exceptions: the Outdoor Recreation Resources Commission found that the leading form of outdoor recreation is automobile riding, while pleasure cruising has largely replaced point-to-point movement as the leading use of oceangoing passenger ships, and private boating has experienced a spectacular boom in recent years. But most transportation does not satisfy a primary demand for transportation per se. It represents a cost, in time, money, and inconvenience, of satisfying other needs. Therefore, in general, the most effective transportation is that which is fastest, lowest cost, and most convenient.

Spatial Friction

Transportation overcomes space and takes place on lineal routes. Therefore, distance is the attribute which transportation is designed to overcome. Distance, on the other hand, is not normally measured exclusively as a direct line from origin to destination—a "desire line"—but rather as a cost. The usual measure of cost is in monetary terms, and for some movements, such as those of certain bulk commodities, the lowest-cost route, in monetary terms, is that which offers the greatest competitive advantage and which secures the most traffic, limited only by the capacity of the route. But there are other costs. Time is money, and delays involve substantial costs for most movements, other than those in which continuous flow and dependable arrival times are more significant. Convenience is also an advantage, and some forms of transportation, of both people and goods, justify a premium rate or fare for passenger comfort or amenities or for centralized responsibility and minimal paperwork in connection with goods movement.

Distance, then, may be measured as the cost of the movement from origin to destination, and it is multidimensional. We may represent distance as d [Figure 7-1] and plot it along the horizontal axis, while the cost of a movement is c, on the vertical axis. If the cost for a given distance were constant, the curve would be a straight line, on an arithmetic scale, with constant slope. However, economies of scale come into play, so that the cost for a given distance, generally, decreases with increasing length of trip or shipment. The curve, therefore, tapers, and the thousandth mile may cost substantially less over the road than earlier miles; in other words, the cost of line-haul or over-the-road movement varies as the square root of the distance for many modes of transportation.

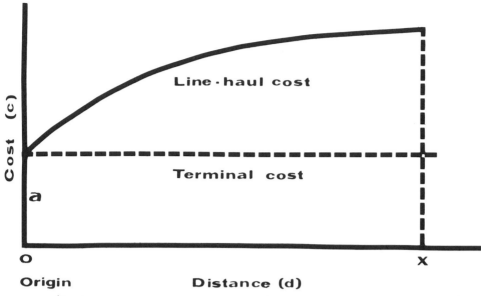

$c_x = a + \sqrt{d}x$ where

cx = cost of transportation over distance d, between origin and destination x

a = terminal cost at origin and destination and at intermediate transfer points, if any.

Figure 7-1   Movement distance-cost relationship.

But few forms of transportation, if any, are designed to handle individual movements of people or goods. The movements are aggregated, whether of individuals in an automobile, on a highway in which many vehicles move, or shipments loaded aboard a railroad car—which must then be placed in a train—or a ship or aircraft. Traffic density, therefore, produces scale economies up to the point at which capacity is approached, where congestion and delays then represent added costs and the curve may invert. The facilities used for assembly and distribution of traffic in order to effect scale economies on the line haul are called *terminals,* and the terminal costs must be distinguished from and added to the line-haul costs. Terminal costs may represent a very large proportion of the total cost of origin-to-destination movement. Therefore, a major concern of the transportation planner is the reduction of terminal costs and delays, and the improvement of terminal efficiency. Since most transportation terminals are in urban areas, an understanding of terminal problems, involving location, design, and operation, is an indispensable part of the urban planning process.

One transportation geographer has pointed out that there are three general prerequisites to movement or spatial interaction: complementarity, intervening opportunity, and transferability or substitution.[1] Complementarity is almost synonymous with regional or areal specialization; it simply refers to the fact that one area or region will specialize to

1. Edward L. Ullman, *American Commodity Flow* (Seattle: Univ. of Washington Press, 1957), pp. 20-27; also Ullman in William L. Thomas (ed.), *Man's Role in Changing the Face of the Earth* (Chicago: Univ. of Chicago Press, 1956), pp. 862-880.

the extent of producing goods or services in excess of its own requirements, and therefore can transfer or "export" them to other areas which, in turn, produce surpluses of other goods or services. Similarly, differences in economic or other opportunities give rise to movements of people from one area or region to another; the result is interregional migration, or, internationally, immigration and emigration. Economists refer to the law of comparative advantage in which a region or nation produces those goods and services in which it has a comparative, though not necessarily an absolute, advantage over other regions or nations. Obviously, without complementarity there would be no demand for transportation, and, by the same token, transportation is indispensable for producing economic and social complementarity, or areal specialization.

Intervening opportunity refers to the competition among places, and the fact that a demand may be satisfied by any one of many places which produce given goods, services, or personal satisfactions. Other things being equal, a demand may be satisfied, assuming that costs at each point are equal, at least costs where transportation is least expensive; in many instances this would be the closest point.

Transferability refers to the possibility of substitution, whether of transportation carriers or routes between the same origins and destinations, of alternate locations at which the demands can be met, or alternate sources of supply, alternate markets, alternate materials or inputs, or of alternate methods of satisfying a demand. Communication, for example, may in some instances substitute for transportation.

Traffic Generation

A useful device for estimating the amount of transportation required to meet the demand (handle the traffic) is the gravity model, which is a generalized analog descriptive of the amount of traffic that may be generated between pairs of points. It is analogous to Newton's law of gravitation, and states that the traffic generated between two points may be proportional to the mass (population, purchasing power, or other relevant measure) of the two points and inversely proportional to some exponent of the distance between them. The equation is very simple:

$$T_{ij} = \frac{kP_iP_j}{d^e}$$

where T_{ij} = traffic between two points, i and j
k = a constant, since the level must be calibrated on the basis of empirical knowledge
P_i, P_j = population, or other relevant measure, at each of the two points
d = distance between i and j, as an exponential function (e)

The gravity model is widely used to estimate the required capacity of highways connecting two points, the amount of service required on a railroad, airline, or shipping route, or the need for extension or new service. If a route serves intermediate points, the estimated traffic must be cumulated between each pair of points served by and along the route, making allowance for intervening opportunities and competition or substitution.

Although the gravity model cannot be applied mechanically without judgment, it is a useful concept.

A transportation route or terminal rarely handles exclusively the traffic between only two points; more commonly many origins and/or destinations will generate movements over a route or through a terminal. It is therefore necessary to estimate the potential traffic at a terminal to and from a large number of points served by the routes converging there. Parking requirements at traffic-generating concentrations within urban areas should be estimated; acceptance rates for aircraft at airports should be considered in the location, design, and operation of the facility; the number of shoppers at a shopping center should be anticipated; and, in general, facilities at a transportation node or terminal should be planned in relation to the volume anticipated, or congestion and ultimately diversion will occur. From the gravity model is derived the potential model, which simply sums the total gravitative pull, or traffic generation, at a terminal point or node, resulting from the traffic generation along each of the routes, or between the given node and all other points connected with that node by the transportation network. Algebraically it is expressed as

$$T_i = k \sum_{i=1}^{n} P_n$$

where T_i = the total traffic at point i

k = a constant, empirically derived, to calibrate the level

P = population (or purchasing power, or other relevant variable) at a point

n = the number of points, or zones, connected with i, actually or potentially

In applying the potential equation, it is important not to overlook the internal traffic, such as within the city, which will be generated, hence $i = 1$.

Frequently it is necessary to evaluate the relative gravitative pull of one place as compared with others. Such knowledge may be essential in deciding upon the location of a facility or land use, such as a retail, wholesale, or industrial establishment or a recreational facility. It is a simple matter to apply the potential concept to an area of any size which contains any number of traffic-generating points or zones, and to derive an imaginary surface of potential, represented by contours or isolines passing through points having equal potential. On such a surface the values can be read along the contours and interpolated between them, just as elevations above a datum plane such as sea level can be read or interpolated from terrain representation on a topographic map. The figures, of course, are themselves arbitrary and meaningless, but the relative evaluations of the points are proportional to their traffic potential, and hence are useful in evaluation of the relative accessibility of locations within the mapped area to the prospective market, and to each other. As in the gravity and potential models, appropriate variables must be selected which are significant in relation to the problem at hand. Total population may be useful, or purchasing power, which in turn is a function of total population and disposable income, or specialized attributes such as farm population may be selected, in estimating the market for agricultural machinery relative to each point in the set of points within the mapped area. Such potentials have been mapped for the United States and for many areas within it. Since the number of points is very large, aggregates are commonly used; these include counties or, in urban areas, the zones which are set up in connection with origin-destination studies, and distances can be measured between the centroids, or centers of gravity of population, within such zones.

Several potential maps have been prepared for the United States.[2] A population or marketing potential map of the nation shows that the point of highest potential is in the New York metropolitan area, and that a ridge of high potential extends westward, paralleling the southern Great Lakes, to just west of Chicago and north of Milwaukee. Along this ridge Chicago is represented by a high peak, though lower than New York's, and peaks also occur at Detroit, Cleveland, Pittsburgh, and other major metropolitan areas. Similarly, a ridge of high potential occurs along the Pacific Coast, with peaks in the Los Angeles and San Francisco Bay areas.

Transportation Corridors

The maps of potential reveal clearly that there are areas, generally lineal, of high potential. These are served by transportation routes which handle high densities of traffic, and commonly several routes, of different modes, serve the same terminal city-pairs and also serve either the same or different intermediate cities. The area between Chicago and the east coast has long been recognized as the dominant or core region of the United States, containing a preponderant proportion of the urban population, manufacturing and commercial activity, and transportation facilities of the nation and of adjacent Canada. The best-known of these corridors is the Boston-to-Washington Megalopolis, containing one-fourth of the population of the United States in a 600-mile lineal conurbation.[3] A Great Lakes Megalopolis is also identifiable,[4] and within it there are several subsidiary lineal corridors which define intermetropolitan coalescence, such as Cleveland-Pittsburgh and Chicago-Milwaukee.[5] Since transportation provides the access which promotes spread of urbanization, the existence of two cities in proximity, with consequent high mutual gravitative attraction, stimulates provision of transportation routes connecting them, and they in turn accentuate lineal development along the routes. As travel time is reduced, the respective urbanized areas, growing toward each other along the routes, eventually

2. Chauncy D. Harris, "The Market as a Factor in the Localization of Industry in the U.S.," *Annals of the Association of American Geographers,* Vol. 44, No. 4 (Dec. 1954), pp. 315-348; William Warntz, "A New Map of the Surface of Population Potential for the United States, 1960," *Geographical Review,* Vol. 54, No. 2 (April 1964), pp. 170-184.

3. Jean Gottmann, *Megalopolis, The Urbanized Northeastern Seaboard of the United States* (New York: The Twentieth Century Fund, 1961), 810 pp.; Senator Claiborne Pell, *Megalopolis Unbound; The Supercity and the Transportation of Tomorrow* (New York: Frederic A. Praeger, 1966), 233 pp.

4. Myrto Bogdanou, "Great Lakes Megalopolis: General Considerations on National Transportation Axes," *Ekistics,* Vol. 27, No. 163 (June 1969), pp. 429-435; Constantinos A. Doxiadis, *et al., Emergence and Growth of an Urban Region: The Developing Urban Detroit Area,* Vol. I, *Analysis* (Detroit: Detroit Edison Co., 1966), pp. 75-113.

5. Irving Cutler, *The Chicago-Milwaukee Corridor: A Geographic Study of Intermetropolitan Coalescence* (Evanston, Ill.: Northwestern Univ. Dept. of Geography Studies in Geography No. 9, 1965), 310 pp.

coalesce. Along such corridors, the distinction between internal urban and intercity transportation is vague. In accordance with the gravity model, traffic volumes decrease outward from each of the respective city centers and outlying nodes in accordance with a negative exponential curve. The profile of traffic flow reveals, accordingly, a series of peaks along a ridge of high density and volume.[6] These concentrations of population and traffic are intensifying relative to the rest of the country, and the corridor concept is becoming increasingly significant not only in terms of radial routes within the respective cities and metropolitan areas, but also as basic elements of the geographic structure of transportation in the nation and continent. One projection indicates the possibility that, by the year 2000, most of the nation's population, and hence demand for transportation, will be concentrated in three such corridors, which the authors of the study term "Boswash" (Boston-Washington), "Chipitts" (Chicago-Pittsburgh), and "Sansan" (San Francisco-San Diego).[7] Whether this extreme projection is valid or not, it is clear that greatly improved intercity transportation will be essential along the major corridors. That this geographic pattern is becoming officially recognized is evident in the creation of the Northeast Corridor high-speed ground transportation project, which includes the "metro-liners" between New York and Washington and the "turboliners" between New York and Boston, and by the fact that the overwhelming proportion of service provided by Amtrak, the National Railroad Passenger Corporation, is along the Boston-New York-Washington corridor, with relatively little service elsewhere.

The urban planner should be especially concerned with the terminals and "interfaces" along the corridors, where passengers and goods are transferred between carriers, whether of the same or different modes. The express highways, intercity trains, buses, trucks handling LTL (less-than-truckload) shipments, airplanes, and other high-density intercity carriers must receive traffic from a multiplicity of origins within the respective cities and metropolitan areas and distribute the passengers and goods to many destinations. Corridor passenger trains cannot be effective unless connections with local intracity transportation is efficient and convenient; local transit access and adequate parking must be provided at the terminals.

Terminals and Line-Hauls

As indicated earlier, a movement between origin and destination involves terminal arrangements at each end, often intermediate transfers as well, and line-hauls. From

6. John E. Brush and Howard L. Gauthier, Jr., *Service Centers and Consumer Trips: Studies on the Philadelphia Metropolitan Fringe* (Chicago: Univ. of Chicago Dept. of Geography, Research Paper No. 113, 1968), 182 pp.; C. F. J. Whebell, "Corridors: A Theory of Urban Systems," *Annals of the Association of American Geographers,* Vol. 59, No. 1 (March 1969), pp. 1-26; *The Corridor Concept: Implications for Illinois* (Urbana, Ill.: Univ. of Illinois Dept. of Planning, 1968), 197 pp.; *Multiple Use of Transportation Corridors in Canada, Part I: Conceptual and Legal Aspects* (Vancouver: School of Community and Regional Planning, Univ. of British Columbia, 1969), 42 pp.; Darwin G. Stuart, *Joint Project Concept—Integrated Transportation Corridors,* prepared for the U.S. Dept. of Housing and Urban Development by Barton-Aschman Assocs. (Washington, D.C.: Government Printing Office, 1968), 129 pp.

7. H. Kahn and A. J. Weiner, *The Year 2000: A Framework for Speculation on the Next Thirty-three Years* (New York: Macmillan, 1967), p. 61.

Figure 7-1 it is evident that terminal costs are major elements in the overall cost of the transportation service. Also, the time consumed in collection and delivery within cities, in the assembly and distribution of passengers and goods between carrier terminal (or expressway access and egress) on the one hand and ultimate origin and destination on the other, constitutes a major consideration. Nearly everyone is familiar with the problems of access to airports through city traffic, and of the time consumed on city streets in gaining access to an expressway. Railroad freight cars spend most of their time in terminals, yards, and on sidings, awaiting loads or available labor for unloading, and, in addition, much time is lost in intermediate yardings in the assembling and breaking up of trains. Similarly, conventional general cargo ships spend more than half of their time in ports. It is clear that, as speeds increase, the "payoff" in reducing terminal delays and costs will be more than proportionately increased. From the viewpoint of the urban planner, the problem is threefold: (a) provision of adequate access to terminals; (b) provision of adequate land areas for the terminals themselves, in the best locations with relation to both the transportation systems and the general pattern of the vicinity, the city, and the region; and (c) planning of the proper relationships between terminal and adjacent areas in order to minimize the adverse effects of the facility and capitalize upon the values, both monetary and otherwise, created by the proximity of the access which the terminal provides. In this chapter we will consider some of the planning problems associated with each of several types of transportation terminals.

Intermodal Movements

A very high proportion of the movements of goods and people between cities, and between urban areas on the one hand and nonurban on the other, involves transfer between transportation modes, at "interfaces" or intermediate terminals. Minimizing costs and time at such interfaces is vital, and the planner must have an understanding of the technology and organizational structure involved.

The time is long past when planning can be confined to a single transportation mode. The entire phalanx of transportation organizations and facilities of a region or nation, and, indeed, of the world, should be regarded on one scale, as a series of interlocking systems, and on another as a single multimodal system. An express highway system is simply one element in a complete system of vehicular circulation. A railroad is an element in a system of such carriers which in turn constitutes but a part of a multimodal system, involving other forms of transportation, commonly, between the railroad terminals and the origins and destinations, especially in the case of merchandise traffic. Except for bulk commodities delivered directly between ships and waterfront industries, movement by water carriers also involves land carriers. Air traffic must be delivered to and from airports.

Each mode is, by its inherent characteristics, especially adapted to carry certain types of traffic under certain conditions. The shipper or traveler chooses the mode, or combination of modes, to secure the most efficient combination of time, cost, convenience, and safety.

In the United States most intercity passenger travel is by private automobile. As for local intracity travel, the automobile is the only mode which furnishes door-to-door convenience and which is available at all times. It furnishes privacy, flexibility, comfort. A terminal is associated with virtually every residential building, and an overwhelming proportion of trips, intercity as well as intracity, begins or ends at a residential location. In 1967, it was estimated that 86 percent of all travelers and 79 percent of all movements were by automobile; the proportion varied with length of trip, from 95 percent of the trips under 50 miles to 56 percent of the trips of over 1,000 miles. In 1970, automobile travel accounted for 1,026 billion passenger miles, or nearly 87 percent of all passenger miles of travel in the United States. Nearly all of these trips were door-to-door and the terminals at traffic-generating nodes were shared by both intercity and intracity movements. Hence the problems of automobile circulation and parking are discussed in Chapter 8. Nearly half of all automobile travel is on rural roads, and much of that is intercity travel. A significant, but unknown, proportion of the movements of the nearly 90 million automobiles in the United States involves intercity (rural-urban) travel. To accommodate this travel, the United States has 3.710 million miles of roads and streets, including 3.162 million miles in rural areas and 0.549 million miles within municipalities [Table 7-1]. Because of their door-to-door characteristics, nearly all passenger trips, by whatever mode of transportation, ultimately involve automobile travel. In the case of other modes, the provision for automobile access and egress—at airports, railroad depots, bus stations, and passenger ship terminals—is an important consideration. The intermodal character of air travel, for example, is epitomized by the widespread use of rental automobiles in destination areas.

The "modal split," or choice of mode, is a function of cost, transit time, convenience, and safety of passengers or goods. In the case of passenger travel, amenities may play a role. The nature of the goods to be moved is a major consideration in the choice of mode for freight transportation; the more compact and valuable the goods, the higher the transportation cost that can be absorbed in the delivered price. Some modes incur high terminal costs and delays, while others have greater terminal efficiency and flexibility but higher line-haul costs. The relationships for overland goods movement are generalized [Figure 7-2]. Trucks, with the flexibility of small units and door-to-door service, are most efficient in terminal areas, but, because of being small, they incur high labor costs on line-hauls. In contrast, barges, which are large units, cannot efficiently be utilized in terminal areas, but realize great scale economies for bulk commodity movements over relatively long distances. As shown in Figure 7-2, for example, the lowest-cost transportation for relatively short distances is by highway; motortrucks incur the lowest terminal costs but high per-ton-mile line-haul costs because they involve small flexible units. Truckload shipments normally require no terminals other than the shipper's loading dock, unless they are transferred from the routes of one carrier to another, or unless consolidation of less-than-truckload is required. In the figure, any shipment, other than bulk movements in large volume, over distances up to point A or OA, are most economically moved by highway, while movements over distances greater than OA would move by rail, provided that sufficient volume is available to realize the economies of scale. If the origin and destination as well as the character of the shipment and the volume permit, movements beyond distance OB would most economically move by waterway, even

TABLE 7-1
Roads and Streets in the United States, 1969

Classified by System and Type of Surface
(In Thousands)

System	Nonsurfaced Mileage Primitive and Unimproved	Nonsurfaced Mileage Graded and Drained	Surfaced Mileage Low Type 1	Surfaced Mileage Inter-mediate 2	Surfaced Mileage High Type 3	Total Surfaced	Total Mileage
Rural Mileage:							
Under state control:							
State primary system	0	3	10	118	275	403	406
State secondary systems[4]	3	1	9	65	43	117	121
County roads under state control[5]	10	7	50	58	27	135	152
State parks, forests, reservations, etc.[6]	3	8	8	2	5	15	26
Total	16	19	77	243	350	670	704
Under local control:							
County roads	230	251	811	316	124	1,252	1,733
Town and township roads	57	53	287	88	25	400	511
Other local roads	8	5	12	3	1	17	31
Total	296	310	1,111	408	150	1,669	2,275
Under Federal control:							
National parks,forests, reservations,etc.[6]	71	59	41	5	6	53	183
Total rural mileage	383	387	1,229	656	505	2,391	3,162
Municipal mileage							
Under state control:							
Extension of State Primary system	—	—	—	6	50	56	56
Extension of secondary roads under State control	—	—	—	8	8	16	16
Under local control:							
City streets	10	15	66	208	177	451	476
Total Municipal Mileage	10	15	67	221	235	523	549
Total U.S. Mileage	394	402	1,296	878	740	2,914	3,710

[1] Soil-surfaced, slag, gravel, or stone.

[2] Bituminous surface treated, mixed bituminous, or bituminous penetration having combined thickness of surface and base less than 7 inches and/or low load-bearing capacity.

[3] Mixed bituminous and bituminous penetration having a combined thickness of surface and base 7 inches or more and/or a high load-bearing capacity with or without portland cement concrete base; bituminous concrete and sheet asphalt with or without portland cement concrete base; and portland cement concrete with or without bituminous wearing surface less than one inch in compacted thickness. Segregation of some bituminous surfaces according to thickness and load-bearing capacity is not uniform for all States.

[4] Includes mileage designated as farm-to-market in Louisiana and as State-aid in Maine.

[5] Includes mileage of county roads under State control in all counties of Delaware, North Carolina, and West Virginia; 10 counties in Alabama; all but two counties in Virginia; and some county mileage in Nevada.

[6] State and national park, forest, reservation, toll, and other roads that are not a part of the State system.

Source: U.S. Dept. of Transportation, Federal Highway Administration, Table M-2.

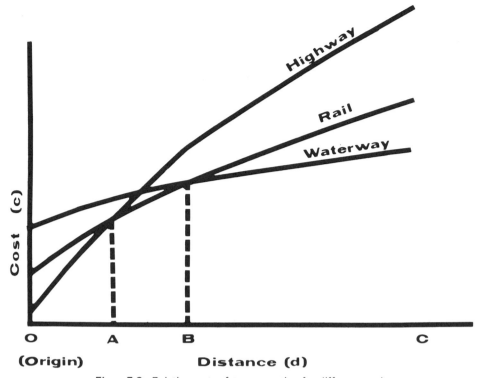

Figure 7-2   Relative costs of transportation for different modes.

though the waterway system, because of its circuity, may involve substantially greater distances than would the overland routes.

The horizontal axis (in Figure 7-2) represents a radius, along a transportation route, from origin O. If one were to consider all radiating routes and were to rotate the figure through a 360-degree circle, the resulting contours would be concentric and would bound the areas within which the most economic mode of transportation could be determined. Since not all points within a given distance are equally provided with transportation, the actual configuration would be star-shaped, with the major available routes forming the ribs or axes, and along such axes transportation costs for any given distance would, of course, be less than on other radii; therefore, greater distances could be covered at equal cost in those directions corresponding with the most highly developed transportation.

Since transportation within any area should be considered as a set of systems involving several modes, and many shipments or trips involve transfer among two or more modes, as well as commonly among carriers of the same mode, the friction represented by delays and costs at the interchange points constitute impedances, and the planner should be concerned with minimizing such impedances. A movement [in Figure 7-3] is represented which involves an intermediate transfer, either between carriers of the same mode or of different modes. An interline rail movement, or a transfer between rail or truck on the one hand and ship or barge on the other, would be such an example. A shipment between O and B, involving a transshipment or transfer at A, would incur additional costs at the

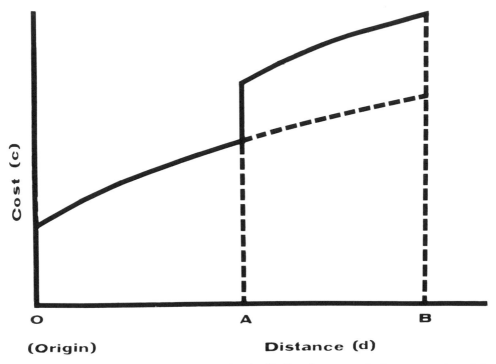

Figure 7-3 Intermediate terminal costs at a break-of-bulk point or transfer between carriers of the same or different modes.

transfer point. In addition, since there is a "distance taper," the distance-related curve would be resumed with a steeper gradient beyond the transfer point, thereby further adding to the origin-to-destination cost. This, of course, would be an incentive to maximize the distance of movement on the initiating carrier, and the incentive for interline or intermodal transfer would be greatly reduced. Diseconomies result from the present national policy with regard to common carriers. It discourages, and in many instances prohibits, a carrier from operating more than a single mode. Railroads in the United States, for example, cannot generally operate or control truck or barge lines unless such lines are feeders to the rail line; they must not normally involve parallel routes or common points. This is in conspicuous contrast to the Canadian policy, which involves primarily two nationwide organizations competing in many modes.

In order to minimize costs of intermediate transfer and break-of-bulk insofar as the shipper is concerned, two devices are invoked by many carriers: (a) "in transit" privileges, and (b) unitized cargo handling.

"In Transit" Privileges

"In transit," used in connection with overland bulk commodity movements, involves a through origin-to-destination rate regardless of intermediate handling. The principal in-transit privilege is "milling-in-transit" in which wheat, for example, from the western

Great Plains can be unloaded at an intermediate point, there converted into flour, and the flour reloaded for onward movement to the final destination. Since the rate (slope of the curve in Figure 7-3) per mile is higher for flour, which takes a higher classification than does wheat, the rate without the in-transit privilege would be represented by the upper curve beyond the intermediate point (A). However, the in-transit privilege involves not only absorption of the intermediate terminal costs but also the continuation of the rate based upon the original classification of the commodity; the actual rate is represented by the lower of the two curves beyond the intermediate milling point. Because of this feature, Minneapolis and other major centers, located between the origin and the market destination areas, have been enabled to develop processing industries such as milling.

Communities should be constantly aware of the changing rate structures of carriers, which affect the competitive positions of their existing and prospective industries, and, of course, the land and other requirements not only for the affected industries, but also for the transportation facilities required for the operation of the carriers. Chambers of commerce and other civic organizations in many cities maintain traffic specialists whose primary responsibility is to maintain knowledge of the local transportation rate patterns and to defend or oppose, as the case may be, prospective changes in the pattern before regulatory agencies. Many cities delegate portions of such responsibilities to their respective port or airport authorities. Since federal and state regulation of transportation rates and services is, at best, fragmented and confused, the task of the local community in defending its position on the rate structure is complex and requires specialized knowledge.

Unitized Handling

Unitized cargo handling is a term which is applied to any method of simplifying the movement and transfer of goods between or among carriers by combining shipments into larger units. The object is to achieve economies of scale by minimizing the number of units to be handled, and thereby reduce the cost to shippers, stimulate additional movements, and expedite these by reducing the time involved in transfers at terminals and intermediate transfer points. As the vehicles are becoming larger, increasing economies are effected in the line-haul; the costs both of capital plant and of labor do not increase proportionately to increases in capacity as the 5,000-ton general cargo liner of a generation ago is replaced by the 25,000-ton container ship of today, which not only has five times the capacity, but moves twice as fast. The economies of the line-haul (sea voyage) would be insignificant unless there were substantial reductions in the time and cost of loading and unloading in the ports. In general cargo transportation the object is to secure scale economies comparable to those achieved in bulk commodity transportation, in which the shipments are handled as continuous flows, by gravity, suction, pumping, and other methods of loading and discharging vessels, or, better still, by continuous-flow movements all the way between origin and destination. On land, railroads compete only with pipelines for large-scale bulk transportation, and then only for liquid commodities; solids pipeline transportation is in its infancy although it has considerable potential. Railroads, however, have been handicapped by the costs and time involved in loading and unloading freight cars, and in assembling and breaking up trains in the classification or marshaling yards; they are less economic for many bulk commodities than are barges and pipelines, and less flexible, hence less adequate, than are trucks for the handling of merchandise. Railroads, therefore, must inevitably be involved in the development of larger-scale units to achieve economies and to compete more effectively with other modes. Trains are becoming longer and heavier; between 1929 and 1970 the average freight carload has increased from 35.4 to 54.6 tons and the average freight trainload from 804 to 1,820 tons, while ton-miles per train hour in the same period has increased from 10,580 to 36,578. But unless terminals increase in efficiency at least proportionately to the increases in efficiency of the line-haul, much of the advantage is lost. The current and prospective trends in the nature and location of terminals of all types are considered later in this chapter. One fact, however, is outstanding: great savings in cost and time can be achieved by consolidating the items to be handled into larger units. This, however, requires substantial investment, and the substitution of capital-intensive operations for labor-intensive operations, in all transportation modes, involves substantial, and frequently traumatic, dislocations of the labor force, with serious social implications of which the planner should be aware. In one mode, railroading, for example, employment decreased from 1,660,850 in 1929 to 566,278 in 1970, although the railroads handled far more traffic in the latter year: 776 billion ton-miles as compared with 455 billion ton-miles in the earlier year. In other modes, too, units are becoming larger; supertankers of 350,000 tons are increasingly common as contrasted with the standard T-2 tanker of World War II, which was 16,000 tons; barge tows on the inland rivers frequently handle more than 40,000 tons; the 747 cargo plane has many times the capacity of the DC-3; and the "double-bottom" truck trailer on a modern express highway can carry several times the load, and much faster, than its counterpart of a few years ago. Labor requirements, however, are decreasing as capital costs increase. It becomes increasingly imperative to expedite the "turn around" of railroad cars, trains, trucks, aircraft, and other vehicles, each of which represents substantial capacity and capital investment, and to effectuate this, substantial investments must be made in the mechanization of terminals. The fewer items passing through the facilities, the greater the efficiencies. Interchange between carriers, of the same or different modes, calls for increased unitization of the loads. Materials handling equipment has been vastly improved; forklifts, straddle carriers, conveyor belts, and cranes represent substitution of capital for labor.

The more uniform the units of cargo to be handled, the more satisfactorily can mechanical devices be introduced to effect transfer, loading, and unloading. Bulk commodities either flow or can be handled by conveyor belts, tubes, pipes, buckets or other devices. On the other hand, general cargo, including merchandise, consists of a tremendous variety of items, each with a different combination of size, weight, and shape. If more-or-less uniform containers can be handled, the scale economies resulting from the continuous-flow characteristic of bulk shipments can be approached. The simplest forms of unitized cargo packaging consist of bales, crates, barrels, and other containers of standardized design. A generation ago pallets were introduced along with forklifts and other devices to handle containers as larger combined units. The most significant trend in general unitization of cargo is the standard intermodal container, which can be transferred between rail, highway, and waterway carriers without unloading the contents, and which can be stacked, since it is a standard module. These can be handled over the highways on flatbed trucks or can be equipped with "bogies" or wheels and handled as semitrailers. They can be loaded on railroad flatcars with the bogies, providing that special equipment is provided for tie-down, and in that case they are carried "piggyback." This form of transportation is called TOFC (trailer on flat car). When the semitrailers are handled on railroad cars without the bogies, they are carried COFC (container on flat car). Devices for effecting the transfer between highway vehicle and railroad car are varied. Cranes can be used for container transfer, but many railroads have adopted special devices on the flatcars, such as turntables. Huge straddle cranes, usually mounted on rubber tires, are commonly used to transfer both trailers and containers between flatbed trucks or tractor units alongside the railroad cars. An older and less efficient method still in widespread use is known as "circus" loading, because it was originally used in the nineteenth century for loading of circus wagons onto trains; it consists of transfer along the length of the train end to end, with the ends of the flatcars connected by hinged "bridges" along which the truck wheels can move. The latter method, unlike the use of straddle cranes, has the disadvantage that the units must be loaded or unloaded in consecutive order, since access to the middle of the train cannot be obtained without switching the railroad cars or waiting until all of the preceding units have been handled.

Transfer to and from ships is effectuated by cranes; the earlier container ships, as well as later ones intended for service to smaller ports and to areas where substantial investment in land-based equipment is not justified, had specially designed gantry cranes aboard ship, with retractable extensions that spanned portions of the wharf area. More recently, it was realized that the large investments in cranes aboard ship would be unproductive while the ship was at sea. Consequently, where volume justifies, the newer container terminals are equipped with wharfside cranes which can span, on the one hand, truck and rail vehicles on the wharf and, on the other hand, the hatches and decks of the ships, with transverse movement between them.

During the late 1960s and early '70s, most of the ocean cargo liner operators on the major trade routes, including at first offshore routes to Puerto Rico, Hawaii, and Alaska, and later the transatlantic, transpacific, and Europe-Far East routes, replaced their fleets of break-bulk cargo ships, including many relatively new vessels, with all-container ships or with combination container-break-bulk ships which could efficiently utilize the new technology. Such vessels carry up to 2,000 containers, although 800-1,000-container ships are more common. Smaller vessels are used on local and feeder routes.

On the railroads of the United States and Canada, piggyback and container traffic grew rapidly. In 1954 the Interstate Commerce Commission authorized a series of rate practices which, in effect, legalized the unitized cargo concept for American railroads in intermodal transportation on a national scale. The railroads have a series—five, with additional modifications—of types of rates for container and piggyback transportation, the rates depending upon whether the railroads, the shipper, or a trucking organization furnishes the containers or trailers, and the railroad cars as well. In the late 1950s and throughout the 'sixties, TOFC and COFC railroad traffic grew rapidly, but then leveled off, due in part to the economic recession; meanwhile, many railroads discontinued handling less-than-carload freight altogether, unless it was carried as forwarded traffic in carloads, or as TOFC or COFC. Thus, unitized handling of merchandise traffic by railroads is a technological response to the competitive forces introduced by the growth of trucking and other modes, which have greater short-haul and terminal flexibility. The TOFC and COFC railroad traffic is analogous to the container ship traffic in producing long-haul scale economies without sacrifice of short-haul and terminal flexibility.

Gateways

Transfer of goods and passengers between carriers of the same or different modes is generally effected where a number of routes converge. The traveler or shipper may have the option of onward movement via any one of several or many carriers who compete for interchange traffic at the gateways. Since operation of transportation terminals and the servicing of the carriers involves substantial concentrations of labor and facilities, the gateways are generally cities of some size. Also, since competition is keenest where traffic potential is greatest, the larger gateways generally attract additional carriers from time to time. The shipper and traveler has, at the gateways, the widest choice of transportation services, and, to meet the competition, the carriers tend to concentrate their efforts there. In addition, where competition is at a maximum, the rates tend to be lower. This has a cumulative effect, for lower transportation rates and more varied and frequent service tends to attract additional commerce and industry. The role of transportation in urbanization has long been recognized.

With intercarrier competition, rates tend to be lower at gateways than at intermediate points. This effect can be diagramed [Figure 7-4] indicating the normal rate for distance (d) to a gateway (G) from origin (O) would be the curve OG'', without the effects of competition at the gateway. But because of the many options available at G for the traveler or shipper in contrast to those at intermediate points which, because of varying routes between O and G, have fewer carriers serving them, the rate OG is depressed below the level at intermediate points. OG' represents the rate for movement between O and G.

One important constraint exists in the United States. The fourth section of the Interstate Commerce Act prohibits a regulated common carrier under the act from charging a higher rate for a shorter haul than for a long haul. In other words, intermediate points (I) would benefit from the competitive rate at the gateway (G), so that all points between I and G would have been equalized. Apparently, then, the advantages of a gateway location would be widespread, well beyond the gateway. This is commonly true insofar as rates are concerned, but the wider choice of carriers at the major gateways still proves to be an inducement to industries and commercial establishments because of the greater frequency and variety of services at the gateways.

Equalization at competitive gateways is a major consideration in determination of traffic flows, industrial location, and port development, for it constitutes an important aspect of the ability of a gateway to develop traffic. Two examples illustrate this point: (a) airline competition between the East and Midwest on the one hand and the Pacific Coast on the other, and (b) port competition between the North Atlantic East Coast ports.

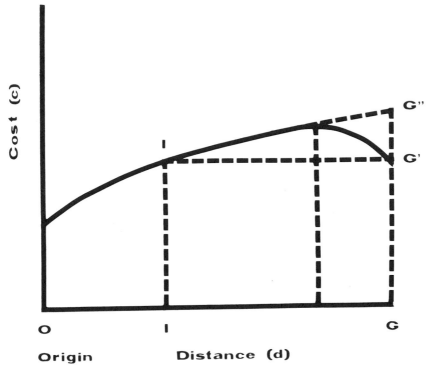

Figure 7-4 Effect of gateway on rates to gateway and to intermediate points: the "long-haul short-haul" effect.

An air passenger between New York, Chicago, or other eastern or midwestern city bound for the Pacific Coast, is charged the same fare whatever his Pacific Coast destination, from San Diego to Seattle, inclusive. There are direct routes serving San Diego, Los Angeles, San Francisco, Portland, and Seattle, among other points, but, in addition, many other airline-served points involve indirect service, with transfers at the major gateways and involving additional distance between such gateway and the ultimate destination. Fresno, for example, is served through airports in the Los Angeles and San Francisco Bay areas, transferring to local flights, but the New York or Chicago rate to Fresno is the same as the rate to the major Pacific Coast gateways.

The North Atlantic ports, from the Canadian border on the north to Hampton Roads in the south, have long been in competition for the oceanic trade, with the railroads serving the various ports favoring one or another, depending upon their route patterns and terminal facilities.[8] When the ocean steamship lines were established, New York became the dominant port, with the greatest number of services and ocean routes.

8. There is a vast literature on port competition. Typical studies include: James Kenyon, "Elements in Inter-port Competition in the United States," *Economic Geography*, Vol. 46, No. 1 (Jan. 1970), pp. 1-24; Donald J. Patton, "General Cargo Hinterlands of New York, Philadelphia, Baltimore, and New Orleans," *Annals* of the Association of American Geographers, Vol. 44, No. 4 (Dec. 1958), pp. 436-455; Edwin H. Draine, *Import Traffic of Chicago and Its Hinterland*, (Chicago: University of Chicago, Dept. of Geography, Research Paper No. 81 1963), 138 pp.

For transatlantic traffic New York is located closer to Europe than are the more southern ports but involves greater overland hauls to and from the common midwestern hinterland. Since the cost per mile of overland transportation is generally higher than that of ocean transportation, Philadelphia, Baltimore, and the ports of Hampton Roads were advantaged on the landward side, and the disadvantage on the ocean side was somewhat less. In contrast, Boston and other New England ports, being farther from the Midwest common hinterland, were disadvantaged landward but were closer to overseas points. When the ocean carriers, because of longer voyage times, charged higher rates to the southern outports than to New York and lower rates to Boston and other New England ports, the overall origin-to-destination rates by combinations of land and ocean carriers were generally comparable. However, later the practice in ocean rate-making was to equalize rates at ranges of ports; the transatlantic general cargo carriers charged the same at all ports between the Canadian border and Cape Hatteras, the so-called USNH or North Atlantic range of ports. In this situation, ports south of New York were advantaged and those in New England disadvantaged because of differences in the overland rates. The Interstate Commerce Act, however, prevents discrimination among localities. The southern ports, being closer to the Midwest, charged differential rates on many commodities below the New York rate: Philadelphia two cents and Baltimore and Hampton Roads three cents per ton less, while Boston was equalized with New York but nevertheless disadvantaged because of the longer overland haul. Equalization of all North Atlantic ports was decreed a few years ago, but further rate reductions by the southerly ports reopened the issue. After decades of litigation before regulatory bodies and the courts, some degree of equalization was achieved, but it is constantly attacked or defended by the ports, railroads, and other affected interests.

In the United States, what makes equalization possible is the fact that, where carriers are adversely affected at certain gateways or other points by competition, particularly by carriers of other modes, they may apply for "fourth section relief" and, if granted, may then reduce their rates to levels which would enable them to compete with other carriers, of different modes, at the major gateways.

A nationally significant effect of gateway competition and fourth section relief is the rate structure which resulted from the opening of the Panama Canal. It has vitally affected most of the nation and set in motion a chain of events which have significantly altered the fortunes of many cities and metropolitan regions, both coastal and inland. In spite of the fact that the distance by ocean carrier through the canal is twice that of overland carriers between the Atlantic and Pacific coasts, the cost of many shipments by intercoastal steamship was reduced sufficiently to be competitive. The cost of transfer at the coastal ports was absorbed in the greatly lowered line-haul costs, and many ports on both coasts, as well as on the Gulf Coast, shared the traffic. Eastbound lumber movements constituted a base cargo for many of the vessel operators, while on the westbound voyages the ships carried steel products and general cargo. Legislation was passed which prohibited railroads from operating or controlling competitive carriers, and they therefore had to face the steamship competition on their longer east-west hauls. Combined rail-water rates were set up, and many movements developed between inland points via the very circuitous route to the nearest coast, then through the canal to the opposite coast, followed by a rail haul inland, in a direction opposite to that of the originating haul (e.g., steel from Pittsburgh via Baltimore to Oakland, thence rail to Salt Lake City).

The result of the Panama Canal was to place interior regions on a rate divide, with traffic moving to the coasts which formerly moved across the continent by rail. Locations along the coasts or short distances inland then had a decided advantage as to transportation costs, not only for import and export movements, as formerly, but also for domestic movements which could use the intercoastal ships through the canal. Intercoastal traffic became a major element for many ports, and many inland points began to feel the effects of the diversion.

Later, as the costs of building and operating American-flag vessels in domestic trade, as elsewhere, increased, the differential cost between water and overland movement became less significant, and intercoastal vessel traffic declined, only to be revived with the advent of the large container ship and its consequent scale economies both in port and at sea. Once again, intercoastal shipping is becoming, for many movements, an effective competitor of the overland long-haul carriers. In order to meet this competition, pipelines have proliferated, and the railroads and truckers are seeking new ways to achieve further economies of scale. Among the latter measures are, of course, TOFC, COFC, unit trains, "run through" trains in which different railroads joining at major gateways run solid trains with locomotive pools through the gateways, the use of interstate express highways for trucking, and the introduction of double trailer combinations on roads which physically and legally permit them.

Since the opening of the Panama Canal, the interior regions have been vigorously seeking ways to mitigate their transportation disadvantages. One way has been to advocate development of inland water transportation, which produces many of the economies of scale of ocean transportation once the initial costs of the waterway improvements have been overcome. A basic public issue has always been the allocation of costs, which is very different for the various modes; traditionally all inland waterway improvements in the United States which affect interstate commerce have been free of user charges (except international waterways such as the St. Lawrence Seaway). The overland carriers justifiably have opposed, in general, the improvements of the waterways as public investments when they are not only adversely affected by traffic diversions but also must pay taxes which are used to reinforce their competition. Railroads, especially, must short-haul themselves or lose traffic, while at the same time they not only must maintain their rights-of-way but are taxed for them as well. Nevertheless, inland waterway improvements have proliferated in order to mitigate the locational disadvantages of the continental interior, not only by furnishing lower-cost water transportation, but also by forcing lower rates from the overland carriers. Two major groups of inland waterway improvements have been of particular importance since the opening of the Panama Canal: (a) improvement and canalization of the Mississippi River system, and (b) improvement of the Great Lakes and opening of the enlarged St. Lawrence Seaway. Space is not available here to discuss either of these vast complexes of waterway improvements in detail, except to point out that they offer interior points a series of alternatives, for both domestic and international shipments, which lower the general level of *all* rates on competitive traffic. Development of port terminals and associated facilities has constituted a major planning focus in many cities along the waterway systems.

THE EXISTING SYSTEM

The United States has a transportation system which is very imperfectly coordinated as among the modes, which has excess capacity in many areas, and which is subject to no consistent national policy, with ownership, operation, and regulation fragmented in an extremely complex manner. National planning of intercity transportation as a whole has not effectively been achieved, and overall planning regionally has been virtually nonexistent. As in the case of internal urban transportation, intercity and interregional transportation is faced with intolerable congestion at peak times in certain areas, while at the same time there is an excess capacity in many instances. The multiplicity of modes and organizations creates a situation which at best is confused and at worst is chaotic. Recently, there has been some interest in the development of a national transportation policy.[9] The creation of the cabinet-level Department of Transportation is a step in that direction, but that agency (DOT) is limited in its authority in many respects. The separation of regulation of common and many contract carriers between the Interstate Commerce Commission, the Civil Aeronautics Board, the Federal Maritime Board, and other agencies has been an impedance to the formulation of national policy. In addition, the regulatory agencies, by their decisions, may at times make policy which should be the prerogative of the Congress. Also, there is often a conflict between policies of the federal agencies and those of the states, as for example, in the "full crew" laws which affect operation of interstate as well as intrastate trains, and in the lack of uniformity of size and weight limits for trucks among the states.

A second major characteristic of the national inventory of transportation facilities and organizational practices is the competition between regulated and unregulated movements, and among the common, contract, and private carriers, as well as among the several modes. As in the case of urban transportation, an important trend in recent years has been toward an increased use of private transportation, not only for passengers, but for goods as well. Private trucks, ships, barges, aircraft, and pipelines are not dependent upon the schedules or routes of common or contract carriers, and they greatly affect, by the competition which they furnish, the operations and rates of all other types of carriers. Although virtually all American railroads are regulated common carriers, with the exception of a few short industrial, switching, and mining lines, trucks are in common, contract, and private operation, and the private sector of motor trucking is the most rapidly growing. Ocean shipping, Great Lakes vessels, inland waterway barges, air transportation, and pipelines may be any of the three types, and of them, only the common carriers are completely regulated as to routes, schedules, and rates, while contract carriers are under partial regulation.

9. *A Statement on National Transportation Policy* (Washington, D.C.: U.S. Dept. of Transportation, Sept. 8, 1971), p. 49.

In recent years, much thought has been given to the coordination of the various types of carriers, as to types of services, degree and character of regulation, and modal relationships. The implications of these complexities are too lengthy to include here, but some of the trends which are of great significance to the urban planner should be covered.

Modes

Most modes of transportation perform several types of services, either simultaneously or consecutively. Highways, for example, carry common, contract, and private carriers of both goods and passengers, as well as service and emergency vehicles.

The distribution of domestic intercity freight and passenger traffic by modes [Table 7-2] shows the trend in total volume and in distribution for each of the modes. It will be noted that during the four decades the total volume of freight traffic, measured by ton-miles, increased more than threefold, while passenger-miles increased nearly fourfold. During approximately the same period the gross national product increased ninefold, from $103.1 billion in 1929 to $932.3 billion in 1969. In other words, transportation, in spite of the great increases in volume, became relatively less important in the national economy.

RAILROADS   The railroads of the United States have been transformed, during the past several decades, from the basic form of intercity and interregional transportation into a specialized type of carrier. They are preeminently the carriers of bulk commodities over long overland distances. This they are especially able to do because of the economies of scale inherent in the technology of the railroad, with its long, heavy trains moving at relatively high speeds. But the inflexibilities of the collection and delivery of goods within the terminal areas precludes the railroads from realizing effective scale economies in the movement of small shipments of relatively high value, especially over short distances. As passenger carriers, they cannot meet the competition of air transportation on the one hand and the automobile on the other. With few exceptions, the railroads have turned their intercity passenger operations over to a quasi-public organization, the National Railroad Passenger Corporation, or Amtrak, while their metropolitan commuter train operations are increasingly performed directly or indirectly by or for public authorities.

Railroads in the late 1960s and early 1970s have been handling greater tonnages of freight than ever before, even exceeding the peaks of World War II. They are accomplishing this with far fewer employees and with less train movement. The number of employees declined from 1,660,000 in 1929 to 566,000 in 1970. While some of the decline is due to the diminution in passenger service, which is especially labor-intensive, the record is nevertheless impressive. During the same period, freight train miles decreased from 613 million in 1929 to 427 million in 1970, while the number of freight car miles remained almost constant. The latter situation is explained by the fact that the number of cars per average freight train increased from 47.6 to 70.1, and the average freight carload from 35.4 to 54.6 tons. During this period, as a result of these trends, the average freight trainload increased from 804 tons to 1,820 tons. Many technological improvements were introduced: among them are centralized traffic control, heavier rails, improved communi-

TABLE 7 - 2

Volume of U.S. Intercity Freight and Passenger Traffic

Millions of Freight Ton-Miles and Percentage of Total (Including mail and express)

Year	Railroads	%	Trucks	%	Great Lake	%	Rivers and Canals	%	Oil Pipelines	%	Air	%	Total
1929	454,800	74.9	19,689	3.3	97,322	16.0	8,661	1.4	26,900	4.4	3	—	607,375
1939	338,850	62.4	52,821	9.7	76,312	14.0	19,937	3.7	55,602	10.2	12	—	543,534
1944	746,912	68.6	58,264	5.4	118,769	10.9	31,386	2.9	132,864	12.2	71	—	1,088,266
1950	596,940	56.2	172,860	10.3	111,087	10.5	51,657	4.9	129,175	12.1	318	—	1,062,637
1960	579,130	44.1	285,483	21.7	99,468	7.6	120,785	9.2	228,626	17.4	778	—	1,314,270
1969	780,000	41.0	404,000	21.2	115,235	6.1	187,666	9.9	411,000	21.6	3,200	.2	1,901,101
1970p	776,000	40.8	400,000	21.0	117,000	6.2	190,000	10.0	415,000	21.8	3,400	.2	1,901,400

Millions of Passenger Miles and Percentage of Total (except automobiles)

Year	Railroads[a]	%	Buses	%	Air carriers	%	Inland waterways	%	Total (except autos)	Private automobiles	%	Total (including autos)
1929	33,965	77.1	6,800	15.4	—	—	3,300	7.5	44,065	175,000	—	219,065
1939	23,669	67.7	9,100	26.0	683	2.0	1,486	4.3	34,938	275,000	—	309,938
1944	97,705	75.7	26,920	20.9	2,178	1.7	2,187	1.7	128,990	181,000	—	309,990
1950	32,481	46.3	26,436	37.7	10,072	14.3	1,190	1.7	70,179	438,293	—	508,472
1960	21,574	27.8	19,327	24.9	33,958	43.8	2,688	3.5	77,547	706,079	—	783,626
1969	12,300	8.1	24,900	16.4	111,000	73.0	3,800	2.5	152,000	977,000	—	1,129,000
1970p	11,000	7.2	25,000	16.2	114,000	74.0	4,000	2.6	154,000	1,026,000	—	1,180,000

a—Railroads of all classes, including electric. p—Preliminary (partially estimated by AAR).

Source: Yearbook of Railroad Facts, 1971 Edition (Washington, D.C.Assoc. of American Railroads, 1971), p. 34.

cation, electronic data processing, conversion from steam to diesel-electric power, lighter-weight but larger cars, and electronically controlled yards. Railroads, like many other industries, have become more capital-intensive and less labor-intensive. This trend would have been even greater except for many operating practices which are anachronistic but which are "built in" to the system because of long-standing labor agreements and "full crew" laws in many of the states. It is obvious that the maximum effectiveness of railroads is in the large-volume transportation of homogeneous bulk commodities, in which handling, particularly at the terminals, can be largely mechanized and automated, while such transportation also is particularly adapted to long, heavy trains. At the other end of the scale, the railroads have virtually abandoned the handling of small less-than-carload shipments except where consolidated into carloads by freight forwarders or carried as container or piggyback traffic. Even in the movement of bulk traffic, the railroads face increased competition from other modes: motortrucks are ubiquitous, and heavier high-speed movements are favored by the proliferation of intercity express highways; river and harbor improvements have facilitated the development of inland barge traffic with improved technology vastly different from that of the steamboat of earlier periods; and the technology of air transportation, especially with the "jumbo jets," is beginning to be felt in major ways. Water transportation is especially important in competing with the railroads for bulk commodities, and the railroads are particularly vulnerable because such a high proportion of their total traffic is of such commodities. In 1970 coal counted for 19 percent of all railroad carloads, or more than three times as much as any other major commodity category. This was followed in rank order by metallic ores, chemicals and allied products, and metals and their products.

More significant to the urban planner than the trends in volume of railroad freight traffic is the composition of the traffic. Bulk traffic is originated and terminated primarily by industries which, for other reasons, are regarded as "heavy" and usually capital-intensive; they generally require large tracts of land, and they have other operational characteristics which, in spite of the recent and current interest in environmental protection, find their best locations on and beyond the peripheries of the high-density urban areas. Railroad freight movements, therefore, no longer, for the most part, originate or terminate in central city areas. Even those movements involving high-value merchandise typically can be handled by motortruck to and from railroad freight terminals, team tracks, and container and piggyback ramps, which need not be centrally located. The proper reuse of redundant railroad land in central city areas, therefore, becomes a major concern of the urban planner.[10]

Nor is the problem of excess land formerly used by railroads, or in prospect of being released for non-railroad use, confined to land occupied by freight terminal facilities. Passenger terminals, where required at all, now need no longer be centrally located, and where they have central locations, they require remodeling to provide adequately for

10. *Rail Lines and Terminals in Urban Planning,* "Planning Advisory Service No. 82" (Chicago: American Society of Planning Officials, 1056), 22 pp.; Harold M. Mayer, "Some Aspects of Rail Passenger Transportation and the Development of Cities and Metropolitan Areas," *A Report on the Brotherhood of Railroad Trainmen's 1966 Conference on Mass Transportation* (Cleveland: Brotherhood of Railroad Trainmen, later United Transportation Union, 1967), pp. 66-76.

connections to local urban transit facilities, as well as adequate parking. In most cities, the decline of intercity rail passenger service has made the large, often monumental, depots surplus, as it has the extensive coach yards and passenger train servicing facilities, which commonly have occupied valuable centrally located land in large cities. Depots were so located in order to avoid empty back-hauls to and from the downtown terminals and to gain maximum access to the urban and metropolitan labor force which found employment in the servicing of passenger trains. Except in a few cities which continue to have extensive suburban and local commuter train service, the large phalanxes of passenger train terminal and servicing facilities are no longer needed, and additional reserves of centrally located land, often on the fringes of the central business district, become immediately or potentially available for non-railroad use. The planning of such uses then becomes an integral part of comprehensive central-area planning.

Circumstances thus have dictated that many railroads have extensive real estate interests in urban areas. In a number of instances, the railroads have set up special departments to dispose of or to develop their central city landholdings. In other instances, holding companies have been established, with separate railroad and real estate or development subsidiaries. Most noteworthy, perhaps, in the past have been the New York City developments associated with the former Pennsylvania and New York Central railroads which, in the first decade of the twentieth century, engaged in extensive development of air rights over the terminals and associated railroad facilities in midtown Manhattan. Their successor, the Penn Central, has inherited the problem of disposing of these real estate developments, which include some of the most valuable centrally located urban sites in the world. In Chicago, the Illinois Central is developing large-scale lakefront downtown properties which are adding substantially to the office-building and high-rise apartment inventory of the city. Within New York, and many other cities, centrally located railroad properties are similarly being developed: in a few instances in connection with air rights over those railroad lines or terminal facilities which are being retained, in other instances in areas where excessive railroad facilities are being or have been eliminated or consolidated.

The current pattern of railroad lines in the United States [Figure 7-5] includes about 206,000 miles of railroad routes. This mileage is slowly but steadily being reduced as branch lines are eliminated where their traffic volume is light, noncompensatory to the railroads, and not essential to the public interest. The peak route mileage of railroads in the United States was in 1915, when nearly 254,000 miles were in operation. Since then, a few trunk lines were abandoned, but most of the reductions were of branch lines; meanwhile a few new extensions, several cutoffs and other new routes intended to shorten overall distances, and spurs into newly established industries were constructed, but the reductions substantially exceeded the additions in nearly every year. Mergers greatly reduced the number of operating railroads from 1,380 in 1905 to 361 in 1969. From the viewpoint of the planner, mergers and consolidations are advantageous in general, because much of their economic justification is through reduction in terminal and interchange facilities, heavily concentrated in urban areas. Freight traffic, however, is more heavily concentrated than formerly on the lines which remain; the national average revenue freight ton-miles per mile of railroad route increased from 735,352 in 1900 to 3,600,683 in 1971.

Figure 7-5 Railroad network of the U.S.

Source: Association of American Railroads.

219

The characteristics of railroads differ widely in various parts of the country. In the Northeast—the area between the Mississippi River and the Atlantic Seaboard and north of the Ohio and Potomac rivers, known as "official" territory—the density of railroads is especially great and the preponderant population and industrial development—hence rail traffic generation—takes place. This area, being primarily a consuming region, terminates more rail traffic than it originates, and the average length of haul, hence terminal cost, is relatively high. Therefore, the railroads would gain maximum advantage from simplification of the pattern of terminal facilities and routes in this region in contrast to the West and South where line-hauls are longer and hence terminal costs represent a lower proportion of the total cost of the railroad service.

The location of industry in urban areas is especially significant in relation to the internal pattern of railroad lines and terminals. In the past, much of the industrial activity was concentrated close to the central city cores, in the fringe areas surrounding the central business districts, where each of the carriers sought to locate its terminals, as close as possible to the shippers' and consignees' plant locations. Commonly, industrial locations were along waterfronts where the industries could benefit from direct water transportation access, for water transportation antedated, in many cities, the coming of the railroads, which at first were essentially feeders to the water routes. Also, waterfront locations usually offered access through easy grades, along floodplains or other low-gradient approaches to the cities, and at the same time offered large extents of relatively level land. Such locations, combining centrality with water access, were magnets which attracted railroad freight terminals, as well as industries. Less-than-carload freight was collected and delivered by "trap" or "peddler" cars and consolidated into carloads at the "freight houses," while wagons and teams performed collection and delivery services to and from establishments not at trackside locations. Industrial development, in order to minimize distances, was high-density, often in multistory buildings, which in the course of time became inadequate for modern operations because of general congestion, vertical movements, inadequate off-street vehicular loading and parking, inadequate floor-load capacities, and general obsolescence. As the industries moved peripherally, so did the major railroad freight-handling facilities, which also required more extensive but peripherally located land areas. Industries generating less-than-carload shipments no longer needed trackside locations, and they became footloose, able to locate in a wider range of sites throughout the urban areas, with highway pickup and delivery, involving either carload consolidation or container and piggyback transfer at railroad interfaces, which could then largely replace the older team tracks and freight houses, typically in congested central locations. Modern railroad freight terminals, like an increasing proportion of the industries they serve, seek uncrowded locations, where land costs are relatively low, where access by highway is good, and where extensive industrial development can take place nearby.

The railroads have always been active in industrial development and continue to be so. They pioneered in the establishment of organized industrial districts in the United States in the early twentieth century, and some of the most notable examples, such as the Central Manufacturing districts of Chicago and Los Angeles and the Clearing Industrial District in Chicago, began as railroad subsidiaries, symbiotically linked to nearby railroad yards and terminals, and using railroad-surplus land in accessible locations. Many of the more important industrial districts which have been or are being developed are closely linked, both organizationally and locationally, to the local railroad patterns.

The railroads have two major interests in industrial development: (a) to generate traffic, directly if possible, but indirectly in any event, for their lines, and therefore locations accessible by private sidings for industries which receive or ship in carload quantities are especially sought; and (b) as users of railroad land, in order to create sale or rental revenue for the use of the land itself with, preferably, additional benefits to the railroads in the generation of freight in carloads, containers, or piggyback trailers, as the case may be.

On the other hand, land along railroad routes represents a special set of problems for the urban planner. The immediate proximity to the railroad—except in very few instances of proximity to a commuter train stop—represents an undesirable location for residences, and the general level of land values along the railroad route, for a few hundred feet on either side, may be lower than the prevailing level a few hundred feet farther back from the right-of-way. In a number of cities, railroads have complained that sites which would be appropriate for industrial development adjacent to the rights-of-way have been selected for development as residential areas, thus contributing to a scarcity of suitable sites for those industries which could benefit from direct railroad access. Because of the noise and unsightliness of some such sites and their consequent undesirability for private development, public housing authorities have located projects there. In several instances, zoning battles between the railroads and industrial interests on the one hand and public housing authorities on the other have occurred.

In a number of cities and metropolitan areas, the several railroads serving the area have joined in forming special terminal arrangements by which several, or in some instances all, of the line-haul carriers gain access to the terminals and industrial sidings of each. One such arrangement is reciprocal switching, in which the participating railroads switch cars for each other's account. In some instances, switching or terminal districts are designated, within which uniformity of switching practices and charges may exist. In some switching and terminal districts the line-haul carriers have access to some or all of the terminals and industrial sidings in addition to those on their own lines, absorbing the switching charges on line-hauls of over a designated distance, so that the shipper has greater freedom of choice of location for his plant or can ship to a greater number of locations within the terminal area than would otherwise be the case. The busiest such arrangement is the Chicago Switching District [Figure 7-6]. Within this district are located facilities of 19 trunk-line railroads and 12 switching and industrial railroads, with approximately 12,000 terminals and private sidings, to and from all of which the Chicago rate applies on line-haul movements of over a minimum distance. Some of the belt and terminal lines are subsidiaries of the line-haul railroads individually, some are joint enterprises of several or many of the participating railroads, and some are essentially plant facilities of large industries, even though legally they may be common carriers. One of these terminal railroads—the Belt Railway of Chicago—is jointly owned by 12 trunk line railroad companies, which includes the majority of the railroads serving the Chicago area; it operates about 440 miles of track, handles about 400,000 cars of revenue freight per

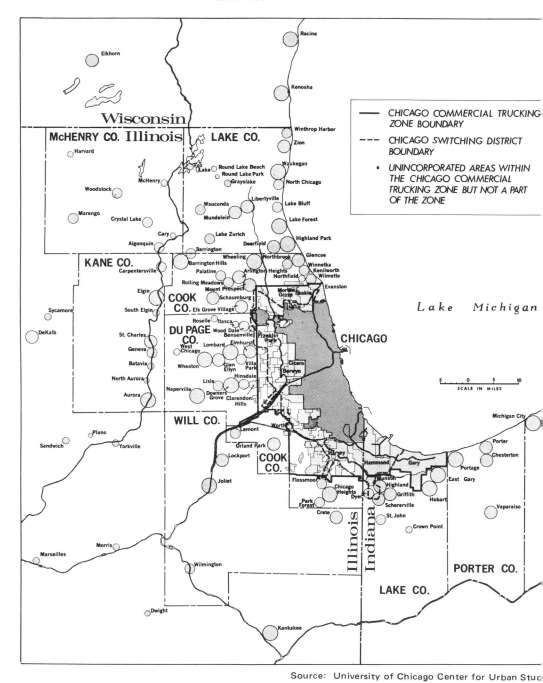

Source: University of Chicago Center for Urban Stud

Figure 7-6 Chicago commercial trucking zone and switching district boundaries.

year, and operates the famous Clearing Yard, a central classification yard for the participating railroads, which interchange thousands of cars per day. The railroads serving the St. Louis-East St. Louis Gateway have a similar arrangement; the Terminal Railroad Association of St. Louis has about 330 miles of track and annually handles about 850,000 loaded cars; it also owns and operates the Union Station.

The urban planner should be aware of the complexity of arrangments within terminal areas by which the several or many railroads gain access to each others' facilities and industries, including joint ownership and operation of lines, yards, and terminals, trackage rights, reciprocal switching arrangements, and many complex forms of leases and other agreements. The technological changes in railroading, the shifts in industrial locations from central to peripheral areas, the central locations of many surplus and redundant railroad facilities, and the location of many railroad lines and facilities where they may constitute serious obstacles to desired developments all indicate that, in general, it will be both possible and desirable, both from the viewpoint of the public and the railroads, to simplify and in many instances consolidate or eliminate railroad facilities, providing that the maze of agreements and property rights can be reconstituted to mutual advantage.

INTERCITY HIGHWAY TRANSPORTATION   More than three million miles of highways and streets give access to virtually every usable parcel of land in the United States. This, together with about 90 million automobiles and nearly 20 million trucks and buses, constitutes the basic transportation system. Roads and streets located within cities and metropolitan areas are not a concern of this chapter, but, as previously mentioned, such facilities also constitute routes for intercity traffic, and they give access to the origins and destinations of intercity trips; therefore, they are considered in part as intercity facilities.

As previously noted, automobiles are responsible for between 85 and 90 percent of all intercity personal movements, as measured in passenger-miles. However, because the average length of an automobile trip is shorter than that for most other forms of passenger transportation, the actual number of automobile trips between cities, and between city and nonurban origins and destinations, is actually considerably greater than the passenger-mile figures would indicate. Furthermore, every household and business establishment, indeed, every parcel of occupied land, is a possible origin and destination for an intercity trip. The problems of planning for internal urban movements are discussed in Chapter 8. Since the proportion of external to internal trips by highway is relatively small—although it tends to vary inversely with size of city—the external trip terminal problem for automobiles is subsumed in the total automobile problem of cities.

Intercity bus transportation has apparently reached a plateau level and has not significantly increased during the past two decades. Growth of nationwide carrier organizations has resulted in an increase in through long-distance services, but most intercity bus trips are relatively short. The development of the expressways, and especially the interstate highway system, has encouraged scheduled bus operators to speed up transit times between the larger cities at the expense of many smaller communities, which are less adequately served, since the operators are somewhat reluctant to divert the buses from direct routes on the expressways in order to serve intermediate stops. Since the decline of long-distance intercity railroad passenger service, the buses have been the recipients of some diverted rail traffic, and in most instances bus transit times and frequencies are more favorable than those of the trains. But fewer communities, nation-wide, have adequate intercity bus services, and there are increasing numbers of small and medium-sized communities which have none, or virtually none.

Since buses, like other common carriers, cannot provide door-to-door service, intercity buses must depend upon feeder services, whether by private automobile, taxicab, or local transit, to collect and deliver their passengers; therefore, as with most intercity carriers, the bus constitutes a link in an intermodal trip. This should be considered by the planner in the location of terminals of intercity buses. In the past, the tendency has been to locate such terminals in the downtown areas. Such locations, however, have several inherent disadvantages, which may or may not be counterbalanced by the advantage of centrality with respect to the traffic-generating nodes within the city. One disadvantage is the necessity, in most instances, for the buses to use the city streets in order to reach the terminals, either from their intercity routes, or from the garage and servicing facilities. Another disadvantage is the space required for access by local transpor-tation, including automobiles and taxicabs. Few of the intercity bus terminals provide sufficiently for automobile parking or for loading and discharge of passengers between buses on the one hand and automobiles and taxicabs on the other.

Bus terminals should be located with convenient access to the expressways which constitute parts of, or connect with, the intercity routes, and should involve minimal distances of movement over city streets. Compromise locations between the "inner belt" circumferential expressways surrounding most downtown areas and the "core" of the central business district would give direct access to buses from the expressways and at the same time provide good access from downtown. In New York the two Port Authority bus terminals are located at the east end of the Lincoln Tunnel and the George Washington Bridge, respectively; in Chicago the principal bus terminal is located within a block of a double-decked circumferential boulevard, where the buses gain access to the terminal from the lower level of the boulevard through a short tunnel, avoiding the surface streets altogether in the downtown area.

Consideration should be given to the development of general passenger transporta-tion terminals in proximity to downtown areas, as well as at major outlying nodes within the metropolitan areas. These "transportation centers," such as those proposed for the New York area by the Regional Plan Association, and the one developed at Journal Square in Jersey City by the Port Authority of New York and New Jersey, provide for interchange between local and intercity buses, other local transit, automobiles, taxicabs, commuter and intercity trains, and in some instances buses—or even helicopters and V/STOL (vertical or short takeoff and landing) aircraft connecting with nearby airports. Such centers can serve well as intercity bus depots, with convenient interchange to and from local and other intercity carriers.

One aspect concerning intercity buses which is frequently overlooked is their role in goods transportation. Just as passenger airliners also carry cargo and mail, most intercity buses carry small packages. Shippers benefit from the fast direct service and the frequen-cy, which most other forms of common-carrier goods transportation cannot match. With the scarcity of railroad passenger trains and the airline emphasis upon larger planes and longer inter-city stage lengths, the availability of buses for movement of small packages and mail should be given increased attention in the location and design of bus terminals. With more conveniently located and designed terminals and with improved intracity access, the bus may very well have greatly increased importance in future intercity person and goods movement, and the urban planner should be aware of the necessity for provision of appropriate sites and approaches to future facilities for intercity buses.

Except for bulk commodity movements by water, rail, and pipeline directly to and from large industries, practically all goods movements in urban areas originate and terminate by truck. The motortruck is the overwhelmingly dominant form of urban goods transportation, and it is also the basic intercity carrier of most goods. It is very unlikely that any other mode, present or prospective, will replace it in the foreseeable future. The motortruck provides door-to-door service, and is virtually the only way in which small shipments can be picked up at the origin and delivered at the destination. Heretofore, the routes and problems of truck movement in cities has received less attention than have passenger movements, but several recent conferences, including international ones, have been devoted to the subject of internal urban goods movement, which, of course, is overwhelmingly by truck.[11]

The growth of intercity trucking and the chaotic state of the industry led to the beginning of regulation of interstate trucking by the Interstate Commerce Commission in 1935. Intrastate trucking by common carriers is also regulated. By 1970, truck registrations in the United States approached 18 million. It was estimated that in that year about 400 billion ton-miles were moved intercity by trucks, accounting for approximately 21 percent of all intercity goods moved by all modes. However, because a high proportion of the goods, in contrast with other modes, was freight of relatively high value in proportion to its bulk, the average ton-mile revenue to the truckers was high, and the estimated $13.5 billion received by the regulated truckers accounted for more than 51 percent of total revenues of all intercity common carriers. Growth of intercity trucking has been proportionate to the total growth of all intercity goods movement in the United States, accounting for about 21 percent of the total in each year throughout the 1960s, although the volume during that period increased more than 70 percent.

Not only does the motortruck compete with most other modes of intercity freight transportation, in spite of the fact that it is usually the originating and terminating mode for most intermodal shipments, but the commercial trucking industry is increasingly finding competition from private trucking. About 40 percent of the total volume of intercity trucking is handled by common and contract carrier "for hire" trucks, with the remainder handled by private and unregulated trucks, such as those used in "exempt" service, including the hauling of certain agricultural produce.

The competitive position of intercity trucking has been substantially improved with development of the interstate highway system and other limited-access high-speed high-

11. *The Urban Movement of Goods: Proceedings of the Third Technology Assessment Review* (Paris: Organization for Economic Co-operation and Development, Oct. 1970), 238 pp.; *Urban Commodity Flow: Report of a Conference Held December 6-9, 1970* (Washington, D.C.: Highway Research Board, 1971) 205 pp.

ways which not only connect virtually all of the major cities, but also provide greatly improved circulation to, from, and between the major freight traffic-generating concentrations within the urban areas. A substantial volume of truck traffic, for example, is generated in the form of container and piggyback services, between rail, water, and air freight facilities and the ultimate origins and destinations within the urban areas. In some instances the transfer of rail freight between railroads across major gateways—as, for example, Chicago and St. Louis—may be faster and easier by hauling the container or trailer across the urban area between railroads on the highways rather than by switching the railroad cars.

The basic network of long-haul intercity motor truck movement is the system of interstate highways, created as a result of the Highway Act of 1956 [Figure 7-7]. This system, almost entirely consisting of limited-access grade-separated expressways, connects all major cities and thousands of smaller urban places, with no cross-traffic, and with easy horizontal and vertical curves, permitting uninterrupted high-speed operation. As part of, or supplementary to, the system, most cities are provided with circumferential expressways or "beltways" which intersect the radiating intercity routes, providing circulation to all parts of the metropolitan area. Along many of these routes, substantial industrial development has taken place, and motortruck access involves a minimum of movement on conventional highways or city streets.

The interstate system, originally proposed in 1944, was over 80 percent completed by 1973 and was expected to be finished by 1976. It involves approximately 42,000 miles of highway to carry about 20 percent of the total highway traffic of the nation. It is financed by special taxes on motor fuel and other items, placed in a trust fund, with which the federal government pays up to 90 percent of the cost of land acquisition and construction, the remainder being a responsibility of the states and local governments, who are also responsible for maintenance of the completed portions of the system. By the early 1970s, however, it became apparent that local opposition to the completion of the system was developing in some areas, due to a combination of concerns for effects of the highways on the environment, the disruption and relocation problems created by the routes through some of the more heavily populated urban areas, and the financial burdens imposed upon states and local governmental units because of the costs of maintaining the completed portions of the system. Those portions which have generated, or are expected to generate, heavy trucking traffic, are especially vulnerable to opposition.

Although every residence and commercial and industrial establishment generates motortruck traffic, the major industrial and commercial concentrations constitute nodes on the traffic network, and access by motortruck thus becomes particularly significant in the selection and development of such nucleations. Since heavy trucking is especially undersirable in proximity to residential areas, the planner should be especially careful to provide adequate trucking capacity on the expressways, and on the access and egress ramps, as well as between the expressways and the traffic generators, involving a minimum of movement on surface arterials and other streets.

Provision must be made for meeting the requirements of the truckers at the points of access and egress along the expressways and major arterials. There are many studies of the impact of express highways upon land uses, but especially significant are the new

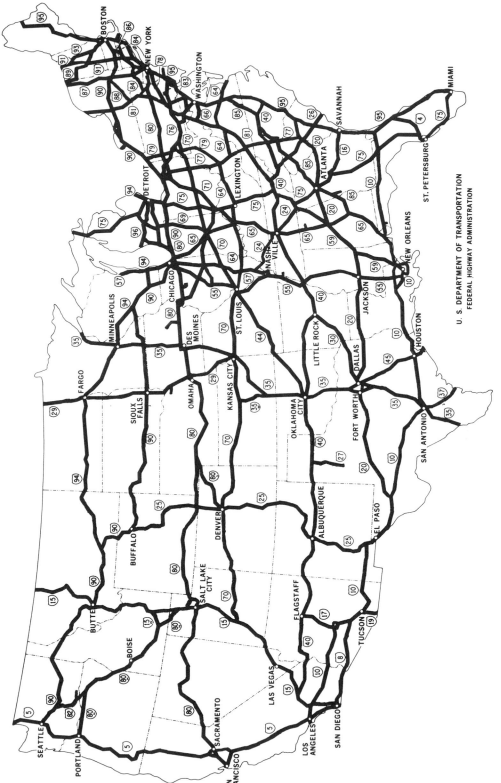

Figure 7-7 The national system of interstate and defense highways.

227

concentrations at the points of access to the limited-access routes. Typically, such concentrations include marshaling yards, somewhat analogous to the railroad classification yards although smaller, for the assembly and breaking up of "double bottoms"—the two-trailer truck trains—which are permitted on the expressways and freeways in many states. Where only single trailers or semitrailers are permitted on ordinary streets and highways, trailers are added to form double units on the expressways; at the same time, at such marshaling yards, trailers and semitrailers are interchanged among the tractors of the same or different carriers. Where these operations take place there is also the need for other facilities to serve the requirements of the truckers; such facilities may include break-of-bulk truck terminals, hotels and motels for the personnel, repair and fueling facilities, etc. Thus, concentrations of highway-oriented land uses occur at access points and interchanges on the major highway network within cities and metropolitan areas, and zoning and other provisions should reflect this condition. Compatibility with other land uses should be given adequate consideration, as well as the control of "ribbons" which may tend to develop along the major surface arterial routes connecting with the expressways and other limited-access highways.

In a few instances, such as within the city of Chicago, special truck terminal districts have been zoned. These districts, located with convenient access to the major highway routes and in proximity to major industrial concentrations, are quite extensive, and within them the zoning permits only truck-oriented uses; such uses include truck terminals, marshaling yards, hotels and motels, restaurants, repair facilities, and similar establishments.

The truck terminals themselves are typically operated by single carriers, although in some instances several over-the-road truck operators may combine in a joint or union truck terminal; in a few instances such terminals have been established by public agencies, with facilities leased to the individual trucking companies, as in the case of facilities in Manhattan and Newark which were established by the Port Authority of New York and New Jersey. Truck terminals perform several functions: (a) they permit interchange of trailers among the several connecting over-the-road carriers, each of which is certificated as a common carrier, to operate over certain routes, or as a contract carrier within certain territory, thus, on through movements, necessitating interchange among carriers; (b) they are sites for interchange between the over-the-road trucks or trailers and the "mosquito fleets" of the same or different carriers which perform the collection and delivery functions within the cities and metropolitan areas; and (c) they are the locales for much of the administrative, maintenance, and repair activities of the truckers.

One of the most significant aspects of urban and metropolitan trucking operations is the designation by the Interstate Commerce Commission of so-called commercial zones, which include the central cities and certain designated adjacent suburban areas within each of the respective metropolitan areas. The boundaries of the trucking commercial zone for Chicago are shown in Figure 7-6. Around each of the larger cities, the ICC has designated the boundaries of a similar commercial zone, while around medium-sized cities the zone is designated as a fixed radius from a designated point in the central core. Within each of the respective zones so designated, common and contract carriers certificated to serve the city can accommodate any terminal or individual establishment, at interstate rates on hauls which are common to all points within the zone. Under regulation by state authorities, similar provisions generally apply to intrastate shipments. Within the respective metropolitan areas, however, locations outside the boundaries of the zone cannot be served by such carriers, except insofar as the same carriers have been certificated to serve the individual communities. Rates are established in which hauls to and from such points external to the commercial zone may or may not be the same as those to and from points within the zone, but on external movements which involve assembly, distribution, or interchange at terminals or other points within the zone, frequently transfers between an over-the-road trucker serving the zone and another trucker connecting the external but nearby point are necessary, with additional costs to the shipper. Clearly, as in the case with railroad switching districts, it may be to the advantage of a commercial or industrial establishment to locate within the zone in order to take advantage of the flexibility as well as the greater number and variety of trucking services available within the commercial zone. Thus, the existence of the commercial zone may serve to inhibit to a greater or lesser extent the deconcentration of industry within the metropolitan areas. This is particularly true in the many instances in which the extension of the commercial zone does not reflect adequately the deconcentration of industry which may have taken place, or which, from the viewpoint of the region as a whole may be considered desirable. Once established, the commercial zones can be extended only with great difficulty, because there are many local truckers, both common and contract carriers, who depend upon interline hauls between points internal and external to the respective zones. It is apparent that the planning of industrial and commercial areas within any large or medium-sized metropolitan region must include designation of an appropriate commercial trucking zone boundary, or consider its modification where an existing boundary is inappropriate. Planners should be prepared to testify before appropriate administrative bodies, such as the ICC, where it becomes apparent that the commercial zone boundaries are inappropriate from the point of view of general planning considerations.

MARITIME TRANSPORTATION   Maritime transportation in the United States may be divided into several components; although these components share some characteristics and problems, each is distinctive in many respects, and the planner should recognize the nature of the problems and take them into consideration in the preparation and implementation of plans for any city or metropolitan area which is situated on navigable water. The components are (a) ocean shipping, including international deep-sea shipping and offshore shipping to such areas as Puerto Rico, Alaska, and Hawaii, (b) intercoastal and coastwise shipping, (c) Great Lakes shipping, and (d) inland waterway shipping.

Because the United States is a large nation, and consequently can meet the majority of its needs from domestic sources, many people fail to realize the significance of its international shipping. This handbook is not concerned with the problems of the United States Merchant Marine, which has been carrying a declining proportion of the country's foreign trade; it is concerned with problems of ports and port development as they involve the urban and metropolitan planner, regardless of the nationality of the ships, wherever there is existing or prospective port development.

As indicated earlier, recent shifts in the technology of transportation have been particularly effective in changing the physical requirements for handling waterborne shipping. The economies of scale of bulk handling of cargoes, which makes possible the dependence of the United States upon worldwide imports of strategic raw materials, as well as the export of many of its products such as grains and coal to world markets, is dependent not only upon the development of very large vessels, but also upon the efficient handling of such commodities, and the vessels which transport them, at the ports. Recently much of the advantage of water transportation for large-scale movement of bulk goods, both at sea and on the inland waterways including the Great Lakes, has inspired developments and techniques for handling general cargo which are rapidly transforming the nature and requirements of ports in general.[12] The planner should be aware of these developments and anticipate them.

Among the major considerations of maritime port development which will affect city planning are the increasing size of ships, requiring deeper channels and more extensive land areas for access to more sophisticated port terminals, the dislocations of the labor force resulting from creation of surpluses of shoreside labor through increasing technological efficiency, and the concentrations of maritime traffic which are resulting from the necessity to assemble larger loads, with fewer ports and fewer but more efficient ships.

The total foreign trade of the United States in the late 1960s amounted to nearly $60 billion and constituted somewhat over 7 percent of the gross national product. Many estimates of future volume of foreign trade have been made; one, made by the Stanford Research Institute, indicates a doubling to tripling of the total volume by the year 2000. At the same time, many of the port facilities for handling this trade are obsolete, both in location and in design, and will require replacement. Not only are there shifts in areas of production and consumption within the United States as well as in the mode of inland transportation to and from the ports, but also major changes in the nature of the required port installations due to the necessity for maximizing the economic advantages of larger vessels and more concentrated loads at the ports in order to facilitate vessel turnaround time. Specific problems of port location and design for maritime traffic are discussed later. Since ocean shipping, regardless of whether it is international or domestic, has generally similar port requirements, no differentiation between them is included. However, the requirements for inland waterway and Great Lakes shipping are in many respects different and require somewhat separate consideration.

At the outset, there are several aspects to ports that should be dominant in the planner's consideration. There is no national plan in the United States which designates or anticipates future requirements in terms of numbers or locations of ports. Although several agencies have advocated the preparation of such a plan, as of 1972 none existed, nor had basic studies been made which would be prerequisite to such a plan. The American Association of Port Authorities firmly opposes any actions which could even

---

12. Several periodicals specialize in descriptions and analyses of port installations; among them are: *The Dock and Harbour Authority, World Ports, Container News,* and *Fairplay International Shipping Journal.* A general discussion of port technology is: R. B. Oram, *Cargo Handling and the Modern Port* (Oxford: Pergamon Press, 1965), 173 pp.

remotely lead to designation of specific ports for development or phasing out, maintaining that interport competition will lead to survival of the most appropriate and fittest. However, modern ports are extremely expensive both in terms of land and money, and virtually all of them are built, maintained, and operated by public agencies; therefore, it would appear in the public interest to have some concept of the scale of future development which would be required.

Maritime traffic is divided into two categories: (a) bulk traffic, both liquid and dry, and (b) general cargo. The former is characterized by continuous flow, and the latter generally consists of discrete items, although, as previously indicated, recent developments include consolidation of items ("unitization") such as in standardized containers or truck trailer units.

Bulk cargoes are generally handled in specialized terminals, either publicly owned and controlled, or privately operated in connection with industrial installations, which may be in immediate proximity or at remote locations. In either event, the availability of facilities for handling bulk cargoes, in spite of the fact that such traffic may require very little labor force for its direct handling, is a major stimulus to industrial location in the general port area. Linked activities, such as trade in the commodities, ship repair, customhouse brokerage, banking services, etc., may also be directly generated at ports which primarily are concerned with handling of bulk goods, and therefore such traffic may indirectly contribute to the multiplier effect upon the economic base of the city and region.

Bulk cargo vessels require very large loads to be economic. Few ports can regularly generate sufficient traffic, and, as the trend toward large size continues, fewer ports can justify the enormous expenditures which are necessary for channel improvements and port terminal installations.[13] The result, in general, is concentration of traffic at fewer ports, with decline and eventual disappearance of those which lose out in the competition. Each port city or region should carefully consider whether it should or could embark upon the very expensive course of attempting to encourage bulk shipping and receiving industries which not only require specialized facilities, but also may dominate its waterfronts, to the exclusion of other desired uses.

The fact is that there is at present no port in the United States which can accommodate the largest and most efficient bulk-carrying vessels. The major problem is their draft, which requires ever-deeper channels. The problem is especially acute in the case of tankers. The modern supertanker, which exceeded 200,000 tons in the 1960s, reached nearly 400,000 tons by 1970, and was expected to exceed 500,000 tons deadweight in the mid-seventies, requires greater depth of water than is available at any coastal port in the nation. New York Harbor, for example, has a low-water depth of 40 feet, which has been sufficient for the largest passenger liners in the heyday, now past, of the "superliner," which at most drew 38 feet; modern tankers have been built exceeding 80 feet of draft, and a more typical draft is about 60 feet. Undoubtedly, these amounts be exceeded in the near future. The St. Lawrence Seaway, which was designed with a

13. A comprehensive study of the increasing size of bulk-carrying vessels, particularly tankers, in relation to required channel depths is: *Merchant Vessel Size in the U.S. Offshore Trades by the Year 2000* (Washington, D.C.: American Association of Port Authorities, 1969), 54 pp.

depth of 27 feet, was obsolete before it was opened, for a declining proportion of the world's ocean ships can use that waterway, and the Great Lakes once again are isolated from access by the more efficient modern ships.

The problem is especially acute in the case of tankers; none of the larger supertankers can serve any United States port directly. The trend is the result of several considerations which are mutually reinforcing: (a) construction costs increase at a slower rate than vessel size and capacity; (b) operating costs also decrease with increasing size of the vessel; and (c) most oil companies for economic reasons prefer to use large tankers for single-product crude or residual oils on very long hauls. Whether the United States will depend in the future more than at present on imported and offshore oil, including from Alaska, remains to be seen. All present indications are that substantial amounts will be landed in the United States. If that is the case, the costs of terminal arrangements must be minimized, or the importations will be less economic.

Many proposals have been made for accommodating to these trends. One is for transfer of oil from larger to smaller tankers at points outside the United States, in effect using the smaller tankers (but still very large vessels) as lighters. Another proposal, which has been seriously considered, is the creation of extensive areas on the continental shelf offshore for the receipt of oil, its storage, and possible processing, and then eventual movement to the consuming areas by smaller vessel or by submarine pipeline. Early in 1971, the state of Delaware enacted legislation which prohibits the development of offshore terminals within its coastal waters. Much concern has been expressed relative to the ecological effects of offshore terminals upon the coastal waters and the oceans. Whether the effects of such terminals would be more adverse than installations onshore in or near the major urban consuming areas is an unresolved question and a very controversial one.

Two problems of special concern to the urban planner emerge: (a) the possible effects of offshore terminals upon the economic base of existing ports and the urban areas within or near which they are located, if the bulk terminals at such ports become redundant as the result of terminals at offshore locations, with respect to employment and shoreline land uses; and (b) the effects of elimination of the necessity of deeper channels. Many ports could not, perhaps, justify extensive channel maintenance without deep-draft tanker traffic. Some ports cannot, in any event, provide for much deeper drafts feasibly because of locations up narrow, shallow, meandering rivers, or because of man-made obstructions down the channel. An example is the tunnel at the entrance to Chesapeake Bay which for generations to come will prevent Baltimore and other ports up the bay from being provided with deep-channel access from the sea.

In the United States, it is a federal responsibility to provide the channels by which shipping can gain access to the port area. This is done by acts of Congress, which authorize river and harbor improvements in annual bills, which must then be followed by specific appropriations. Many projects which are authorized are not built because of changing conditions which render them unnecessary, or because escalating costs change the benefit-cost ratio sufficiently to make the project less attractive, or because of political pressures from rival ports or areas. The actual channel improvements are carried out as authorized, by the Army Corps of Engineers, who may do the work themselves or contract with civilian organizations.

The responsibility of the federal government generally stops at the edge of the channel, unless there are joint benefits other than transportation which may extend beyond the edge of the channel. The development of terminal facilities at the shoreline is a local responsibility, and this may be done by private industries, shipping companies, land transportation companies, or they may be developed by public agencies such as municipalities, states, or special ad hoc port authorities, which may be independent taxing bodies, may depend upon user charges, or may be components, such as departments, of city, county, or state governments. In a few instances interstate port authorities have been set up, following the lead of the Port of New York Authority, which was established by interstate compact in 1920.[14]

Petroleum port facilities, in general, are operated by private interests and, aside from the provision of channels, local port authorities are concerned primarily with the effects of tanker traffic on the ecology of the port areas, including the dangers resulting from oil spills due to collisions, groundings of vessels, and otherwise, and with the possibilities of fires and explosions. In a comprehensive port which handles petroleum along with other traffic, the terminals for tankers should be separated, preferably in a relatively remote portion of the waterfront, and special anchorages should be provided for the tankers apart from other maritime traffic.

Dry-bulk vessels, like tankers, are becoming larger and have deeper drafts than formerly. They are becoming more specialized, and the speed of loading and discharge is increasingly critical; loading and discharge, therefore, require highly specialized facilities. Such facilities may be privately owned and operated, or may be public, commonly with operations carried on by contract or lease with private operators. Grain elevators, ore loading and discharging facilities, and similar installations are characteristic of both specialized and comprehensive ports. Ports which anticipate extensive general cargo traffic benefit also from the availability of specialized bulk-handling facilities, such as grain elevators, where the traffic justifies, because the prospect of "bottoming" cargo, to be loaded when there is available capacity before scheduled sailing time of general cargo liners, may be an inducement to regular liner traffic which otherwise may not provide the desired regularity and frequency. With prospects of filling the available capacity with bulk cargo, the port, on the other hand, may prove additionally attractive for regularly scheduled services.

One phenomenon in recent years which prospective port developments must serve is the combination liquid-dry bulk vessel. A decade ago, with the uncertainties relative to the Suez Canal, the supertanker, with its fantastic economies of scale, was developed. Such vessels released many smaller tankers, which proved uneconomic on shorter movements; since most of them were foreign-flag, they were unavailable for the coastal trade of the United States, and they found difficulty in seeking employment elsewhere. Consequently, they began to compete with dry-cargo tramp vessels of conventional type in the dry-bulk trades, particularly in the movement of grain. Since they were larger than the traditional types of dry-cargo tramps, they became a major factor in the availability of shipping at many ports. Also, petroleum traffic is generally one-way, and tankers do

14. The most comprehensive, although somewhat out-of-date, analysis of port organizations is: Marvin L. Fair, *Port Administration in the United States* (Cambridge, Md.: Cornell Maritime Press, 1954), 217 pp.

not have the routing flexibility of more generalized cargo carriers, often having to make return voyages in ballast. To mitigate this condition, combination-type vessels were developed, to carry liquid and dry-bulk cargoes on consecutive voyages; these vessels, which are becoming increasingly common, are known as OBOs (oil-bulk-ore). Some of them are comparable with large tankers in size, and most are considerably larger than the conventional types of dry-cargo ships.

Planners should be aware of the need for more sophisticated facilities for repair and maintenance of the increasingly large and complex vessels. Shipyards are the epitome of "heavy" industry, and major ports must provide waterfront areas for them, appropriately separated from incompatible uses.

While dry-cargo vessels of conventional type continue to operate on many trade routes, both as liners on regular schedules and as tramps in unscheduled service as well as industrial private carriers, there have been several noteworthy trends in the design and employment of such vessels which planners in port cities and regions should recognize in considering the demands for waterfront terminal land uses. We have already touched upon the growth of the container ship which, along with the supertanker, represents the most noteworthy trend in maritime shipping in the past decade. The container ship is employed on high-density routes, such as on the North Atlantic and North Pacific, where regularity of scheduled sailings is important. On many other routes, combination container and break-bulk ships are employed; the latter may or may not require to be loaded and discharged at specialized container terminals. Originally, the early container ships carried their own cranes on board; later container ships typically do not have specialized cranes, relying instead on shore-based ones, which must be provided by the terminal operator. Container ships in general are considerably larger and faster than conventional break-bulk cargo vessels, and the problems of shoreward access are multiplied by the necessity for fast turnaround, which involves extensive areas for sorting and handling of the containers with minimum delay.

The typical dry-cargo facilities a generation or two ago consisted of "finger" piers and slips, in order to maximize the amount of berthage for vessels in proportion to the land area. The result was a series of narrow piers jutting into the water, with almost inevitable congestion at the landward end as the trucks and railroad cars sought entrance. Frequently, as on the west side of Manhattan, or on Atlantic Avenue in Boston and the Embarcadero in San Francisco, the congestion in the marginal streets was very costly and time-consuming. The landward supporting areas could not be extended, because the port was largely developed in and near the older sections of the city, where intensive development, commonly associated with the central business district or adjacent wholesale-light manufacturing areas, had taken place. With the decline of such landward areas, renewal programs commonly featured developments which could more appropriately be situated in such locations than could port-oriented uses. As in the case of many other industrial activities, the port facilities tended to be relocated farther from the cores of the cities, usually on much more extensive land areas, with more adequate landward access by rail and truck, with extensive areas for associated industrial development and with considerably lower land costs. In order to minimize vessel turnaround and voyage time, as well as channel dredging, such new port developments generally are located not only toward the urban periphery, but seaward.

The decline of the older portions of ports presents the planner with major opportunities for renewal and attractive treatment of former port areas. The redevelopment of the North and East river waterfronts of Manhattan, of the Delaware River frontage in Philadelphia, the downtown waterfronts of Boston, Baltimore, Jacksonville, New Orleans, San Francisco, Seattle, and many other cities which formerly had intensive general cargo terminals of inefficient design, are noteworthy. They are possible only because of the changing requirements of larger—and hence fewer—vessels, and more efficient land transportation, which demands more rapid movement of cargo, and which, at the same time results in changed land requirements.

To illustrate: the typical general cargo vessel in the 1920s, built just after World War I, and which survived in world trade until after World War II, carried about 5,000 tons, and required as much as 10 days in port to unload and load a full cargo. Thus, with 10,000 tons to be handled, the berth typically handled about 1,000 tons per day. A modern container ship may carry 25,000 tons, and can turn around in one or two days; thus a berth must handle up to 25 times as much cargo as formerly. Even with the efficiency of the container, the land requirement for backup, behind the berth, has increased severalfold. A modern container ship berth may require more than 30 acres of backup land area. Because such land has specialized location and other physical requirements, there is relative inflexibility and limited choice for location of such uses, and the planner should adequately provide for them in the comprehensive city or regional plan.

The same principles of minimizing cargo handling at the ports which stimulated development of the container ship apply to several other types of vessels which are becoming increasingly important. These are the Roll on-Roll off (RoRo) ship, and the LASH (lighter aboard ship) and Seabee types of vessels.

The RoRo is an evolution from the long-familiar vehicle ferry, in which loading ramps or bridges at the stern, and sometimes at the bow, of the vessel permit wheeled vehicles to be put aboard on their own wheels, either under their own power or by means of tractor units. Large ocean-going ships with stern-loading, and sometimes bow doors, have been constructed; some have ramps within the vessel enabling wheeled vehicles to reach each of several decks. In a few instances, tracks may accommodate railroad cars, as in the case of the Lake Michigan car ferries, from which RoRo has adapted many design concepts. A significant number of vessels combine container and RoRo capability, both with and without break-of-bulk cargo. RoRo vessels can handle a wide variety of cargo which conventional or container ships cannot accept, or can handle only with difficulty; for example, wheeled earth-moving machinery, military equipment such as trucks and tanks, and truck trailers with wheels. From the viewpoint of the planner, RoRo vessels constitute no special problem, for landward access requirements do not differ much from those for other types of general cargo traffic.

Perhaps more significant is the LASH or Seabee type of vessel, which became significant on certain trade routes in the early 1970s. These vessels, currently in the North Atlantic and North Pacific trades, carry the unitized cargo concept a step further than previously in that they take loaded barges aboard. Once loaded, the barges need not be relieved of their cargo until they reach their ultimate destination, which may be in ports not accessible to the larger vessels, including the barge-carrying ships. The barges are put aboard and refloated by means of large cranes on the deck of the vessel, which span a stern opening. The LASH and Seabee vessels theoretically do not require any shoreside installations whatever in the port and, in fact, can load and discharge the barges on board without even a harbor under certain conditions. In practice, however, the barges are handled within the port areas, and the larger vessel commonly is tied alongside a wharf.

The LASH and Seabee vessels make many conventional port installations redundant, and make possible the growth of direct non-break-of-bulk traffic at a variety of inland ports, such as those along the Mississippi River and its tributaries, and on the Great Lakes where the larger vessels cannot operate because of draft restrictions. New Orleans, Baton Rouge, Montreal, San Francisco, Oakland, Portland, and other ports on the lower portions of many navigable rivers are logical places for transfer of barges to and from ocean-going ships, and inland ports need to be aware of the possibilities of extensive river-ocean barge traffic, including international movements. The types of terminal facilities, however, would be similar to those required for internal barge traffic, except for the addition of customs and other facilities for whatever international traffic may be developed. The LASH and Seabee barges present many legal problems when they are handling international traffic on the inland rivers, but these need not specifically concern the urban planner.

The prospect of bypassing conventional port terminal facilities with the proliferation of barge-on-ship movements should be considered in the planning of ports which may or could be served by such vessels; but because the development of the technique is so new, specific design and site specifications should benefit from the experience of the few ports which currently or prospectively handle this type of traffic.

Further in the future, but in prospect, is development of more exotic methods of transferring cargo between ships, or from ship to shore. Experiments have been technically successful in the use of helicopters for such transfers. Replenishment of naval vessels at sea by this means has been experimentally successful, and it is possible that the technique could be extended to merchant ships. If so, traffic so handled need not go through conventional coastal ports at all, but could be handled directly between the ship, which may be at sea rather than in a port, and inland points within range of the helicopter.

With the prospects of offshore terminals, extensive use of barge-on-ship transportation, and possibilities of aerial transfer between ship and shore, conventional coastal ports cannot be complacent, and the planner should be very careful to consider such possibilities in planning for port installations which must, because of expense, be amortized over long periods of time.

Transportation on the Great Lakes and the inland waterways constitutes a major portion of the total goods transportation within the United States, while the Great Lakes are also vital to the economy of Canada, and there is a considerable volume of international traffic, both United States-Canada and direct overseas, moving through Great Lakes ports.

Great Lakes and inland waterways ports resemble ocean types in many respects, but in several ways their requirements are specialized. On both waterway systems, traffic is almost entirely bulk, except for a limited amount of general cargo moving directly between the Great Lakes and overseas ports.

The inland waterway system of the United States, excluding the Great Lakes, has developed as a major factor in the nation's domestic transportation very rapidly in recent years: in the early 1970s it was carrying 10 percent of the total ton-miles of domestic intercity freight, with the volume increasing rapidly, both relatively and absolutely.

The inland waterways constitute approximately 25,000 miles of navigable routes. The principal part of the system constitutes about 12,000 miles of the Mississippi River and its tributaries, extending from western Pennsylvania to Sioux City, Iowa, from the twin cities of Minneapolis-St. Paul to the Gulf of Mexico, and from the upper Tennessee River to near Tulsa, Oklahoma, on the newly improved Arkansas River. Principal routes are on the Monongahela, Kanhawa, Ohio, upper Mississippi, Illinois, Missouri, Arkansas, Cumberland, Tennessee, and lower Mississippi rivers, connecting with the Gulf Intracoastal waterway which extends from western Florida to the Mexican border. Virtually all of these waterways have been extensively channelized, and in the upper portions of the system a series of dams and locks provide a sequence of pools, within which a minimum channel depth of nine feet is maintained. On the Gulf Intracoastal Waterway, connecting the Mississippi system with ports on the Gulf of Mexico, the minimum low-water depth is maintained at twelve feet.

On the Mississippi River system, and many of the other navigable inland waterways, the transportation technology is utterly different from that made familiar by Mark Twain in the days of the packet steamboat. Modern river navigation is by means of "tows," consisting of a set of standard-sized barges, pushed by a powerful diesel towboat; the latter has twin screws, recessed in tunnels under the stern to protect them against bottom obstructions. The towboat may develop as much as 10,000 horsepower and it may push as many as 30 or more barges, each of which may be loaded with from 1,000 to 3,000 tons of bulk cargo. As with railroad freight trains, barges may be added or dropped at various points en route; the crews may be delivered to or removed from the tows as these move along the channels without stopping. Ton-mile costs of barge transportation are the lowest of any mode, with the possible exception of pipelines in some instances. In 1970, the inland waterways, other than the Great Lakes, handled 190 billion ton-miles of traffic, and employed about 80,000 people in direct transportation service. Both the waterways and the vessels are being constantly improved, and the traffic continues to increase rapidly.

From the viewpoint of inland port cities, the principal advantages of the inland waterway system is that the low-cost movement of bulk commodities gives industries along, and tributary to, the system a competitive transportation advantage, not only because of the low-cost water transportation directly, but also because of the effects that it has in lowering the freight costs by competitive overland transportation. The existence of the system has gone a long way toward removing the previous rate disadvantages to the Midwest, previously discussed.

Originally, impetus was given to development of the inland river system by the congestion on the nation's railroads during and immediately following World War I. The federal government, realizing the opportunity which the waterways provided, organized the experimental Inland Waterways Corporation (Federal Barge Lines), to demonstrate the advantages of low-cost barge transportation, and at the same time to develop "know-how" in the techniques. At the same time, extensive river improvements, including the system of pools, made possible by locks and dams, were begun on the upper rivers; the nine-foot channel on the Ohio was completed in 1929, and the Illinois Waterway was completed in 1933; at the same time the Tennessee Valley Authority began canalization of the Tennessee River to the standard nine-foot depth. The latest major extension of the system was on the Arkansas River, where a nine-foot channel was opened to Catoosa, Oklahoma, near Tulsa, in 1971.

Barge transportation on the inland waterways is almost entirely of bulk commodities. The early Federal Barge Line experiments in merchandise transportation were unsuccessful, largely because of the competition of railroads and especially the development of modern highways. Barge transportation is of maximum advantage for those movements in which transit time is immaterial, and where the commodities are of low value in proportion to bulk. Consequently, the principal interest of the planner in barge transportation is the stimulus that it may furnish to the local economic base, by attracting bulk-shipping and bulk-using industries, not only to riverfront locations, but also to inland locations where joint rail-barge and truck-barge rates extend the hinterlands of the river ports well inland beyond the actual rivers themselves.

A major concern relating to inland navigation, however, is the subject of bridge clearances. The Army Corps of Engineers has established clearance regulations for each of the inland waterways, and no structure may extend in any way into the vertical and horizontal clearances which are designated. This in many instances affects the design and costs of highways and other structures, for in order to achieve the requisite clearances, the bridge approaches may extend well beyond the shore, and thus affect interchanges and other links far shoreward of the waterfront. On the Great Lakes and St. Lawrence system, for example, the international standard is 120 feet above high water, permitting vessels with masts up to 117 feet above the summer load line to pass underneath. If bridges are lower than these standards, they must be movable, and must be manned in such manner as not to constitute obstructions to vessel movement. On the other hand, a movable bridge is an intolerable condition on an express highway, and they are not permitted on those highways which constitute parts of the interstate system.

Great Lakes ports are very similar to ocean ones in many of their requirements. Since the Great Lakes are not tidal, water levels fluctuate through a narrower range than at either coastal or river ports; maximum range, over an 11-year cycle, is less than 7 feet, so that vessels can be continuously worked without special provisions for changes in water level. Vessels in the Great Lakes are required to have certain special installations not normally required of ocean-going ships; these include holding tanks or sewage disposal facilities, constant-tension winches for Seaway navigation in the locks, and English-speaking officer personnel.

Most Great Lakes traffic, except for direct overseas general cargo, like that of the rivers, is bulk traffic. Within the lakes it is handled in specially designed vessels, called "lakers," which have hatches designed on standard modules, 12 or 24 feet between centers, to permit handling at terminal facilities which, in the upper lakes ore trade, also have standard modules. An increasing number of lake bulk carriers are "self loaders," which include provision for unloading by means of rotating conveyer booms, making discharge of their bulk loads independent of shore-based mechanical devices. Stockpiles of ore, coal, and limestone at waterfront industries, therefore, are normally located within range of such booms, not usually over 250 feet from the wharf edge.

Domestic and United States-Canada internal traffic within the Great Lakes has not been growing significantly in recent years, but has fluctuated, depending upon business conditions, at something over 100 billion ton-miles annually. It consists principally of iron ore from the Lake Superior and northern Lake Michigan areas, downbound to the steel plants along Lake Michigan and Lake Erie and to the interior plants served from those areas by rail; coal upbound from Lake Erie ports and South Chicago to utilities and industrial plants in the upper lakes and to the Canadian side of Lake Ontario; limestone, used as a flux in the blast furnaces, from the Lake Huron shore of Michigan; and several minor commodities, such as cement, oil and petroleum products, newsprint paper, and chemicals. Recently, the nature of the most important commodity, tonnage-wise—iron ore—has been changing, with the advent of concentrates, notably taconite, largely replacing hematite and other direct-shipping ores, as the high-quality reserves have been reduced. Taconite has a much higher iron content per ton shipped than the other ores, consequently, even though more iron is consumed, the volume of ore moved across the lakes has not significantly increased.

From 1959, the year the St. Lawrence Seaway opened, until 1971, the maximum-sized vessel operating in the Great Lakes had a length of 730 feet, a beam of 75 feet, and a loaded draft of 26 feet; these dimensions were limited by the size of the locks in the St. Lawrence Seaway, the Welland Ship Canal, and the locks at Sault Ste. Marie, which permitted entrance into Lake Superior. Such vessels could not only operate within the lakes, but also to the lower St. Lawrence with downbound loads of grain and upbound eastern Canadian iron ore. With completion of a larger lock at Sault Ste. Marie in 1969, larger vessels could reach the Lake Superior ores, but would necessarily be landlocked, since they could not have access to the area east of Lake Erie. Several such vessels were built, and placed in service in the early 1970s, with length up to 1,000 feet, beam of 105 feet, and, on a draft of 26 feet, they could carry up to 53,000 tons of ore, compared to a maximum of about 28,000 tons aboard the earlier "maximum lakers." Standard depth in the Seaway, connecting channels, and principal Great Lakes ports is 27 feet, permitting a draft of 26 feet. But access to the Lakes through the St. Lawrence Seaway is denied to an increasing proportion of the world's ocean ships, since the more competitive ones all have drafts considerably in excess of 26 feet.

Direct overseas traffic to and from the Great Lakes has been increasing rapidly, as has also the traffic between the Great Lakes and the lower St. Lawrence. By 1970 the total annual traffic through the Seaway had reached 50 million tons, but, in spite of such increases, the Seaway itself was somewhat of a disappointment to its enthusiastic promoters. It is now clear that planners in the Great Lakes port cities need not seriously concern themselves with possible great increases in general cargo traffic. In general, such traffic can be handled at existing facilities, with some local improvements. Seaway and Great Lakes traffic will continue to be primarily bulk traffic, carried in both "lakers" and "salties," but with decreasing emphasis on the latter.

At coastal, inland, and Great Lakes ports, the trend in recent years has been, and in the future will continue to be, toward increasing concentration of traffic at fewer but more efficient ports. Scale economies dictate that, the larger the vessels and the greater the volumes of traffic, the greater can be the economies realized from concentration at those ports which have the most modern and efficient facilities, and where the maximum number and variety of sailings and services are offered. The excess of port labor, not only at the smaller ports which will suffer from decreasing shares of the traffic and eventual atrophy, but also at the relatively few major ports where capital-intensive operations and greater efficiency will continue to replace the older labor-intensive cargo handling, will constitute an increasingly urgent problem for the city planner. Such ports must, if they are to survive as economically viable cities, find alternative types of economic base to replace the employment which will rapidly decline as port characteristics change.

AIR TRANSPORTATION   Air transportation has rapidly developed into the major mode of intercity passenger movement, other than the private automobile. In addition, increasing quantities of goods are transported by air. By 1970 air carriers, including both scheduled airlines and charter operators. produced three-fourths of all the passenger miles, other than private, of transportation in the United States. In addition, about two-tenths of one percent of all ton-miles of goods movement was by air, although of course the latter represented a much higher proportion of the value. General aviation, which includes all air transportation activities other than those by regular carriers, has also been rapidly increasing in importance.

The urban planner is concerned with several aspects of air transportation; these include: (a) the external transportation services which sustain the activities of the city and region, (b) the employment furnished by activities in connection with operation of air carriers and other aviation, including operation, maintenance, equipment manufacture and repair, and accessory activities related to airports, (c) access between airports on the one hand and traffic-generating nodes within cities and metropolitan areas on the other, (d) ecological and environmental aspects of air transportation, including air pollution and noise, (e) locations and sites for airports as essential elements of city and metropolitan plans, and (f) land uses and their control in the vicinities of airports.

Airports are extensive users of land. A modern regional airport requires at least ten square miles within the airport boundary, and its presence vitally affects the character of development for a considerably more extensive area outside the boundaries. In major metropolitan regions, the principal airport may constitute the largest single parcel of land under unified and continuous ownership and control, and, in addition, there may be a number of additional airports to serve general (noncarrier) aviation activities, as well as additional carrier airports. Airports, furthermore, may constitute significant nodes of employment and ground traffic generation, comparable in some instances with the central business districts.

In the United States, two federal agencies divide responsibility for the promotion, regulation, and operation of aviation. The Civil Aeronautics Board (CAB) regulates rates, routes, and services of carrier airlines, while the Federal Aviation Administration (FAA) within the Department of Transportation is responsible for federal activities in connection with airports and the operation of the federal airspace system, including air traffic control, and the development and sponsorship of improvements in airport and air navigation operation. The latter agency also administers a federal-aid airport program, and operates the Dulles International and Washington National airports. Of vital concern to planners is the FAA-operated advisory service to communities in the design and construction of airports, and the implementation of the National Airport Plan, by means of which aid to communities in the financing of their airport developments is determined. In Canada, analogous activities are carried on by the Department of Transport. The urban and metropolitan planner is confronted by the necessity to reconcile the requirements, in the interest of air safety, of the federal government agencies with those involved in other aspects of the preparation and implementation of city and regional plans. Very often, the resolution of mutual incompatibilities between the demands of air transportation and those of other aspects of city and regional development is very complex and difficult.

Few fields of human endeavor have witnessed as rapid evolution and change as has aviation. Rapid obsolescence means that investments in aviation equipment and facilities must be amortized very rapidly, but, on the other hand, the plant and equipment which are required necessitate extremely large investments. A large hub airport, developed "from scratch," may involve not only many square miles of land which consequently would be unavailable for other uses but financial commitments in excess of a billion (thousand million) dollars. Some of the most pervasive and difficult decisions relating to the physical problems of cities and regions arise from the need for airports. Because of the nature of airports, which are relatively few in number compared with most other types of urban and metropolitan land uses, the widespread impact that an airport has beyond its own boundaries, and the tremendous investments involved, the planning for airport location must involve not only consideration of the interrelationships among the several or many airports within a metropolitan region, but also the complex of relationships among all the communities within the region. Most airports cannot be financed solely by a single municipality, nor would that be desirable, since any given airport would have effects upon a much larger area. The planner must, therefore consider airports in relation to the entire metropolitan region, and, beyond that, to the national, continental, and intercontinental patterns of air transportation and air-space utilization. Because the latter is the responsibility primarily of the federal government, close collaboration is necessary between city and metropolitan planning agencies on the one hand and federal agencies on the other.

Coordination of airport planning at all levels of government on the one hand, and of airport planning with other aspects of urban and metropolitan development on the other, is facilitated by the availability, under certain circumstances, of federal planning and financial assistance, which is usually channeled through the regional, state, or metropolitan planning agency which has been designated as the clearinghouse under the Demonstration Cities and Metropolitan Development Act of 1966. The FAA administers, under the Airport and Airways Development Act of 1970, a program of planning grants under which as much as two-thirds of the cost of area-wide airport system planning studies are financed by grants to appropriate area or metropolitan planning agencies. In addition, Section 701 of the Housing Act of 1954 provides some funding of planning in terms of metropolitan areas and more extensive regions. Many of the states, also, have prepared statewide airport plans.

As in all transportation facility planning which involves the commitment of vast sums of money and which, because of magnitude, may require many years for effectuation, the airport system planner is faced with the dilemma that the time period for amortization of the investment may exceed the useful life of the projects, because of the speed of technological change and shifting social requirements. The commitment of vast areas of land, with consequent widespread effects upon the urban and metropolitan pattern, further complicates the task. In the early 1970s, the rapid introduction of new aircraft, differing in many significant ways from the earlier planes in many basic performance characteristics, increased the difficulty of projecting requirements and consequently accentuated the need for planning a variety of types of airports, each with its specialized characteristics.

There is no space in this chapter to consider the problems of military air activities, although the location of a military air base in or near a metropolitan area brings a host of associated problems. On the other hand, the demand for new military air bases in the United States is not likely to confront many urban planners, for the development of missiles to replace manned aircraft for combat purposes has greatly reduced the amount of military air traffic, and the likelihood of many additional bases is not great. Typically, the urban and metropolitan planner will be concerned with the provision of civil airports to meet the varied transportation needs of his area.

In the early 1970s the development of civil aviation seems to be heading in several different directions. On the one hand, economies of scale indicate the continued development of "jumbo" or "wide-bodied" aircraft, such as the 747 and the DC-10, with high capacity and long range, requiring extensive airports and complex terminals. On the other hand, such aircraft cannot be handled at airport locations close to the city centers, which would be the optimal locations from the viewpoint of landward accessibility to the ultimate origins and destinations of the passengers and cargo. At the other end of the scale, convenience—which means frequent schedules and easy access to and from the airports—indicates the prospective development of aircraft which are considerably smaller and which are economic on shorter flights. In addition to conventional fixed-wing aircraft, such services may increasingly be performed by STOL (short takeoff and landing) and VTOL (vertical takeoff and landing) aircraft, the later including helicopters. In addition, general aviation continues to grow, and provision must be made in a metropolitan airport plan for such activities, which range from instruction and pleasure flying in light planes to extensive high-speed long-distance business travel in executive jets. The performance characteristics and hence airport requirements of this latter are not unlike those of the smaller commercial airline jets. Airport planning for metropolitan areas must, normally, include provision for most or all of these varied types of aviation activities. With the vast areas required for airports, the tremendous investments in their development, and the complexities of both air-space and ground utilization, it is apparent that, in the future, virtually all airports in urban and metropolitan areas, regardless of type, may be assumed to be under some form of public ownership: municipal, county, or ad hoc special-purpose authority. In many instances, it has become evident that the resources of even the largest city may be insufficient to build or operate those airports which serve the entire metropolitan area or more extensive region. In such cases, the municipal airport may be operated, under lease or some other arrangement, by a higher level of government, or by a special-purpose authority or district. The Port Authority of New York and New Jersey, for example, operates the municipal airports of New York City and Newark. In many instances, nearby cities and metropolitan areas may join to operate, or to form an operating agency, for one or more of the metropolitan airports, as in the examples of Minneapolis-St. Paul and Seattle-Tacoma. On the other hand, San Francisco and Oakland each have their own airports, as do Dallas and Fort Worth, although a large regional airport will soon serve the latter two metropolitan areas. In the early stages of planning for a metropolitan airport system, considerable thought must be given to the nature and extent of the most appropriate airport agency or agencies, in the light of existing facilities and arrangements, possible locations, and administrative and political feasibility. No one solution is applicable to all cities and metropolitan areas. Whatever the form of organization, however, it is essential that the airport agency coordinate its planning and operation on the one hand with the other local, metropolitan, and regional governments and agencies, and on the other hand with those state and federal agencies concerned with aviation, land use planning, and ground transportation systems.[15]

Civil airports may be classified into several types: (a) air carrier or transport airports, (b) general aviation airports, and (c) V/STOL airports, including heliports. These are not mutually exclusive; air carrier airports may also handle general aviation, and feeder or connecting services may be by V/STOL aircraft, while general aviation airports may have some carrier activity, particularly of local scheduled airlines, supplementary carriers (charter operators), and V/STOL scheduled or unscheduled commerical services. In many metropolitan areas, general aviation airports serve as "relievers" to the major airline airports, by handling a significant volume of private flying as well as some short-haul airline operations. The planner must consider the role of general aviation airports in reducing the need for, or extending the time period for, development of extended or additional major airports and facilities. In the New York region, for example, Teterboro and Stewart airports are "relievers" for Kennedy, LaGuardia, and Newark; the North Philadelphia Airport is supplementary to the Philadelphia International Airport; Detroit City and Willow Run airports are relievers for Detroit Metropolitan; Burke Lakefront handles general aviation and short-haul airline services relieving Cleveland Hopkins, etc. One may regard a metropolitan or regional airport system as a hierarchy of airports of differing types and characteristics. Obviously, the planning of such a system must be based upon forecasts of the level and rate of growth of each of the aviation services that the airports will be expected to handle. This involves a considerable degree of uncertainty not only relative to the future economic base and population of the region, but also the direction and rate of change in the technology of air transportation, as well as of the ground transportation access to, from, and between the various existing and prospective airports.

In the development of a regional or metropolitan airport plan, the studies of

15. Federal Aviation Administration, *Planning the Metropolitan Airport System* (Washington, D.C.: Government Printing Office, 1970), 108 pp.

population and economic base made for other purposes are useful, and the estimates of future air traffic should utilize them. Air traffic, on the other hand, is subject to many additional variables, and the long-range plans should have considerable "play" as to timing. But it is important to reserve land as far in advance as possible for the location of future airports, for, once developed for other uses, the land cannot probably later be reclaimed for airport use. Should the need be overestimated, however, the costs, in social, monetary, and physical terms of withholding land from development for alternative uses would be enormous. It is necessary to balance the prospective future benefits and the degree of uncertainty relative to an airport against the other requirements of the community. For this reason, if no other, planning of a metropolitan airport system must be an integral part of a comprehensive metropolitan plan.

The system of air carrier operations within the United States (and Canada) includes a hierarchy of airlines, at several different levels. The main lines are comprised of domestic and international trunk carriers connecting large population centers. These carriers are certificated over definite routes, and are subject to federal regulation relative to rates and services. By 1970 virtually all of the trunk line operations entailed the use of jet aircraft of large capacity. In recent years, the number of trunk-line carriers has been reduced by mergers, which tend to rationalize the route structure by increasing the flexibility of equipment utilization; at the same time competition among carriers serving common points is retained as a matter of federal policy. In the 1960s the number of routes and the frequencies of service—hence the number of available seat-miles—increased rapidly, and late in the decade several of the major air hubs were operating at close to capacity during certain periods, with consequent excessive burdens on the air traffic control system, upon the terminal facilities, and, in some cases, the ground access routes in the vicinities of the airports. In the early 1970s, however, the economic recession and consequent slowing up of the growth of airline traffic, together with the introduction of the "jumbo" aircraft, resulted in a substantial decline in the numbers and frequencies of scheduled airline flights, thereby relieving to some extent the congestion in the air over and near major metropolitan areas, but on the other hand, creating intensified congestion and "peaking" problems when the larger aircraft clustered their arrival and departure times. The airlines were faced with the problems of excess capacity, but it was anticipated that the continued growth of air travel, at whatever rate, would eventually catch up, and the lead time needed for planning dictated that major airports would once again be overburdened unless their capacities and numbers were increased.

The domestic trunk-line carriers are further, unofficially, subdivided into two groups, the "Big Four" (United, American, TWA, and Eastern), and the others, each serving either the entire United States or at least several major regions, with some, in addition, having intercontinental routes. The trunk lines are basically long-haul carriers, and their economies of scale are greatest with large planes, providing that the traffic volumes justify such aircraft. On the other hand, many of the trunk lines also provide short-distance services, particularly in the heavily urbanized corridors; for such services the smaller jets, such as the DC-9 and 737, are generally used. These aircraft can utilize runways shorter than those of the larger jets such as 707s and DC-8s. New York's LaGuardia, Washington National, and Chicago Midway airports—in each case the smaller of the air carrier airports of the respective metropolitan areas—are served mainly by such smaller jets.

The second level of air carrier service is provided by the so-called regional airlines, such as North Central, Ozark, Allegheny, and Air West. Originally, these airlines served intermediate points between the major air hubs, connecting with the trunk lines; they were known as "feeder" airlines. More recently, the regional airlines were certificated to serve city-pairs at considerably greater distances apart, and in some instances they compete with trunk line routes, though their primary function is still to serve the smaller cities where trunk line service is not economic. Most of the regional airlines are increasingly using the smaller jets, and their services more and more resemble the secondary services of the trunk carriers. The latter, in turn, very often have relinquished service at smaller and medium-sized cities to the regional lines, with connections being maintained at the larger hubs. Thus, many of the regional airline services and routes represent a "filtering up," with services and airport requirements resembling those of the trunk lines. Services of certain "offshore" airlines, such as the major internal carriers in Alaska and Hawaii, as well as a few intrastate carriers, such as Pacific Southwest and Air California, resemble those of the major routes of the regional airlines, and these carriers supplement, and in some cases supplant, both the trunk lines and the regional carriers within their respective areas.

In the larger metropolitan areas, where more than one carrier airport exists or is in prospect, a difficult problem which the planner must consider is that of provision of adequate numbers and frequencies of connecting services, both among the trunk lines, and between trunk lines and regional airlines, for the traveler and shipper will not willingly accept the inconvenience of transfer between airports, which, of necessity, must be many miles apart. For this reason, Dulles Airport, Chicago Midway following the development of O'Hare, Ontario International (California), and others in areas where nearby large air carrier airports are operating have had great difficulty in attracting air carrier services which depend in part on receiving passengers and cargo from and delivering them to connecting airlines. Until a "critical mass" of schedule frequencies is reached, dividing airline services among more than one metropolitan airport results in substantially less frequency at each than if the traffic were concentrated at fewer locations; on the other hand the busiest airports produce intolerable congestion, both in the air and on the ground.

Just as the trunk lines have relinquished service at many small and intermediate-sized cities to the regional airlines, so the regional carriers, with their larger and faster planes, have abandoned service to still smaller communities. Many of the latter, also deprived of rail passenger service, and, with the advent of express highways, and of intercity bus service as well, would have no common-carrier interurban passenger service whatsoever were it not for the rapid growth of "third level" or "commuter" airlines to fill the gap. The latter, an outgrowth of "air taxi" or "fixed base" operations, perform both scheduled and charter services with light planes, not exceeding 12,500 pounds weight; such planes can carry up to about 19 passengers, and their routes extend up to several hundred miles in length. In recent years, CAB has implemented a "use it or lose it" policy, in which certification of airlines to serve smaller communities has been rescinded in instances where traffic did not reach certain minimum levels. In many instances, the "commuter" airlines have stepped in to fill these gaps. Typically, such carriers can use general aviation airports, because their aircraft are not unlike those used for many noncarrier purposes. In some cases, they have arrangements with trunk and regional airlines for through ticketing, baggage transfer, and through movement of cargo shipments. They, like the regional airlines, commonly connect with the trunk lines at important centers, and estimates of capacity requirements for airports from the largest down should include "third level" traffic.

Because of the short "stage lengths" or distances between points served by the commuter airlines, and because of the small size of the aircraft used, such airlines offer good prospects for intrametropolitan operations, and particularly for some types of corridor operations between nearby cities. They require much shorter runways than do other types of carrier aircraft, they can "turn around" with less time on the ground, and they commonly can utilize air space on approaches and takeoffs which are outside of the approach and takeoff zones of the larger carrier aircraft, thereby contributing little to the congestion in the air spaces surrounding major airports. In the near future, such air services may increase more rapidly than the services of the trunk and regional carriers, particularly in view of the prospects for improved V/STOL fixed-wing and helicopter aircraft. Such aircraft, in the future, may be more economical, as measured in seat-mile costs, than conventional aircraft in short flights, and thus may be able to offer greatly increased frequency, thus overcoming the disadvantage of low capacity.

These advantages may well, in the future, be manifest in greatly increased use of air space for local, suburban, and short intercity transportation, supplementing, and perhaps eventually reducing, the demand for ground transportation. Helicopters, originally performing local intrametropolitan and interairport services within such areas as New York, Chicago, Los Angeles, and San Francisco-Oakland, have, in some instances, been supplanted by V/STOL fixed-wing aircraft. The provision of STOL ports and heliports should be an essential element of a metropolitan airport plan. Such facilities may substantially help to solve the problem of airport access from and to the major nodes of traffic generation within the urban areas, and contribute to the slowing up of the rate of growth of gound traffic in major metropolitan areas and urban intercity corridors. They can, in effect, bring the major airports close to the city centers and other major traffic-generating nodes within the urban complex. STOL ports and heliports require far less land area than do airports for conventional fixed-wing planes, and in many instances the land requirements are such that the facilities may be developed in proximity to, or within, central business districts, with shuttle services to the major metropolitan airports and to nearby cities.[16] In any event, the planner should be aware of the competitive cost relationships, at any stage of technological development between helicopters and VTOL and STOL aircraft on the one hand, and ground transportation, including rapid transit and express highways, on the other.

Another type of air carrier service, with an uncertain future, is that of the "supplemental" carriers. These carriers are the "contract" or "charter" air carriers, performing a

16. Federal Aviation Administration, *Planning and Design Criteria for Metropolitan STOL Ports* (Washington, D.C.: The Administration, 1970), 42 pp.

variety of passenger and cargo services, without, however, being permitted to operate on regular schedules. They range from fixed base operators with light aircrafts to large corporations, comparable to some of the medium-sized scheduled carriers in size, and from purely local operations to worldwide intercontinental operations; their equipment includes every type of aircraft, from the smallest to the largest. Consequently, the airport and air terminal requirements of supplemental operators do not differ basically from those of the scheduled carriers, and we need not give them separate consideration.

METROPOLITAN AIRPORT PLANNING   Because airports must be located and developed not only in relation to other elements of the city, metropolitan area, and wider region, but also in relation to air space, which is a national resource, the federal governments both in the United States and in Canada, are actively engaged in the process of airport system planning, and airports must conform to national requirements. In the United States, the FAA has evolved, and annually revised, a National Airport Plan (NAP), which serves as a guide for Congress in the appropriation of funds, and to the FAA in the allocation of funds under the Federal-Aid Airport Program (FAAP). Inclusion of an airport in the National Airport Plan does not assure federal financial aid, since the availability of funds falls far short of the demands, but such inclusion is essential for such funding.

The National Airport Plan, logically favors, in any given metropolitan area, a minimal number of intensively used sophisticated airports, rather than a larger number of smaller airports of limited capacity. There are several reasons for this. The economy of scale is such that larger and more efficiently utilized airports can more nearly approach financial viability, the utilization of air space and air traffic control is more efficient with fewer airports, and there are fewer environmental conflicts. Federal policy generally favors concentration of air carrier traffic at a minimum number of airports within a metropolitan area—one wherever possible—accompanied by the development of "reliever" airports to handle general aviation. Of course, it is not usually possible to exclude general aviation entirely from the major air carrier airports, for much of the general aviation activity is supplementary to, and in connection with, the carrier operations, but it is generally accepted that an effective way of increasing the capacity of major airports for the carrier traffic is to siphon off as much as possible of the general aviation, and thereby maximize the use of available capacity for carrier movements, which, per landing and takeoff, directly serve more passengers than do other forms of aviation activity. Smaller airports, specially designed for VTOL and STOL operations, are in prospect, and are encouraged by federal policy, although, in the early 1970s, it was not clear the extent to which or the rate at which technology, including availability of suitable aircraft and the area requirements for such airports would permit inner-city operations. One of the major considerations in the development of such airports in central city locations, aside from availability of sites, is the problem of noise; another is safety of operations in areas of high-density urban development. Some cities, where waterfront development is possible, such as on landfill, may be particularly favorable for the development of such types of airports, which require shorter runways and hence much less land than do conventional airports.

Federal policy in the United States is generally one of excluding terminal buildings and associated facilities from federal aid, except insofar as necessary to secure maximum efficiency from those portions of the airports, such as runways and navigation facilities, which do receive federal aid.

In the early 1970s, the FAA had under consideration a major revision of its classification of airports, in order to provide a better description of the hierarchy of airports in the national system, and to facilitate evaluation of airports in connection with the federal-aid program. Two criteria are used: function and density. Three major categories are identified: airports in the national system, airports of "local interest," and military types. The airports comprising the national system in turn are divided into three categories: high-density, medium-density, and low-density, and each of these, in turn into two categories: air carrier airports and general aviation airports, although, of course, the former commonly handle general aviation activities, and the latter may handle a small amount of air carrier traffic.

At the end of 1968, there were, in the United States, 10,470 airports, a total which included 555 heliports and 411 seaplane bases. Of the total, 3,986, or slightly less than two-fifths, were owned by cities, states, counties, or the federal government, the remainder being privately owned. Approximately one-third, or 3,312, had lighted runways, and approximately the same number, 3,353, had paved runways. All of these figures have been increasing steadily in recent years. At these airports, 127,164 aircraft were based, including slightly less than 3,000 air carrier aircraft. Thus, the overwhelming proportion of aircraft serviced by the nation's airports are engaged in general aviation. On the other hand, air carrier operations are far more important to the general public than their relative numbers would indicate. Furthermore, since air carrier aircraft are, for the most part, considerably larger than those in general aviation, their terminal requirements, traffic generation, ecological effects, and economic effects are proportionately significant.

Similarly, a very high proportion of air carrier activity is carried on at relatively few airports, and these are located in a few large metropolitan complexes. Communities served by air carriers are classified into several categories, termed large, medium, and small hubs, and nonhubs; these refer to communities and metropolitan areas rather than individual airports, since some of the hubs may be served by more than one carrier airport. The categories are delimited by the proportion of the total air carrier passenger traffic of the nation, as measured by annual enplaned passengers, handled by each community or metropolitan area. In 1968, the large hubs, defined as those generating at least 1 percent of the enplaned air carrier passengers, numbered 22, and included 36 air carrier airports. Each of these hubs had annually at least 1,409,359 enplaned air carrier passengers, representing 1 percent or more of the national air carrier total. In 1968 the largest hub was, of course, New York (Newark was classified as a separate hub), and the busiest airport in the New York area—John F. Kennedy International Airport—enplaned 5.5 million passengers, or about half of the 10.8 million enplaned passengers at the four airports constituting the New York hub, again excluding Newark, which enplaned 3.2 million passengers. By contrast, the busiest single carrier airport in the nation, and in the world, in 1968 was the Chicago O'Hare International Airport, which enplaned nearly 13.4 million passengers, although Chicago ranked second to New York as an air hub. These rankings continued into the early 1970s. The magnitude of the air traffic at these major hubs and airports is indicative of the nature, scale, and character of the problems faced by planners at other important metropolitan areas as the volume of air traffic and hence the airport requirements are expected to approach, in the late 1970s and subsequently, those of the largest hubs of a few years earlier.

In one respect, however, the physical planning problems for future major air hubs may differ from those of the past. This is in terms of the numbers and types of aircraft. On the one hand, there is a growth of "jumbo" aircraft, such as the 747 and DC-10, and, prospectively, a civil version of the massive military C5A; these aircraft handle from 250 to nearly 1,000 passengers in addition to considerable volumes of cargo and mail. With this tremendous capacity, obviously a greatly reduced number of aircraft and movements can handle the present volume of traffic; or the present number of movements, with much larger aircraft, can handle a very much greater volume of traffic. On the other hand, the prospects for shorter flights in smaller aircraft with frequent service at the larger hubs and new services to smaller communities, connecting at the large hubs, may result in an even greater number of plane movements than previously, with cumulative effects upon passenger, cargo, and mail traffic volumes. It must be assumed that the slowing up in the rate of growth of air carrier traffic in the early 1970s, due to economic recession in phase with the introduction of much larger aircraft and consequent excess capacity, was temporary, and that the principal advantage to the planner is that it provided him with a small amount of additional time to anticipate the increases in demand for air travel and associated services and facilities which were forecast.

General aviation airports, of course, constitute the most prevalent type, and typically the urban planner will be concerned with communities which have or will plan for one or more of them. As commuter or "third level" air services proliferate, the demand for general aviation airports will include the handling of such services, in addition to other types of general aviation.

As has been indicated, most general aviation airports are privately owned, either by operators who are in the airport business, or less commonly, as adjuncts to industrial or commercial establishments. Privately owned airports, whether serving the public or not, involve no assurance of permanency, and it is therefore in the public interest to see that the necessary aviation services will be provided for a community, by some form of public ownership or operation. A private airport, generally located on or beyond the periphery of an urbanized area because of the extensive land requirements, is especially vulnerable to conversion to other uses, such as residence, commerce, or industry, as urbanization proceeds to engulf or surround the airport, which generally represents a lower-density, and hence economically less productive per acre, use. In many metropolitan areas, the decrease in number of airports, and particularly those with relatively close-in locations, has become a major inhibitor of further general aviation growth.

Because of the extent of the required sites, the effects upon surrounding areas, the catalytic effect upon both the economic base and the land use pattern of the communities and metropolitan areas, the possible adverse ecological effects, and the amounts of time involved in site selection, acquisition, and development, the location of airports constitutes one of the most important types of decisions that confronts the urban planner.

As in the case of most urban land uses, airport location involves a balance between centripetal, or centralizing forces, and centrifugal, or decentralizing ones. The conventional concept of a negative exponential curve of density and land values, grading away from the core of the city, is of little help to the planner involved in airport location studies, for airports tend to fall outside the normal concepts of urban density because of their unique attributes, including their relatively large size and their relations to their surroundings and the entire metropolitan complex. The largest airports, as has been mentioned, tend to develop, both within and in proximity to their boundaries, as major nuclei of the metropolitan pattern in their own right, and therefore the planner cannot limit his site selection criteria to those of the airport alone.

Availability of land is a major inhibitor in airport site selection. In general, of course, the major metropolitan airports cannot be located close to the metropolitan center, not only because of lack of availability of sites, but also because of difficulties of site assembly, due to relocation, title clearance, zoning problems, and approach zone obstruction clearance problems, in addition to high land values. Thus the major airports serving a metropolitan area will be located at some distance from the center, preferably near the edge of the urbanized area in order to maximize the possibilities of control of the development in the vicinity and to ensure a minimum of incompatible development. But, on the other side of the scale, the airport must be accessible to the major portions of the metropolitan region which constitutes the origins and destinations of the passengers, cargo, and mail, and thus landward access becomes a major factor in site selection. Site conditions, including drainage, slope, bedrock, and soil factors, and local microclimate also constitute important variables, and an initial screening of prospective sites will eliminate many on these grounds.

In the larger metropolitan areas with considerable existing or prospective carrier traffic, a basic decision may be required early in the planning process as to whether the region will have a single major carrier airport, a major one with one or more "reliever" airports with carrier operations, or two or more major carrier airports. On the other hand, it may be feasible to join with other nearby or contiguous cities or metropolitan areas to share a carrier airport at an intermediate location. In any event, the size and character of the site will involve a series of negotiations with the many interested communities and with governmental agencies at all levels, as well as citizen groups having vested interests in locating, or, perhaps more commonly, preventing location of, an airport in their immediate vicinity.

Three major considerations in airport location and development usually involve the planner in extensive discussions and negotiations with special-interest groups. These are: (a) landward access, (b) securing the necessary airspace against obstructions, and (c) ecological effects, including especially noise and air pollution. Transcending and overlapping all of these considerations is the necessity for comprehensive planning of land uses in the areas outside the airport boundary which would be directly affected by the development and operation of the airport and associated facilities.[17]

Access to the airport involves coordination of airport site selection with comprehen-

17. U.S. Dept. of Housing and Urban Development, *Airport Environs: Land Use Controls* (Washington, D.C.: Government Printing Office, 1970), 35 pp.

sive transportation-land use planning for the region. Except for the very largest airports in major air hubs, it may be assumed that access will be by highway. The planner must, therefore, determine the optimal points of accessibility to existing and prospective nodes of traffic generation, in view of the highway network. He should estimate the capacities of existing and future highways throughout the region, balance these against prospective traffic generation, which, in turn, involves considerations of future land use and density patterns, and modify these patterns, using a model which includes alternative locations and numbers of metropolitan airports. Ideally, therefore, airport site selection should be concurrent with, and indeed, a part of, the comprehensive transportation and land use planning operation for a metropolitan area, for the effects of airports and other elements in the metropolitan pattern are reciprocal.

Few airports justify extensive expressway or freeway construction, except, perhaps, in the largest hubs, and then only in the immediate vicinity of the airport. On the other hand, connections between elements of the major freeway or highway network of the metropolitan area and the airport itself may, in many instances, be justified, and determination of the capacity of such connections thus becomes a part of the task of airport planning. Included in such planning is consideration of the extent to which, if any, feeder air services, including the use of V/STOL aircraft, connecting the airport with nearby cities, the central business district, and other traffic-generating nodes, may be provided to relieve ground transportation routes of the total burden. In rare instances of waterfront airport locations, it may be possible, if the "state of the art" develops in the near future, to provide high-speed overwater connections, by hydrofoil, hovercraft, or conventional vessels, to and from the airport.

Rapid transit has attracted much attention in connection with ground access to airports in large metropolitan areas. Early in the 1970s direct rapid transit access to airports was available only in Cleveland, where the Cleveland Transit System line, passing through the central business district, was opened in 1968, but, subsequently, the volume of traffic at the airport station declined. The major traffic there was generated, not by the airport, but by nearby industries only partly associated with airport activity, and by suburbanites who drove to parking lots at the airport or other transit stations along the extension and then rode the transit trains into downtown Cleveland, often using the parking facilities which were primarily intended for airport users, and necessitating a major expansion of parking provision at the airport. In an attempt to remedy this situation, the transit system assessed an extra fare for use of the airport station, thereby further reducing the use of the airport transit extension. In short, America's only existing airport rapid transit direct access, as of the early 1970s was, in many ways, not a very useful model for application elsewhere. Outside the United States, the airport for Brussels is served by a spur of the national railway system with service from downtown stations, the Gatwick (London's second) Airport is on a stop on a main railway route with frequent electric train service, and Tokyo's main airport is connected to the central city by an eight-mile monorail line. Several other cities were, in 1973, planning rapid transit access: Los Angeles by means of an unconventional guide-rail system, New York's Kennedy and Newark airports by branch-line extensions of existing commuter rail systems, and Philadelphia, among other cities, by transit extensions. In a few cases, such as Boston's Logan International Airport, and to some extent LaGuardia Airport in New York, short bus connections from nearby rapid transit lines give access to the airport terminal. But in none of these instances is a major portion of the transit traffic on the line generated by the airport itself. It is clear that only in the very largest metropolitan areas can rapid transit be considered an important means of airport access, and then, in most instances, only if airport-associated industrial and commerical activities are generated by the presence of the airport. Whether access is by highway alone, or in combination with transit, various federal programs of financial assistance can be drawn upon.[18]

Possibly the most troublesome and complex aspect of planning in relation to airports, even more than the planning of the airport itself, is the protection of the area in the vicinity of the airport from development incompatible with the airport, and vice versa. While the urban planner is generally not competent to prepare the detailed plans for the airport proper, the planning of the land uses associated with, or in the vicinity of, the airport but outside its boundary, is of the very essence of urban and metropolitan planning.

In the determination of the extent of the airport proper as well as in the boundaries of its property, it is important that sufficient land be designated, within the boundary, to serve as a buffer between the aviation activities and the land uses outside. A buffer would assist in insulating the surrounding area from a portion of the noise generated by the airport activities, and at the same time would constitute a safety factor, particularly beyond the ends of the runways, where much of the hazard is concentrated during landings and takeoffs. In this context, planners should recognize the reciprocal relationships between the control and guidance of land uses outside the airport boundary on the one hand, and the runway alignment, volume, and type of airport use, and location of terminal facilities within the airport boundary on the other. Not only are noise and environmental pollution problems involved, but also the protection of the air space for effective utilization and safety.

Unfortunately, relatively little can be done to ameliorate noise conditions in the vicinities of existing airports where intensive surrounding development has taken place, other than improvements in the operating characteristics of aircraft and their engines and, in some instances, the establishment of flight patterns associated with approaches, landings, and takeoffs to minimize the annoyance to residential and other developments near the airports, to the extent that such patterns do not jeopardize the safety of air transportation.

Much research has been done on reduction of aircraft noise at the source.[19] It is generally agreed that substantial noise elimination is impossible, but that, through noise suppression devices on engines now in use, and design of future engines, significant improvements may result. In the early 1970s, some of the types of large aircraft which were introduced, including the 747 and DC-10, proved less noisy than their smaller predecessors, and, indeed, the federal government now requires that new aircraft produce

18. Highway Research Board, *Public Transportation to Airports—Seven Reports,* "H. R. B. Record No. 330" (Washington, D.C.: The Board, 1970), 36 pp.
19. U.S. Office of Science and Technology, *Alleviation of Jet Aircraft Noise Near Airports* (Washington, D.C.: Government Printing Office, 1966), 167 pp.

noise below specified thresholds, which are lower than those of many aircraft types in current operation. The supersonic transports, in this context, do not constitute a special problem, because they will operate at subsonic speeds for considerable distances beyond the airports, and in such operations they will be within the permissible noise thresholds. The sonic boom, on the other hand, is an unsolved problem which transcends the problems of urban and metropolitan planning per se.

Aircraft noise abatement strategies involving land use planning and control will differ as between existing airports and prospectives ones. It is not easy, and in many cases impossible, to change significantly the nature of the land uses in the vicinities of existing airports. One reason is that airports, being a relatively new form of urban activity on the time scale of urban development, have served as nuclei around which development, typically, has taken place relatively recently, and the amortization of existing physical developments in their vicinities will take many years. In many instances, changing general urban patterns, together with changes in the technology of air transportation, may indicate eventual abandonment of the older airports with their conversion to other land uses, or major changes in the character of airport use itself may take place as for example, the gradual conversion of smaller carrier airports into general aviation facilities (for example: Detroit City Airport and Akron Municipal Airport). Meanwhile, palliative measures, such as modifications in flight patterns, and perhaps—as at Washington National Airport—the prohibition of certain types of operations during the night, may be used.

Noise will continue to be a major consideration in the location of future airports. As has been mentioned, some reduction in the effects may be obtained by planning the runway configurations so that approach and takeoff flight patterns will pass over areas where the land uses that would adversely be affected will be minimal. Conversely, zoning to guide land uses into locations where the adverse noise effects will be minimal may be an effective approach, although the fragmentation of most urban areas in the vicinities of airports into numerous political units necessitates a high degree of coordination; here the regional or metropolitan planning agency can be invaluable.[20]

A useful device in the evaluation of noise in airport vicinities is the noise contour diagram [Figure 7-8]. Noise contours are directly related to the configuration of the runways, the operating characteristics of given types of aircraft, the configuration of land and water (noise travels farther over water), and wind directions. In addition, the flight paths after takeoff may bend the noise contours. A common measure is the amount of perceived noise, in decibels (PNDB). Another, and more sophisticated measure, used, for example in the recent study which resulted in the decision not to extend New York's JFK International Airport, is the Noise Exposure Forecast (NEF), which is a measure of the intensity and duration of each noise exposure and the time of day at which it occurs, as well as the number of such exposures in a day. As a result of such measures, it has been determined that adverse noise effects may be felt as much as seven or eight miles from an airport.

Regulation and control of land uses in airport vicinities not only can mitigate the effects of noise, but are essential to ensure "clear zones" for air navigation, and to

20. *A Study of the Optimum Use of Land Exposed to Aircraft Landing and Takeoff Noise* (Washington, D.C.: National Aeronautics and Space Administration, 1966), 140 pp.

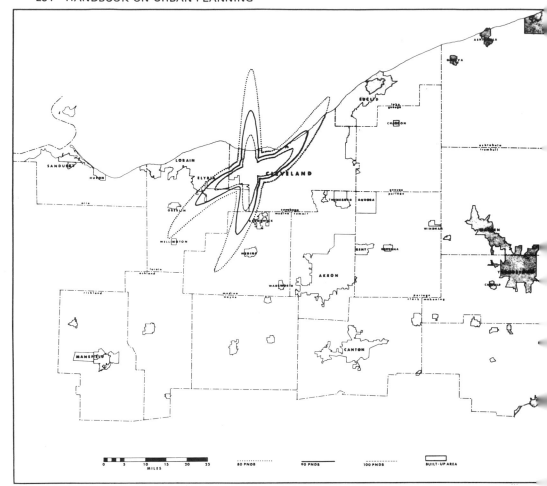

Source: Center for Urban Regionalism, Kent State University

Figure 7-8 Cleveland-Hopkins Airport noise contours.

maximize the safety of landings and takeoffs. To this end, the FAA, and analogous agencies in countries other than the United States, require assurance that the clear zones will be provided. The configuration of such zones will vary, depending upon the type of airport and the character of the anticipated air traffic. Air-space zoning, particularly involving restrictions as to the heights of structures, is therefore an essential prerequisite for any airport, and the urban planner must be aware of the applicable regulations in the vicinity of each existing or prospective airport. In general, height restrictions apply within an air space defined by a sloping surface from the end of each runway, extending outward for several miles, and widening, forming a trapezoid in ground plan, but with the addition of other surfaces at right angles to provide clear approaches for turning movements. Generally, the most restrictive height limitations are applicable to runways used for instrument approaches, and such restrictions involve a slope of 1 foot vertically for each

60 feet horizontally from the end of the runway. At Chicago's O'Hare International Airport, for example [Figure 7-9], the instrument approach zones begin 200 feet from the end of the runway (but well within the airport boundary), and are 50,000 feet long, fanning out in width from 1,000 to 16,000 feet. Noninstrument approach zones extend for 10,000 feet, fanning out from 1,000 to 4,000 feet, and with a slope of 1:50. In addition, there are further restrictions within 20,200 feet of the geometric center of the airport. The high density of air traffic and the large size of the aircraft using O'Hare are indicative of conditions that are, or will be, applicable at major metropolitan airports in many locations.

On the other hand, V/STOL airports will require very substantially less air-space restriction, and can therefore be placed much closer to built-up high density urban areas.

In planning for a metropolitan airport system, not only must the air space in the vicinities of airports be kept clear of obstructions, but the distances between airports must take cognizance of the flight paths of the respective airports, in order to avoid conflicts; this, of course, creates minimal distance thresholds within which adjacent

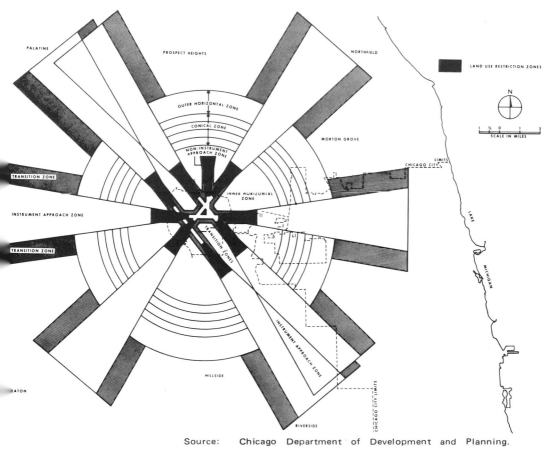

Source: Chicago Department of Development and Planning.

Figure 7-9 Land use restriction zones in the vicinity of Chicago-O'Hare International Airport.

airports cannot be developed; such distances, obviously are a function of the character of the respective airports and their types of traffic. The planner should work in conjunction with the FAA, or the counterpart national agency in other countries, to ensure that such conflicts will not arise.

The guidance and control of land uses under the "clear space" zones, related to the flight paths, is a major challenge to the planner. In most instances, it is necessary to secure coordination of the zoning and land use planning of several or many municipalities, and, in most instances, of unincorporated areas as well; in the latter case county zoning may be applicable. Not only must height restrictions be compatible with the air-space regulations described, but the character and density of land uses and structures below the restricted zones must be such as not only to minimize the adverse effects, in terms of noise and safety, under and near the flight paths, but also to secure maximum economic and other advantages from the proximity of the airport. Near some of the largest airports, for example, more than 50,000 people may be employed, directly or indirectly, as a result of the airport location, and industrial and commercial activities there may constitute major nodes in the metropolitan fabric, rivaling the central business district, or other important industrial and commercial concentrations. In addition, the presence of major airports may exert a metropolitan-wide "pull," the effects of which can significantly alter the entire metropolitan land use and functional structure.

In general, land uses under the "clear paths" should be of low density, and close to the airport boundaries under such paths, building should be avoided wherever possible. Ideally, such land should be in public ownership, but practically the costs in most instances dictate some types of private use. Residential use should generally be prohibited under at least the inner portions of the clear zones, and schools and other establishments involving dense concentrations of people should in no instance be placed there; preferable uses would include open types, such as parks, golf courses, cemeteries, and forest preserves, or other open forms of institutional use. Where airport sites are adjacent to extensive water areas, the problems of land use are, of course, reduced, although there may be other considerations, such as local meteorological and ecological conditions, which must be considered in deciding for or against airports at such locations.

CONCLUSION

The urban and metropolitan planner, as has been shown, must consider the provision and protection of land for transportation routes and terminals which link his city or region to the rest of the world as a major essential in the formulation and effectuation of comprehensive plans. The very nature or urban development rests upon the specialized functions that cities perform, and the functions in turn depend upon such external links.

All transportation, regardless of mode, constitutes elements in a single interrelated system, and all land uses, in turn, depend upon the accessibility provided by that system. The planning of transportation and the planning of land uses must go hand-in-hand, and the two together form the physical and functional pattern of city and region.

The planning of a transportation system, or of any of its components, is a complex task, not only because such system forms the skeleton of the entire urban and regional pattern, but also because of the numerous interests involved, including, usually, a complex of reciprocal relationships between transportation and other elements of city and region; lack of centralized authority, since the system is comprised of a mixture of public and private ownerships and operations; a multiplicity of local governments; and, in many instances, seemingly incompatible competitive relationships among the elements of the system. Paradoxically, in many instances there is a redundancy of transportation while at the same time intolerable congestion and inefficiency exists in some parts of the system. In addition, the planner is faced with the difficulty resulting from rapid techno-logical change while at the same time transportation involves long-term investment in physical plant which is largely fixed in location. In spite of new and unconventional modes now being introduced, such as monorail, guideway vehicles, ground effect vehicles including hovercraft, and "people movers" or continuous-flow devices such as moving belts, it is generally agreed that the existing modes will continue to dominate in the foreseeable future, and the planner should therefore operate accordingly, but with sufficient flexibility so as not to retard the introduction of new modes in suitable situations. In any event, land transportation will continue to carry most of the passenger and goods traffic, supplemented by water and air traffic in some situations; land traffic requires rights-of-way, and all modes require terminals. Whatever forms may develop in the future, individual passenger vehicles—the automobile or some modification of it—will continue to be important, along with the motortruck, and these will continue to require rights-of-way. On the other hand, intercity mass transportation of people and goods will continue to demand sites for terminals in and near urban areas, and such terminals will continue to be major foci for a multitude of activities constituting import nodes in the urban structure. Therefore, the urban and metropolitan planner must be familiar with the elements of the intercity, interregional, national and international transportation system, its intermodal character, its main elements, and, in particular, its right-of-way and terminal requirements, as well as its complex of effects upon urban, metropolitan, regional, national, and international economic, social and especially physical, develop-ment.

   Since the internal transportation system of a city and metropolitan area is not only complementary to, but also a part of, the external system, the next chapter is concerned with the planning of the internal circulation of city and region.

TRANSPORTATION FACILITIES PLANNING– INTERNAL

Herbert A. Goetsch

The subject of transportation facilities planning covered in Chapter 7 has special implications when applied to the internal transportation needs of a municipality. The basic task of an urban transportation system is to move people and goods from one place to another. This bears restating so that the primary purpose is never forgotten. It further implies certain starting and terminal points as well as channels of movement. We see the basic land uses and activities connected by a street network and recognize the inseparability of city land use planning and transportation planning.

THE TRANSPORTATION PLANNING PROCESS

The Federal Aid Highway Act of 1962 provided that in order to be eligible for federal aid cities over 50,000 in population had to have an approved transportation plan which was "comprehensive" as well as "area wide." The term "comprehensive" was subsequently defined by the U.S. Bureau of Public Roads to mean that the transportation planning process must concern itself with both highway and transit facilities including terminal facilities and traffic control systems. It must be based on the collection, analysis, and interpretation of all pertinent data concerning existing conditions and historical trends. The transportation planning process must, therefore, include the collection and analysis of basic data on the following elements: (a) economic factors affecting development; (b) population; (c) land use; (d) transporation facilities, including those for mass transportation; (e) travel patterns; (f) terminal and transfer facilities; (g) traffic control features; (h) local plans and zoning; (i) financial resources; and (j) social and community value factors such as preservation of open space, historical sites and buildings, parks and recreational facilities, and environmental amenities and aesthetics.

The process must also include provision for the establishment of community goals and objectives; the preparation of forecasts of future land development and travel patterns; and the selection from alternatives, adoption, implementation, and continuing evaluation, refinement, and updating of land use and transportation facility plans.[1]

Stated another way, the transportation planning process should include three distinct steps in the attempt to improve mobility. First, the plan should provide for ways to obtain the maximum benefit from existing transportation facilities and services. Second, the plan should outline the evolutionary changes to be undertaken within a specific and reasonable time by coordinating all existing equipment and technology to provide for all required travel modes. Third, the plan should include basic and applied research into new technology and equipment which will be needed to meet the future transportation objectives of the municipality.

INTERNAL TRANSPORTATION SYSTEM OBJECTIVES

The objectives of the internal transportation plan should coincide with the overall community objectives. They should be concerned with the social, economic, health, safety, aesthetic, and other environmental values of the municipality. Transportation systems, like all community facility systems, must exist solely to serve and sustain the more basic land use activities. They should serve the people with safe, efficient, reliable, convenient, and economical transportation. This must include all segments of the population with varying and sometimes conflicting needs.

While some of the expressed short-range objectives may aim to relieve congestion, increase safety, provide greater service, and reduce pollution, the long-range objectives of an internal transportation plan should be to assist in improving the spatial organization of the municipality to provide new activities and increased opportunities for its people.

BASIC PLANNING DATA

Because of the impetus given by federal requirements cited previously, much basic transportation planning data is available in larger cities. An analysis of some of these planning studies and the results achieved gives the urban transportation planner a wealth of information in determining the type of data required for his municipality. These can

1. *Southeastern Wisconsin Regional Planning Commission Newsletter*. Vol. 8, No. 3 (June 1968), p. 4.

be readily found in local planning and engineering departments, in the offices of regional planning agencies, and in the files of state and federal transportation agencies. Some of the factors are briefly described here.

Inventory of Existing Facilities

An inventory of existing facilities involving the street system, rights of way, transit systems, equipment, terminals, and technology is essential. The public has a substantial investment in these facilities. They currently serve the transportation needs of the municipality, if not adequately, at least to a substantial degree. Many of the facilities are rather permanent in character. Some of these will be described later under the subject of components of local transportation systems.

Existing and Projected Land Use

Since World War II, the United States and Canada have experienced drastic changes in land use, especially in the move from central cities to suburbs and rural areas. This has been true of residential, industrial, and commercial activities. This trend must be researched to determine its magnitude, its rate of change, and the reasons for such change. Projections of these trends, together with desired modifications, must be made.

Population

Throughout the history of the United States the population has grown and there has been a steady trend from rural to urban population. Since World War II much of this growth has been in suburban areas, with central cities in many instances losing population. The population trends give rise to the consideration of entire metropolitan areas for transportation planning. The trend to lower overall densities has substantially altered transportation needs.

Economic and Social Trends

Improvement in living standards and the economic well-being of people have contributed to the demand for greater transportation opportunities. At the same time this has been a factor in the increased cost of transportation. The shortage of local funds derived to a large extent from property tax has resulted in more state and federal funds normally from user taxes being applied to local transportation activities.

General affluence has affected social trends also, with more people seeking work and recreation at greater distances from their homes. However, the realization of the breadth and depth of social requirements in our urban areas is just emerging. Much research is needed to determine their impact on the transportation plan. Although the transportation system may benefit the community as a whole, many individuals or groups may be adversely affected thereby. The needs of certain groups, such as the poor, the elderly, racial minorities, and the handicapped, may not be reflected in the traditional data gathering methods.

External Systems

The presence or absence of external traffic facilities, such as airports, railroads, freeways, and interurban buslines which provide traffic service between cities or metropolitan areas, will greatly affect local traffic facilities. In order to properly plan the local transportation setup, the current impact of and the future anticipated additions or alterations to these external facilities should be determined. Any local transportation plan should purposely be extended beyond political boundaries as required.

Jurisdictional Systems

No transportation plan will have any value unless it contains the details leading toward implementation. Transportation responsibilities have traditionally been divided among several units and levels of government. Normally local units of government, county transportation agencies, regional or special authorities, state departments of transportation, and the U.S. Department of Transportation will all be involved except in minor local plans.

Financial Resources

A variety of sources for financing local transportation projects exist. These may include user taxes, user charges, property taxes, benefit assessments, state and federal aid, revenue bonds, and general obligation bonds. Conditions may vary greatly from one locality to another and from one point in time to another. Proper research and evaluation of this factor is critical.

COMPONENTS OF A LOCAL TRANSPORTATION SYSTEM

A local transportation system contains a multiplicity of components whose nature, function, and influence need to be evaluated and understood. These can be broadly grouped into three physical categories. These are: (a) roadways, (b) mass transportation, and (c) terminals.

Roadways

The principal transportation arteries for land transportation in an urban area are the various roadways. They are the arteries on which automobiles, trucks, buses, and pedestrians move from place to place. Standards regarding right of way, roadway and lane widths, alignments, clearances, and similar design requirements have been well defined by traffic engineers and frequently adopted by local planning agencies and state and federal transportation departments.

Freeways are fully controlled access roadways which have the ability to carry high volumes of traffic at relatively high speeds with a high factor of safety. In many large cities they have become the framework around which other transportation is planned. Most freeways appear to be superimposed on the urban area as a combination of radial and circumferential arteries, including generally a loop around the central business district [Figure 8-1]. Freeways greatly affect developed areas by causing displacement of people and activities. This has led to objections on the part of the general public. Freeways in undeveloped areas have stimulated substantial industrial and commercial development. This has been true in the case of belt-line freeways around urban areas [Figure 8-2]. Comprehensive planning is required to assure maximum benefits with the least disruption of the urban environment. This should include joint usage of the right-of-way and possible excess land acquisition to provide for open space and other public uses. Somewhat less elaborate than freeways are expressways and parkways which have partial control of access and serve special traffic needs.

Arterial streets provide for through traffic movements between areas and across the city. They may serve as collectors and distributors of freeway traffic. They do not provide direct access to abutting property. Collector streets serve subdivisions or districts

Source: Denver Planning Departmen

Figure 8-1 Part of a modern urban freeway system—Denver's Valley Highway, Interstate 25.

Source: Howard, Needles, Tammen, and Bergendoff.

Figure 8-2 Milwaukee interchange on Interstate 94.

of a city and provide for traffic movement between arterials and local streets. Direct access to abutting properties is provided on collector streets. Local streets are for local traffic movements only and serve abutting properties with direct access. The gridiron street pattern found in older sections of cities permits some through traffic movement. Newer subdivision layouts provide for curving streets and cul-de-sacs which discourage through traffic. Access to properties abutting on arterials is furnished by alleys or service roads.

Every automobile or mass transit vehicle rider becomes a pedestrian at some time in his trip from origin to destination. Sidewalks are provided along major arteries and collectors and on certain local streets, especially those leading to schools. Concern for the safety and convenience of the pedestrian may dictate complete separation of pedestrian and vehicular traffic in congested areas. This has led to the construction of pedestrian overpasses and underpasses. Both have cost and operational disadvantages, but these can be minimized by proper planning and design.

In the late 1960s several cities, notably Minneapolis, Minnesota, and Cincinnati, Ohio, began the installation of elevated pedestrian walkways in connection with downtown redevelopment activities. Rather than merely bridging a street these walkways are designed to be a continuous network of pedestrian walks at the second level.

Street rights-of-way contain a number of features which perhaps affect the abutting property as much as they affect the traffic movement. Streetlighting facilities can greatly increase the feeling of security in the city by deterring crime. Street trees not only beautify the city but reduce the effects of noise and automobile exhaust fumes.

Proper planning will permit the use of certain streets as ceremonial and parade routes. Other purely local streets may be temporarily barricaded for neighborhood recreational and civic activities. This may have great community value in areas of the city where there is insufficient open space.

Mass Transportation

Movement of large numbers of persons in a single vehicle or train is normally performed by some form of mass transit, sometimes referred to as public transit. This mode of transportation serves many workers during peak hours. It also serves the so-called "captive" rider who has no other means readily available. This includes the young, the old, the infirm, and the poor. Most transit services are provided by rubber-tired buses, with fixed rail transit being used in certain large cities where rail facilities and rights-of-way are available.

Mass transit usage was at an all-time high in the United States during World War II, but in the 20 years 1945-65 it declined nearly 64 percent. This decline is largely attributable to the enormous increase in the use of the private automobile for travel to and from work. Because of the pattern of development of American cities during these years, transit is faced with several operational difficulties. These are the passenger collection problem, the passenger distribution problem, and the "peak" problem. The latter is caused by riders commuting to and from work. This leads to high operating costs, since a much larger capacity of equipment and manpower is required to meet peak loads for only 3 or 4 hours per day than is required for the average operation.

Public transit systems in a city are generally a combination of local service, express service, and rapid service. Local transit uses the public streets and makes local stops. Express service uses local streets but stops only at major points along the way. Rapid service may be provided by either rail or bus and uses high-speed service rights-of-way that have grade separated crossings with other traffic arteries.

The transit network of a region should include (a) the collection of persons located in relatively scattered residential areas using facilities such as feeder bus systems, automobile park and ride, walking, etc., (b) the delivery between residential areas and the downtown area using line-haul rapid transit systems, and (c) the distribution of persons to ultimate destinations. The distributor system in the downtown area can take a variety of forms, ranging from simple pedestrian paths or bus systems on existing street to mechanized loops on exclusive rights-of-way.[2]

2. Lester A. Hoel, *The Planning Environment for Urban Transportation*, "ASCE Meeting Preprint 666," May 1968.

Terminals

Terminals for people, goods, and vehicles are important components of the total transportation system. They may serve highway-oriented vehicles like automobiles, trucks, and buses, or railways, airports, or water ports. Whatever their function, they should be carefully incorporated into the transportation plan. Their locations and functions should be coordinated with the land use plan of the area.

Perhaps the most critical terminal problem involves the setting aside of space for automobiles to park. With the spectacular increase in the use of the automobile since World War II came the demand for more parking. The most acute need occurred in the CBD of cities. Parking can be provided at the curb, in lots, or in structures. Requirements of zoning and building codes that owners of commercial properties be required to provide a proportionate amount of off-street parking have been found to be impractical in the CBD. Private enterprise generally has not been able to meet the demand, so municipal governments have invested deeply in off-street parking lots and garages.

Parking needs are closely related to the size of a city, vehicle ownership, and intensity of downtown development. Parking study procedure has become rather well standardized and guides for conducting parking studies can be readily obtained from traffic or highway agencies.

Parking facilities should be located in areas where there are unmet demands for parking. They should be closely associated with parking generators such as banks, office buildings, hotels, and retail establishments, so that walking distances will not be too great. They should also be so located that they will attract parkers on their primary trip and consequently minimize circulation in the CBD. Access to and from the street system should be convenient. Parking charges should be structured to make the facility economically sound but should not be so high that usage will be discouraged.

Fee structures have in many cases favored the long-term parker, whereas turnover parking is the most profitable. There are many examples of financially profitable parking facilities, while others are deliberately subsidized. In some cities parking fee receipts, including those from meters at the curb, are segregated and used to develop and maintain parking facilities.

Private enterprise will generally provide the parking required in the operation of a specific facility such as a hotel or bank. Municipal governments have the advantages of eminent domain in the acquisition of land, a tax-exempt status and lower interest rates on bonds. Some cities have established public parking authorities which enjoy many of the advantages of a municipal t peration without governmental and political pressures.

A municipality may encounter many parking demands outside the CBD. Older residential areas developed before the automobile was used extensively may now have a greater automobile population than can be accommodated on private property. Schools, colleges, hospitals, stadiums, and some older industries may have major parking needs. Outlying shopping centers have provided their own parking. These and other outlying lots should be integrated with freeway and rapid transit systems.

Bus and train terminals for passengers coming from other cities or suburban areas should be so located that they will serve the core of the CBD. There should be a convenient interface with taxis, private cars, local buses, and pedestrian faciliites. Freight train terminals in urban areas are generally on the fringe of the densely developed core, so that goods can be readily distributed. The necessary freight transit buildings and motor-truck facilities should be available, as should ready access to the freeway or arterial street system.

With the development of freeways and other high-type highways in the United States has come an increase in trucking of freight. The large trucks and trailers travel long distances via highway and the trailers in some instances "piggyback" on railroads. As they reach their destination it is desirable to restrict such trucks to certain major highways leading to truck terminals where loads are broken down for distribution. These terminals or distribution centers generate their own needs for fuel, food, and lodging facilities which should be considered when planning these centers.

Airport planning has become extremely important in most urban areas since World War II. The usage of airline passenger and cargo service has been growing at a rate greater than past predictions indicated. While early airports were planned without respect to the community design this situation has changed greatly as maximum benefits to the area were sought and major environmental problems were created.

An airport system consists of the publicly owned airports which serve a city, county, or metropolitan area. There should be a determination of the geographic area to be served by the system, its economic characteristics, and its air travel market demands. The airport planner should consider several factors. Local air travel market characteristics and distribution should be determined for economic justification and to establish priority with regard to other municipal needs. Air space utilization and control should be studied to determine the proper location and layout of an airport and aircraft operating capability at that site. Present and proposed land uses should be evaluated to determine availability and cost of land, impact of airport operation on adjacent land uses, and ability of related land uses to develop. The accessibility of the airport-to-ground transportation should be studied to determine whether full airport potential can be obtained.

The plan should provide for a balanced design in which all components complement each other. The operating air space must be in balance with the airport capacity, which must be in balance with terminal capacity, which in turn must be in balance with the ground access and parking system [Figure 8-3]. The major ground transportation services for air passengers consist of the franchised airport bus or limousine, public bus, taxis, private autos, and rental cars. In a few instances direct subway or surface rail or helicopter service is available. Since air travel demand tends to peak in the morning and evening, access travel should be planned to accommodate this.

Airport planning should include the consideration that certain land uses in the commercial, industrial, and recreational categories may well be located near airports, since they are not greatly affected by the noise of the aircraft nor will they be any significant compromise to safety. As the demand for air travel increases, the planner must carefully evaluate the effects of expanding existing facilities or establishing satellite airports. Several federal agencies provide financial assistance for comprehensive community and airport planning.

Ports and harbors are the terminals of waterborne traffic in cities located on the seacoast or on inland waterways. While some passenger service is provided, the major water traffic involves bulk cargo. Special transportation planning is required to provide the required highway, trucking, and rail facilities for the transport of goods to and from the port. Provisions must also be made for safe accessibility of employees, passengers, and sightseers.

TRANSPORTATION SYSTEM EVALUATION

The evaluation of any system is determined by how well it meets the goals that have been established. For a transportation system, two general categories of goals are recognized, those of movement and environment. The first involves the desire of the individual for convenient, efficient, economical, and safe transportation, whereas the second involves the social, economic, and physical impacts that the transportation system makes on the individual, his neighborhood, his city or region. What makes any evaluation more difficult is the fact that certain of the goals conflict. Untold instances have been encountered by traffic planners where the public demanded a particular transportation facility but no one wanted it in his neighborhood.

Meaningful criteria should be established to measure the degree of goal achievement. Some measurements can be expressed in objective, highly quantified terms such as of dollars, or passengers per mile per hour. Others must be expressed in subjective, nonquantitative terms. All must be expressed in terms which are meaningful to the general public and to public officials. Normally an evaluation of a series of alternates is made. This may involve the comparison of one route versus another or one transportation mode as against another. Where possible, the evaluation should be made of alternatives involving multimodal systems, since this is what most systems are.

Transportation system characteristics which can be measured are: (a) public investment requirements; (b) user movement effects; (c) environmental effects; and (d) implementation considerations. Public investments include the cost of construction, mainte-

Source: Photo by Colorado Visitors Bureau.

Figure 8-3 Stapleton International Airport, Denver, showing access and parking facilities.

nance, and operation of the system compared to available financial resources. User movement effects include all the qualities of the transportation system which directly affect the user and his ability to travel. Among these are: (a) the cost to the user as it relates to his ability to pay; (b) availability; (c) speed, travel time, and delay; (d) flexibility; (e) convenience; (f) reliability; and (g) safety. Environmental effects are those benefits and disadvantages to the residents of the area and the environs of the system. These effects are not as readily understood as those affecting the user directly. They include (a) influence on desired and undesired growth and development; (b) amount of social disruption caused; (c) disruption of existing activities; (d) effect on aesthetics; (e) degree of noise created; (f) pollutional effects; and (g) effect on natural geographical features. Implementation considerations involve coordination with other development programs; availability of legal, financial, and administrative resources to implement; and necessity for public action such as zoning.

Evaluation can be done in several ways. One employs the threshold approach in which minimum values are assigned to the criteria. Unless the plan meets these values it is rejected. Another is the comparative approach in which values are assigned to the criteria for each alternative and then measured as the difference between them as a ratio of one to the other, or as the degree by which each meets an established ideal value. A combination of the two approaches can be used by comparing only those that meet threshold values.

It is often desirable to apply a cost-benefit analysis when analyzing transportation systems. The object is to compare the input cost with the output consequences. These results may include increased monetary profits, reduction in cost of operation, increased personal or community satisfactions, or adverse or beneficial social, environmental, and community effects.

Another type of analysis that can be used to evaluate transportation systems is the cost-effectiveness analysis. According to this method a determination is made as to what input costs are required to produce different degrees of success toward reaching a goal. This analysis will show the trade-offs of economy of the transportation system required to reduce undesirable social or environmental consequences.

These analyses offer considerable assistance to the public and to the decision-makers in understanding the relative merits of alternative transportation system plans.

FUTURE SYSTEMS

As we look toward the future, we see a greater need for planning. Despite many experiments and research projects that have been carried on to develop new transportation technology, the changes are likely to be incremental in character, with no drastic breakthrough and consisting mainly of improvements to current facilities. Transportation planning and urban planning must proceed together [Figure 8-4] . As in the past transportation plans and modes will attempt to respond to public needs, but their application may continue to lag behind the demand. This is not because technology is lacking, but because of the many other constraints, such as the investments in current facilities, lack of

Source: Perry Park, Colorado, Lee Stubblefield, Developer, and Charles Gathers and Associates.

Figure 8-4 Example of integrated land and transportation planning—New City of 120,000 population.

financial resources, institutional inertia, and reluctance to undertake change.

In the early 1970s we saw the evidence of the development of major activity centers (MAC), low-density expansion on the periphery of urban areas, and an increase in overall travel demands. Development of pedestrian distribution facilities such as moving belts and escalators will become a necessity in major activity centers. In low-density areas the automobile will continue to be the major vehicle, with dial-a-bus or special taxi service for nondrivers. For longer trips there will be faster buses, some on exclusive rights-of-way, increased use of rail mass transit in special corridors, and the continued use of the automobile.

The automobile may undergo some changes in involving its power source and additional safety features and exhaust control. The dual-mode vehicles, automated vehicle control systems, tracked air-cushion vehicles, and gravity-vacuum or tube systems are technologically possible, but their application on a large scale does not appear imminent. The transportation planner must, therefore, reckon with future transportation technology as well as the future urban form and scale.

BIBLIOGRAPHY

1. Wilbur S. Smith, *Urban Planning Guide*, "ASCE Manuals and Reports on Engineering Practice No. 49" (1969), Chap. 7, "Transportation Planning."
2. John W. Dyckman, "Transportation in Cities," *Scientific American*, Sept. 1965, pp. 163-174.
3. Robley Winfrey, *Economic Analysis for Transportation—A Guide for Decision Makers*, Highway Users Federation for Safety and Mobility, March 1971.

9 | REGULATORY AND INCENTIVE MEASURES

Russell H. Riley

Several of the preceding chapters have discussed the planning of physical facilities—streets, parks, schools, and public buildings, among others. These are essential for the satisfactory functioning of urban areas and should ensure many conveniences and economies. The plans for these facilities are, however, intended as general guides for future improvements, rather than as assurance that the improvements will be completed in the exact location and character shown on the general plans. Planning legislation in many states provides that, after such general plans have been officially adopted by the Planning Commission (some also authorize concurrence by the legislative body), any improvement proposed by a public agency which is similar to the facility planned for shall be submitted to the Planning Commission for study and report before the project is initiated. If the commission does not approve the project, it can still be initiated, usually by a two-thirds approval by the sponsoring agency. Even though the Planning Commission does not have complete control over its official plans, there are many advantages in the procedures requiring that improvements affecting them be submitted for study and report before they are initiated. This assures that public agencies will become familiar with the comprehensive plan and usually adjustments can be agreed upon that will be advantageous to all.

REGULATORY MEASURES

Regulatory measures are an important part of comprehensive planning, but have different characteristics than the general plan. As the name implies, they are regulations and controls rather than guides. While prepared and approved by the Planning Commission, they are officially adopted in ordinance form by the legislative body—usually after a study and report by the Planning Commission. They have such an immediate and direct control upon citizens, and especially property owners, that they are officially adopted only after duly advertised public hearings have been held thereupon.

In earlier decades, there were two major types of regulatory measures directly related to comprehensive planning; these were zoning and subdivision regulations. A few states, particularly New York and Wisconsin, have also enacted enabling regulations authorizing municipalities to adopt and enforce official street maps. Even before these, municipalities had adopted and enforced building codes for sound design and construction of buildings in order to protect the health and safety of the general public. In more recent years, regulatory measures directed toward prevention of air and water pollution are receiving widespread attention and are being adopted in many areas. Each of the several major types of regulation is separately discussed in this chapter.

Zoning

Following is a discussion of the more important factors regarding zoning regulations.

EARLY HISTORY   The first comprehensive zoning ordinance in this country was adopted in New York City in 1916. Prior to this date, several California cities had adopted ordinances controlling land uses; but the New York City ordinance was the first to contain height and area regulations, as well as land use controls. Even before the New York City ordinance had been enacted, the United States Supreme Court had upheld, in the well known case of *Hadacheck* v. *Sebastian*, an ordinance of the city of Los Angeles, California, prohibiting brickmaking within a designated area.

In November 1926, the United States Supreme Court issued a second outstanding decision upon zoning. This was the well-known Euclid Village decision. In the case of *Euclid* v. *Ambler Realty Company*, it held that the legislative body of the village of Euclid, Ohio, had the right to adopt and enforce comprehensive zoning regulations.[1] This decision was a major influence in encouraging American cities and towns to adopt zoning regulations.

In 1921, Herbert Hoover, then Secretary of the Department of Commerce, appointed an advisory committee to draft a model zoning enabling act which would serve as a standard or guide for state legislatures, and thus authorize their municipalities to adopt and enforce zoning regulations. The committee approved the act a few years later, and by 1925, it was adopted in whole or part by nineteen states. The standard or model act was further amended in 1926.

Although the first comprehensive zoning ordinance was not adopted until 1916, zoning activities spread rapidly thereafter, especially during the 1920s. According to data compiled by the Department of Commerce, only 48 cities and towns with a total

1. *Village of Euclid* v. *Ambler Realty Company (Ohio)* 272 U.S. 365 S. Ct. 114, 71 L. Ed. 303

population of less than 11,000,000 inhabitants had adopted zoning regulations by September 1921 whereas on January 1, 1926, there were at least 425 zoned municipalities comprising more than one-half of the country's urban population. More and more cities and towns have continued to adopt zoning regulations, particularly since the federal government began financial assistance to planning projects under the "701" programs. While no recent data has been released regarding the present number of zoned municipalities, they probably represent about 90 percent of all incorporated areas. As late as 1971, Houston, Texas, was the only large city in the United States that had not adopted a zoning ordinance. Because of increase in population and new zoning techniques a large majority of the older ordinances have been revised in recent years.

In addition to municipalities, zoning regulations are also being adopted in counties and, in some states, in townships—especially in Michigan, Wisconsin, and Pennsylvania. The need for county and township zoning arose from the spreading of urban development beyond corporate limits and the need to guide and protect this new growth, especially where cities were not authorized to exercise extra jurisdictional control. There was also a need to prevent scattered and objectionable development in the rural sections, and especially to protect good farmland from premature residential subdivisions. County zoning is becoming increasingly popular, particularly around or near large urban areas. A separate enabling act is necessary to authorize counties or townships to adopt zoning regulations.

Hawaii is the only state that has adopted statewide zoning regulations. Such a practice is more feasible in this state since counties, rather than municipalities, are the smallest local units of government. Officials and citizens of other states have considered the potential advantages of statewide zoning or land use controls, but no enabling legislation has been enacted.

ELEMENTS OF ZONING   Practically all state zoning enabling acts authorize municipalities to adopt and enforce three major types of regulations. They are: (a) *use* regulations—namely the uses that may be made of land and structures; (b) *height* regulations, specifying the maximum heights to which buildings may be erected; and (c) *area* regulations, which include two different types of controls—one is the minimum amount of open space in the form of front, side, and rear yards that must be provided around buildings and structures; and the other is lot area per family. This latter regulation controls the minimum size of lots that must be provided for single-family dwellings, as well as the maximum number of living units that may be provided in multifamily dwellings (apartments).

While it is seldom specifically authorized, modern zoning ordinances also control the minimum number of off-street parking spaces that must be provided to serve the uses made of the lots. Such regulations are essential under modern conditions due to the extensive use of automobiles.

It should be emphasized that zoning regulations exercise no controls over the cost of a building or over its design and structural details. The latter is controlled by the building code.

State enabling acts usually clearly state the objectives of zoning regulations and factors that should be considered in developing them. Typical of these is the following section from the Missouri Enabling Act:

"The regulations shall be in accordance with a plan to lessen congestion on the public streets, to promote public health, safety and general welfare, to avoid congestion of population, to facilitate adequate provision for a system of transportation, sewage disposal, water supply and other public requirements. It further provides that the regulations shall give reasonable consideration, among other things, to the character of the districts, their peculiar suitability for particular uses, the conservation of property values, and the general trends and character of building and population development."

The portion of the foregoing requirements regarding lessening of congestion and the promotion of the public health, safety, and general welfare are usual requirements for regulations adopted under the police power. They are of basic importance, however, and it should be noted that it is the public rather than individual interest that should be improved or protected.

PREPARING THE ZONING ORDINANCE   The zoning ordinance consists of two separate items. The first is a district map showing the location and extent of the several zones within the area being zoned. Normally, the zones are for residential, commercial, and industrial uses and there are usually several different zones under each of these major classifications. The text of the ordinance contains the regulations within each of the zones shown on the district map. Current practice is to first describe or list the permitted uses and then to prescribe the maximum height; the minimum front, side, and rear yards; and the minimum lot area per family requirements [Figure 9-1]. The off-street parking requirements for different uses are usually contained in a separate section of the ordinance and are related to floor area, seating capacity, or number of employees.

The text of the ordinance also contains procedures for changes and amendments in both the regulations and district map, as well as procedures for variations and adjustments. The latter are normally handled by a special board (Board of Adjustments or Board of Appeals), although in some states the final decision thereon can be made only by the legislative body. Zoning regulations are enforced by checking applications for permits for new buildings, or the enlargement or alteration of existing buildings, to determine that they conform thereto.

The data compiled in the studies and proposals for other elements of the general plan will be of major assistance in preparing the zoning ordinance and district map. Accurate, up-to-date base maps are essential. They normally are at scales ranging from 1″ to 200′ to 1″ to 500′. In townships and counties, the scale can be larger (up to 1″ to 1 mile) but any unincorporated urbanized area should be shown as an insert at the larger scale. The base map should show location of streets, railroad rights-of-way, parks and water areas, and lot lines.

Information essential to the preparation of zoning regulations is a map showing location and extent of existing land uses. It will be recalled that enabling acts provide that zoning regulations should consider existing conditions, and the land use map graphically

KENT COUNTY, DELAWARE

Zoning District	Maximum Height		Maximum Overall Density	Minimum Lot Requirements			Minimum Yard Requirements			
	Feet	Stories	A. Dwelling Units Per Acre B. Average Lot Size Per Dwelling Unit	Lot Area In Square Feet	Width of Lot (Measured At The Bldg Line)	Depth of Lot	Depth of Front	Width of Each Side Yard (Two Required)	Aggregate Width of Side Yards	Depth of Rear Yard
A-C agricultural-conservation	35	2½	A. 0.5 D.U./acre B. Two acres	43,560	200	200	50	30	60	50
A-R agricultural-residential	35	2½	A. 2.0 D.U./acre B. One half acre	18,000	100	125	30	20	50	40
R-1 Single-family residential	35	2½	A. 3.6 D.U./acre B. 12,000 sq.ft.	8,000	65	100	25	10	20	25
R-2 Multiple-family residential	40	3	1-Fam. or 2-Fam. A. 11.6 D.U./acre B. 7,500 sq.ft.	7,000	60	100	25	10; 3-sty.: 15	20; 3-sty.: 30	25; 3-sty.: 30
			3-Fam. A. 11.0 D.U./acre B. 4,000 sq.ft. ea.	12,000	80	100	25	10; 3-sty.: 15	20; 3-sty.: 30	25; 3-sty.: 30
			4-fam. A. 14.5 D.U./acre B. 3,000 sq.ft. ea.	12,000	80	100	25	10; 3-sty.: 15	20; 3-sty.: 30	25; 3-sty.: 30
			Town house A. 9.0 D.U./acre B. 4,840 sq.ft.	2,000	18	100	25	10	20	25
RMH residential mobile homes	—		A. 8 units/acre B. 3,600 sq.ft.	See special regulations contained in article 4						
PUD planned unit development	See special regulations		Determined by district in which property is located	See special regulations contained in article 4						
B-1 neighborhood business	35	2½	Dwellings must be associated with business use				50	For dwellings: same as R-1		
			Other bldgs.: none	none	none	none		None except adjacent to R zone. See art. 4		
B-2 general business	40	3	Dwellings must be associated with business use				50	For dwellings: same as R-1		
			Other bldgs.: none	none	none	none		None except adjacent to R zone. See art. 4		
M-1 limited industrial	35	2½	Dwellings not permitted Avg. lot size: 43,560	40,000	150	200	50	20	50	40
M-2 light industrial	45	3	Dwellings not permitted	None	None	None	50	None except adjacent to R zone. See art. 4		
M-3 heavy industrial	125	—	Dwellings not permitted	None	None	None	50	None except adjacent to R zone. See art. 4		
HP historic preservation	See special regulations contained in article 4									

Source: Kent County, Delaware, Zoning Ordinance by Harland Bartholomew and Associates.

Figure 9-1 Permitted uses, height, density, area and yard requirements.

shows these conditions. The map should be based upon a careful field survey and recording of the use of all property. The uses are grouped into major classifications and recorded by different colors or patterns upon the map [Figure 9-2] . When the field survey is made, data should be recorded regarding the number of stories in all buildings containing three or more and also the number of living units in all residential structures other than single-family dwellings. The latter data enables determinations to be made of existing lot areas per family, which will indicate what such requirements should be in the zoning regulations. After the map of existing land use is completed, computations should be made to determine the area occupied by each major use. The field survey and land use map should be prepared as a part of the general planning program, but if this has not been done, it should be prepared separately for zoning purposes.

For zoning purposes and for most planning purposes, the land use classifications should be related to the several uses that will be permitted in the zoning regulations. Past experience has indicated that the following classifications are adequate for all but the larger cities:

Single-family residential	Heavy industrial
Two-family residential	Railroad property
Multiple-family residential	Public and semipublic areas
General commercial	Parks and recreation
Highway commercial	Streets and alleys
Light industrial	Vacant areas

Within recent years, publications upon land use classifications have been issued by departments of the federal government. The first was published by the Bureau of the Budget and was primarily intended for economic and employment studies.[2] The latest publication was primarily intended for use in the transportation studies that have been underway in all larger urban areas.[3] While the latter publication contains many classifications, several could be grouped together to provide the data essential for zoning studies.

Within more recent years, many cities are recording data obtained from the land use surveys so that it can be stored on cards, tapes, or disks and processed in computers. This enables use of the data for many different purposes and facilitates keeping it up to date.

After careful consideration of the analysis of existing conditions and needs, as well as recommendations regarding the amount and character of future growth developed in the studies of the comprehensive plan, work should begin upon the district zoning map. The land use plan should show the existing location of land uses, and field inspections (or information in the general plan) should indicate the adaptability of areas for future use. From this, the boundaries of the proposed zoning districts can be determined [Figure 9-3] .

It is important that the area within the proposed districts be related to land use requirements of the estimated future population. Data are available regarding percentage of developed area occupied by the different uses and amounts of land used by units of

2. *Standard Industrial Classification Manual*, U.S. Bureau of the Budget, 1957.
3. *Standard Land Use Coding Manual*, Housing and Home Finance Agency and Bureau of Public Roads, 1965.

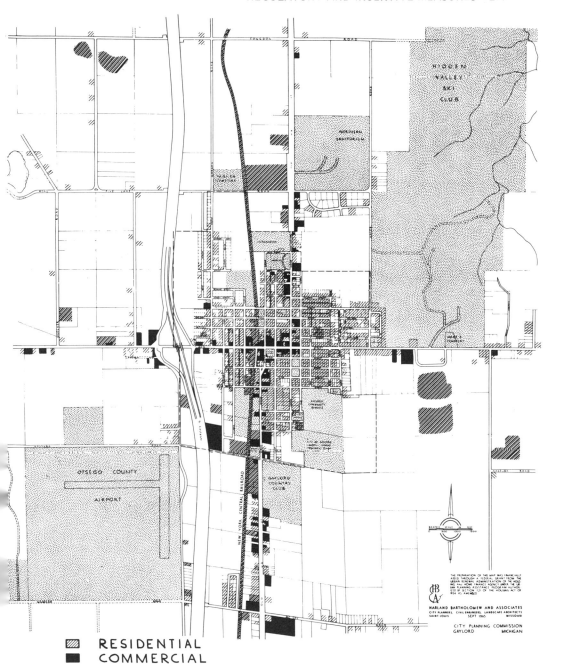

RESIDENTIAL
COMMERCIAL
PUBLIC AND SEMI-PUBLIC
INDUSTRIAL AND RAILROADS

Source: Harland Bartholomew and Associates.

Figure 9-2 Existing land use—1965.

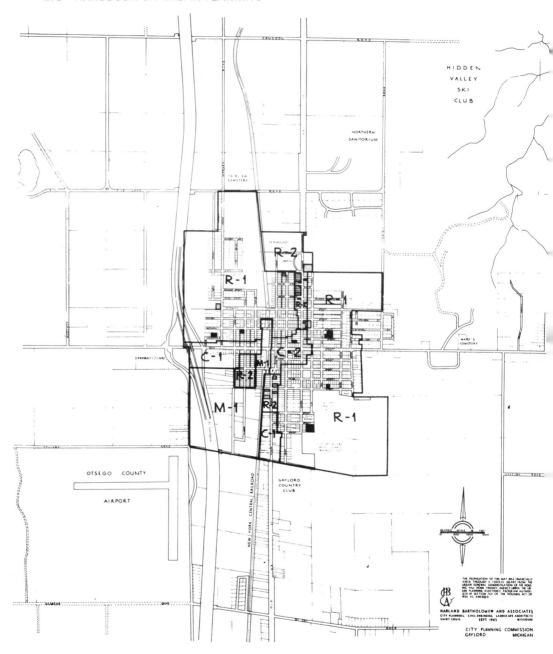

NONCONFORMING COMMERCIAL USES
NONCONFORMING INDUSTRIAL USES

Source: Harland Bartholomew and Associate

Figure 9-3 Zoning district map.

population—usually expressed in acres per hundred persons.[4] By comparing these data with the local percentages and ratios, reasonable estimates can be prepared for future land use needs and the areas within the several zones can be related thereto [Figure 9-4].

The final step in preparing the zoning ordinance is writing detailed regulations for each zoning district, sections upon variations and exceptions, changes and amendments, and other requirements that are needed in the regulations. Legal assistance, especially the assistance and cooperation of the city attorney, should be obtained for this phase.

TRENDS IN ZONING PRACTICES   Early zoning ordinances were comparatively simple instruments, with the uses permitted within districts usually limited to single-family dwellings, apartments, commercial establishments, and light and heavy industry. Any restricted use was permitted in a less restricted district—for example, single-family dwellings were permitted in any district. Further, there were comparatively few, but broad, use categories listed as being permitted in each district. Separate sections of the ordinance usually contained regulations for the height and lot area or density requirements for each district.

The majority of the modern ordinances are much more voluminous. There is a much longer and more detailed list of uses permitted in each district. Further, the more restricted uses are not permitted in all districts since residences are now normally not permitted in industrial districts. In addition to the permitted uses, many ordinances now include a list of conditional or special uses that might be permitted in the district if they conform to certain desirable standards that would protect surrounding development. Examples are colleges, hospitals, nurseries, and clubs. The Planning Commission makes a report upon the desirability of any such use and the legislative body has final decision regarding its approval or rejection. This practice affords flexibility to zoning and still ensures a desirable character of development—especially in residential sections.

Another important innovation is the use of what is commonly known as "Planned Districts" or "Planned Unit Development" (PUD). They may provide for either residential, commercial, or industrial development [Figure 9-5]. Planned residential districts may provide any type of living units, including apartments, but the total number of units would not exceed the number of units permitted under the existing zoning. However, any area dedicated to open space or recreational use is usually included in the total area for determining the number of living units permitted. Planned commercial districts are primarily intended to accommodate large, modern shopping centers. They usually are located upon vacant or sparsely developed tracts that may be initially zoned for residential purposes. The applicant submits a complete plan of the proposed development including types of uses, architectural sketches, drives, parking, and landscaping schemes. The plans are studied by both the Planning Commission and the legislative body. After a public hearing, the area may be changed to a planned commercial district. Official approval usually requires adherence to the approved plan and to a minimum time period for initiating the project. The principles and details of a planned industrial district are

4. Harland Bartholomew, *Land Uses in American Cities*, (Cambridge, Mass.: Harvard University Press, 1955).

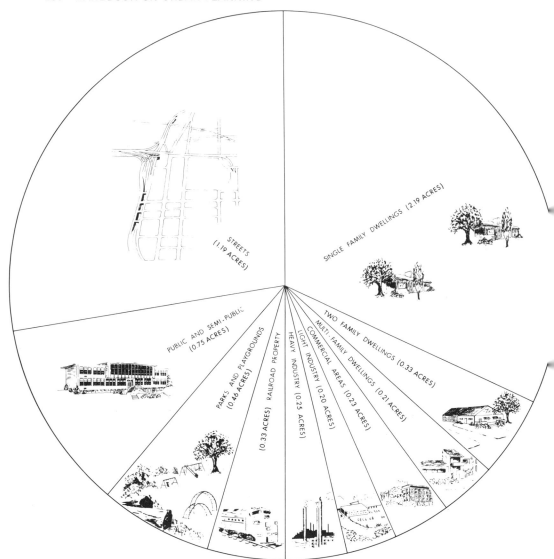

Source: Harland Bartholomew, "Land Use in American Cities," Harvard Univ. Press, Cambridge, Mass., 1965.

Figure 9-4   Areas of land used per 100 persons (averages in 53 central cities).

very similar to the commercial one. They are primarily intended to facilitate the development of the modern "industrial park," or planned industrial district, or organized industrial areas.

Some control of advertising signs, including billboards, is contained in most zoning ordinances, but·many communities are now effecting detailed control over advertising signs in separate sign ordinances. This has advantages in that it tends to reduce opposition to zoning controls which contain enough essential regulations.

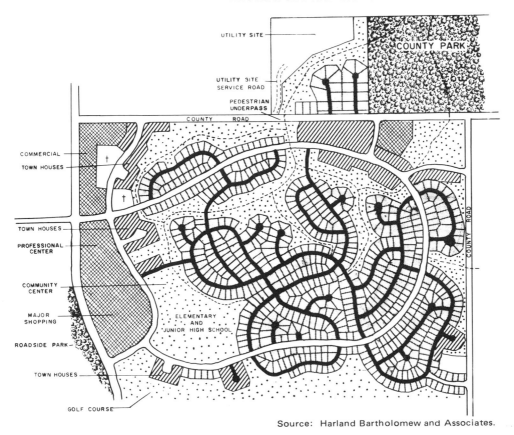

Source: Harland Bartholomew and Associates.

Figure 9-5 Planned unit development.

Zoning of floodplains so as to assure protection of life and property is becoming an increasingly popular part of zoning regulations. It is expected that this trend will continue, but it is essential that the regulations be based upon sound, factual data regarding the location of past and probable future areas subject to damaging floods.

A current zoning problem of relatively recent origin is the matter of encouraging, or even permitting, more multiple-family dwellings within suburban communities. In addition to permitting this use, there is a growing demand for these dwellings to have rental rates that would make them available for moderate- or lower-income families. Suburban communities normally have more vacant land than central cities and the large majority are predominantly occupied by single-family homes, many of which are located upon large lots—areas of from one to five acres. Naturally, officials and citizens of these communities strongly oppose the intrusion of less desirable types of living facilities, but with the widespread discussion of the serious need for good, medium-priced living units, the demand for zoning changes in suburban areas will undoubtedly continue.

The problem of distributing living facilities that would be available for medium-to-lower-income families throughout large metropolitan areas has aroused much consideration and discussion. The possibility of creating a Regional Agency with authority to require such distribution has been mentioned and tried in some modified form in a few areas. This may prove to be the eventual solution if coercive efforts are not successful. However, it would require new enabling legislation and, since it would usurp important zoning controls from local legislative bodies, would be strongly opposed.

It is rather surprising to note that comparatively few states have amended or changed their original enabling acts, many of which were enacted in the 1920s. However, during the 1971 legislative session of the state of Illinois, a completely new Zoning Enabling Act was introduced. This was substantially different from early acts and was very comprehensive in context. Among the major changes was authorization to adopt regulations regarding floodplain zoning and preservation of historical, agricultural, and conservation areas. It also required a thorough review of all zoning ordinances every five years. The legislation was not adopted, but it is encouraging that such a comprehensive act was prepared and considered.

TRENDS IN COURT DECISIONS   Mention has been made of a few of the early decisions upholding the legality of comprehensive zoning regulations. Several books and articles have been published upon legal problems and practices, including Yokley's works,[5] among others.

Thousands of court decisions have been given upon zoning cases since the 1920s. Practically all of these have been based upon the reasonableness of the zoning regulations as applied to a particular lot or tract. For the most part, these decisions have upheld the local zoning and two major policies have emerged. The first is that the potential value of property is not the determining factor in deciding upon proper zoning classification, but rather that the welfare of the general public is the controlling issue in zoning. The second is that courts are unwilling to substitute their judgment for that of the legislative body whenever there is reasonable doubt or question regarding the proper zoning.

Within the past few years, a few state supreme courts have refused to uphold large lot area requirements—two or more acres—in zoning regulations, especially where extensive areas are included in such classifications. With the current efforts to disperse satisfactory housing facilities for lower-income families and minority groups, such decisions may become more frequent.

Another important trend in court decisions within recent years (but less publicized because there have been fewer of them) is that of upholding aesthetic considerations in zoning. While aesthetic considerations may never equal the importance of economic or social factors, it is encouraging to note that they are being recognized and accepted. With the rapidly increasing interest in the environment, it is expected that their importance will increase in the future (see below under architectural controls in this chapter).

Subdivision Regulations

Urban areas grow and expand primarily through the development of new subdivisions and the locating of structures therein. Thus, the subdividing of vacant land, or the

5. E. C. Yokley, *Zoning Law and Practice*, 3rd ed. (Charlottesville, Va.: Michie Co.: 1965).

resubdividing of existing plats, have major influences upon the future area. It establishes a street pattern that should exist for many years, and also influences the type and character of development that will occupy the land. Regulations controlling new subdivisions have been an integral part of comprehensive planning for many years. The planning enabling acts in many states clearly outline the authority and method of procedures for exercising such controls. Other state acts also authorize legislative bodies to exercise this type of regulation. The Federal Housing Administration has developed suggested subdivision regulations[6] and the American Society of Planning Officials has published reports upon the subject.[7] These are useful guides, but careful consideration must be given to local needs and practices.

Modern subdivision regulations exercise two major types of controls, namely (a) design and (b) improvement standards.

DESIGN   The location and width of streets and easement, arrangement of lot lines, and the location and extent of any public areas are the major items of control in the design of the subdivision. From the standpoint of streets, it is especially important that if the major street phase of the comprehensive plan proposes a thoroughfare through the subdivided area, the plat should provide a right-of-way of appropriate width for this route. The width for minor or normal streets serving residential lots varies in different communities, but a right-of-way width of 50 feet is normally adequate. Where large lots are provided, a 40-foot width is frequently permitted. Some cities, especially in colder sections, require a 60-foot width—primarily to facilitate the removal and storage of snow from the pavements. Wider rights-of-way are needed for apartment and industrial developments.

The street design should avoid hazardous intersections and the use of curvilinear and cul-de-sacs (dead-end streets) should be encouraged in residential development. The width and length of blocks should be related to lot sizes, but block lengths of 1,200 feet are not objectionable in residential sections. There should be a minimum of minor streets intersecting major thoroughfares. While all streets within the new subdivision need not extend to its boundaries, enough should do so to assure reasonable movement of vehicular traffic and access to adjoining development.

Lot sizes and widths should conform to the requirements of zoning regulations applicable to the subdivided area. The commission, or its staff, can frequently assist in improving the lot arrangement. Several regulations contain requirements that the depth of lots shall not exceed three times the width [Figure 9-6].

Easements should be required over the lots to accommodate the necessary utilities— water, sanitary and storm water sewers, gas, electric and telephone lines. In addition, easements should be established to preserve streams and natural drainage channels. Utility easements are usually located along rear lot lines, although some may be needed along sidelines. Normally, water, sewer, and gas lines are located within the street rights-of-way, but sewers are sometimes desirable in easements along rear lot lines. Overhead poles and wires should be along rear lot lines. Many jurisdictions are now requiring that all electric and telephone lines be placed underground in new subdivisions.

6. *Suggested Land Subdivision Regulations*, Housing and Home Finance Agency, Supt. of Documents (Washington, D.C.: Government Printing Office).

7. *Information Report 174*, (Chicago, Ill.: American Society of Planning Officials, 1963).

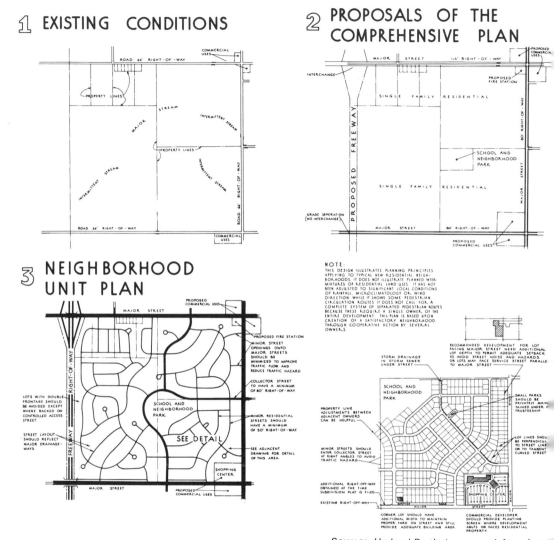

Source: Harland Bartholomew and Associates

Figure 9-6 Subdivision design principles.

Efforts should be made to assure that parks and school grounds will be dedicated in new subdivisions, especially when their location is recommended in the park and school phase of the comprehensive plan. Some jurisdictions—but far from the majority—require that the developer of a new residential subdivision dedicate at least 10 percent of the total area to public agencies. If the area is small or the comprehensive plan does not propose any such facilities within the subdivided area, an equivalent amount of money shall be deposited with the agency. This type of regulation is not widespread, but is being used more frequently.

IMPROVEMENT STANDARDS   Controls for improvement standards are of more recent origin than those for design standards. They primarily affect the construction of physical improvements that must be completed in new subdivisions before the final plat can be recorded and lots sold therefrom. In lieu of completing the improvements, the developer may file a bond for the estimated costs thereof, assuring that they will be installed within a two-year period. The improvement standards are primarily concerned with grading, streets, walks, water, sewers, and disposal of storm water.

Grading primarily is allied to streets, but it is also concerned with assuring that a satisfactory building site will be provided upon each lot and that streets will not have excessive grades for vehicular traffic movements. The standard of street pavement is of major importance and a lasting, impervious surface is essential. The width of pavement and standard of surfacing varies in the local communities.

Water and sanitary sewers are essential in most urban developments. If a public water supply or sanitary sewer system is within a reasonable distance of the subdivision, the developer should connect and extend the facilities to each new lot. If neither water or sewers are reasonably accessible, developers are required to provide a source of same. For water, this will probably require wells or an impounded supply with proper treatment and mains to the lots. For sanitary sewers, package treatment plants with connecting sewer lines to each lot are now commonly used.

Utilities (especially gas, electric, and telephone) are normally provided by the respective companies without any cost to the developer. However, the placing of wires underground may involve some cost by the developer.

Official Maps

A few states have enacted legislation authorizing cities to adopt official maps. This was primarily to protect major street rights-of-way. The widened or proposed location of the street is shown upon the map and regulations provide that no new building can be constructed within the proposed right-of-way. New rights-of-way must be accurately located by surveys, but this procedure can result in substantial reduction of land acquisition costs. Parks, school sites, and sites for public buildings can also be shown upon the map.

This regulatory measure is not widely used, but a description of its operation in Wisconsin should be studied.[8]

Building Codes

Building code regulations have been in effect for many years and were adopted long before zoning. They are primarily concerned with protection of the public health and safety. In its strictest sense, the building code is concerned with the functional and

8. Kurt W. Bauer, "Planning and Engineering Consideration for the Official Map," *Journal of City Planning*, Division of ASCE, Vol. 87, No. CPI, Proc. Paper 2931, Sept. 1961.

structural aspects of buildings, but it may also include regulations for electric, plumbing, gas, and other mechanical equipment.

Building codes contain detailed regulations and it is important that they be closely adjusted to changes in building materials and types of contruction. Otherwise, unnecessarily high construction costs might result. Because of the involved details and changing conditions, the majority of cities (especially smaller communities) adopt, by reference, all or portions of one of the national codes, which are continually being revised to include the latest tested and approved materials and practices.

An important characteristic of the newer building codes is the reliance upon performance standards for materials rather than requiring only those that have been in standard use for many years. With the introduction of many new materials and techniques, much more flexibility and frequently economies are permitted. HUD's "Housing Breakthrough" program should provide many useful examples.

Included in the recognized national codes are: Building Officials and Code Administrators (B.O.C.A.) International; Southern Standard Code; Uniform Building Code, by the International Conference of Building Officials; and National Building Code, developed by the National Board of Fire Underwriters (now called American Insurance Association).

Minimum Housing Standards

Adoption and enforcement of minimum housing regulations have been accomplished in many municipalities within the past two decades—especially since the adoption of the Housing Act of 1949 (Public Law 81-171), as amended.

These regulations establish minimum standards for all living units in single-family, two-family or multiple-family (apartment) dwellings. The regulations usually include minimum standards for size of sleeping rooms, size of windows, availability of a bathroom and toilets, hot and cold running water, satisfactory supply of heat, screens and other protection from insects and rodents, satisfactory disposal of storm water, adequate protection from rain and weather, removal of any unsanitary conditions, and general structural conditions of the unit that will protect the health and safety of the occupants.

Unlike building codes which control new structures or the enlargement or alteration of existing structures, the minimum housing standards apply to both new and existing living units. After representatives of the building department have inspected a living unit and listed all defects not meeting minimum standards, the owner is furnished a list of changes and improvements to be completed within a stated period of time. If the corrections are not made, the owner may be ordered to demolish the building.

The enforcement of minimum housing standards requires a comprehensive program of inspection and checking of older living units, especially in older sections of the city. This inspection is commonly known as a "Code Enforcement Program" and is an important part of most urban renewal projects.

Architectural Controls

It has been indicated that building codes are concerned with structural details of buildings to protect the health and safety of individuals and the general public. They are only indirectly concerned with the appearance of the structure. Within comparatively recent years, several municipalities—especially suburban communities—have enacted regulations effecting some controls over the design and appearance of buildings. These are commonly known as architectural controls.

This new type of control is adopted as an ordinance which indicates the objectives of the regulations, establishes standards to be considered, and creates an official agency to pass upon the architectural design and appearance. The administrative agency usually includes architects, as well as persons experienced in building and real estate values. Some communities have adopted such controls as an amendment to their zoning ordinance.

Since the controls are primarily concerned with appearance or aesthetic values, care must be exercised in establishing sound standards or a basis for disapproving any proposed design. After all, there are many different opinions as to what is attractive, and it is not intended that the members of the enforcing agency completely substitute their ideas for those of the owner and his architect. Instead, judgment should primarily be based upon avoiding serious conflict with surrounding or nearby development, and with preventing obvious monstrosities that would detract from established character and affect property values. The administrative agency is not expected to consider all new or altered buildings, but only those referred to it by the Building Commissioner when he feels that there is considerable question regarding the appropriateness of the design.

Formerly, there was considerable question regarding the legality of this type of municipal control, and there were some adverse court decisions. However, within recent years, the supreme courts in some states (Wisconsin, Ohio, and Missouri are examples) have upheld this type of regulation and especially aesthetic considerations. One of the more recent decisions was in Missouri, during the latter part of 1970.[9]

A few larger cities have enacted regulations requiring approval of the design of new structures fronting upon public parks, plazas, and similar open spaces—other than public streets. Such a regulation has been in effect within the city of St. Louis, Missouri, for several years, and satisfactory results have been obtained therefrom. The original ordinance providing for these controls established a separate commission (formerly known as the Art Commission) to approve or disapprove the building plans. This ordinance was amended in recent years and the name of the enforcing agency was changed to Landmarks and Urban Design. It is also authorized to designate buildings of historical significance as landmarks and to prevent their demolition or alteration.

With the increased interest and activity in improving the environment, it is encouraging that courts are giving more support to aesthetic considerations. There is certainly need for improving the appearance and beauty of urban as well as rural areas.

Environmental Controls

Governments and citizens are becoming increasingly active in improving the country's environment, with the interest therein growing rapidly during the past several years. Countless articles and books have been published upon the subject and many meetings and conferences held. Many national and local citizen organizations have been created to

9. *State of Missouri* ex. rel. *Stoyanoff* v. *Robert Berkely, Building Commissioner,* City of Ladue, Missouri, 458 S.W. (2d.) 305.

study and deal with the subject and it is widely discussed at most conferences of professional organizations. Obviously, it must be included in the comprehensive planning program. The major environmental problems are found within larger urban areas which are expected to increase in both size and complexity. Unless adequate controls are effected over the polluting influences, the environment can only become more undesirable and objectionable. Since the several pollutions directly affect the health, safety, and general welfare of most citizens, the increased attention they are receiving is quite understandable.

Three levels of governments have major interests in environmental controls—namely, federal, state, and local. The federal government can be especially effective in several phases of control; included are research, development of overall standards, legislation (such as controls for the amount of pollutants that can be emitted from autos and requiring comprehensive basin plans for conservation of water and controlling its pollution), and financial assistance. The federal government recently created a new Environmental Protection Agency charged with the responsibility of consolidating the many federal agencies concerned with pollution control programs.

The states should also adopt standards for pollution controls, generally conforming to federal standards. The states can be—and many have been—especially effective in preventing water pollution. This can be effected by controlling the use of septic tanks, requiring installation and setting standards for sewage treatment plants, maintaining or improving water quality in streams and lakes, and approving source, treatment, and distribution of public water supplies. States should also be concerned with pollution from pesticides, fertilizers, and solid waste disposal.

Cities and urban areas also need regulations for controlling pollutants, but these should be closely related to those of the federal and state governments, with suitable adjustments as desirable for unusual local conditions. The enforcement section of the local regulation is much closer to the possible sources of pollution and thus can ensure more effective control.

Currently, the major concern of pollution is with air, water, solid waste, and noise. In some areas, there is also concern with radiation problems.

AIR POLLUTION   Regulations to prevent or lessen air pollution were adopted in several of the larger cities many years ago. The primary objective of these earlier ordinances was to control the amount of smoke emission, either by prohibiting the use of fuels that resulted in large volumes of noxious smoke or by using improved types of furnaces or combustion devices. The marked success achieved in at least two larger cities—Pittsburgh, Pennsylvania, and St. Louis, Missouri—indicated the value of these regulations.

Smoke control is still an important phase in improving the condition of our air. There are many elements or pollutants that should be controlled. For example, practically no coal is burned within Los Angeles, California; yet the city has a very serious pollution problem with its well-known smog. Automotive vehicles and airplanes powered by internal combustion engines are very serious sources of air pollutants, primarily because of their increased number and use in urban areas. Jet aircraft are also serious polluters. As previously indicated, the federal government has initiated research programs, as well as directives, to many manufacturers and airline companies to develop equipment and to use fuels that will reduce the emission of pollutants to reasonable levels. Local governments will substantially benefit from these improvements and should make necessary adjustments in their controls to ensure proper local enforcement.

There are several other sources of air pollution. Dust particles and fly ash are emitted from many types of manufacturing plants and some of this can be effectively controlled by precipitators, while other sources may require other methods. The emission of gases and noxious fumes or odors is far from uncommon in many different types of manufacturing or processing establishments. The emission of dust from city streets and from demolition of buildings can be objectionable in cities. Even the usual outdoor burning of leaves and trash is now prohibited in many urban areas.

Currently it is impracticable to suggest any standard type of ordinance for air pollution regulation that would be satisfactory for local areas. Local officials can maintain a careful study of regulations and recommendations developed by both federal and state governments. The appropriate regulations could then be selected and adopted for local conditions.

WATER POLLUTION   The pollution of lakes, rivers, and underground supplies of water is logically of national concern. An adequate supply of water is essential for human, animal, vegetable, and marine life. It is also essential for industrial operations and important to recreational activities. The extensive damage that has already resulted from pollution of lakes and rivers is widely recognized—Lake Erie is an example—but damage to underground supplies is not understood by most citizens.

The rapid increase in population and industrialization has resulted in major increase in water consumption and concern about the availability of an adequate supply for future needs. A committee of the United States Senate has indicated that by the year 2000, a total of 496 billion gallons of water will be used daily for municipal, industrial, rural, and irrigation purposes within this country. While all of this water need not be completely potable and free of pollutants, a substantial portion must be. Unless the amount of pollution is reduced, the treatment costs to assure potability will be very high. Further, the possible loss of marine life, damage to vegetation, and limitation of recreational activities must be avoided.

There are many different sources of water pollution, but included within the major ones are: (a) discharge of untreated or inadequately treated industrial wastes, (b) untreated sanitary sewage, (c) dumping of solid wastes, (d) discharge of heated water from certain industrial uses, and (e) storm water carrying large amounts of noxious material. Discharges of industrial wastes and untreated sanitary sewage are the most common and serious causes of water pollution and can be largely prevented by proper treatment of the waste material. Dumping of solid waste occurs often near large bodies of water and can be prevented by developing other means of disposal. There are many different types of storm water problems and each will require separate study for satisfactory solution.

The federal government has a major interest in controlling water pollution, especially where more than one state adjoins the body of water; actually, this would include all streams, for their waters eventually discharge into the Great Lakes, major rivers, or oceans. Consequently, standards should be developed to enforce the control of such pollution which would be a guide for all states.

All the states have designated agencies to adopt and enforce standards for control of water pollution, as well as approval of public and private water supply, and practically all are also actively engaged in enforcing regulations for treatment of sanitary and industrial sewage and control of individual septic tanks. Much of the inspection and control is frequently handled by local, city, or county departments—quite frequently, the health department. The cooperation of local agencies is helpful because of their familiarity with local conditions and problems. The state should, however, maintain sufficient contact to assure that its standards and requirements are being properly enforced. Additional standards and stricter enforcement will probably be required in the future, especially for industrial wastes.

Many urban areas, and those becoming urbanized, are preparing or implementing area-wide plans for sewage systems that are interconnected or operated by some central authority. This has the valuable advantage of making available centralized design, maintenance, and operating personnel that might otherwise not be available to small fragmented sewer systems. In addition, an area-wide authority can plan for an entire basin or watershed rather than can just the boundaries of one municipality or subdivision. New federal guidelines require consideration of regional or basin-type planning to bring about joint systems rather than a number of separate sewage treatment plants discharging to the same small stream.

SOLID WASTE DISPOSAL   The rapid growth of urban areas has resulted in substantial increases in the amount of solid waste which require removal and disposal. The problem is further complicated by the increase in urban land uses, leaving little, if any, available land where the waste might be deposited. Previously, the most common methods of solid waste disposal were: (a) incineration, (b) sanitary landfill, and (c) transporting it some distance from shorelines and then dumping it into large bodies of water. Within recent years, there has been a marked increase in garbage disposal units in individual living quarters which discharge directly into the sanitary sewer systems; but cans, bottles, and other solid materials still require manual disposal.

The federal government, as well as many states, are becoming increasingly interested in this problem and the former has allocated funds for research projects for developing new methods of disposing of waste material. Considerable research is also being done by private industry. Among methods being investigated are compaction, which primarily reduces the volume rather than complete disposal; recycling; use of waste as fuel after treatment; and others. The disposal of abandoned or junked cars represents an increasingly difficult portion of the problem. Recently, machines have come into operation that shred the old autos and separate the different types of metals so that they can be reused in making new material. Because of the pressing need and the current concentration upon the problem, it is not unreasonable to anticipate that improved solutions and methods will be developed within the next several years.

The comprehensive plan should include a study and recommendations regarding the method of solid waste disposal within the planned area. This should involve an analysis of all potential methods and selection of the one best suited for local conditions and needs. Assistance and advice from appropriate state agencies and officials would be desirable. After the most appropriate and economical plan has been decided upon, regulations should be adopted to ensure that it is followed and that no violations occur.

NOISE POLLUTION   Currently, there is probably less noise in cities than in earlier decades. This has resulted from the widespread use of air conditioning, abandonment of streetcars, and changes in manufacturing and construction techniques. However, there is still a substantial amount of noise in larger uban areas. One of the major noise problems is related to plane operations at major airports accommodating scheduled commercial operations. More controls will gradually be developed and enforced over these and other noise producing operations.

PLANNING INCENTIVES

Comprehensive planning has been practiced for so many years that much tangible evidence is available regarding the many benefits and advantages that result therefrom. This alone is a dominant incentive for initiating planning programs. There are, however, many other incentives for this activity. Following is a summary discussion of some of the more important ones.

Federal Financial Assistance

Many federal agencies have programs that give financial grants to municipalities or counties. The type of assistance and details thereof undergo changes, but publications are issued from time to time containing details of all federal programs.[10]

The federal government has given financial assistance for highway development for many decades. The current program is under the Federal Aid Highway Act of 1966, as amended by the Federal Aid Highway Act of 1968. The major provision of the new legislation is that cities and urban areas containing more then 50,000 persons must have a Comprehensive Transportation Plan and a Continuing Planning Program before the area is eligible for future federal aid. The federal government will participate in financing the planning program. In some respects, this may appear as a negative approach, but it is certainly a strong incentive and financial reward for comprehensive planning. The federal government also gives financial assistance for mass transportation improvements which, of course, require comprehensive planning.

An excellent example of incentives for comprehensive planning and controls is the program for highway beautification. Under the 1968 act, the normal federal allotment to each state is reduced by 10 percent, unless the state develops a plan and enacts

10. *Catalog of Federal Domestic Assistance* (Washington, D.C.: Government Printing Office).

regulations controlling billboards and junk yards on federal-aid highways—especially interstate routes. Several states still have not adopted such controls.

The government has several forms of financial assistance for housing and urban renewal programs. These are discussed in Chapters 4 and 11, but comprehensive plans are mandatory and additional studies are required in many phases of the program.

Important federal assistance is available in acquiring and developing open space and recreational facilities. Again, a comprehensive plan is required to justify the need and soundness of the proposed facilities.

With the current interest and activity upon control of pollution, the federal government makes substantial financial contributions thereto. Of particular importance to communities is the financial assistance for developing or improving public water supplies, as well as collection and treatment of sanitary sewage. The amount of contribution varies according to conditions, but is generally in the vicinity of 50 percent. If the project is approved by a regional council of governments, a bonus of 5 percent of the amount of federal assistance is usually given. Obviously, all participation is based upon the availability of a comprehensive plan, which clearly indicates the financial advantage of such planning.

Practically all urban areas, except some suburban communities, are competing for new industrial development, which is so important to the growth and economic welfare of most towns and cities. The availability of a comprehensive plan and evidence that it is consistently followed is an important, but admittedly not controlling, factor in attracting new industries.

Some states authorize municipalities to adopt and enforce zoning regulations within unincorporated areas for specified distances beyond the corporate limits—usually about one and one-half miles. However, if the city does not exercise this authority, then the county can control the zoning within the area. This is an important incentive for municipalities to exercise such controls.

Many of the modern zoning ordinances also provide incentives for developers. For example, bulk or floor area controls are now a normal means of controlling building heights. Thus, an ordinance may permit more floor area or higher structures if additional open space is provided, beyond the minimum required by the yard regulations. Mention has previously been made of permitting more intensive types of residential use in planned residential units.

It is obvious that many incentives are available for comprehensive planning. While the advantages and conveniences that become available to the citizens should be adequate, the potential financial assistance from federal and state governments is currently of major importance.

Private Incentives

The preceding discussion has described incentives available to urban public agencies from comprehensive planning. Many similar incentives and advantages are also available to individuals, corporations, and organizations. The protection of property values is primarily possible through soundly enforced zoning regulations. These, together with active neighborhood organizations, are the most logical methods of maintaining the character and desirability of residential sections, especially single-family districts.

The discussion of trends in modern zoning regulations in the earlier part of this chapter briefly mentioned incentives available to developers if they would provide more open and landscaped space around tall structures. Likewise, modern provisions for planned units, especially residential areas, afford many incentives and advantages for the developer. These clearly encourage developments on the basis of sound, large-scale development rather than using individual lots. A few modern ordinances have gone further, such as permitting more living units in apartment buildings if higher fire and soundproofing standards are adhered to or if additional landscaping, recreational, or guest parking facilities are provided. Similar incentives should be expected and encouraged in the future.

Preceding chapters have indicated the necessity of comprehensive planning, especially in urban areas, and the advantages that accrue therefrom. The possibilities of assuring sound land use patterns, adequate physical facilities, and an improved environment benefit all persons. It is the soundest way of assuring better living conditions—a major goal of citizens—and thus, the latter should fully cooperate in and assist such programs for they are the beneficiaries.

10 CAPITAL IMPROVEMENTS PROGRAM

Russell H. Riley

High on the list of more important functions of municipal governments is the provision of public facilities and services. The type and character of most of these facilities was discussed in Chapter 6. The facilities include physical improvements such as streets and their appurtenances, parks, buildings and utilities—especially water, sanitary, and storm water sewers. Other public agencies (school districts, county, state, and federal governments) also provide physical improvements in urban areas. Services include fire, police, and health protection, garbage and trash collection, administration, including enforcement of codes and regulations, and maintenance and repair of physical facilities.

With the rapid increase in population and land uses within most urban areas, there is a continuing need for new physical improvements. Further, many existing improvements are becoming obsolete and need enlargement, major repair, or replacement. There is also a growing demand for new services or expansion and improved standards of existing ones. The problem is further complicated by increasing costs—higher wages and prices for materials and supplies. In brief, municipalities and urban areas are experiencing unusually difficult financial problems.

Because of the extensive need for physical improvements, it is essential to separate those that can be classified as capital improvements from those that are more properly considered repair and maintenance, as well as replacement or purchasing of new equipment. A basic determinant for capital improvement is that it should provide a long period of usefulness and service. The period should not be less than fifteen years and preferably twenty years or more. Certainly, major streets, parks, public buildings, and utilities should be expected to serve twenty years and longer, although within rapidly growing areas, some enlargement or extension may be necessary during that period. With the rapid progress in technology, some improvements become obsolete as to their usefulness before they are actually worn out. Another consideration for capital improvements is that they serve all or a major portion of the area and its population, rather than small sections thereof. In some instances, it is entirely possible that expensive and durable equipment, such as some construction devices, would meet these standards and thus could be considered as capital improvements.

In contrast to capital improvements are the manifold expenditures for repairs, maintenance, and operation. These include patching and seal-coating street pavements, painting and minor repairs of public buildings, and replacing of lawns and landscaping in parks and open spaces. The maintenance or minor repair of all equipment, including office facilities, is another example. However, a modern electronic computer might logically be considered a capital improvement. The aforementioned and other similar projects may not be encountered annually, but the majority recur every few years. Such expenditures should be included in the normal budget for the respective departments, rather than in a long-range capital improvement program.

Preceding chapters have discussed the many physical improvements that would be proposed in a comprehensive plan. Collectively, they would require such large expenditures that they would have to be initiated over a long period of time and, fortunately, all would not be needed immediately. The major function of a capital improvement program is to determine the general order in which the many projects should be undertaken and how they can be financed. Such programs are intended to cover only a comparatively short period of time rather than the entire period considered in the comprehensive plan. It would be impracticable to estimate land acquisition and construction costs for fifteen or twenty years in the future. Some state enabling acts specify the number of years that should be considered in the improvement program—for example, the Michigan act provides for a six-year period—and most programs are normally based upon a five-year program. General improvements planning beyond 5 or 6 years up to 20 years informs public officials and citizens of long range needs. However, this type of public improvements plan is separate and distinct from a capital improvements program.

FINANCING CAPITAL IMPROVEMENTS

Several means are used for financing capital improvements such as current revenue, general and revenue bonds, and special assessments.

Current Revenue

Paying of all municipal expenditures from established sources of annual income—commonly known as "pay as you go"—is a desirable procedure in many municipalities. It has sound advantages, but is also fraught with difficulties and is seldom practicable in the larger communities. The major problem is that the large proportion of annual income is needed for administration, services, and maintenance. Citizens are normally more conscious of the need for services than for physical improvements. Further, the cost of a large physical improvement will usually require an increasingly large proportion of the annual income. As previously mentioned, capital improvements should have a long life and payments therefore can be extended over a long period.

General Obligation Bonds

These bonds are a popular and logical method of financing capital improvements. The payment or amortization of such bonds extends over a long period—usually fifteen years or longer—yet funds become immediately available for financing the project. They do involve extra costs in interest payments, but require, except under unusual conditions, only nominal amounts each year. Normally, these bonds carry relatively low interest rates because the interest is tax exempt.

Citizen approval is required before general obligation bonds can be issued since they are financed by an annual tax upon local property. In some states, such approval requires a two-thirds majority of all persons voting upon the issue, while in others, only a simple majority is necessary. It is thus essential that citizens understand and favor the improvements for which bonds are to be issued and educational campaigns therefore are usually conducted. In practically all instances, state legislation controls the total amount of obligation bonds that may be outstanding at any time, which is related to the total assessed valuation. It is difficult to compare one state with another because of the range of assessing policies and practices, but generally the allowable bonding limit is about 10 percent of assessed valuation.

Revenue Bonds

The interest and amortization of these bonds are financed from the net income of a municipal operation. Among the more common types are those issued for the water system, sanitary sewers, and off-street parking facilities, but some communities are also charging fees for admittance to certain public facilities such as zoos and museums. Revenue bonds do not require citizen approval, nor is there any legal limit upon the amount that may be outstanding. The amount of the issue is controlled by the willingness of bonding and financial institutions to purchase same which is directly related to the amount of net revenue available for interest and amortization of the bonds.

Special Assessments

Certain physical improvements that primarily benefit individual properties or neighborhoods, but also help the entire community, are frequently financed by assessing all or a portion of the costs against benefited private properties. The more usual types of such projects include resurfacing of minor streets, sanitary sewer laterals, streetlights, sidewalks, and facilities for disposal of storm water.

The determination of the property to be assessed and the amount of the assessment varies according to the type of project. For a street resurfacing, sidewalk or sanitary sewer project, only the abutting property is affected and the assessment is levied on a front foot basis. For street widenings or openings or for a storm drainage project, a benefited district should be established.

The proportion of the cost assessed against the benefited property frequently varies among communities and according to the type of project. Special assessment bonds may be issued, but usually for shorter periods than general obligation bonds, and the entire project requires the approval of at least the majority of affected property owners.

Assistance From Other Public Agencies

Several capital improvement projects are eligible for financial assistance from other public agencies. Among the more common of these are streets and highways, public buildings, flood control, and water and sanitary sewer systems.

As mentioned in Chapter 9 and elsewhere, the federal government has many programs of financial assistance for urban communities and the number of such programs has been continuously increasing. States also give financial assistance for local improvements, especially highway and major street projects. Some states also now assist in financing projects that will assist in controlling water pollution, such as collection and treatment systems for sanitary sewage. Counties may assist in financing some local improvements, especially highways and streets. In some areas, special taxing districts have been established to provide separate services such as water, sewer, and drainage districts. Currently, assistance from other governmental agencies is an important source of income for local improvements.

Another potential source of income in smaller urban areas, and especially in resort communities, is gifts and contributions by individual property owners. There are many examples of parks and cultural facilities that have been donated by individuals or families; but in smaller communities, general donations are made to assist financing of services and improvements. An incentive for such contribution is that they are tax exempt. It is difficult, if not impossible, to forecast the amount of revenue that may be received from this source.

ESTIMATES OF ANNUAL REVENUE

The first step in developing a capital improvement program is preparation of careful estimates for the annual general revenue for the period covered in the program. This is essential to determine the income that may be available for improvement after expenditures for administration, services, maintenance, and similar purposes have been allocated.

Such estimates should be based upon analysis of past trends in revenue during the past five, or preferably, ten years, as well as upon appraisals of probable future changes.

Sources of Municipal Income

For many years, the major source of municipal income has been a tax levied upon assessed valuation of all real and personal property under private ownership [Figure 10-1]. State legislation or special municipal charters determine the maximum tax rate that may be levied in any year. This is a major reason why cities are continually seeking to increase the assessed valuation by attracting new industrial and commercial development. Where cities operate their own utilities, such as water and sewer systems, some of the net income may be transferred to the general revenue fund. However, much of the income from utilities is needed for operating and maintenance purposes and for amortization of the investment. Other common, but less important, sources of income are fines, licenses, and charges for services, such as inspections, building permits, and frequently for garbage and trash collection.

Other important sources of income in some areas are refunds from state taxes collected locally. These may include gasoline, liquor, or sales taxes and possibly state income tax. The practice varies among the several states and according to state legislation.

Because of the growing need for additional revenue and the limitations upon the property tax rate, many cities are utilizing new sources of income. The most important of these are a local income tax and tax upon local retail sales. State legislation is necessary before such taxes can be levied and the citizens must also vote approval thereof. It is expected that these potential sources of income will be more widely used in the future.

Currently, there is widespread discussion of the burdens imposed by the property tax. A major reason is that several different public agencies levy a tax upon property within the municipality. In addition to the city tax, taxes are levied by the county, school districts, sometimes the state, and special taxing agencies, such as a community college or draining and sewer districts. The latter districts are not found within all urban areas, but their number is increasing. Expenditures for educational purposes absorb the major portion of public tax funds, usually about half to two-thirds of the total. With the exception of state and federal contributions, the school income is primarily derived from the property tax. While state legislation imposes some limits upon the tax rate for school purposes, practically all such laws provide that the rate can be increased by approval of the voters. In some states, this approval requires only a majority vote, while in others, a two-thirds majority is required. Thus, the total property tax may become very high upon individual plots within most municipalities [Figure 10-2].

Municipal Expenditures

Since cities utilize different classifications for many of their expenditures, it is difficult to cite comparative amounts expended for most purposes. Studies reveal, however, that normally the majority of municipal expenditures are made for three major purposes—namely, (a) administration and maintenance, (b) fire and police protection—

ASSESSED VALUATION

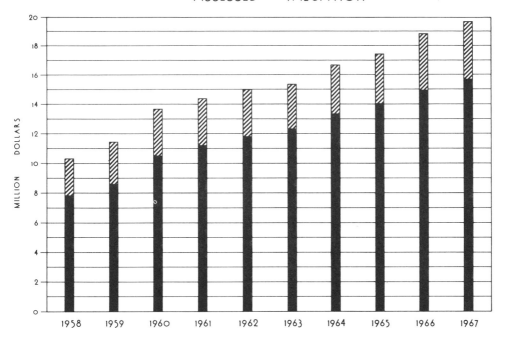

PERSONAL AND UTILITIES

REAL ESTATE

TAX RATES

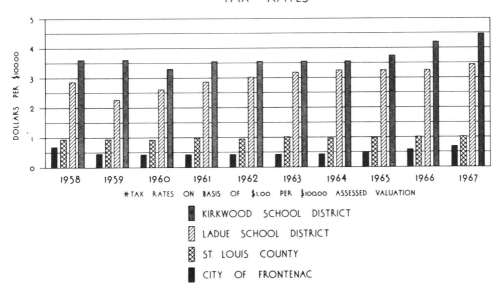

*TAX RATES ON BASIS OF $1.00 PER $100.00 ASSESSED VALUATION

KIRKWOOD SCHOOL DISTRICT

LADUE SCHOOL DISTRICT

ST. LOUIS COUNTY

CITY OF FRONTENAC

Source: Harland Bartholomew and Associates.

Figure 10-1 Trend in assessed valuation and tax rates 1958-1967, Frontenac, Missouri.

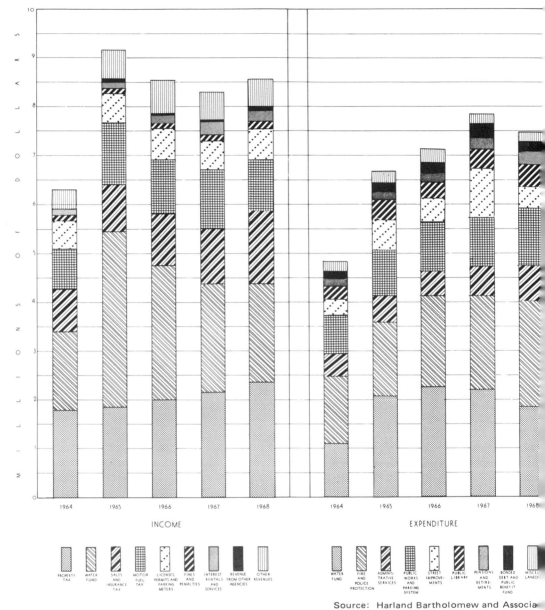

Source: Harland Bartholomew and Associa

Figure 10-2   Trend in annual income and expenditures 1964-1968, Skokie, Illinois.

public safety—and (c) special services, including parks and recreation, garbage collection, and airports. In communities with large bonded indebtedness, fairly substantial amounts may be required for interest and amortization.

While the percentages may vary between cities, the expenditures for administration and maintenance normally represent about one-third of the total. This depends primarily upon the type and cost of improvements included as maintenance rather than classified as capital improvements. Fire and police protection usually absorb between 30 and 40 percent of the total. Obviously, only a minimum portion of the total income is available for a long-range capital improvement program. Because of increased costs of labor and material, the expenditures required for most municipal services are also increasing and it will be increasingly difficult to reserve funds for large physical improvements.

DEVELOPING THE PROGRAM

Preceding discussion has indicated the more important financial analysis that should be made in the initial phase of developing a long-range improvement program. It is important that normal public services, including maintenance and repair, be continued, which may leave only limited annual amounts available for financing the program. However, data must be developed regarding the potential amount. Other essential steps or studies involve: (a) preliminary selection of improvement projects, (b) cost estimates of the projects, (c) estimates of potential funds that should be available from the various sources, and (d) final selection of projects within the financial ability of the municipality.

Preliminary Selection of Projects

The comprehensive plan should consider a complete appraisal of existing and probable future needs and many proposed improvements would be related to such needs. Thus, there should be useful data regarding the comparative importance of many improvements. A list of the most needed projects should be selected by the Planning Commission and its staff for inclusion in the improvement program.

This first list of projects should be discussed with respective department heads who will be responsible for construction and operation. The comments and suggestions of the several departments should have a major influence upon final inclusion of each project and its comparative order of importance.

Since the program is for the entire community, several factors must be considered in selecting each project as to its effect upon the community. Among the more important are: (a) protection of life; (b) maintenance of public health; (c) protection of property; (d) conservation of services; (e) replacement of obsolete facilities; (f) reduction of operational costs; (g) public convenience; (h) preservation of natural resources; (i) recreational value; (j) economical value; (k) new growth and development; (l) preservation of historical landmarks; and (m) equitable distribution in major sectors of the community. These criteria are not necessarily in order and must be established by the individual community.

Cost Estimates

Construction cost estimates must be prepared for each of the initially selected projects. These need not involve working drawings and specifications, but preliminary sketches should indicate extent of improvements and type of construction so that quantities and unit prices can be determined. Several projects such as parks, schools, major streets, and new public buildings may require acquisition of land and the probable cost thereof should be included in the project cost. Some projects may also require new equipment before becoming operable, and this should be included in the total project cost. An example would be a new fire station, where new fire fighting equipment would be required before protection could be provided.

Consideration should also be given to probable operating and maintenance cost of any capital improvement. While not affecting the improvement program, these could increase other city expenditures, thus reducing the amount remaining for future capital improvements. Current inflationary trends must be carefully considered in developing estimates of future costs [Figure 10-3].

Source and Amounts of Available Funds

This phase requires careful and detailed study. It involves estimates of assessed valuation for each of the impending five or six years, as well as any change in property tax rates. Probable income from other sources such as fines, licenses, and state refunds should also be made. Similar estimates will also be required of other major sources of income such as sales and income taxes. The objective is to have accurate forecasts of the annual normal income that can be anticipated during the period studies.

Similar estimates should be prepared of the probable annual expenditures for normal government activities—administration, repair, and maintenance and the many services that are provided or will be required. Estimates of interest and amortization for outstanding bonds is also necessary. These data, together with the estimates of the total income, will enable close approximations of the annual amount of current funds available for the capital improvement program. Close cooperation with the city's fiscal officers is essential during the preparation of estimates of income and expenditures.

Each of the proposed improvements should be carefully studied to determine the possibility of obtaining financial assistance from other governmental agencies. Projects such as parks and open space, schools, major streets, water and sewer facilities, and urban renewal projects afford good possibilities for such assistance, especially from the federal government. Proposed projects should be discussed with appropriate representatives of governmental agencies to determine the possibilities of their approval and participation, as well as the amount of funds therefor.

Final Selection of Projects

After cost estimates and estimates of potential income are available, the projects that can be initiated each year can be finally selected. Consideration must be given to the fact that some of the larger projects, especially those requiring land acquisitions, will probably require one or two years before construction can be started. This will affect the year in which they are included within the entire program. If a bond issue is to be used for financing a portion of the program, conferences should be held with financial

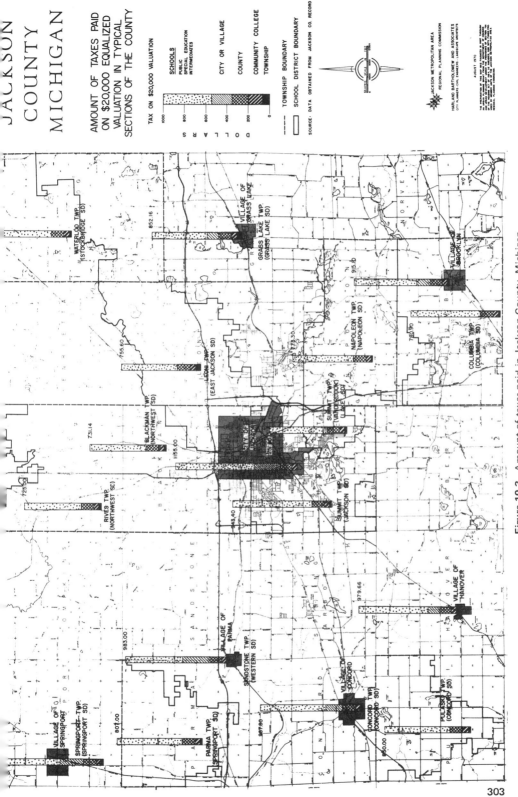

Figure 10-3 Amount of taxes paid in Jackson County, Michigan.

consultants or financial institutions to secure suggestions regarding interest rates and the life of the bonds.

The final improvement program should be presented in both graphical and tabular form and a brief, descriptive statement is desirable so the program can be readily understood by the citizens.

CONTINUING REVIEW

The first capital improvement program will cover a period of five or six years, but thereafter, it should be reviewed annually. As projects are completed, they will logically be removed from the program and new ones will be added for an additional year. Unexpected changes in local conditions and needs may also require addition of projects not previously considered or adjustments in the starting dates that were first proposed.

The Planning Commission is the logical agency to develop and revise the capital improvement program. In fact, some state enabling acts provide that the Planning Commission shall develop and revise annually such a program to assist in carrying out the comprehensive plan. In general, the same steps should be followed in revising and updating the improvement program as were used in developing the initial one. It is especially essential that the commission and its staff work closely with local department heads and financial officials as well as with appropriate federal and state representatives.

11 URBAN RENEWAL AND PLAN REALIZATION

Wm. H. Claire

One of the most significant approaches in connection with parts of a general plan to be implemented is through urban renewal and community realization of needed facilities, such as a new school or the widening of a street substandard in width. Urban renewal usually is the best method for bringing about these improvements and correcting a number of other deficiencies simultaneously.

The process of formulating renewal techniques could be thought of as having gained its impetus from the slums of the late nineteenth century, when the Industrial Revolution spawned workers' row houses near factories in large eastern manufacturing complexes. Living conditions became unbearable and the first efforts to correct them were privately sponsored and funded. These efforts were social experiments of lesser magnitude than the problem called for, yet paved the way for other and larger low-rent private housing developments of an eleemosynary nature in the larger cities of the United States. This finally led to the Housing Act of 1937 that included for the first time a public housing program, funds for which were guaranteed by the federal government.

The public housing program supplied a desperate need for adequate housing but usually in areas where the worst slums were located and with incompatible land uses nearby, often in the form of industry, railroads, or substandard areas. Most of these public housing projects are still operating.

The next step was the Housing Act of 1949 that included additional public housing allocations, as well as the first slum clearance and urban redevelopment legislation nationwide in the United

States. Several states had passed similar enabling statutes, some of the more notable of which were New York, Illinois, California, and Pennsylvania in 1946 or earlier.

For the first time a national housing policy was set forth (in the Housing Act of 1949) and is sufficiently significant to repeat in part here as follows:

> Sec. 2. The Congress hereby declares that the general welfare and security of the Nation and the health and living standards of its people require housing production and related community development sufficient to remedy the serious housing shortage, the elimination of substandard and other inadequate housing through the clearance of slums and blighted areas, and the realization as soon as feasible of the goal of a decent home and a suitable living environment for every American family, thus contributing to the development and redevelopment of communities and to the advancement of the growth, wealth, and security of the Nation.

As beneficial as the slum clearance and urban redevelopment program administered by the Housing and Home Finance Agency proved to be, there were still some shortcomings in the process. Relocation was not adequately provided for, correcting pockets of blight left remnants of blight surrounding the redevelopment project, and a more comprehensive attack on substandard conditions was needed. Consequently, a broader scope was taken to deal with blight that was growing faster than it was being eliminated, and the Housing Act of 1954 established urban renewal and its three-pronged assault on blight—conservation, rehabilitation, and redevelopment. Similar programs were in progress in Canada, though under different nomenclature and methodology.

The term "blight," as applied to an urban location, may be defined as applying to an area, which because of lack of development, cessation of growth, decrease in economic activities, deterioration of improvements, or characteristics of occupancy, age, obsolescence, high incidence of vacancy, substandard buildings, or other factors impairing values or preventing normal development of property or use thereof, has become undesirable for or impossible of normal development or occupancy. A "slum" may be defined as an area with advanced conditions of blight, usually indicating redevelopment or clearance and rebuilding as the most effective corrective action. "Substandard" as defined in Chapter 4 regarding housing should also be considered applicable to other buildings or structures not in keeping with modern standards for such development.

Presently the renewal program in the United States is being developed into a still broader concept, the Neighborhood Development Program (NDP) stemming from the Housing Act of 1968 with promise of greater benefits and a hope of eventual elimination of substandard housing and other conditions of blight. This act also included a program to provide 26 million housing units during the ensuing 10 years. The current program designed to achieve this goal is known as Operation Breakthrough.

These housing acts, coming every year or two since the first one in 1937, contain other provisions related to renewal. One may mention the General Neighborhood Renewal Plan, the Feasibility Study, the Community Renewal Program, Code Enforcement, and others that are discussed below. The widespread use of these programs, though disappointing from the standpoint of number of projects completed, nevertheless indicate the need for renewal in the country. Appropriations of federal grants between

1949 and 1971 have amounted to over $10 billion for more than 2,000 projects, with less than 600 completed in that time. A look into the reasons for this poor record is included hereafter in this chapter—not as criticism but to lead toward an improved record. Examples of renewal programs in a number of cities in the United States and Canada are shown graphically throughout the chapter.

A description of the urban renewal process should start with the three aforementioned renewal tools of conservation, rehabilitation, and redevelopment.

TOOLS OF RENEWAL AND THEIR APPLICATION

The degree of blight usually determines the tool to use to correct unwanted conditions. Early signs of growing blight in a fairly acceptable neighborhood may indicate only the light treatment of conservation, while more advanced deterioration may also require rehabilitation, and predominant conditions of substandardness may be corrected only by clearance and redevelopment.

Conservation

This renewal tool should be categorized as one that prevents blight more than correcting it and may be applied in a neighborhood of near standard quality with a few deficiencies, that if left untreated would eventually affect the surrounding area adversely. Examples of this might include a machine shop or junk yard in a residential neighborhood, lack of a neighborhood park, a street system that invites heavy volumes of traffic through a neighborhood rather than around it, or an old house converted to commercial or industrial use in a neighborhood otherwise free of such incompatible conversions.

Corrective measures for such deficiencies may consist of individually treating each trouble spot or doing so collectively in a conservation or code enforcement project, depending upon the degree of deteriorating conditions. If say, five or less homes out of a hundred need code enforcement, a project would hardly be justified but, with 20 percent or more one probably would be. Normally a housing code, if properly enforced, should take care of areas with less than 20 percent substandard housing. Availability of federal grants and loans for a code enforcement project should be carefully considered in determination of the type of corrective action to be taken. The action necessary to break the continuity of the street that carries traffic through the neighborhood in an effort to divert it around the neighborhood may be accomplished as a separate municipal chore or as a part of a conservation or code enforcement process, and the same is true in acquiring space for the neighborhood park or new school.

Rarely does an urban area fit neatly and entirely into a conservation, rehabilitation, or redevelopment type of renewal project, but rather a combination of two or all three of these tools are necessary. Conservation is the "light" touch, a preventive measure, and the least controversial of the three types. Rehabilitation is the middle course in renewal and is considerably more complicated than conservation, largely because much more is wrong and needs to be corrected.

Unfortunately, the term "conservation" as used in urban renewal has been replaced by or combined with rehabilitation. However, conservation is a renewal technique necessary by itself to protect good neighborhoods and to keep them from deterioration, and may not involve rehabilitation at all.

Rehabilitation

The big thrust toward rehabilitation came with the Housing Act of 1954 and the loans and grants provided for therein and in subsequent legislation. The slow start of the slum clearance and redevelopment program in the late 1940s and early 1950s was due to the complications of the redevelopment process, the controversies it has survived, and the realization that, as rich as the country is, there was not enough money to correct all blight by clearance and redevelopment. The bulk of it would have to be adjusted or mitigated through rehabilitation.

One plus feature rehabilitation has going for it is that persons retain ownership of their property and rehabilitate it themselves through improvements that would bring the property up to a predetermined standard, such as FHA's *Residential Property Rehabilitation Standards*.[1] In this manner, the use of condemnation powers or eminent domain are obviated and family relocation is less than it would be in redevelopment. The social aspects are more acceptable too; neighborhood continuity is more likely and fewer families would leave their homes, churches, convenience of the corner store, and other familiar places.

The rehabilitation process in an urban renewal project consists of setting goals for the project; drawing up standards for residential and nonresidential properties; surveying each property in sufficient detail to decide if it is standard, conservable, or should be acquired and cleared; planning public improvements where necessary; and formulating a financial plan consisting of federal loans and grants, the city's share of the deficit or net project cost, and private funds, if any.

A word of caution in the field of rehabilitation is that most old structures are infeasible of rehabilitation. Forcing rehabilitation on a homeowner whose house is not large enough, or too obsolete, or improperly constructed originally is a hardship he should be spared. This is particularly true if the house should eventually need to be acquired and cleared for public improvement reasons, such as a change in street patterns, a new school or park, or a public housing development. Many old structures in both Canada and the United States have been successfully rehabilitated and certainly many more should and will be. However, the test is in the arithmetic; the question is: (a) will the cost of rehabilitation be recouped in additional rent in the case of a duplex or multifamily structure or in added resale value in the case of a single family dwelling, (b) is the cost of rehabilitation in excess of the rule-of-thumb norm of 50 percent of the market value of the structure, (c) or is the cost of rehabilitation of the structure more than the

1. HUD-FHA Publication PG-50, Washington, D.C., Jan. 1968.

cost of tearing it down and building a new one of comparable size and accommodations? The rehabilitation project should be constituted to provide answers with facts and figures to each of these questions and a negative response in case of any of them would indicate clearance and redevelopment is in order.

One reason why a rehabilitation or code enforcement project often also uses redevelopment is that some studies of feasibility of rehabilitation may prove negative or that rehabilitation is infeasible, and at least spot clearance, if not more widespread clearance, is usually a necessity. An acceptable method of shortening this process is developing rehabilitation "typicals" in sufficient detail to answer the three questions above by selecting a small percentage of structures which are typical of many others in the project such that results of the study could logically apply to the others. The example of a typical rehabilitation that proved feasible [Table 11-1 and Figure 11-1] and another infeasible [Table 11-2 and Figure 11-2] were made in 1971 in a renewal project in Memphis, Tennessee. Notice how questions above are answered in the analyses. These examples are from the Kansas Street Neighborhood Development Program Area in Memphis, Tennessee [see Figure 11-3].

Redevelopment

The ultimate tool in renewal when conservation and rehabilitation are unable to bring about the desired cure is redevelopment, or acquisition, clearance, and rebuilding. All structures in an urban renewal project need not necessarily be acquired and cleared, though acquisition and clearance of some standard structures may be necessary for a sound plan to be implemented.

The core of a city or the fringe of the core is more often than not a likely location for redevelopment because land uses are incongruously mixed, the street system may be outmoded, most structures are obsolete or have deteriorated beyond feasible repair, and the public utilities are inadequate for modern structures. These physical deficiencies, as troublesome as they are, do not equal the deplorable sociologic situations and debilitating economic drag on the community usually predominant in these locations.

The redevelopment process is much like that for a rehabilitation project in that surveys are made, an urban renewal plan is formulated, a public hearing is held on the plan, approval is obtained from the LPA (local public agency—housing authority or renewal agency), HUD, and the local governing body of the city upon recommendation of the Planning Commission; funding contracts are drawn up between HUD and the LPA; and finally the project is ready for development or carrying out of the approved urban renewal plan by the LPA.

A difficult part of renewal is setting the project boundary. Normally there is not a definite border between a blighted and unblighted area. Urban areas usually are good or bad and the space between these extremes is a mixture of both, known as the gray areas. If neglected, these areas customarily get worse and, the sooner they are renewed, the less the cost. The extent of an urban renewal project should be measured against the ability of the community financially and administratively to accomplish the project before the project boundary is set.

TABLE 11-1
Feasible Rehabilitation Typicals Study (See Figure 11-1)

For: Memphis Housing Authority   By: Harland Bartholomew and Associates

Date: 16 July 1971

Description: One-story, frame and brick veneer duplex, one bedroom each side, tenant occupied.

Total Building Area: 1,137 SF   Total Lot Area: 5,000 SF

Proposed Lot Area: 7,000 SF

Proposal: Four-bedroom, two-bathroom single-family dwelling. Lot would become standard by closing of Fairview Street and the widening of Goodloe Avenue.

Cost Estimate: Costs shown are the sums of all items considered under each major item and include labor and materials in place.

Roofing	$ 450
Doors	590
Windows	300
Exterior repairs (painting, tuckpointing, etc.)	417
Floors	567
Moulding (interior and exterior)	139
Heating unit	800
Sheetrock (painting included)	198
Paper (interior)	331
Painting (interior)	108
Plumbing	685
New framing	90
Wainscoting in two bathrooms	360
Miscellaneous	277
Incidental job cost	170
Subtotal	$5,482
Overhead and Profit (25%)	1,371
Total Cost of Rehabilitation	$6,853

Estimated Value: $7,250 for house and lot

Conclusions: The cost of rehabilitation of this structure as a one-bedroom duplex or a four-bedroom single-family dwelling is greater than one-half the estimated value. According to the 50 percent rule, this structure is infeasible for rehabilitation. However, a cost of $14,378 (estimated value plus rehabilitation cost plus cost of net additional land at $0.50 per SF) for a four-bedroom house is reasonable on today's market.

A new house of this size at $11.00 per SF construction cost and a lot of 7,000 SF at $0.50 per SF would cost $16,007. The house could, therefore, be considered feasible for rehabilitation, be useful as a relocation resource, and save $1,629 on the grant requirement for a homeowner to be relocated or for a tenant relocatee to become a homeowner. Consequently, rehabilitation by MHA is recommended.

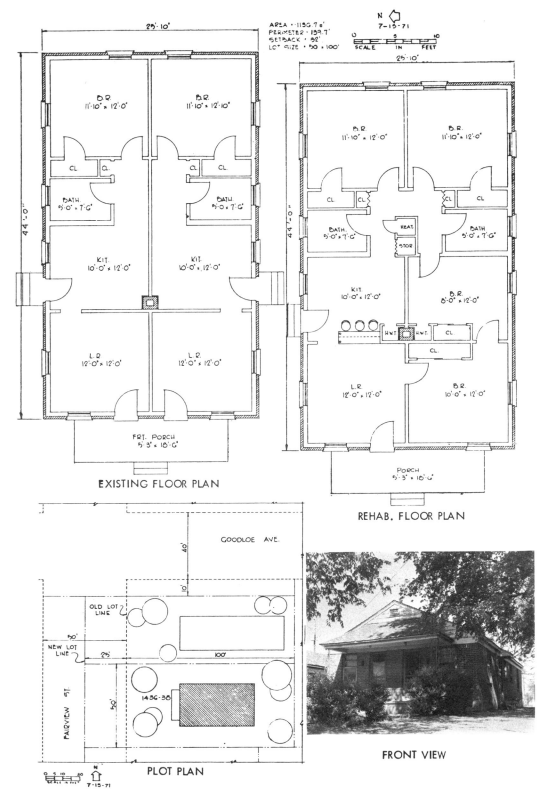

AREA · 1156.7 □'
PERIMETER · 139.7'
SETBACK · 32'
LOT SIZE · 50 × 100'

N
7-15-71

SCALE IN FEET

EXISTING FLOOR PLAN

REHAB. FLOOR PLAN

PLOT PLAN

FRONT VIEW

Source: Memphis Housing Authority and Harland Bartholomew and Associates.

Figure 11-1 Feasible rehabilitation typical.

TABLE 11-2
Infeasible Rehabilitation Typicals Study (See Figure 11-2)

For: Memphis Housing Authority   By: Harland Bartholomew and Associates

Date: 16 July 1971

Description: One-story, two-bedroom, frame, single-family dwelling, owner occupied.

Total Building Area: 800 SF   Total Lot Area: 5,000 SF

Proposed Lot Area: 6,000 SF

Proposal: Two-bedroom house with alterations where necessary to conform to FHA standards.

Cost Estimate: Costs shown are the sums of all items considered under each major item and include
labor and materials in place.

Foundation	$ 580
Removal of old siding	100
Brick veneer	1,048
Windows	280
Alterations	206
Insulation and 1/2″ fiberboard	196
Repairs	140
Floors	259
Plumbing (replace bath fixtures)	650
Sheetrock	486
Heating unit	250
Electrical	380
Doors	445
Miscellaneous	416
Incidental job cost	170
Subtotal	$5,607
Overhead and Profit (25%)	1,401
Total Cost of Rehabilitation of Structure	$7,007
Add 1,000 SF of land at $0.50 per SF	500
Total Rehabilitation Cost	$7,507

Estimated Value: $5,650 for house and lot

Conclusions: The rehabilitation cost of this structure is well above the estimated value. The structure
is economically infeasible for rehabilitation. The cost of a new 800 SF structure at $11.00 per SF plus
the cost of 6,000 SF of land at $0.50 per SF would be approximately $11,800. The total investment
after rehabilitation would be $13,157 (estimated value plus rehabilitation cost). Consequently,
rehabilitation is not recommended.

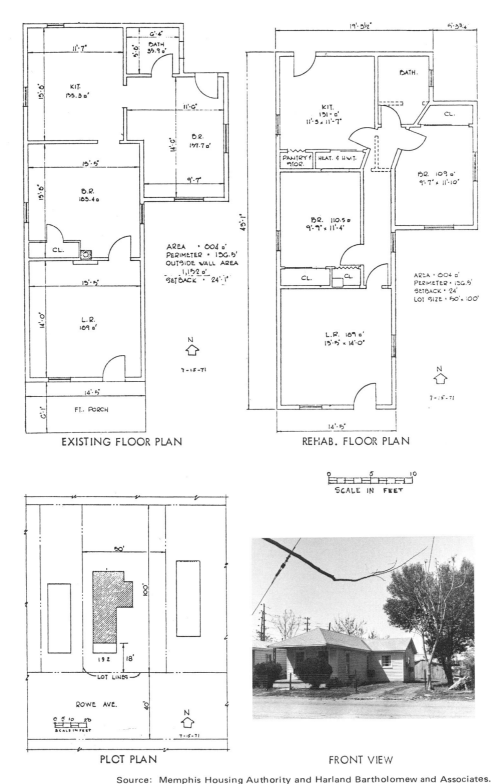

EXISTING FLOOR PLAN

REHAB. FLOOR PLAN

SCALE IN FEET

PLOT PLAN

FRONT VIEW

Source: Memphis Housing Authority and Harland Bartholomew and Associates.

Figure 11-2 Infeasible rehabilitation typical.

313

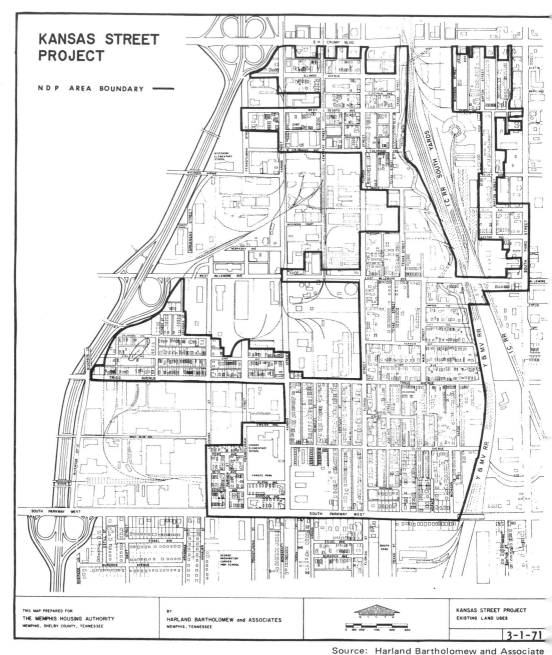

Source: Harland Bartholomew and Associate

Figure 11-3   Kansas Street NDP Project, Memphis.

One feature added in recent years is the PAC (Project Area Committee) composed of residents of the project area elected by the people (owner-occupants or renters) in the project to represent them in the entire renewal process from plan formulation through development. This HUD requirement has the express purpose of involving the people in the renewal of their neighborhood and avoiding the lack of communication that often occurred between project site occupants and the LPA.

PAC is a social experiment intended to spread understanding of the renewal process to the people most affected by it—those who dwell in the project areas, and to encourage their participation in the process in a positive manner. PAC can be a progressive force in renewal, if those responsible for its leadership in the LPA, in the city offices involved, from consulting firms, and in PAC itself use the necessary degree of patience, objectivity, tolerance, knowledge, and kindness. An example of the planning goals arrived at in a series of PAC meetings in Memphis in 1971 [Table 11-3] indicates the mutual understanding and respect of opinions on both sides that took more than a year to develop.

The financing of a renewal project, whether by conservation, rehabilitation, or redevelopment is by means of federal loans and grants. The loans are short-term as needed for acquisition, clearance, and site improvements, and are repayable at the going federal rate of interest. Federal grants for renewal pay for up to two-thirds (three-fourths in cities under 50,000 population) of the net cost of the project. The net cost is the difference between gross project cost and proceeds from the sale of cleared land. Relocation payments, customarily a 100 percent federal grant, are part of the gross project cost as of July 1, 1972.

A shortcoming of the renewal process was (and still is in many communities) the lack of a coordinated program for renewal efforts to fit into the whole scheme of improvements and the absence of corollary systems necessary to realize the desired coordination. The Housing Act of 1954 (Section 101C) initiated the Workable Program for Community Improvement (WPCI) and made it a requirement that a community would commit itself to before certain federal loans and grants would be available to the community.

WORKABLE PROGRAM FOR COMMUNITY IMPROVEMENT

The simple logic of systems engineering that made possible the fantastic achievements in space travel and exploration could have been the motivating force behind the WPCI. Urban renewal should make more sense and the tax dollars used should be spent more wisely and effectively with the WPCI than without it.

A WPCI is an official plan of action of a community for utilizing appropriate private and public resources to deal effectively with urban slums and blight and for the establishment and preservation of a well-planned community with well-organized residential neighborhoods of decent homes and suitable living environment for adequate family life.

The general objectives or requirements of the WPCI are to (a) establish responsibility

TABLE 11-3
Kansas Street (Memphis, Tenn.) NDP Project Planning Objectives

1. Standard [a]residential neighborhoods with living environments that are safe, sanitary, quiet, and beautiful.
2. A system of standard [a]major, collector, and minor streets.
3. Convenient public transportation facilities.
4. Standard [a]community facilities such as schools, parks, neighborhood centers, and appropriate utilities.
5. Improved relationships between living and employment centers with separation of and/or provision for buffers between incompatible land uses, wherever feasible.
6. Convenient shopping facilities within a reasonable walking distance.
7. Improved worship environment.
8. First priority for development is to be land which is vacant or occupied by an incompatible use within a residential neighborhood.
9. Standard [a]housing adequate for and within economic reach of each family or individual in the area who wants to remain in the area shall be provided wherever feasible in accord with the following:
    a. The total number of housing units in the area after renewal shall at least equal the number of families who live and want to remain in the area.
    b. The number of single-family dwellings for sale in the area after renewal shall at least equal the number of acquired and cleared single-family dwellings occupied before renewal by owners who wish to remain in the area.
    c. Every effort shall be made to rehabilitate or retain as many housing units as is feasible.
10. The total net amount of land used for housing before renewal shall at least equal the same after renewal except that land used for parks, schools, and other community facilities may be substituted for housing.
11. Site occupants who must be moved shall be relocated as follows:
    a. Relocation shall be into standard housing only and those who wish to remain in the area shall have first priority on relocation housing in the area.
    b. Relocation housing shall be provided for the elderly who want to remain in the area.
12. The Kansas and Trigg residential neighborhoods shall be the least area in the Kansas Street Urban Renewal Project devoted to residential and related commercial or public, but not industrial, land uses.
13. The area bounded by Trigg, Louisiana, Omega, and Kansas Streets shall, if feasible, be added to the above described area and be made available for housing in order to:
    a. Link up with the Kansas neighborhood.
    b. Eliminate industry next to Kansas Street school.

[a]"Standard" here may be defined as equal to or better than a minimum set of requirements established for a building, facility, or an entire neighborhood.

Source: Prepared for Project Area Committee and Memphis Housing Authority by Harland Bartholomew and Assocs.

in the hands of the chief executive of the community (the mayor or city or county manager, for example), (b) establish administrative mechanism to execute the WPCI, (c) set forth the relationship between the chief executive and the administrative entity responsible for the WPCI, and (d) to list, schedule, and delegate responsibility for various actions proposed under four principal headings—codes and code enforcement, planning and programing, housing and relocation, and citizen involvement.

The motivation to establish a WPCI rests with the desire for federal funds as evidenced by the fact that 3,763 communities each had a certified WPCI as of the end of 1969.[2] Also significant and indicative of the complications associated with using federal funds is the fact that the WPCI in 1,523 of those communities at that time was allowed to become inactive. HUD requires recertification of the WPCI every two years after the initial certification. The continuing efforts to make renewal work properly are behind this last statistic and new management techniques required in recent HUD directives as well as completely new approaches to community improvement in the proposed revenue sharing program are ongoing methods discussed below.

Most communities with a WPCI meantime are finding long-lasting benefits from its use and are continually improving living conditions through the four basic components of the WPCI. The HUD requirement for each of these components is quoted[3] below verbatim.

Codes and Code Enforcement

The primary HUD requirements are twofold: "(a) The adoption of the latest published edition of one of the nationally recognized model housing, building, plumbing, electrical, fire prevention and related codes and ordinances, as amended, or state or local codes with comparable standards. (b) The establishment of an effective code enforcement program."

The related codes may include a sign, traffic, sanitary, elevator, oil drilling, or other codes that would help a community control dangerous operations or nuisances.

The codes are listed in the WPCI application of a community, reasons are given for deviations from model codes, a description is provided as to how the codes are proposed to be used to eliminate slums and blight, maps are included showing areas proposed for code enforcement activities, a budget for code enforcement work is included. Finally a chart is furnished showing the number of structures and dwelling units inspected, found in violation, whether violations abated, or buildings were razed. Reasons are also required as to why the proposals in the previous application were not accomplished if this were the case, and what the community intends to do about it.

Too often code enforcement work has been carried out on a hit-or-miss basis without regard for predetermined objectives or to pacify pressure groups demanding action. Sound planning including dovetailing of code enforcement with other community action such as redevelopment, is the answer to this problem.

Planning and Programing

The HUD requirement here is "The development of an effective continuing planning and programing process which engages in the development of comprehensive plans and

---

2. *HUD Statistical Yearbook* (Washington, D.C.: Government Printing Office, 1969), p. 312.
3. From Application for Workable Program Certification or Recertification, HUD-1081 Form, Washington, D.C., Nov. 1968.

translates such plans into action programs to help overcome the major physical, social, and economic problems of the slum and blighted areas within the community."

A description is required of the status of the general plan as to its completion and adoption as well as its elements or components of land use, transportation, housing, community facilities, public improvements program, and the like.

Then a program of action is indicated to resolve the problems or portions of them during the ensuing five or six years with estimated budgets of city and other funds and the professional and other personnel retained or to be retained to carry out the program.

Finally, the relationship of these activities to the chief executive of the community is described together with the role of local agencies and organizations both of a public and private nature.

These activities and programs are often frustrated by a lack of appropriate preparation for housing and relocation of those displaced by governmental action of one kind or another.

Housing and Relocation

The housing requirement of this double-faceted element of the WPCI is to "Identify and analyze the gap between the community's low and moderate income housing needs and the resources available to meet the need, and develop and implement a meaningful action program to help overcome the gap."

This calls for an inventory of low- and moderate-income families, by size, income, and race, living in substandard housing and the number of standard housing units presently vacant and available at prices or rentals such families can afford to pay. Next a program should be set forth indicating how required housing is to be provided and the responsibility of private or public agencies involved, with schedules to meet relocation and other housing needs.

The relocation requirements are "The development of a centrally administered or coordinated relocation program for all families and individuals displaced by governmental action in the community; the provision of a sufficient volume of decent, safe, and sanitary housing within the means of such displacees in appropriate unit sizes; and the provision of services to such displacees comparable to those under the urban renewal program."

First, relocation needs are determined and categorized as renewal or other governmental action and the responsible relocation entity is identified. These needs are set forth in a table by numbers of families (minority and nonminority) and businesses and whether relocation was into standard or substandard accommodations. Next, a determination is made of the relocation workload anticipated in the next two years and how it is proposed to be handled. This requires housing size needed, income, race, and other pertinent information. Finally, the agencies involved are described and also how any relocation housing deficiencies are proposed to be overcome.

Clearly, the three elements of the WPCI described above necessarily involve a broad spectrum of the community and this involvement can mean the success or failure of the renewal program.

Citizen Involvement

The HUD requirement is that " . . . the community provides and continues to expand opportunities for citizens, especially those who are poor and members of minority groups, to participate in all phases of the related HUD-assisted renewal and housing programs. The particular organizational means for community involvement is left to the discretion of each community, but the latter must demonstrate in its Workable Program submission that it provides clear and direct access to decision-making, relevant and timely information, and necessary technical assistance to participating groups and individuals in programs covered."

This element of the WPCI should identify and describe the types of participating groups in HUD-assisted programs and the program of the community to expand low- and moderate-income housing and which groups are involved in each program. Then efforts to coordinate involved groups and opportunities offered individuals to participate are described. Next, the steps taken to provide information and technical assistance to groups and individuals are related and, finally, the nature of issues relating to the programs of the community and subsequent recommendations are made and results therefrom are described.

Some idea of the technical surveys, the professional determinations, and the administrative workload involved in the four WPCI elements may be realized in the brief descriptions above. The first exposure of most community officials and leaders to this apparently enormous red tape produces astonishment, bewilderment, or indignation, unless a good number of the requirements have already been fulfilled or at least initiated in the community. However, the WPCI is more flexible than the seemingly rigid requirements imply, and the gradual implementation of the elements over a period of years is implied and actually practiced. The reasonableness of the WPCI application from the community and the reasonableness of its review by HUD are keys to a sound and successful WPCI. The benefits of the WPCI to a community are worth the efforts, patience, and tough decisions required to get it certified and recertified in the years ahead.

THE GENERAL PLAN AND URBAN RENEWAL

There are several reasons for the ponderous slowness of the urban renewal program in the United States, some of the principal ones of which are lack of organization for a program of this magnitude, adjudication of state and federal renewal legislation, controversial issues involved in the program, administrative red tape, political machinations, insufficient funding by the Congress and/or the President, or lack of adequate comprehensive or general planning in some of the approximately 1,200 communities in the United States with renewal programs.

The WPCI, though no longer a prerequisite for federal funding of public housing, must be certified by HUD before a community may enter into a contract with HUD for federal financial assistance in urban renewal. All four elements of the WPCI provide a logical foundation for renewal and general planning. The relationship between general planning and renewal, if properly understood and observed by the Planning Commission, the renewal agency, and the public and private leadership of the community can mean a more efficiently operated renewal program.

The frustrations of renewal result in considerable measure from a lack of a general plan, or a plan too general to serve as a basis for land use and other determinations to be made in renewal planning, or a general plan incomplete in blighted areas where planning decisions are delayed because they are tough ones to make or the planner has no backing for his decisions.

The general plan, if adequate, would prevent the undesirable practice of a code enforcement program followed soon after in the same area by an urban renewal project. A property owner who brings his property up to prevailing codes at his own expense or even with governmental financing and a few years later finds his property condemned for urban renewal has a legitimate complaint. The general plan should so definitely determine the corrective action to be taken in blighted areas that this difficulty will be mitigated. The excuse is often that the owners of standard property put pressure on their councilmen to force the substandard property owners to improve their properties and renewal, though intended for the area eventually, is already committed, as to funds and manpower, elsewhere in the community. Thus, the councilman gets relief from the pressure of his constituents by arranging for a code enforcement project in the subject area, a year or two, in some cases, before the renewal agency gets around to the area.

Making decisions as to the appropriate renewal process to use in each blighted area of a city is no easy task and, fortunately, there are several types of special studies to turn to for these difficult answers. Some of these studies are the CRP (community renewal program), the feasibility survey, GNRP (general neighborhood renewal plan), model cities, concentrated code enforcement project, demolition project, interim assistance program, certified area program, and NDP (neighborhood development program). Confusing? Could be, except that each has a particular application and reason for being. They are listed, not in chronological order as they came into being but as to their comprehensiveness and coverage geographically or functionally.

CRP

This useful planning tool provides grants to communities of up to two-thirds of the cost of surveying conditions of blight and preparing a program to cover the full range of urban renewal needs of an entire community. The details of the CRP may be found in the Housing Act of 1959.

Feasibility Survey

This is a study of a blighted area that may be too large to renew as one project and may be more feasibly renewed as two or more, depending on findings of relocation workload, cost to the city of the local share of net project cost, and the ability to market land for redevelopment as it is cleared. The feasibility survey was authorized by the Housing Act of 1956.

GNRP

This is similar (from Housing Act of 1956) to the feasibility survey except that a plan is formulated for the projects studied and a commitment to proceed with a project of at least 10 percent of the subject area is included in the GNRP contract between HUD and the community.

Model Cities

This is correctly titled Model Neighborhoods in Demonstration Cities and was authorized by the Metropolitan Development Act of 1966. The Model Cities Program (there are more than 150 in operation) provides grants and technical assistance to plan, develop, and carry out comprehensive programs for rebuilding or restoring slum and blighted areas through coordinated use of all available federal programs and private and local resources. Plans cover housing, jobs, and education, and such associated problems as health and social services, transportation, crime, and recreation.

Code Enforcement

This program, authorized by the Housing Act of 1965, provides technical assistance and grants for planning, reviewing, and administering concentrated code enforcement programs in selected local areas and is used where clearance and redevelopment are not needed or desired.

Demolition Project

This program, authorized by the Housing Act of 1965, provides technical assistance and grants to communities to finance up to two-thirds of the cost of demolishing structures which state or local law determines to be structurally unsound. The structures may be located in or outside of urban renewal areas and provide the necessary action in a conservation project where more extensive renewal is not required or desired locally.

Interim Assistance

The Housing Act of 1968 authorized this program to provide interim actions to alleviate harmful conditions in slum and blighted areas planned for comprehensive renewal but in which some immediate public action is required, such as rat control, waste disposal, demolition of vacant and dangerous structures, weed abatement, and the like.

Certified Area Program

This program provides for rehabilitation of residential properties within areas planned for either urban renewal or code enforcement activities within a reasonable time and was authorized by the Housing Act of 1968.

NDP

This program has considerable promise of renewal being accomplished more expeditiously and was authorized by the Housing Act of 1968. NDP consists of urban renewal activities in one or more urban renewal areas that are planned and carried out on the basis of annual increments. Financing is based on the amount of loan and grant funds needed to carry out the activities planned during a twelve-month period and beginning with the first such period. Thus, renewal development starts the first year and the application to HUD from a community must include a plan for a selected section of an urban renewal area in sufficient detail for renewal activities (rehabilitation or property acquisition) to begin during the first year. The more general and definitive planning a community has accomplished, the better it is prepared to satisfy NDP requirements. NDP federal grants are calculated the same as for a conventional renewal project, two-thirds of the net project cost (three-fourths in communities of 50,000 or less population). The maximum allowable rehabilitation grant is $3,500. After June 30, 1972, relocation grants were split federal and local on the two-thirds formula instead of 100 percent federal, as mentioned above.

Other

Several other programs are available including disaster projects, public housing, cooperatives, public facilities, historical preservation, neighborhood facilities, low-income home ownership, demonstration programs, and others directly or indirectly of benefit to renewal.

The degree of use made of these programs should give an idea of their acceptance and effectiveness throughout the United States [Table 11-4] and yet the whole urban renewal process needs additional expediting, more efficiency, less politics, improved management, and considerably more money. The comparison of several cities as to the degree of utilization of renewal geographically [Figure 11-4] indicates that renewal has only just begun.

Several innovations recently established by HUD should bear watching to learn if they improve the renewal process. One is a proclaimer certificate that an LPA may submit to HUD in place of lengthy detailed proof that such and such an activity was performed or a condition exists. Another is a policy of no amendatory grant increases that puts it up to an LPA to request a carefully calculated grant amount to sustain a project through to completion. One other is a management control using CPM (critical path method) and computerized systems to monitor costs and schedules so that weak links in the complicated urban renewal chain of activities may be discovered and strengthened in good time.

The foregoing has traced the evolutionary process of urban renewal trial and error, improved techniques, new management controls, and the like. The process of refinement is still active and new programs, such as community development and revenue sharing, are being tried. These and others are treated below in this chapter. However, regardless of the formation of new renewal methods, the old rules and regulations govern renewal efforts now and some pointers on how to make them work are covered at this juncture.

TABLE 11-4

Summary of Urban Renewal Programs as of June 30, 1970
(dollars in thousands)

Type of Program	Local-ities	Proj-ects	Federal Grants
I. Programs With Federal Grants			
A. APPROVALS			
All Programs - Total	1,079	2,850	$8,980,660
Urban Renewal Projects - Total	967	2,073	7,618,525
Approved for Execution	818	1,683	6,367,040
Completed	330	520	614,661
Active	679	1,163	5,752,379
Approved for Planning	342	390	1,251,485
Planning under way	320	360	1,194,689
Applications under preparation within			
General Neighborhood Renewal Plans	30	30	56,796
Neighborhood Development Programs - Total	129	129	1,014,091
Active	129	129	914,248
Reserved	xxx	xxx	99,843
Code Enforcement Projects - Total	132	151	245,494
Completed	—	—	—
Active	132	151	245,494
Demolition Projects - Total	102	123	21,877
Completed	19	22	1,311
Active	91	101	20,566
Interim Assistance Programs - Total	25	27	13,268
Completed	—	—	—
Active	25	27	13,268
Certified Area Programs - Total	8	8	6,017
Completed	—	—	—
Active	8	8	6,017
Community Renewal Programs - Total	221	234	51,953
Completed	99	99	7,174
Under Preparation	129	135	44,779
Demonstration Programs - Total	x	105	9,435
Completed	x	51	3,030
Active	x	54	6,405
B. DISBURSEMENTS			
All Programs - Total	xxx	xxx	4,025,797
Urban Renewal Projects	xxx	xxx	3,476,936
Neighborhood Development Programs	xxx	xxx	406,908
Code Enforcement Projects	xxx	xxx	86,802
Demolition Projects	xxx	xxx	5,586
Interim Assistance Programs	xxx	xxx	5,738
Certified Area Programs	xxx	xxx	847
Community Renewal Programs	xxx	xxx	36,518
Demonstration Programs	xxx	xxx	6,462
II. Other Programs			
General Neighborhood Renewal Plans - Total	243	279	xxx
Completed	193	215	xxx
Under Preparation	60	64	xxx
Feasibility Surveys - Total	88	94	xxx
Completed	70	75	xxx
Under Preparation	18	19	xxx

Source: Urban Renewal Directory, HUD, Washington, D.C. June 30, 1970

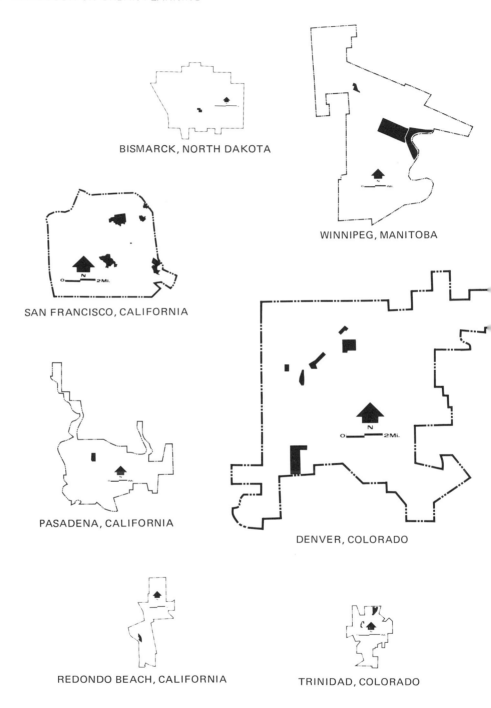

BISMARCK, NORTH DAKOTA

WINNIPEG, MANITOBA

SAN FRANCISCO, CALIFORNIA

PASADENA, CALIFORNIA

DENVER, COLORADO

REDONDO BEACH, CALIFORNIA

TRINIDAD, COLORADO

Figure 11-4   Urban Renewal Projects in selected cities.

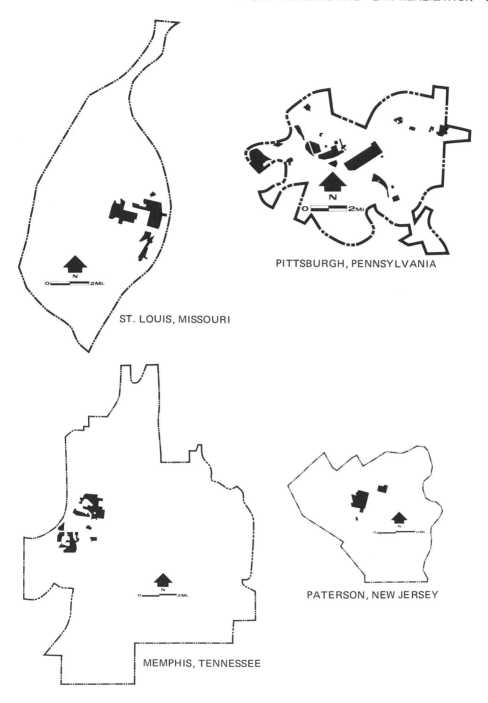

ST. LOUIS, MISSOURI

PITTSBURGH, PENNSYLVANIA

MEMPHIS, TENNESSEE

PATERSON, NEW JERSEY

Figure 11-4   (continued)

HOW RENEWAL SUCCEEDS

There are many activities in the renewal process that need to proceed smoothly for the whole process to be successful, but several critical activities are essential for success. They are financial feasibility, relocation capability, a market for cleared land, and an understanding of the renewal program.

Financial Feasibility

One difficult step in renewal is setting the boundary for the area to be renewed. Making the area too small usually results in much higher renewal cost for adjacent blighted areas, which would be renewed later. Making the area too large burdens the city with a local share of net project cost, which the city may be unable to produce. Somewhere between is the size of project that may be considered feasible for the city, taking into account other financial needs of the place.

There are other feasibility tests an urban renewal project should pass. One is the accuracy of acquisition cost estimates and, later on, of appraisals. Another is the accuracy of reuse appraisals or the proceeds to be expected from cleared land to be sold. The value of the cleared land may be written down or sold for less than actual market value to encourage a type of development essential to balanced community growth, such as public housing, nonprofit housing for the elderly, or a neighborhood park. This reduction in proceeds from cleared land may strain the financial feasibility of the project and can be avoided with more accurate foresight of eventual use of cleared land and more accurate financial planning and cost estimating.

HUD usually catches oversights or miscalculations of these types, but it is well to remember that HUD offices have many projects they are responsible for and few persons to review them, some with limited experience. If the application for renewal funds has been prepared by the LPA without these errors or miscalculations, success in HUD review will more likely follow, as well as success of the entire project. The secret of success here is to contact HUD before and during the application period.

One other facet of financial feasibility is determining the correct budget for site improvements in the project. This usually varies from $10,000 to $50,000 or more per acre for demolition, sanitary sewers, storm drains, and street work, depending upon the age, size, and density of the area. Estimating site improvement costs accurately after they are known is much easier than knowing definitely what the improvements are to be. This is where a sound general plan for the community is important, not only to determine land uses, major thoroughfares, and community facilities in the project area but the future needs in adjacent areas as well and their relationship to improvements proposed in the renewal project.

Relocation Capability

There are two aspects of relocation that are critical to renewal success, reduction of renewal delay because of relocation and the attitude of relocatees toward renewal. The cycle of activities in a renewal project from planning and approval through development includes acquisition, relocation, demolition, site improvements, sale of cleared land, and rebuilding.

RELOCATION DELAY   Relocation can be the most time-consuming activity in renewal, if not properly handled. HUD loans, usually in millions of dollars, are drawing interest charged to the project as soon as acquisition begins and the date of sale of cleared land is the point in the process that reduces the loan and interest. Land can be sold before site improvements are completed and even before demolition, but not before relocation is accomplished.

RELOCATEES' ATTITUDE   The reaction of relocatees to renewal and relocation is a result of the degree to which the LPA has taken the trouble to prepare them for renewal activities, particularly relocation. This is a painstaking educational and public relation obligation of the LPA, no part of which should be left to chance. The media through which this renewal process is imparted to the prospective relocatees is the newspaper, TV, radio, PAC, explanatory leaflets, public hearings, and especially face-to-face conferences with affected parties. A few actual relocation examples showing before and after housing [see Figure 11-5] are convincing evidence that relocation can be done well. The most effective way to expedite relocation is to do a good job and thereby gain the confidence of those to be relocated.

A thorough knowledge of available housing in all localities of the community and all price ranges is a prerequisite to relocation capability determination. Regardless of how well relocatees have been indoctrinated as to their role in relocation, if there is no vacant housing in their price range, some will have to be built or older housing rehabilitated. This takes time and will need to be programed accordingly. Temporary relocation is only an expedient and should be avoided wherever possible for the sake of the relocatee as well as the relocation budget.

Summarizing, the relocation function can be the most delaying one of all renewal activities and needs to be planned humanely and soundly and the plan should be implemented firmly and expeditiously with kindness and tolerance and business acumen. Relocation is done a family at a time and a business at a time and if done in an orderly, planned manner need not be the delayed and delaying function it often is.

Market for Cleared Land

One of the most undermining happenings in the early and uncertain days of the renewal program was going to all the trouble of acquiring property, relocating families, and clearing the land with no ready market for its sale. This happened in Detroit, St. Louis, Memphis, and several other cities and left a bad image of redevelopment in the minds of leaders of cities contemplating renewal.

Impressed with the importance of having a ready market for cleared land San Francisco, Chicago, New York, Los Angeles, and many other cities began to get redevelopers interested in their renewal projects before plans for them were completed.

BEFORE

AFTER

BEFORE

AFTER

Source: Memphis Housing Authority, 1971.

Figure 11-5 Homes of renewal relocatees before and after relocation.

This technique was and is especially effective in those states with enabling legislation that permits direct negotiation with a redeveloper for sale of cleared land without competitive bids, the case in most of the states. Thus, at least an interest was promulgated by the LPA and, when the cleared land was ready for sale, a buyer was more likely to be available and willing to buy, particularly if options to redevelop were legally allowable, offered by the LPA, and accepted by developers.

Gradually this led to redevelopment corporation concepts that several states have passed enabling legislation for—New York, California, and Missouri, among others. The Missouri statute is of interest in that it allows the development corporation to use the power of eminent domain, if necessary, to acquire property, clear it, and redevelop it.

Profits are limited to a maximum of 8 percent. The LPA and the governing body of the city must approve the contract with the redevelopment corporation.[4]

Normally cleared land in renewal projects is in demand, if the market is favorable at the time of sale for the land uses proposed. One difficulty here is the time lag between plan approval and availability of cleared land. This is usually several years even in NDP, though less than a conventional renewal project.

The objective is to leave no stone unturned in seeking a buyer for cleared land well in advance.

Understanding Renewal

The planner and renewal director have a joint responsibility to inform those involved with renewal as to their particular assignments and how and why these should be conducted. This should start with the mayor and councilmen with specifics on the purposes of renewal and methods to be employed under applicable law. Other city officials affected should be informed how their input influences the renewal process. This especially applies to each appointed member of the LPA, directors and staff as well. The next group that needs to know about the renewal process are the residents and property owners of the project as to the scope and nature of their involvement.

The people as a whole are also an important part of the information dissemination process, especially where a renewal bond issue or similar objective is at stake. Then the power structure of the community should certainly be on the list to receive information on the program and should include such groups as the Chamber of Commerce, Urban League, labor unions, professional groups, and the like.

The press and other news media should periodically receive information on the renewal program that includes not only specifics about a certain public hearing or land sale, for example, but general information about the renewal program and its objectives.

PRIVATE ENTERPRISE AND RENEWAL

A serious blunder in renewal is to assume the program is primarily governmental. Renewal is a joint effort of private enterprise and government. Private enterprise includes the redeveloper as well as a variety of types of consultants who assist the LPA in planning, appraising, counseling, property title investigations, engineering, architecture, and other studies.

Redevelopment corporations, mentioned above, are an important segment of renewal from the private sector, where the entire process of development (exclusive of planning) is performed by private corporations. It is just as important for employees of a redevelopment corporation to know their assignments and the objectives behind their efforts as it is for an LPA staff that does this work without the assistance of a redevelopment corporation. The mistakes, especially regarding relocation, made in the early days of redevelopment corporation activities in the city of New York, brought the

---

4. See Norman Murdock, "Unusual Missouri Law," in *Planners Notebook*, Vol. 1, No. 2, American Institute of Planners, Washington, D.C., May 1971.

renewal program to a halt for months there with considerable hardship on site occupants and others and resulted in an adverse opinion of renewal on the part of many observers throughout the country. Now periodic checks on the renewal process, particularly the relocation function, have eliminated much of this poor management and the process is running more smoothly. A good example of this may be found in Missouri, where progressive legislation on redevelopment corporations and tax incentives is working well, as mentioned.[4]

A private-enterprise feature in renewal that may be practiced only in California is the owner-participant privilege under the California renewal enabling statute. This provides for an owner of property in an urban renewal project to retain ownership of his property, if it fits into the approved urban renewal plan for the project and if he agrees to alter (at his own expense) or use his property in accord with the plan. This feature can relieve an LPA of costly acquisition and alteration or demolition expenses, as the case may be, but it is difficult to administer fairly and equitably. Some states, other than California, have this feature in a different form and under a different title than owner-participation.

More than one city in the United States has turned down urban renewal as too complicated, too controversial, or too costly for the benefits to be gained. This may have resulted from lack of courage, a status quo syndrome, or ignorance of the benefits that renewal offers a community.

BENEFITS FROM RENEWAL

The wide range of benefits to be derived from urban renewal include both obvious and subtle benefits too obscure to observe let alone measure but are described here as physical, social, and economic benefits.

Physical Benefits

These are the benefits that can be seen and experienced and include (a) provision for urgently needed facilities in the urban area, such as a city hall or at least land for it, a hospital, school, bus terminal, park, etc.; (b) traffic betterments in the form of rearrangement of an obsolete street system, increased traffic-carrying capacity of streets by widening or channelizing them, providing space for transit facilities, correcting deficiencies in street grades and sharp curves, etc.; (c) enhancement of utilities by replacing worn-out or obsolete waterlines and sewers, installing drainage facilities to eliminate flooding in low-lying areas, and reducing water pollution by installation of sewage treatment facilities, and (d) increasing public safety by means of adequate streetlighting, modern fire alarm systems, and grade-crossing elimination at railroad tracks. The list could go on for pages and some of these benefits would also contain social benefits.

Social Benefits

These benefits are not as easily evaluated or measured and yet may have more impact than physical ones. An example is the breaking up of juvenile gangs through relocation in a neighborhood where Mexican-American and Negro gangs were attacking each other, keeping the neighborhood in an uproar—an actual, not a fictitious example. Another actual case was the relocation from an extremely substandard frame shack to adequate yet simple accommodations appropriate for an elderly blind woman caring for her imbecile son confined to a wheelchair by polio. Cases like these are not well known and many go unnoticed for years in both urban and rural slums. Broader social benefits include new schools and recreation facilities, a community center building with programs for the poor and aging, a health clinic, or a job training program. Probably the most impressive social advancement renewal offers is the elimination of substandard housing and the creation of standard housing in standard neighborhoods.

One other benefit of a social nature stems from the relocation process. This can be a very perfunctory function, unless a dedicated person is in charge of the work. There is a unique opportunity in relocation to overcome objections many not-too-well-informed people have to renewal—namely, that the people in the slums just make another slum where they move. This can be true if the relocation worker does not take advantage of the opportunity of advising and educating the relocatees in appropriate behavior and attitudes that make for a better life for themselves and their neighbors. Many families in substandard urban districts have recently migrated from rural areas and are confused and intimidated by city life. They need help in just about any facet of urban life imaginable and relocation can be a constructive vehicle for adjustment and acclimation.

Like physical benefits, social ones have much in common with economic ones. As may be discovered in the following section, some of these social benefits of renewal are tangible and may be measured in dollars.

Economic Benefits

If hardheaded business leaders in a community are unimpressed with physical and social benefits of urban renewal, the economic benefits should convince them that not only do tax revenues from an urban renewal project far exceed those before renewal than after but the cost of city services in a blighted area far exceed those costs after redevelopment. Consequently, the longer the tax liability of a blighted area is allowed to remain, the longer will be delayed the tax asset to be realized through renewal of the blighted area. Statements like these are more meaningful if backed up with statistics.

Few examples exist of a cost analysis of city services in a substandard area as detailed as those in the Bunker Hill Urban Renewal Project in Los Angeles. The planning for this 136-acre substandard area adjacent to downtown was completed in the late 1950s with the longest public hearing on record in the United States for an urban renewal project and possibly a record for any other project. The City Council hearing was in 1959; opposition to the project coupled with the policy of the council to let anyone in that city of over two million speak on anything caused the hearing to last over six months. This gave the opposition ample opportunity to question every fact the project eligibility under the law was based upon, and yet gave the Community Redevelopment Agency of the City of Los Angeles ample opportunity to answer each one of those questions with statistical details never before investigated. Some of these details reveal the economic benefits of urban renewal.

The tax revenue to the city of Los Angeles in 1958 from the Bunker Hill Area was $106,120 while the cost to the city of only fire, police, and health services was $754,101, creating an annual deficit of $647,981. The citywide average for police costs during the 1957-58 fiscal year was $15.60 per capita, while in Bunker Hill during the same period it was $83.00 per capita for the 9,485 persons living there.

The average annual cost of fire control and inspection in the city of Los Angeles for fiscal 1957-58 was $10,849 per acre, while in Bunker Hill it was $83,300 per acre. A fire service comparison was made between Bunker Hill and a standard area, Park La Brea in Los Angeles on 155 acres with 12,000 persons housed in 18 13-story modern high-rise apartments and about as many 2-story garden apartments. During a 12-month period from June 26, 1955, there were the following fire services performed by the Los Angeles City Fire Department:

Fire Service	Bunker Hill	Park LaBrea
Total alarms	110	14
False alarms	21	3
Times booster tank used	8	3
Hours worked	42.7	4.8
Feet of 1" hose used	1,300	0
Feet of 1½" hose used	1,500	0
Feet of 2½" hose used	700	0

The extent and seriousness of the fires may be gauged by the length of hose used. During the year there was one fire fatality in Bunker Hill and none in Park La Brea.

One of the greatest economic benefits renewal provides is the increase in assessed valuation and tax revenue from a renewal project area. In 1958 before renewal of Bunker Hill, the tax revenue to all taxing bodies (City, County, Board of Education, Flood Control District, and Sanitary District) was $400,000 and in 1959 was estimated at $4,400,000, an increase of $4,000,000 annually after redevelopment. In December 1970 the annual increase in tax revenue had risen to $2,700,000 with the cleared land only partially built upon or redeveloped. The estimated $4,000,000 tax revenue increase apparently will be exceeded within the next few years.

Housing was mentioned above in connection with social benefits of renewal but an economic gain may be realized here too.

Urban renewal gets blamed for many urban shortcomings because it is where the action is, where people meet change face to face, and where more and more people are going to be involved as time passes. Renewal is an effect of urban problems and, besides not being the cause of them, is solving many of them.

HOUSING AND RENEWAL

National renewal goals set by HUD in 1968 required a renewal project application to observe at least one of the three goals: (a) include the worst substandard housing first, especially where minority groups are located, (b) provide a standard housing unit in the community for each substandard housing unit eliminated by renewal (referred to as the one for one rule), and (c) provide employment for the unemployed and underemployed in the community by means of the renewal activity.

HUD recently revised these national goals but the one for one rule is still in force. This wise decision provides a ready tool to hack away at substandard housing and still maintain a supply of standard housing in the community and country at least equal to the number of substandard units eliminated by renewal. Gradually this process should put an end to substandard housing, but not too gradually. As mentioned in Chapter 4, Operation Breakthrough and the public housing and renewal programs generally should expedite the goal of a decent, safe, and sanitary home for every American family.

Housing is one of the features in the renewal program that are difficult to resolve on a citywide basis and should be administered regionally.

REGIONAL PLANNING AND RENEWAL

Several aspects of renewal have grown in recent years to the point of being regional instead of only community-wide problems. They are housing, relocation, financial, and other aspects of renewal. Chapter 12 covers the subject well, but a few points relating to regional aspects of renewal are touched on here.

Housing

The emphasis in the past few years on low- and moderate-income housing in HUD, including the Federal Housing Administration and the Farmers Home Administration, has stretched the housing problem into a region-wide one in both large and small metropolitan areas. High cost of urban land is one definite reason for this trend, as well as the desire for escape from ghettos and higher-density areas in the urban core. Few can afford the luxury of this escape and many are subsidized in this effort by the provisions of both FHA programs above. Chapter 4 discusses this problem in more detail.

Relocation

As the renewal program grew from its start nationally in 1949 there was increasing awareness of the necessity for relocation to be administered on a community-wide basis and soon after a regional concept of the activity was necessary. Renewal agencies in cities were accused of diverting their relocation responsibilities to adjacent cities or unincorporated areas in the county nearby. This was quickly discovered by those counties where this occurred which had housing authorities. Their housing facilities soon were full or had a waiting list.

The relocation function should be planned and operated on a regional basis to put all agencies on notice sufficiently in advance of these shifts in population caused by the renewal process in the cities in the region.

Financial

This is the critical area of need for a city carrying the burden of renewal expense while the surrounding communities and counties reap the benefits directly, or at least indirectly.

Regional planning commissions and councils of government are growing in numbers across the country but have little more than advisory authority as yet.

One method of coping with this problem is the use by a renewal agency of tax revenue increases from a renewal project to defray local project expenditures including the local share of the net project cost. California and Colorado have this advantageous renewal feature as have a few other states. The Los Angeles LPA is retiring its $10 million bond issue on the Bunker Hill Project with the $2.7 million tax revenue increase from the project in less than 4 years. The key point here regionally is that the city of Los Angeles has taken the trouble and expense to correct a deficit condition of benefit to all taxpayers, city and county. The county tax increase is diverted during indebtedness repayment and when the debt is fully repaid at the end of the four-year payment period, all the tax revenue including the increase flows normally to all the taxing bodies and everybody gains.

Other

Still other renewal matters that warrant regional considerations have not yet been broached or planned for in the magnitude they deserve. These include facilities of a regional need such as mass transit, sanitary engineering requirements (water supply and sewerage), flood control, railroad line rerouting, highway arterials, and other types. They are discussed in the following and concluding section of this chapter.

THE FUTURE ROLE OF RENEWAL IN PLAN IMPLEMENTATION

Those who are enlightened by ideas that could solve problems that others are ignoring or just fretting over often find solace, in their frustration at failing to find a listener for their ideas, by writing a book and at least having the satisfaction that the ideas are down in black and white for anyone to see. This book is no exception and some of the ideas, though not yet tried, should certainly be tested.

There may seem to be a gap in communication catapulting from the subject of urban renewal to mass transit and a bridge over this gap is in order.

Those sections in Chapter 1 on the magnitude of urban problems calling for solutions of equal magnitude are a beginning for building the bridge across this communications gap. Urban renewal has pecked away at a few parcels of blight here and grown up to handle a few blocks of blight there, and all through these 22 years of renewal there has hardly been a single professional involved in this work who has not noticed how much is left undone or uncorrected by renewal. Rarely is a railroad line moved by renewal because of the time or money it would take to do it, but the need is there. Rarely is a mass transit facility involved in a renewal project for the same reasons, but the need is evident here too. The Underground (subway) Authority in London proposed an extension of a line to a new station, the Elephant and Castle Station (a quaint old name). However, the method of this extension was not quaint or old but intelligent and modern. The area to be served by the line extension was blighted and marked for redevelopment. The line was built while the redevelopment was under way. When the line was ready for service, so were high-rise office and apartment buildings arranged within an easy covered walk from the new underground station, integrated into the whole complex complete with a community shopping center. Does this apply to, say Denver or St. Louis? Not today (maybe) but if it does in ten years or less, now is the time to plan for such extensive development.

Conversion of railroad property, particularly passenger lines and facilities now all but dormant in many cities, to uses more pressing, especially in core areas where urban land values are too high for rail freight use, is an urban renewal opportunity to be studied on a large scale as early as possible. Air rights over railroad properties, used remarkably for skyscrapers and other needs in large cities, have application as well in smaller cities not yet but soon to be in the large-city category. Renewal is essential here to solve related and other problems in the vicinity simultaneously and less expensively than if solved piecemeal over a long period of time.

Grade separation of highway and rail traffic is a costly need that should be integrated into a citywide renewal effort like NDP.

The duplication and waste of manpower and money in the one area of acquisition, for example, is astounding. The renewal agency could acquire property for renewal projects, schools, highways, parks, flood control works, water supply facilities, sewerage works, mass transit lines, railroad lines to be removed, airports, and other public properties. The savings would be enormous since planning on a vast scale would be a necessity. This is the summit consideration—planning for such broad-range undertakings. Yet this is exactly what the future requires.

Relocation stemming from renewal or any other governmental action should be managed comprehensively on a regional basis, as mentioned in Chapter 4 regarding housing planning conducted regionally.

Some political boundaries would be absorbed in such a regional approach to urban problems and this too should occur before the entire ungainly urban organism crunches to a halt in city after city. Regional planning commissions are leading the way, including two or more counties and cities. Bigness in business and bigness in government are fears that should be allayed with appropriate checks and mechanisms responsive to the people. The bigness is needed in government to solve the bigness of current urban problems and renewal can be the implementer of plans comprehensively formulated on a regional basis.

The federal government recognizes the need for a bigger approach to these bigger problems. HUD is discussing and Congress is preparing legislation on general instead of categorical grants in urban renewal. The community development program, though not yet funded as it should be, takes a broad approach to many urban problems including renewal with more local determinations of how the money is spent that the city is entitled to. Revenue sharing is established with its implications of still broader local decision-making on the part of governing bodies directly involved in the problems to be solved.

Readiness is the key to these larger programs—readiness with comprehensive planning, regional and other.

METROPOLITAN AND REGIONAL PLANNING

Harold M. Mayer

One of the outstanding characteristics of twentieth-century North America is the rapid expansion of urbanization outward from the older city cores into the surrounding countryside. Modern transportation and communication has enabled lower-density development to spread, so that the former distinction between "urban" and "rural" is much less significant than previously. Rarely, if ever, do municipal boundaries coincide with the limits of the built-up urbanized areas; municipalities are commonly "under-bounded"; the limits of the urbanized area extend well beyond the boundaries of the central municipality. Less commonly, and particularly in the southwestern United States and in a few other places, including some in Canada, annexations and city-county consolidations have produced "under-bounded" cities, in which extensive nonurbanized territory is included within the limits of the city. Furthermore, within the urbanized areas, a phalanx of local governments has tended to develop, giving rise to serious and complex problems in the coordination of public services, duplication of facilities, and constraints to comprehensive planning of areas which constitute, geographically, physically, and economically, logical areal units for many aspects of planning.

Modern transportation and communication have greatly reduced the former distinction between territory which is "urban" and that which is "nonurban" or "rural," and, in many instances, the present hierarchial structure of local governmental units represents a spatial anachronism, a cultural lag which poses many problems for the planner and the public administrator.

THE METROPOLITAN REGION AS A SPATIAL AND PLANNING UNIT

Recognition by the federal governments of the United States and Canada of the significance of the metropolitan region as a unit for planning has come in the past two decades, and in both countries metropolitan and regional planning have recently developed, with promise of greater effectiveness than previously.

The Nature of Regions

What is meant by the terms "metropolitan" and "region"? Both terms imply that there is a set of areal or spatial units which transcend the limits of an individual city or urban place, and which have sufficient functional and physical integrity to justify consideration in the planning process.

Geographers recognize two types of regions: homogeneous ones and nodal ones. Homogeneous regions are those defined and delimited by a set of criteria selected to facilitate a particular purpose, in which, with regard to the attributes and criteria selected, the similarities are more significant among the locations within the region than are the differences between those points and other points outside the region. In other words, a region can be defined for any purpose in which the criteria are not identical within and without the region; it is essentially a device for classifying locations for purposes of description, study, and operation. Thus, there may be urban regions, climatic regions, economic regions, *ad infinitum,* and any appropriate criteria may be selected to bound the regions; boundaries may be precise, as in the case of political and administrative regions, or they may be transitional zones. On the other hand, a nodal region is a point, or a concentrated area, which constitutes a focus, such as a concentration of commercial or industrial activity, or a transportation node. Cities and metropolitan regions have attributes of both types of regions; within cities there are homogeneous regions such as neighborhoods, industrial districts, and other areas of relative physical or functional homogeneity, while the cities themselves constitute, in many instances, parts of larger areas, such as metropolitan regions, which also have homogeneity with respect to certain attributes. Within cities, we also recognize nodes, such as the central business district, major institutional focuses, shopping centers, and other points or zones, characterized by their generation of traffic, an evidence of their nodal or focal quality. Cities and metropolitan regions themselves, with respect to their external areas, are also, at a different scale, nodal regions, for they constitute nodes on the systems of transportation and communication, and they are areas of intensive activity.[1] The definition and classification of regions is of special significance to the planner, for many of the planning activities assume homogeneity or nodality, and the transfer of successful solutions to problems with which the planner is concerned, from one region to another, may involve consideration of the extent to which, if any, the relevant attributes vary within and between regions.[2] Transfer of solutions to planning problems may be effective, in many

1. For further discussion of the nature of regions, see Derwent Whittlesey *et. al.,* "The Regional Concept and the Regional Method," Chap. 2 in P. E. James and C. F. Jones (eds.), *American Geography, Inventory and Prospect* (Syracuse, N.Y.: Syracuse Univ. Press, 1954), pp. 19-68.

2. This theme is expanded in Walter Isard, *Methods of Regional Analysis* (Cambridge, Mass.: M.I.T. Press, and New York: John Wiley and Sons, 1960)

instances, only if the regions involved resemble one another with respect to the pertinent characteristics.

The Concept of the Metropolitan Region

It has long been clear that, with respect to many characteristics, the "city," or municipality, is not the significant spatial unit, and that another type of region would constitute a much more adequate delimitation for planning purposes. During the early years of the twentieth century, many of the outstanding urban comprehensive plans extended well beyond the municipal boundaries. Patrick Geddes, in 1915, recognized the metropolitan region as a logical unit for many planning purposes in his classic, *Cities in Evolution;* even earlier, Ebenezer Howard, in *Garden Cities of Tomorrow,* proposed the creation of "New Towns" in the countryside, well beyond, and separated by greenbelts from, the main urban mass of the central city, but linked to it economically, and by intrametropolitan transportation, physically as well. The famous Burnham and Bennett *Plan of Chicago,* published in 1909, considered many aspects of the physical and economic developments of the region beyond the limits of the central city. The noteworthy Regional Plan of New York and Its Environs, of the 1920s, was concerned with a multicounty region extending well beyond the limits of New York City. The regional concept metropolitan and otherwise, was well established by the 1930s, when the Tennessee Valley Administration and other regions formed the basis of organizations superimposed upon the existing units of government spatially, for treatment of problems, such as water management, which were not contained wholly within any local subnational unit of government. Some precedents had been established much earlier: the Sanitary District of Chicago, one of the earliest and most successful of the metropolitan regional special-purpose governments, was created in 1889, and the interstate Port of New York Authority in 1920. But well before those, recognition of the dispersion and spread of urbanization beyond the limits of municipalities resulted in annexation of suburban territory; most cities extended their boundaries during the nineteenth and early twentieth century by annexing outlying territory, much of which was in advance of urbanization, or which was urbanized but generally not included within the municipal limits of incorporated suburban municipalities. City-county consolidation, not unlike those involving Nashville-Davidson County, Tennessee, Miami-Dade County, and Jacksonville-Duval County, Florida, and, more recently, Indianapolis and Marion County, Indiana, in the 1960s and early 1970s, was a partial solution to the problems involving cities and outlying urbanized areas in the nineteenth century; the city and county of Philadelphia were consolidated in 1854, and those of St. Louis and San Francisco before the nineteenth century ended. The present city of New York was created in 1898 by the federation of five counties. In each of these instances the boundaries of the respective cities have not subsequently been extended by annexation or consolidation of outlying areas, except, to a minor extent, by filling of some of the adjacent waterways; otherwise the areal extent of the cities mentioned has not been changed for many years. In each instance, however, it is probable that, as in the case of the nineteenth-century city-county consolidations, an "overspill" of the expanding urban population beyond the extended city-county boundaries will eventually take place.

Because there is no clear-cut difference in the way of life between residents of urban places and those in nonurban ones, there can be no boundary of a metropolitan or other urban region which is equally useful for all purposes. There are two types of metropolitan delimitation which have been adopted by the United States government for statistical and planning purposes; Canada has somewhat similarly defined its metropolitan complexes.

The most widely utilized definition transcending municipal boundaries of the modern American city, is that of the United States Office of Management and Budget, and it is utilized by virtually all federal agencies concerned with metropolitan statistics, or with urban affairs, including the census. It is the Standard Metropolitan Statistical Area (SMSA).

STANDARD METROPOLITAN STATISTICAL AREAS

In defining and delimiting the functional, geographic city, as distinguished from the municipality, a dilemma arises. Since the actual limits of urbanization, by whatever measure may be used, are undergoing constant change as population expands and land becomes subdivided for urban uses, the dilemma arises as to whether the criteria for boundary determination should be set up so as to shift readily the boundaries as urbanization is extended, or whether relatively constant areal units should be utilized, in order to make comparisons over time for the same areas and at the same time utilize statistics which are more readily available for constant than for shifting units. Obviously, the purposes will determine which of these two approaches to defining the metropolitan area will be used. Since a very large proportion of the available statistics on population, housing, commerce, and industry are compiled by government agencies, the latter are concerned that the boundaries of the statistical areal units be so located as to provide maximum utility to the greatest number of interests. A large body of statistical information is normally available for counties, and the counties constitute general units of government within the states; therefore counties are used as the basic spatial units in constituting the metropolitan areas, for statistical purposes, and, more recently, for many planning purposes.

In 1950, the United States census first published statistics for Standard Metropolitan Areas (SMAs) which were comprised of whole counties, including each county in which there was a city—the "central city"—with a minimum population of 50,000, together with adjacent and contiguous counties which, by certain criteria of commuting and other measures, were economically or socially integrated with the county containing the central city. In some instances, more than one city exceeded the threshold population, and in such instances, the SMA was designated with the name of two or more such cities. In a few instances, two cities which had common boundaries constituted central cities, even though neither had 50,000 population, providing that the total of the two was 50,000 and one had at least 35,000. In the 1960 census and subsequently, such areas, consisting of one or more whole counties, were designated as SMSAs. In New England, where the county has a different status than in the rest of the United States, the SMSA uses the town as the basic areal unit. In any case, a county (town in New England), in order to be included within the SMSA, must have certain ties, as measured by commuting, or by work-residence relationships, with the county containing the central city or cities, and must be contiguous, either to the central city-county, or to a county which is, in turn, contiguous to the county containing the central city or cities; therefore, all SMSAs consist of uninterrupted areas of one or more whole counties [Figure 12-1].

One of the problems in the use of the SMSA is that the use of whole counties involves inclusion within most SMSAs of extensive areas which have not been urbanized, even though portions of such counties have sufficient urban development, and sufficient ties to the central counties of the SMSA to be included; thus, the areas of the respective SMSAs bear no relationship to their relative populations or importance. San Bernardino County, California, for example, qualifies as a part of an SMSA, because the population of San Bernardino, in its southwestern corner, is above the threshold requirement, but most of the county is unpopulated desert, and the area of the county is considerably larger than the combined area of the three southern New England states.

Another problem in the use of the SMSAs is the fact that, in some instances, two or more contiguous ones form a continuous chain or cluster with a somewhat arbitrary boundary between them. In reality, such chains or clusters may, in some instances, form a conurbation or urban corridor, with overlapping labor market and housing market areas. To overcome this problem partially, two so-called Standard Consolidated Areas were defined in 1960, each consisting of SMSAs clustered around large central cities and overlapping into more than one state. The New York-Northeastern New Jersey Standard Consolidated Area consists of four contiguous SMSAs, one in New York State and three in New Jersey, with two additional New Jersey counties; and the Chicago-Northwestern Indiana Standard Consolidated Area consists of a six-county SMSA in Illinois and a two-county SMSA in adjacent Indiana. A number of other Standard Consolidated Areas could readily be designated in other parts of the country, where the SMSAs are intimately linked, and have common boundaries.

In using the SMSAs as areal units for regional planning, a difficulty commonly occurs in situations where the area is comprised of portions of two or more states. In such instances, interstate regional agencies may be set up, or, short of that, mechanisms for interchange of information and mutual agreements relative to planning matters may be needed.

Within the metropolitan areas, for statistical purposes a dichotomy exists between the "central cities" on the one hand and the "suburban ring" on the other. While this distinction is important, it is so general that it tends to obscure significant homogeneities between central city and inner suburbs, and important differences among the suburbs of the respective SMSAs.

During the past few decades, nearly all of the net growth in the population of the United States has been within the SMSAs. During the 1960's, 84 percent of all the net growth was within such areas, in spite of substantial declines in many of the central cities, and in spite of the fact that the rate of growth has been slowing up. Between 1950 and 1960, the SMSAs showed a growth of 26.4 percent, and in the following decade the rate was 16.6 percent. At the same time, the number of metropolitan areas substantially increased as many small and medium-sized cities passed the 50,000 threshold, resulting in

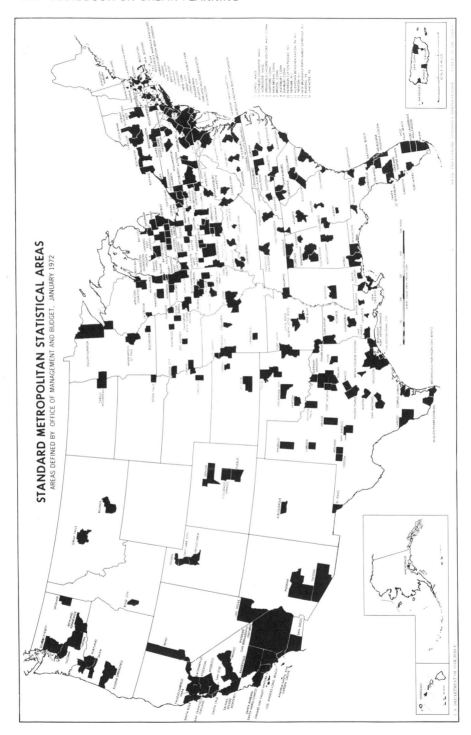

STANDARD METROPOLITAN STATISTICAL AREAS

AREAS DEFINED BY OFFICE OF MANAGEMENT AND BUDGET, JANUARY 1972

Source: Bureau of the Census.

Figure 12-1 Standard metropolitan statistical areas—1972

the designation of new SMSAs. The number of these increased from 168 in 1950, to 212 in 1960, and to 247 at the time of the 1970 census. During the 1960s, although the metropolitan rate of growth slowed up, being only 16.6 percent, it greatly exceeded the national growth rate, which was 13.3 percent, or only 6.5 percent for the non-metropolitan population. In 1970, over 140 million people, or 69 percent of the total national population, lived within the 247 SMSAs, as compared with 67 percent in the same areas in 1960, or 61.5 percent in the 212 SMSAs as they were defined in 1960.

By the time of the 1970 census, the total population of the suburban portions of the SMSAs exceeded that of the central city, for the first time. In that year, the population of the United States was divided roughly into three more-or-less equal portions, that of the central cities of the metropolitan areas (63.9 million), the suburban portions of the metropolitan areas (76.3 million), and the smaller urban places and rural areas (63.0 million). By 1970 the proportion of the metropolitan population living outside of the central cities had reached 54.4 percent. For some time, central city populations in many instances had been declining as the city areas filled up, and "overspill" into the areas beyond their boundaries took place. In some instances as, for example, Boston, Pittsburgh, and Cleveland, the respective central cities contained only a relatively small proportion of the total population of the metropolitan areas. By 1970 many more central cities lost their population predominance to the suburban areas. During the 1960s, twelve of the nation's largest cities lost population, but of the 50 largest metropolitan areas all but one (Pittsburgh) gained substantially in total population; the gains in the suburban areas were much more than sufficient to offset the central city losses.

In most of the metropolitan areas, there are significant differences between the ethnic and socioeconomic characteristics of the populations in major portions of the central cities and in the suburban areas; these differences and their implications for urban planning are discussed elsewhere in this book, but a number of the problems presented later in this chapter have important ethnic and socioeconomic significance in terms of the city-suburban dichotomy.

Urbanized Areas

Although the urban-rural distinction is much less significant, in many respects, than it formerly was, for some purposes it may be desirable to consider specifically those areas which are distinctively urban in character. In the SMSA, as pointed out in the preceding section, much territory is included which is essentially rural; because of the nonhomogeneity in this respect of some of the counties, portions have such character as to qualify the entire county for inclusion in the SMSA. In order to eliminate this difficulty, the United States Census Bureau has defined and delimited a set of areas around the larger and medium-sized central cities which are termed "urbanized areas" and some statistics are available for these, although not in as great abundance as for the SMSAs and the counties comprising them. In the decennial census of 1950, 1960, and 1970, urbanized areas [Figure 12-2] have been designated around central cities of 50,000, as in the case of the SMSAs. Such areas are smaller than the SMSAs. In a few instances the outer ends of tentacles of urbanization, included within the urbanized areas, may extend for short

Figure 12-2 Urbanized areas of the U.S. and Puerto Rico: 1960.

Source: Department of Commerce.

344

distances beyond the SMSA boundaries. The urbanized areas, the precise rules for delimitation of which may differ from time to time, essentially include all territory of the central cities together with adjacent territory which is developed for urban uses and which has a density of 500 housing units or about 2,000 persons per square mile. This corresponds roughly to the developed areas which are characterized by urban street patterns; thus the outer boundaries correspond rather closely to the boundaries of the "built-up" areas. In general, such areas are continuous, to the outer contour of the density threshold as mentioned above; the maximum distance of open area permitted for inclusion of built-up area beyond the interruption is one and one-half miles.

The urbanized area concept gives the planner an option, other than the SMSA, of an area which excludes those peripheral lands not yet urbanized; in many instances the area within the SMSA but outside the urbanized area may be construed as representing area which may be subject to urbanization in the relatively near future. After each decennial census, both the area and the population of the suburban territory associated with the respective central city and which is developed with urban densities may be compared. A major problem in the use of such areas for comparison, however, is the time lag between date of determination of the urbanized area boundaries and the publication of the relevant census statistics; such time lag is normally much greater than for publication of the corresponding SMSA or county statistics. Furthermore, the fact that, by definition, the area included as Urbanized Area is almost never constant will influence, to a considerable degree, the comparisons over time.

INTERMETROPOLITAN COALESCENCE: CONURBATIONS AND MEGALOPOLISES

In the United States, the overwhelming proportion of the population, whether within a metropolitan area or not, is within commuting distance of at least one metropolitan agglomeration, and a substantial proportion of the population is within the "labor-shed" or housing market area of more than one metropolitan area. In Canada, because most cities are smaller and further apart, only in a few areas, mostly close to the United States border, do the commuting areas of two or more metropolitan districts overlap. With the development of effective highway transportation, the outwardly expanding tentacles of urbanization radiating along the major transportation routes from nearby metropolitan centers tend to reach toward one another, and eventually overlap, forming more-or-less continuous "corridors." Residents in or near these corridors may have access to employment and other opportunities in two, three, or even more nearby metropolitan areas, and the overlapping has made a clear-cut separation, for purposes of planning, administration, and even perception and orientation, very difficult.

Clusters of cities with overlapping housing-market areas and labor-sheds, with resulting cross-commuting, have long been recognized. With the virtual ubiquity of automobile transportation, and the reinforcement of urbanization along the major rail-road routes, in high-density areas, lineal development has become characteristic of such multinucleated conurbations. With increasing emphasis upon time and costs rather than distance in commuting, the "desire lines" of internal urban and metropolitan travel, formerly completely dominated by commuting to and from the central business districts and forming radial or star-shaped patterns, have become more diffuse as an increasing proportion of employment and residence has become "footloose," i.e., not dependent upon a limited number of mass transportation routes. The result is a more diffuse pattern of "desire lines" of travel connecting origins and destinations with the CBD still the dominant node, but with many other nodes as well. Much of the growth has taken place along routes not necessarily leading to the older cores, and where the radial routes have witnessed increased travel as suburbanization has taken place, the reinforcement and extension of radii from nearby cities have resulted in a coalescence, with intermediate areas of overlap. In such areas, the resident has a choice of employment in two or more metropolitan areas nearby, while, on the other hand, commercial and industrial establishments can draw upon the resident labor force within the area of overlap. Where transportation by rail, highway, or both is particularly fast or frequent, lineal alignments of cities tend to develop, with intermediate areas accessible to several such cities. Such a geographic pattern is sometimes called a "corridor." In some instances, as along the Carolina Piedmont, a cluster of cities is linked by a network of corridors.[3] Jean Gottmann applied the term "megalopolis" to the lineal set of cities betwen Boston and Washington,[4] and the generic term has been applied to other corridor-type multi-nucleated urban complexes which are characterized by lineal intermetropolitan coalescence, as, for example, along the southern shores of the Great Lakes.[5] The Boston-New York-Washington axis has as its core the New York metropolitan region, and the Regional Plan Association, concerned with that portion of the Boston-Washington megalopolis centering upon New York City, has, appropriately, used the term "spread city." Earlier, in the 1930s the phenomenon of intermetropolitan coalescence was recognized, in the case of Washington-Baltimore-Annapolis, by a number of regional planning reports, stimulated by the National Resources Planning Board.[6] Later, the Friendship Airport was established in the corridor, to serve both the Baltimore and Washington metropolitan areas, as was the new town of Columbia, which not only serves as a dormitory suburb for the residents who work in either metropolitan area, but also itself serves as an employment center, producing two-way commuting outward from both areas.

In many other parts of the United States, intermetropolitan coalescence is taking place along transportation corridors, and the role of transportation is well documented.[7] In the Boston-Washington corridor, the federal government officially recognized the

3. F. Stuart Chapin, Jr., and Shirley F. Weiss (eds.), *Urban Growth Dynamics in a Regional Cluster of Cities* (New York: John Wiley and Sons, 1962). For a general discussion of networks see: Peter Haggett and Richard J. Chorley, *Network Analysis in Geography* (New York: St. Martin's Press, 1969).

4. Jean Gottmann, *Megalopolis, The Urbanized Northeastern Seabord of the United States* (New York: The Twentieth Century Fund, 1961).

5. C. A. Doxiadis and J. G. Papaioannou, "The Emerging Great Lakes Megalopolis: Comparison with the Eastern Megalopolis," in *Transportation: A Service,* "Sesquicentennial Forum on Transportation Engineering" (New York: Academy of Science, 1967), pp. 282-300.

6. *Regional Planning, Part 4, Baltimore-Washington-Annapolis Area* (Baltimore: Maryland State Planning Commission, 1937).

7. For example: Irving Cutler, *The Chicago-Milwaukee Corridor, A Geographic Study of Intermetropolitan Coalescence* (Evanston, Ill.: Northwestern Univ. Studies in Geography No. 9, (1965).

phenomenon in the form of the Northeast Corridor Act, which set up a series of experimental transportation programs. The best-known results are the Turboliner trains between New York and Boston and the Metroliners, high-speed passenger trains between New York, Philadelphia, Baltimore, and Washington. The author of the act, Senator Claiborne Pell, gives credit to Gottmann for not only defining the megalopolis concept, but also for pointing out the role of transportation in the functioning of such a multinucleated urban complex.[8]

Even before the concept of the metropolitan area has become well established in the public's mind, the fusing of development into continuous urbanization between nearby metropolitan nodes has confused the delimitation of appropriate areas for purposes of planning. Nevertheless, the growth of metropolitan planning, transcending the limits of individual local government jurisdictions, gained momentum in the 1950s, and, with the impetus of federal requirements for technical assistance and financial aid for a variety of programs, became generally accepted in the late 1960s.

INTERGOVERNMENTAL RELATIONS IN METROPOLITAN PLANNING

As early as the nineteenth century, it became evident that many of the public functions could not be carried out within the limits of local administrative and political jurisdictions. The multi-tiered concept of a nested hierarchy of jurisdictional units—federal, state, county, and local municipal (townships and other comparable units in rural areas)—is as old as the United States. Implicit in this structure of governmental units is the knowledge that some problems and functions involve areas larger than those within the boundaries of a local jurisdiction but smaller than the nation as a whole. However, such a nested hierarchy of units applies only to governments which have multiple functions, and consequently the limits of such jurisdictions do not, in many instances, coincide with the logical boundaries of the areas within which the functions can best be performed. Water resource management areas most logically would be within the boundaries of drainage basins; air pollution control cannot stop at local governmental boundaries because the air circulates freely across them, and land use controls, such as zoning, may produce gross distortions and deviations from the most desirable patterns if the uses prohibited in a local jurisdictional area cluster just beyond the boundaries.

To deal with such problems, many special-purpose governments have been established. One of the earliest, and most significant, was the Sanitary District of Chicago (now the Metropolitan Sanitary District of Greater Chicago), which was established in 1889 to construct a diversion canal across the drainage divide between the Great Lakes and the Mississippi Basin in order to furnish a route for the sewage of the Chicago area away from Lake Michigan, from which the city's water supply was—and is—obtained. Later, special-purpose governments were established across state lines to deal with interstate problems. In such instances compacts between the states required congressional approval. The prototype of such agencies is the Port of New York Authority, and subsequent to its

8. Senator Claiborne Pell, *Megalopolis Unbound, The Supercity and the Transportation of Tomorrow* (New York: Frederick A. Praeger, 1966), Preface, p. v.

establishment many other interstate agencies were established in metropolitan areas which overlapped state boundaries, such as in the St. Louis-East St. Louis (Missouri-Illinois) and Cincinnati (Ohio-Kentucky-Indiana) metropolitan areas. The principal ties which hold such areas together are the transportation facilities, and it is not surprising that a high proportion of the metropolitan agencies, whether interstate or within states, are concerned with metropolitan transportation.

Metropolitan Transportation-Land Use Planning Studies

Metropolitan transportation planning, and the instrumentalities for effectuating it, evolved rapidly, particularly after World War II. The "City Beautiful" movement of the late nineteenth and early twentieth centuries was only incidentally concerned with transportation, and the tremendous effect of the automobile in later decades was not generally anticipated. The Regional Plan of New York and Its Environs, in the 1920s, was one of the earliest metropolitan plans to involve more-or-less detailed consideration of the automobile; the earlier planning concepts, such as the Garden City movement, led by Ebenezer Howard a decade or two earlier, gave a prominent role to rail transportation.

Metropolitan transportation and traffic studies, until after World War II, were relatively crude. In the 1940s, origin-destination traffic studies were evolved, in which "desire lines" between origin and destination areas, independent of the routes actually taken, furnished the basis for extrapolations, projections, and plans to accommodate travel facilities to the actual desired movements. They were deficient, however, in two respects. First, they were heavily oriented toward highway and street planning, and gave inadequate consideration, in many instances, to the possibilities of mass transit, and second, they were not related to, or integrated sufficiently with, existing or prospective land uses and their patterns. By the early 1950s it was realized that transportation and urban land use were but two sides of the same coin, and that surveys and comprehensive planning operations would not be effective unless both transportation and land use considerations were integrated.[9] Shortly thereafter, origin-destination traffic studies were broadened to include projections of land use trends and patterns, and the testing of alternative physical patterns of land uses and functional areas in terms of their transportation requirements in order to determine the optimal combinations. The surveys concentrated upon the areas within the cordon lines drawn to include the central cities and major portions of the built-up areas of inner suburbs around the respective metropolitan cores irrespective, generally, of the locations of the governmental jurisdictional boundaries.[10] Throughout the mid and late 1950s and early 1960s, the techniques of operating and applying the results of the comprehensive transportation-land use surveys of metropolitan areas were improved, and the transfer of experience, and, in some cases, professional personnel, among the various metropolitan areas which had been subjected to such studies produced a degree of standardization of the techniques, and formats for presen-

9. Robert B. Mitchell and Chester Rapkin, *Urban Traffic, a Function of Land Use* (New York: Columbia Univ. Press, 1954).
10. For more detailed discussion of the techniques of such transportation land use studies see: Roger L. Creighton, *Urban Transportation Planning* (Urbana, Ill.: Univ. of Illinois Press, 1970).

tation of the results. Among the pioneering metropolitan-transportation-land use studies which produced significant development of techniques of operation and presentation, some of the more noteworthy included the Detroit Metropolitan Area Traffic Study (1955-56), and the Niagara Frontier Transportation Sudy (1962-64).[11] In these and most other comprehensive transportation-land use surveys, financing was federal (U.S. Bureau of Public Roads), with state, county, and local units matching funds. Concurrently with the development of such surveys in the United States, comparable surveys, using similar techniques, were operated in several other countries as far apart as Canada[12] and New Zealand.[13] Throughout the 1950s and 1960s, improvements in electronic data processing were reflected in increased use of sophisticated computer methods, without which many of the techniques of the surveys, including the testing of many alternative patterns of land use and transportation arrangements, would have been impracticable.

During the early period of such surveys, one of the outstanding difficulties was the general lack of mechanisms for integrating the results into the total metropolitan planning process, principally because responsible governmental jurisdictions on a metropolitan basis were rare; many of the metropolitan areas had no overall planning agencies, although special-purpose ad hoc agencies were increasingly common. In many instances, in addition to the local general-purpose governments (county and municipal), and the special-purpose districts and authorities, metropolitan planning agencies, often without being responsible directly to any specific governmental authority, proliferated, with duplication and often conflict. In the New York region, for example, the Regional Plan Association, a citizen group growing out of the Regional Plan of New York and Its Environs of the 1920s, the Port of New York Authority, and, later, the Tri-State Transportation Commission, each undertook various aspects of comprehensive regional planning, involving transportation and land use. In 1971 the latter agency was reconstituted as the Tri-State Regional Planning Commission, and became the official planning agency for the region, recognized as such by the three states and accredited by the federal government as the review agency for federally aided improvements within the region of metropolitan significance. In the Chicago region, the quasi-public Chicago Regional Planning Association was subsumed into the Northeastern Illinois Metropolitan Area Planning Commission (later renamed the Northeastern Illinois Planning Commission, or NIPC), which was created in 1957. Coordination among the three principal planning agencies of that region—the city of Chicago's Department of Development and Planning,

11. *Report on the Detroit Metropolitan Area Traffic Study,* Part I, "Data Summary and Interpretation" (July 1955); Part II, "Future Traffic and a Long Range Expressway Plan" (March 1956); *Chicago Area Transportation Study, Final Report* Vol. I, "Survey Findings" (Dec. 1959), Vol. II, "Data Projections" (July 1960); Vol. III, "Transportation Plan" (April 1962); *Pittsburgh Area Transportation Study,* Final Report, Vol. 1, "Study Findings" (Nov. 1961), Vol. 2, "Forecasts and Plans" (Feb. 1963); *Penn Jersey Transportation Study,* Vol. 1, "The State of the Region" (April 1964), Vol. 2, "1975 Projections–F oreground of the Future" (Sept. 1964), Vol. 3, "1975 Transportation Plans (May 1965); *Niagra Frontier Transportation Study, Final Report* (1964).

12. For example: Metropolitan Toronto and Region Transportation Study (MTARTS), *Growth and Travel Past and Present* (April 1966); *Choices for a Growing Region* (Nov. 1967), Ontario Dept. of Municipal Affairs.

13. *Traffic in a New Zealand City,* W. B. Johnston (Christchurch, N. Z.: Christchurch Regional Planning Authority, 1965).

the Chicago Area Transportation Study (CATS), and NIPC—was not fully achieved until the late 1960s, when the last agency was designated the official review one for federally aided projects within the metropolitan area.

The series of comprehensive transportation land use studies of metropolitan areas have had, and their successors have, several important characteristics. With few exceptions, they were carried on as individual studies, representing conditions at the time of the survey, without provision for regular or systematic revision or updating. However, in some areas, as, for example Chicago, Detroit, and Philadelphia, two or three separate surveys, conducted at intervals of a decade or more, have had some utility in determining trends.

The surveys varied with regard to the extent to which interagency cooperation was involved, although subsequently, as discussed later in this chapter, federal actions have encouraged and facilitated interagency cooperation, and, indeed, have made it prerequisite for federal aid.[14]

The surveys generally include a series of alternatives relative to physical patterns of metropolitan development, and some of them include testing of the transportation demands that would be imposed by alternative patterns of land use. However, because, in most instances, there was no comprehensive metropolitan government with authority to direct and control land uses, the plans were to be regarded as general, and flexible, guides, rather than as definitive plans.

Extensive use was made of mathematical models of urban growth and development around the framework of transportation. This, of course, was made possible by the use of computers, with the aid of which the alternatives were evaluated. Some critics have observed that the testing phase of the studies tended to be hurried, and generally not as successful as had been anticipated.[15]

The Multiplicity of Governments in Metropolitan Areas

Probably the principal impedance to metropolitan planning has been the proliferation of governments within the metropolitan areas. These governments are both general-purpose (federal, state, county, and municipal), and special-purpose. The latter include both those which have taxing powers and those which depend upon appropriations and grants from the general-purpose governments, as well as those which depend in whole or part upon user charges for the facilities which they operate. Each of the respective governments has a vested interest either in a territory within the metropolitan complex, or in one or more specific functions within all or part of the metropolitan area. While there are three times as many local governments outside of the SMSAs, there are over

14. The Regional Science Association, in 1960, conducted a session in which the then-current surveys were evaluated. *Papers and Proceedings, The Regional Science Association,* Vol. 7 (1961), pp. 223-262.

15. For further discussion of a number of the comprehensive transportation-land use planning studies, together with a critical evaluation see: David E. Boyce, *et al., Metropolitan Plan Making, An Analysis of Experience with the Preparation and Evaluation of Alternative Land Use and Transportation Plans (Philadelphia:* Regional Science Research Institute, "Monograph Series No. 4," 1970.)

20,000 governments within them. As of 1967, there were 20,703 local governments within the metropolitan areas of the United States. These included 17,538 with property-taxing power; included among the local governments were 404 counties, 4,977 municipalities, 3,255 townships, 5,018 school districts, and 7,049 single- or multiple-function special districts; together, the local governments had over four million employees.[16] The special districts include such diverse ones as transit districts, port districts, airport districts, drainage districts, flood control districts, junior and community college districts, air pollution control districts, mosquito abatement districts, and many others. Of the special-purpose governments, only the school districts have been reducing in numbers, in order to achieve economies of scale. Individual metropolitan areas have as many as several hundred general and special local governments; the New York region has over 1,400, and the Chicago metropolitan complex over 1,000. Commonly, it is difficult or even impossible to determine the actual number of such governments which are involved at a given location; the layers are superimposed in an infinitely complex pattern. Only exceptionally do the boundaries of the territory of more than a small proportion of the local governments affecting an area coincide, in spite of a trend, recently, for the SMSA boundaries to constitute guides for delimination of the territories of some of the recently constituted governments.

It is no wonder that metropolitan planning has been constrained and inhibited by the multiplicity of local governments.[17] Comprehensive planning and its effectuation, as distinguished from ad hoc or special-purpose planning must, of necessity, involve intergovernmental cooperation in the absence of a comprehensive general government covering the territory with which such planning is concerned. In recent years, the situation has been somewhat improved in two respects: (a) increasing participation by the federal government, and by the states, in metropolitan planning and in the facilitation of intergovernmental cooperation, and (b) in some metropolitan areas, a trend toward the creation of new general governmental units, or the expansion of older ones, to cover all or major portions of the metropolitan complex.

Increasing Federal and State Participation in Metropolitan Planning

Encouragement of regional planning by the states and the federal government has significantly increased in recent years, but those governments have been instrumental, in some instances, in stimulating regional planning for several decades. In the 1930s, regional agencies, transcending the territorial boundaries of general-purpose governments, including states, were created for single or multiple purposes. The Tennessee Valley Authority is an outstanding example, but there were others. The U.S. Bureau of Public Roads, as previously mentioned, was instrumental in the operation of origin-destination transpor-

16. U.S. Dept. of Commerce, Bureau of the Census, *Statistical Abstract of the United States, 1971* (Washington, D.C.: Government Printing Office, 1971), p. 414.
17. For a more detailed discussion of the problems arising from the multiplicity of local governments, see: James G. Coke and John J. Gargan, *Fragmentation in Land-Use Planning and Control,* prepared for the consideration of the National Commission on Urban Problems, (Washington, D.C.: Government Printing Office, 1969).

tation studies in the 1940s and 1950s. Such undertakings were extended in scope to include studies of land use, and the federal-aid highway programs depended in major part upon the interpretation of their results. In spite of the broadened scope of the studies, however, the emphasis was heavily upon highways, and, furthermore, there were certain assumptions built into the studies, such as continuation of the existing transportation technology, and no major changes in the social or economic milieu.

The many state and federal programs for urban redevelopment, conservation, and rehabilitation, public housing, and, later, the consolidation of most such programs under the rubric of urban renewal, did not take into consideration for the most part the existence of the metropolitan complexes; most of the agencies created under such programs were confined to the territorial jurisdictions of the individual municipalities.

One of the most significant extensions of federal stimulation of metropolitan and regional planning resulted from the Federal Aid Highway Act of 1962. That act made area-wide planning in metropolitan areas mandatory as a prerequisite for federal assistance in many programs, after July 1, 1965. For such aid, it required that, in each area, an agency be designated to carry on a continuous planning program and to develop comprehensive planning as a basis for review of all projects involved in the federal programs which had metropolitan significance. Each of the local governments in the respective areas was required to submit to such agency all projects in which federal aid, in a large number of enumerated categories, was applied for, and certification of conformance with comprehensive plans was made a condition of such aid. As a result, the existing metropolitan planning agencies were provided with expanded rules, and strong incentives were provided for the performance of such roles. In areas where comprehensive planning agencies did not exist, agencies with limited functions were in some cases expanded, and in other areas new comprehensive planning and review agencies were created. The planning activities of these agencies were—and are—in a large proportion of the areas financed in part by the federal government under the Comprehensive Planning Assistance Program provided by section 701 of the Housing Act of 1954.

The "701" program, expanded and modified in some respects, has furnished support to metropolitan planning since 1955, when the first grant under that section of the Housing Act was made to a metropolitan planning agency. Under that section, the federal government provides financial aid for planning to metropolitan agencies, as well as to local municipal agencies in communities under a given size, the limits of which have varied from time to time. As a result of the Federal Aid Highway Act, federal planning assistance under that act, complemented and reinforced by the 701 program, has been substantially increased.

The effectiveness of federal aid for metropolitan planning is controversial, since there are no guidelines to measure accomplishment. Political scientists have ambivalent feelings relative to the advantages of adding to the already complex phalanxes of local general- and special-purpose governments and authorities an additional level of metropolitan agencies, in spite of the fact that such agencies have, in most instances, encouraged a greater degree of intergovernmental cooperation and coordination. A widespread reservation relative to the federal encouragement of metropolitan planning is the continued emphasis upon physical planning, and especially highway planning, to the relative neglect of housing and social programs, although the later categories have significantly expanded. A measure of the effectiveness of federal stimulation in planning comprehensively for metropolitan areas was a survey by the United States Department of Housing and Urban Development which revealed that less than five percent of the area-wide planning agencies assisted by the 701 program during the fiscal year of 1968 were engaged in housing or housing-related planning activities, whereas over 90 percent of such agencies were engaged in such activities a year later.[18]

Subsequent to the Highway Act of 1962, federal requirements for areawide review, including recommendations as to the conformance of programs and projects to metropolitan comprehensive plans, were broadened. The Demonstration Cities and Metropolitan Development Act of 1966, and its 1970 modifications and extensions, provide for review and recommendations as prerequisite to federal aid for a wide variety of public facility projects and programs. These include hospitals and libraries, sewer, water, and sewage treatment facilities; highway, mass transit, airport and other transportation facilities; and recreation and other open space areas. In addition, land development or uses, which, because of their size, density, type, or location, have public areawide or interjurisdictional significance, are also subject to review by the areawide agency and may be subject to federal financial grants. The Department of Housing and Urban Development (HUD) is the primary agency responsible, at the federal level, for administering most of the provisions of the act.

The appropriate review agencies within the respective metropolitan areas are normally designated by the states or, in the case of interstate metropolitan areas, by the several states, subject to federal approval as to conformance with certain requirements. One of these requirements is that at least two-thirds of the persons on the governing boards of such agencies be local elected officials. This, of course, was instituted in order to make the planning operations more responsive to local desires and objectives. It necessitated, in some instances, major changes in the composition of planning agencies which had been created previously. In 1969, only about one-third of such agencies conformed to that requirement, but by the end of 1971, virtually all of them did.

Where the metropolitan area is comprised of a single county, the county planning agency normally is the review agency, but in other, more extensive areas, considerable confusion has sometimes resulted from the ambiguities relative to the geographic area to be included, and the appropriate agency to cover the comprehensive planning for such areas; this is especially true of some of the largest metropolitan complexes.

In the largest metropolitan region, centering upon New York City, the official planning and review agency, recognized by the three states and the federal government, is the Tri-State Regional Planning Commission, which, as previously noted, represents a change in name and an expansion of functions of the preexisting Tri-State Transportation Commission. In other large metropolitan areas, however, designation of the appropriate agency is sometimes much more difficult. A large part of the difficulty arises from the mutual antagonisms between the respective central cities and the suburbs, as well as among the suburbs. In many instances, the suburbs fear the loss of control of planning to

18. Nicholas P. Thomas, "Effectiveness of the Metropolitan Planning Agency," in *Planning 1971* (Chicago: American Society of Planning Officials, 1971). p. 425.

the central cities, which represent the largest proportion of the metropolitan population, or at least the largest single local governmental unit. A further difficulty arises from the problem of determination of which matters should remain under local control, and which involve considerations that are metropolitan-wide or region-wide. Political partisanship differences between central cities and suburbs, and sometimes among the suburbs, commonly complicate the problem, as do differences in racial and ethnic composition between central cities and suburbs. To illustrate these difficulties, we compare the situation in two large metropolitan complexes, that of northeastern Illinois (metropolitan Chicago) and northeastern Ohio (metropolitan Cleveland and Akron.)

The famous Plan of Chicago, published in 1909, was essentially metropolitan in scope, although, as was common until recent times, it underemphasized social issues, including housing. Nevertheless, it stimulated the creation of two planning agencies which have survived in modified form until the present. One was the Chicago Plan Commission, created in 1910, as a citizen group to lobby for projects included in the plan within the municipal limits of the city of Chicago. The other was the Chicago Regional Planning Association, comprised of both individual and municipal members, to promote the plan in the suburban areas. The Chicago Plan Commission subsequently went through several reorganizations, after each of which it became a more effective instrument, closer to the city government. In 1939 it was reconstituted as a continuing planning agency, quasi-official; in 1957 it was again reconstituted as the Department of City Planning, and later it was combined with effectuation agencies as the Department of Development and Planning, with a large staff headed by a commissioner who is a member of the mayor's cabinet. In this evolution, it typifies the national trends in city planning, with transition from an unofficial citizen's lobbying group to a full-fleged city department concerned not only with plan preparation but also with many aspects of effectuation.

Outside of the city, the Chicago Regional Planning Association was subsumed within, and eventually supplanted by, the Northeastern Illinois Planning Commission (NIPC), created by the state of Illinois in 1957. Later, that agency, in addition to being supported by memberships of local governments and some individual contributions, drew much of its support from the federal 701 program. In accordance with the provisions of the Federal Aid Highway Act of 1962 and Section 204 of the Demonstration Cities and Metropolitan Development Act of 1966, the state of Illinois, with federal concurrence, designated NIPC as the official review agency for the six county northeastern Illinois metropolitan area, coterminous with Chicago SMSA.

In the summer of 1956, before the creation of NIPC, the Chicago Area Transportation Study (CATS) operated its comprehensive transportation-land use study, the results of which were published several years later. Subsequently CATS became a permanent agency, updating the original study and plan proposals periodically. At first, NIPC and CATS were not coordinated in many respects, but after the passage of the federal acts relative to metropolitan planning in 1962 and 1966, CATS became the transportation study and planning agency, with inputs and reciprocal relations with NIPC as well as the Chicago Department of Development and Planning. In recent years, the three agencies have been mutually cooperative.

Between 1962 and 1964, the Chicago Department of Development and Planning, in the preparation of its basic policies plan,[19] consulted frequently, mostly at the staff level, with NIPC as well as with CATS. It was originally contemplated to have, in the city's policy plan, a chapter on the metropolitan aspects of the city's plan, but, although the chapter was prepared by the department's staff and consultants, it did not appear. Two years later, the comprehensive plan for the city was published and accepted; it contained a revised section on metropolitan development, including a statement on "Chicago and Northeast Illinois-Common Goals and Concerns" and "Development Recommendations for the Metropolitan Area."[20]

The Northeastern Illinois Planning Commission, like most metropolitan planning agencies, was concerned throughout most of its existence with essentially noncontroversial physical development projects and programs, avoiding the more controversial social issues. Its accomplishments in the fields of water resource management and solid waste disposal planning were especially significant, and, in collaboration with the United States Geological Survey, it pioneered in the publication of flood hazard maps of the metropolitan area.

NIPC was designated by the state of Illinois, under the Federal Highway Act of 1962 and the Demonstration Cities and Metropolitan Development Act of 1966, as the official review agency for the northeastern Illinois counties (Chicago SMSA) metropolitan area. Even before such designation, substantial progress was made on studies leading to preparation of a comprehensive plan. As noted, communication with the City of Chicago Department of Development and Planning led toward better compatibility between the central city and metropolitan area plans, and collaboration with CATS, after some initial difficulties, assured that the transportation aspects of the plan would not be inconsistent with the CATS findings. Actually, NIPC prepared a series of alternative general plans for land use patterns in the six counties of northeastern Illinois, and CATS tested the alternatives in terms of the transportation requirements. It found that one of the alternatives, essentially a "finger plan" with some modifications, had, by a slight margin, more economic advantages in transportation service requirements than any of the others. The principal alternative plans were published and publicized throughout the region.[21] The advantages of the so-called "finger plan" were pointed out, and exhibits were presented aboard a train which was parked on various railroad sidings throughout the suburban area. A series of public hearings was held in which preferences were voted upon. As a result, it became apparent that the recommended plan met with general public approval. An official, advertised public hearing was held in November 1967, and the modified "finger plan" was adopted by NIPC as the official metropolitan plan on April, 19, 1968, and subsequently published.[22]

19. *Basic Policies for the Comprehensive Plan of Chicago* (Chicago: City of Chicago Dept. of Development and Planning, Aug. 1964).

20. *The Comprehensive Plan of Chicago* (Chicago: City of Chicago Dept. of Development and Planning, Dec. 1966), pp. 26-29.

21. *Diversity Within Order; Coordinated Development for a Better Environment* (Chicago: Northeastern Illinois Planning Commission, March 1967).

22. *The Comprehensive General Plan for the Development of the Northeastern Illinois Counties Area* (Chicago: Chicago: Northeastern Illinois Planning Commission, Apr. 1968); also *The Plan Study: Methodology* (Chicago: Northeastern Illinois Planning Commission, April 1968).

In accordance with federal requirements, turnover among the commissioners of NIPC in mid-1968 resulted in an increased proportion of elected public officials. Subsequent to adoption of the comprehensive metropolitan plan, projects submitted for review by local governments, including those of the city of Chicago, suburban municipalities, special-function governments, and the counties, are evaluated not only in terms of incompatabilities among them, but also in terms of conformance with the adopted metropolitan plan, which itself is subjected to constant study and modification. Thus, although there is no single government to which NIPC is directly responsible covering the metropolitan area as a whole, the agency is a mechanism to coordinate a wide variety of plans and programs more-or-less effectively within the metropolitan area.

The six counties of northeastern Illinois which constitute the Chicago SMSA and the NIPC area, however, constitute but part of a chain of contiguous metropolitan areas along the western and southern shore of Lake Michigan, including the Gary-Hammond (Lake and Porter counties) SMSA in northwestern Indiana (together with the Chicago SMSA constituting the eight-county Chicago-Northwestern Indiana Standard Consolidated Area), and the contiguous Kenosha, Racine, and Milwaukee SMSAs in southeastern Wisconsin. NIPC, under federal impetus, entered into a memorandum of understanding with the Lake-Porter County Regional Transportation and Planning Commission, covering the Gary-Hammond SMSA, under which any project which is likely to affect both of the contiguous metropolitan areas must be approved by both metropolitan planning agencies before being submitted to the relevant federal agencies. A committee consisting of members of both agencies meets periodically to coordinate the operation. Later, a somewhat similar arrangement was made with the Southeastern Wisconsin Regional Planning Commission, which is concerned with the metropolitan areas immediately north of the Illinois-Wisconsin boundary.

It is especially significant to note that the comprehensive plan publication for northeastern Illinois makes specific reference to the problems of housing and of racial non-discrimination as essential elements, without the solutions to which the physical plan would be difficult or impossible to accomplish. Furthermore, the physical plan depends for its essential elements upon the radial transportation, centering upon downtown Chicago. These radii, including railroads, rapid transit, and express highways, are the axes of the "fingers" of NIPC's "finger plan" in the suburban portions of the region, and their inner portions constitute "corridors of high accessibility" which form major elements of the city of Chicago's comprehensive plan. Thus, the concepts of corridors, and of intermetropolitan coalescence along the corridors, achieves recognition as a major element in comprehensive planning for a multinucleated suprametropolitan urban complex of thousands of square miles, with a population exceeding 10 million. This could, perhaps, furnish a prototype for integration of the numerous metropolitan and regional planning operations along the 600-mile northeast corridor or megalopolis, containing close to 50 million people, extending from north of Boston to south of Washington.

Much less effective than the integration of planning in northeastern Illinois, metropolitan and regional planning in northeastern Ohio furnishes an example of the chaos that can result from inadequate support for planning, and from inadequate recognition of the interdependence among contiguous metropolitan areas, thereby producing conflicts as to the appropriate areas of concern. The problem of differentiation of levels of concern within a hierarchy of urban-oriented regions is exemplified by the failure of the several regional and metropolitan planning efforts in northeastern Ohio to coordinate.

The counties of northeastern Ohio constitute a portion of a recognizable corridor extending from Lake Erie west of Cleveland to the Allegheny Plateau region east of Pittsburgh. This corridor, in turn, is a portion of the "Great Lakes Megalopolis" and, except for a break in the Allegheny area, is almost contiguous with the Boston-Washington axis. The dominant urban focus in northeastern Ohio is the central area of Cleveland, but it is not as dominant as central Chicago in the northeastern Illinois-northwestern Indiana complex, or of New York City in the northeast corridor.

The state of Ohio defined, in the 1960s an area which it termed the Lakeshore Uplands Development Region, centering upon Cleveland and containing over 42 percent of the population of the state, and more urbanized land than the total of all the rest of Ohio.[23] This region includes sixteen counties, of which eleven constitute six SMSAs. Five of the latter are contiguous, containing ten counties. They are: Lorain-Elyria SMSA (Lorain County); Cleveland SMSA (Cuyahoga, Medina, Lake, and Geauga counties); Akron SMSA (Summit and Portage counties); Canton SMSA (Stark County); and Youngstown-Warren SMSA (Trumbull and Mahoning counties). Several of the individual counties have active and effective county planning agencies. Where the SMSA is a single county, as in the case of Stark County, the county and metropolitan agencies are identical, but in the multicounty SMSA's, particularly that of Cleveland, serious conflict has existed, to the detriment of the planning process.

For many years, Cleveland constituted an outstanding example of effective city planning; the Cleveland City Planning Commission in the 1950's was nationally known as one of the better operations of its kind. Cuyahoga County also had—and has—a well-established planning agency. The city of Cleveland had, in 1970, slightly over one-third of the population of its metropolitan area. Because it is "under-bounded," with the municipal limits well inside the urbanized area, many of the close-in suburbs have characteristics, which, in many other physically comparable situations, would constitute "inner city" areas. As in many metropolitan areas, the central city population has been rapidly declining, with an increasing proportion, as well as an increasing total, of nonwhites.

In 1963, the Cleveland/Seven County Transportation/Land Use Study (SCOTS) was organized to conduct, with the usual federal and state aid, a comprehensive planning study, in accordance with the procedures and techniques outlined earlier in this chapter. The area involved coincided with no existing governmental jurisdiction. It included the four counties of the Cleveland SMSA, the adjoining area to the west (Lorain County: the Lorain Elyria SMSA), and portions of two contiguous counties to the southeast (Summit and Portage). The latter two counties constitute the Akron SMSA, but the principal urbanized portions of both counties were excluded from SCOTS, because, concurrently, a similar transportation-land use study was under way covering those urbanized areas: the Akron Metropolitan Area Transportation Study (AMATS). The AMATS study, like

---

23. *Use of Land in Ohio; Report of the Land Use Survey and Analysis* (Columbus: Planning Div. of the Development Dept., State of Ohio, n.d., *ca.* 1968).

SCOTS, did not coincide in area with any governmental jurisdiction, but the two studies were to dovetail. The SCOTS study was published in May 1969,[24] and the AMATS study in a series of reports in 1967 and 1968.

With the completion of the SCOTS report, and under pressure from the federal agencies, the Cleveland/Seven County Transportation/Land Use Study was expanded in scope to form the nucleus of a new agency, NOACA, or the Northeast Ohio Areawide Coordinating Agency. In accordance with federal stipulations, the NOACA board was constituted of elected public officials, including those from Cleveland as well as from the suburban counties. NOACA, shortly after its creation, was designated by the state of Ohio as the official review agency, in accordance with federal requirements, and was so accredited by the federal government. Almost immediately, however, several conflicts arose relative to the scope, and the geographic area, of the agency's concerns. First, the suburbanites, both within Cuyahoga County and in the outlying counties of the Cleveland SMSA, claimed that the city of Cleveland was overrepresented and that it exercised undue influence upon area-wide planning; Cleveland on the other hand, claimed under-representation. Early in 1971, Cleveland failed to pay the assessment for its share of the costs of the agency's operations, and a suburban county threatened to withdraw from the agency. Without representation from the central city of the region, NOACA could not truly be a regional or metropolitan planning agency, and the federal government withdrew its recognition of NOACA as the review agency. Many federally aided projects in the seven-county area were thereby stalled. Late in the year, following a change in the municipal administration in Cleveland, that city paid its dues in NOACA, and steps were initiated toward recertification of the agency as the official reviewing and regional planning body. City-suburban and intergovernmental tensions, however, continued.

A second difficulty faced by NOACA, to the detriment of regional planning in northeastern Ohio, arose from the inclusion of several counties beyond the boundaries of the Cleveland SMSA, and in particular three counties to the south which constitute the Akron SMSA. In that area, another regional planning body was created: the Tri-County Regional Planning Commission, which subsumed AMATS as that metropolitan transportation study neared its conclusion. The tri-county agency, however, was concerned with an area that coincided neither with that of AMATS or with the Akron SMSA. AMATS did not include the northern portions of Summit and Portage counties, since that area was covered previously by SCOTS. Furthermore, the Tri-County Regional Planning Commission based in Akron, included within its territory Medina County to the west, a county which is included within the Cleveland SMSA rather than the Akron SMSA.

The Akron-based agency, Tri-County, is not recognized by the federal government as an official planning and review agency, since its entire territory is included within that of NOACA. Akron interests tend to resent the centralization of regional planning in Cleveland, and have frequently threatened to withdraw support of NOACA. Meanwhile, neither of the two regional planning agencies can be effective, until the conflicts are resolved. The territory of the Tri-County Regional Planning Commission, including the

24. *A Framework for Action: The Comprehensive Report of the Cleveland Seven County Transportation/Land Use Study* (Cleveland, May 1969).

Akron SMSA and one county of the Cleveland SMSA, is completely subsumed within the area of NOACA, resulting in inevitable conflict. Since the state of Ohio favors the Cleveland-based NOACA, it is possible that resolution of the conflict must await some form of outside intervention, most likely federal.

Forms of Intergovernmental Cooperation in Planning: New and Expanded Governmental Units

Metropolitan planning must be concerned with the spatial and structural organization of the governmental units within the geographic area of its operation. The planner, therefore, must consider, and make recommendations, relative to reorganization or reconstitution of the units, where existing governmental structures inhibit or constrain effective planning.

A basic problem in planning is the separation of those matters which are of metropolitan and regional concern from those which are of concern to local areas, whether municipal or not, within the metropolitan complexes. A regional park or forest preserve is of metropolitan or regional concern; a major city park is of citywide concern, and a local neighborhood park of local concern. A major university has metropolitan and suprametropolitan aspects, while a local elementary school is of primary concern to the immediate neighborhood even though it may be part of a citywide system. Similarly, an express highway typically is a matter for metropolitan, regional, and even national concern, while a local access street is not. It is therefore necessary to recognize the existence not only of planning mechanisms, but of governmental structures, constituting a nested hierarchy within any geographic region; this is particularly pertinent in metropolitan regions, where fragmentation of governmental responsibilities is a significant element in plan preparation and effectuation.

Several approaches to the problem offer promise; some of them have been successfully applied, and others are relatively recent in origin and await testing before they justify widespread adoption. All of the approaches are concerned with separation of responsibilities in accordance with the level, both organizationally and spatially, which is most appropriate to the particular problem.

One approach through creation of a single metropolitan government to include larger portions, or all of a metropolitan area, is not new. City-county consolidation first occurred in the nineteenth century, and in the 1950s and 60s several have taken place in the United States. These, however, do not eliminate the need for sub-metropolitan governments concerned with neighborhood and community affairs.

Annexation, or the addition of territory to established governmental areas, such as municipalities, occurs as a normal procedure, although the specific requirements vary from state to state. In some of the southwestern states, it has been possible to annex territory to expanding cities relatively easily; in the 1960s several large cities in Texas, New Mexico, and Arizona annexed land well beyond the boundaries of their built-up areas in advance of development, and some more than doubled their population overnight. This occurred in Chicago as early as 1889.

Creation of area-wide government may take one of two forms: general or special-purpose types. The former has the objection that it reduces, or eliminates, the possibility for local citizen participation, by removing the individual from easy access to officials and from direct participation. The individuality of the neighborhood and community tends to become lost in metropolitan complexities. One suggestion that has been made to mitigate this circumstance is to maintain a two-tier set of governments, with the area-wide one taking over from the local municipalities only a portion of the government functions, namely, those which transcend local solution. The sharing of power is at the heart of this dilemma. Within the larger metropolitan cities, it has been suggested that neighborhood government—concerned with neighborhood matters—be the basic units of political and administrative power, in order to avoid the fear on the part of suburbs that a monolithic power structure within the central cities would dominate the metropolitan area, while in the suburban areas, federation of some of the suburban governmental functions would tend to balance suburban powers in comparison with those of the central cities.[25]

Consolidation, or merger, of governmental units can assist in the effectiveness of planning, because economies of scale can be achieved, subject to the constraints noted of reduced opportunity for direct citizen participation. Consolidation of general-purpose governments is extremely difficult because of the vested interests in preserving existing governmental organizations and the officialdom and patronage jobs that scale economies could eliminate; but in some instances it may be feasible. Some special-purpose governments could be consolidated to great advantage: the consolidated school district is the most noteworthy example.

As the population expands peripherally, relatively few cities have unincorporated territory immediately contiguous to their municipal boundaries, so that expansion of their area would involve consolidation with adjoining municipalities.

Short of consolidation or the creation of new units of general- or special-purpose governments, a measure of metropolitan coordination of planning, and of plan effectuation, can be achieved by a cooperative approach.

Many governmental functions, such as fire and police protection, water supply, waste treatment and disposal, air and water pollution control, and others, can be achieved for parts or all of metropolitan areas by intergovernmental contractual agreements for sharing of services. In lieu of the creation of new special-function governments, added complications in metropolitan administrative and political structures would thereby result.

Of particular interest to planners is the provision in many states for extraterritorial powers of municipalities to control land uses for a stated distance beyond their boundaries—usually one to three miles—in unincorporated territory, by means of zoning and subdivision controls, in advance of development. Such extraterritorial planning provisions, if invoked, may save the expanding municipality considerable difficulty later, when the territory may be annexed, if it can be assured that the planning standards outside the municipal limits do not significantly vary from those within. In some instances, other planning activities and services may be shared, for example, the joint use

25. Conrad J. Weller, Jr., "Metropolitan Federation Reconsidered," *Urban Affairs Quarterly,* Vol. 6, No. 4 (June 1971), pp. 411-420; Milton Kotler *Neighborhood Government* (Indianapolis: Bobbs-Merrill Co., 1969).

of planning consultants or staff, which the individual municipality could not afford to employ by itself; such contractual arrangement for sharing of planning services may have the additional advantage that compatibility across jurisdictional boundaries may be improved.

Most significant among recent developments in local intergovernmental cooperation which, among other results, facilitates the preparation and implementation of planning, is the Council of Governments (COG) movement.

COGs are associations, technically voluntary for the most part, of elected governmental officials. Typically, they involve entire metropolitan areas or portions thereof, although some COGs exist also in rural areas. Their membership varies from three governmental units to over a hundred, and the populations from several thousand to several millions.[26] Most of them were created directly as a result of the federal requirement for comprehensive regional and metropolitan planning and project review as prerequisite for federal aid. Many COGs are federally recognized as the official review agencies, although in some instances there are parallel agencies to furnish the planning and review services.

COGs are more acceptable than official governments, in general, because they have no coercive force and create little threat to existing governmental organization, but at the same time relieving some of the pressure for creation of general- or special-purpose metropolitan governments. COGs are not, in fact, governments, since they do not have taxing powers, nor can they pass laws or ordinances.

The first COG was organized in 1954 in the Detroit metropolitan area, but the major spread of the concept was the result of the availability of federal funding contingent upon the creation of planning and review agencies. Because of the general desire to avoid controversy if possible, most COGs have been primarily concerned with physical planning and "housekeeping" operations, rather than the more controversial social issues, such as housing and racial integration. However, due to the impetus of increasing federal concern and intervention in such matters, it is quite possible that the COGs will increasingly become involved in controversy.

In some instances, the COGs have superseded previously existing agencies which carried on planning and other activities. The Metropolitan Washington Council of Governments, for example, became an effective planning and review agency only after a presidential order dissolved the National Capital Regional Planning Council.

Arising from the COG movement, but not a typical COG, the Twin Cities (Minneapolis-St. Paul) Metropolitan Council could be a prototype for a new kind of agency which shares some of the advantages of COGs, but reduces the typical disadvantage that COGs have in their lack of access to tax support and the possibility of dominance by a fraction or segment of the population. More important, the Twin Cities Metropolitan Council, unlike typical COGs, has some real power over planning, because it can suspend local plans, grant applications, and many types of programs if they do not conform to the general pattern or if there are other major objections. No action can be taken on plans or

---

26. "The Councils of Government Movement in the United States," *The Municipal Yearbook 1970* (Washington, D.C.: International City Management Assoc., 1970), pp. 39-59.

programs until after referral to the Metropolitan Council, which is mandatory, and 60 days have elapsed. The council is a central metropolitan body for the local and ad hoc boards and agencies, with power to implement projects and programs in water supply and treatment; sewage collection, treatment, and disposal; airport development; open space; and solid waste disposal. In such fields, the council prepares guidelines and criteria, and it appoints officials to the operating boards. Thus, it is concerned with broad policy issues on a metropolitan basis, while avoiding involvement in minor construction and operating details. Unlike typical COGs, which rely upon local membership contributions, which theoretically are voluntary, and upon federal grants, the Twin Cities Metropolitan Council has authority to impose a tax levy.

In summary, metropolitan planning, long relatively ineffective because of the political and administrative fragmentations within metropolitan areas, and the lack of consensus or community of interest in many matters between central cities and suburban areas and between suburbs, was given a major impetus with the increasing number of federal programs for local and metropolitan assistance, both in planning and in effectuation and operation of projects and programs, during the decade of the 1960s. There is increasing realization at local, regional, state, and federal levels in the United States, and at local, provincial, and federal levels in Canada, that planning is concerned with some matters at the local neighborhood and community scale, and with others at the scale of the metropolitan area or region; that identification of the appropriate level for each matter, and that the creation and operation of appropriate governmental agencies at each level to perform the relevant functions, are essential if metropolitan planning is to be effective. Out of the confusion, new governmental, quasi-governmental, and unofficial organizational structures are emerging, and their effects upon the nature of planning will be very significant. The metropolitan area, like the city in a previous era as well as in the present, represents a frontier for the planner. Beyond the metropolitan area, in turn, is another planning frontier: the multinucleated urban and urbanizing region.

13 | FUNDING AND SUPPORTING PLANNING

K. Woodrow Benckert

HOW PRIVATE ENTERPRISE VIEWS URBAN PLANNING

Having actually attended meetings called for the purpose of starting a movement to establish an orderly plan for community growth and improvement, the author, as a representative of business was greeted by an almost apologetic organizing committee. Their reticence stemmed from the assumption that the business community (being large taxpayers) would oppose any planning effort since planning would automatically be followed by capital expenditures.

Nothing could be more wrong. The complaint most frequently voiced by the business community is not the amount of local and state taxes, but rather how those tax monies are spent. The business community may bitterly oppose the expenditure of a few thousand dollars on a make-work boondoggling project, but will applaud and actively support the commitment of hundreds of thousands of tax dollars over a twenty- or thirty-year period to provide financing for a capital project that will permanently enhance the community. Private enterprise knows, however, that no such project is going to achieve its intended aims *unless it is part of an overall long-range community plan.*

Any business currently successful not only approves of organized planning, but practices it. There are few businesses of any size that do not have, *in writing* (a) long-range plans (with basic goals and general policies to achieve those goals), (b) a five- or seven-year plan (objectives and planned actions leading toward the basic goals), and (c) a two- or three-year plan (in which the objectives have been

363

detailed and are quantitative and which are backed up by detailed plans for reaching the defined objectives).

Those who oppose the expenditure of money for planning will argue that plans do not remain constant over the years, and hence are useless and a waste of effort. Short-range plans are apt to change considerably. These changes are brought about for many reasons. The most common one is the inability to finance or complete a planned project in the original time frame. Changes might also take place in short- and middle-range planning due to developments of new materials, methods, and ideas; the emergence of a new problem not originally recognized; the disappearance or solution of an original problem. Changes in long-range planning generally come about in the form of gradual evolution. This evolution, however, is inevitable, and any plan, as covered by Chapter 14 of this book, must be under constant review and must be updated as the review dictates. The only greater mistake a community can make than not to continually review its basic planning is *not to have any such plan.*

Many people think that formal urban planning is a brand new idea. It is not. It is true that there is now available a relatively small, highly proficient professional group of planners. They have expertise and experience which did not exist twenty or even ten years ago.

Here is an example of what planning *has done* (not what it can do). In the 1940's the author was a field engineer (engineering outside of plant expansion) for one of the Bell System companies. Located in the district in which he worked were two cities about twenty miles apart, City A and City B. Both were along a good-size river ensuring adequate water supply; both had good railroad facilities; both were astride the then-principal highway between New York and Chicago; in both cases their primary industry was heavy, i.e., foundries, steel fabricating, and mining and quarrying machinery.

City A was bounded by a river on the east, a recently annexed borough on the south (peopled by a group generally different than the balance of the community), an independent borough on the west (the logical direction of expansion), and an incorporated township to the north. City B was bounded on the east by a river on the other side of which was a good-size city. On the south, west, and north were unincorporated townships.

City "A" postponed developing a fundamental plan, since it was felt that such planning was not possible until all of the political subdivisions were united. This was never accomplished and only recently has progress been made through the use of consolidated school districts (even this has not been 100 percent achieved) consolidated industrial parks, water and sewerage systems, etc. Even with this progress the city has lost out as a major commercial center to its nearby neighbor, City B. In A the new housing starts are few, new industry is almost nonexistent, and young people move out to greener pastures.

City B on the other hand expanded its boundaries into what was then farm country. It developed plans for a magnificent park system; parts of the riverfront were continued zoned for industry, but upstream was zoned for park and residential use. The school system, established on a sound tax base, is second to none. As a result, dozens of secondary and supporting industries have been established. No longer is the community dependent entirely on heavy industry, with its feast-or-famine cycles, but has a diversification which levels out the former economic peaks and valleys. I am sure that the planners in 1946 did not specifically envision what is currently happening, but they can surely take credit for having paved the way. An area that in many communities would have almost inevitably become a slum, has now been cleared and is giving way to low- and medium-income garden apartment units, housing so located that many employees will be able to walk or bicycle to work. The city has become the hub for an industrial, retail, living area encompassing smaller communities for miles around. The banks and retail and service businesses have developed branches that now not only service the entire county, but parts of four peripheral counties.

One of the seemingly most convincing arguments and one of the greatest falacies against spending money for planning is the oft-repeated statement: "Let's get on with the doing and instead of spending money on planning, let's spend the money on building something." There is no better way to waste money.

WHAT DOES PLANNING COST?

Good planning! In a business such as a utility, hotel operation, etc., which is capital oriented, (a city or community is similarly oriented) fundamental planning represents from 1/2 percent to no more than 1 1/2 percent of capital expenditures. It must be remembered that these are organizations which have had a long time commitment to planning and have developed a great deal of expertise. Furthermore, they have basic plans they are now concerned with keeping modernized.

Any community that does not have a good, basic, long-range plan must face up to a major effort and expenditure to establish such a plan.

How much will this cost? No one can estimate this for a given situation without considerable study. A cheap fundamental plan based primarily on conjecture rather than fact will be worth nothing. On the other hand, large sums can be spent on planning only to end up with a product that is also worthless. However, these alternatives can easily be avoided, and the tools are available so that a community can develop and maintain an up-to-date plan for a reasonable investment—an investment that will pay for itself many times over in savings in capital expenditures.

The American Institute of Planners is a national professional society of urban and regional planners. Its more than 6,000 members are professionals who have met established standards of education and/or experience. The American Society of Consulting Planners is a national organization of planning consultant firms whose members meet stringent criteria. Members of both organizations are governed by codes of ethics, copies of which are available. More important is the fact that the continued success of both the individual professionals and their firms is dependent on a continuing string of satisfied customers. In very few areas of professional endeavor are errors or omissions so widely publicized. Consequently, it is an area wherein the successful organizations must constantly maintain a high level of professional competence.

Not only funding assistance but also technical advice and assistance can be secured from both the state and federal level. The amount of assistance varies due to many factors. In some states enabling legislation, allowing communities to make full utilization of federal funds, has not been passed. In other cases matching funds can be used. Even the size of your community can be a factor. Professional planning consultants and/or the state and federal agencies can be of assistance. Almost all communities can secure financial aid for planning under one or more sections of the 1954 Housing Act.

ORGANIZING FOR PLANNING

Having had a great deal of experience in establishing new organizations or new functions in both business as well as public agencies, there are several basic principles the author has described below regarding planning (also see the Bibliography at end of this chapter).

Planning success depends on the quality of the people involved from the interested citizen to the dedicated professional. As in almost every other endeavor, quality rather than quantity is paramount.

Whether it is called a Planning Agency, Planning Commission, Citizens Committee, Citizens Action Commission (which functioned so effectively under Mayor Lee in New Haven), or has some other title, it is through such a group that planning can most likely become a reality. Ideally, the members of the Board of Directors of the Planning Agency would be persons highly respected by the entire community, of great professional competence, be able to put forth almost 100 percent effort in the agency's work, and be completely nonpartisan. Such persons never exist. The legislation enabling the establishment of the Planning Agency may dictate as to how it comes into being and to some degree who are qualified to become members. Within such restrictions, however, the control group of the agency should consist of people who have the respect and trust of a good segment of the community. Insofar as this assignment is concerned, they should be capable of objective thinking. Their responsibilities are many, but their effectiveness depends on their ability to sell their staff's recommendations to the governing bodies involved and the voter. It is the Planning Agency directors who must take the responsibility for the work of their staff and the planning consultants which they hire.

If funding of planning is separate from general community funds the budgeting and control of such funds is a responsibility of the director of the planning agency. If planning funding is part of an overall budget, the Planning Agency aids the regular governing body in budgeting and dispensing funds.

It is the Planning Agency, often with the help of outside consulting services that outlines the areas to be investigated, estimates costs, i.e., establishes budgets, hires staff, and selects and contracts with a consulting planning service.

As in the case of all contracts for professional services, it is imperative that the services to be provided, the manner of billing for them, and the responsibilities of all parties to the contract all be clearly defined. Most contracts for professional services have well spelled out plateaus (usually identified as major events on a master schedule) at which time a specific product is available for review and both parties to the contract have a "go/no go" option. Such an approach is desirable to both parties since it protects the Planning Agency board from making commitments over long terms without periodic review. It makes it possible for the planning consultants to provide services as required at a minimum cost. It should be borne in mind that in the embryonic stages of planning, fixed-fee contracts of any type must have relatively large cushions built into the pricing structures. It is for this reason that most reputable professionals recommend some type of "payment for services rendered" contract rather than a fixed fee. Fixed-fee contracts are only practical for specific tasks, easily evaluated, which are performed late in the development of a plan.

One of the first decisions (and of primary importance) that must be made when a planning program is contemplated is to determine whether it shall be done by a full-time staff or with a consulting planning service. The professionals (and politicians) can list advantages and disadvantages of both concepts. To those unencumbered by professional pride and with no political prejudices to interfere, the answer is quite obvious—USE BOTH! Develop the smallest, most proficient, highly motivated, least biased staff possible. Then contract with a consulting planning service to do the majority of the work under the surveillance of the staff.

Here are two reasons for this middle-of-the-road recommendation: (a) No city, including greater New York can maintain a staff that will have the expertise to *develop* a *fundamental plan.* They *may* be able to maintain one once developed and this is doubtful. Aside from the problems of key positions being filled by politicians, no one Planning Commission can develop the expertise that is available in a group of professional planners working in many areas under the scrutiny of several planning boards and their respective citizenry. (b) Why then bother with *any* planning staff? There is a sharp difference between delegation and abdication although the difference is frequently not recognized. An example many times repeated where delegation became abdication is apparent to everyone in looking at some of the churches that have been constructed in the last decade. Many may be an architect's dream but they are a parishioner's nightmare. The reason is that most church governing bodies are not knowledgeable in building and hence delegate (abdicate) to the professional architect. The architect (as in the case of most professionals) has an absolutely free hand perhaps for the *first time* in his entire career (he may have designed his own house but his wife was looking over his shoulder), and hence some of the horrible "masterpieces." Every professional plan should contain a reasonable amount of proprietary influence and still observe the objectives of the people who must live with the plan.

STAFFING FOR PLANNING

Organization of a Planning Agency varies with the size of a city. A smaller one (under 10,000 population) usually has no staff, a medium-size city (10,000 to 100,000) may have a Planning Director and a small staff, and a large city (100,000 or more) may have an Executive Director with a Director of Planning, Director of Public Relations, and a Director of Budget [see Figure 13-1].

The membership of the directors of the Planning Agency must be persons who, after reviewing the presentations of their staff, can make decisions and then back up those decisions with persuasion that will convince members of the advisory committee and

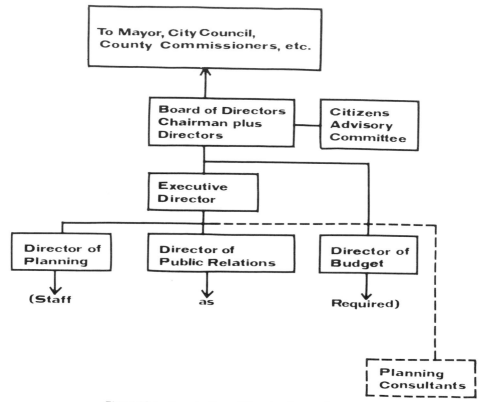

Figure 13-1   Organization of Planning Agency by structure.

ultimately the general public. The broader the membership of the directors, the more effective will be the agency.

The executive director is the key professional of the Planning Agency. He should be not only an administrator, but must be capable of passing judgment on the activities and recommendations of both his staff and planning consultants. It is his responsibility to make recommendations to the Board of Directors. The concept that he should present the options to the board and allow them to make their choice is a weak and uncertain premise. He should not only make specific recommendations but should be able and willing to substantiate them.

The incumbent of this position should have the following minimum qualifications:

1. Have a degree in urban planning or related field.

2. Be a registered professional engineer. (Ideally he would have a degree in urban planning—an almost impossible requirement since even today universities are not meeting more than one-third of the current requirements.)

3. Have had at least seven years experience in positions of increasing responsibility with either a Planning Agency and/or a reputable planning consulting firm.

4. Have taken part in seminars, conferences, etc., on urban planning.

5. Demonstrate or prove ability to prepare and interpret an economic analysis study.

6. Understand and have experience with some form of critical path scheduling.

7. Have a working knowledge of managerial and administrative techniques.

The Director of Planning should meet the same requirements as the Executive Director except that he need not be as experienced, particularly in the administrative area.

The Director of Budget is the chief fiscal officer of the agency. As such he is in charge of administering the funds of the Planning Agency. Seemingly, a very simple, routine job. It is not! Bear in mind that a Planning Agency has no substantial project to show the citizenry who are paying the bills until planning has been completed (at least one phase) and some of the plans have been implemented. It is during the early stages of planning activity that any disclosure of a loose fiscal policy can be especially damaging. Even after planning is well under way, the agency still needs a strong fiscal officer. If a project that in the basic plan was estimated to cost x dollars is completed for $2x$ or $3x$, the Planning Agency must be in a position to explain the discrepancy. The Board of Directors should be made aware of any such events *while they are occurring* not after they have become *fait accompli.* It is infinitely better to have impending disasters brought to light by the Planning Agency than by some other group.

The Director of the Budget should function as does the controller in a modern well-run business. He is shown (Figure 13-1) reporting directly to the Board of Directors with a dotted line relationship to the Executive Director, a practice coming into increasing use in corporate organizations. Thus, in day to day operations of the Planning Agency, he would work through the Executive Director, but in exercising budget control, internal audit functions, and capital budget surveillance he would report directly to the Board of Directors. The Budget Director should have the following minimum qualifications:

1. Have a degree or equivalent in accounting and/or business administration.

2. Have had substantial experience in operating budget control.

3. Have at least three years internal auditing function. This experience could be in the auditing department of a business or government organization or with a recognized accounting firm.

4. A fourth qualification which could be waived but which would be desirable would be experience with capital budget administration. This is a field in which many think themselves adept and few really are. Many progressive planners have found themselves in disrepute not because of their own failings, but because of poor capital administration by another agency or contractor. Keeping aware of capital expenditures in relation to project development, even though not a prime function of the Planning Agency, can yield great dividends, dividends in the form of avoiding embarrassing situations which reduce the credibility of the agency.

When one thinks of a Director of Public Relations (Information) the first image of such a person is a nice-looking, well-dressed, outgoing individual with an ability to recall first names. These are fine attributes for the incumbent to have, but they may contribute little to his effectiveness in his function of supporting a Planning Agency. Many directors have been hired on this basis and have been disappointments to their organizations.

Almost everyone is convinced that they could do a good job as Director of Public Relations/Information; yet, very few could. Keeping the public accurately informed requires skillful use of the public media. The best PR/Info director the author knows insists that no one can function effectively in the PR field unless he has worked a beat on a good daily newspaper. Whether this is true or not it should be borne in mind that in addition to maintaining liaison with a Citizens Advisory Committee the PR director's main function is to see that the planning board activities receive both adequate and accurate reporting in all available media. The most conscientious reporter or newscaster will welcome well-written, *accurate* news releases. Also the best feature writers are not averse to putting their byline over a well-prepared human interest story. In any case the PR position is not an opening for someone's charming nephew but should be filled by a professional who is completely familiar with the news media and how they function. This operation at best is on the fringe of the political area and the PR director should know what moves should be made when and if planning becomes a political football. He must be astute enough to avoid making claims for planning that can never be achieved, but must also capitalize on the attainment of each threshold or plateau.

CITIZENS ADVISORY COMMITTEE

The term Citizens Advisory Committee would appear to describe the primary function of this committee. From this one would conclude that the primary function of the committee is to aid the planning board in their planning function. This is not entirely true. The primary function of the Citizens Advisory Committee is to sell the planning concept and secure acceptance of the plans as they evolve.

When one mentions that the primary function of the committee is not to actually aid in the planning process, this does not mean that the committee should not participate. On the contrary, the more its members are involved the more effective will be the committee. It has been said we dislike people because we do not know them and that we do not know them because we dislike them. If this is true of people it is infinitely more true of ideas, particularly if they are new and unfamiliar. One way to sell the planning concept is to involve the members of the advisory committee. Thus, they will know what planning means and what its advantages are. Knowing this they will embrace the idea and help promote it.

The Citizens Advisory Committee should have broad representation from every segment of the population. It should meet regularly and the meetings should be well organized with handouts, visual displays, or whatever else may be used to (a) educate the members, (b) secure their involvement, (c) provide them with information that they can use in their day-to-day contacts.

One of the prime responsibilities of the Director of Public Relations/Information is working with this committee. It is his job to help keep them informed and also to secure input from the members of the committee in order to make full utilization of their powers, influence, and knowledge.

As mentioned above, this committee should represent all segments of the population involved. It is not necessary and in fact one should avoid selecting people simply because they are easily led. The people who never ruffle the waters, never ask embarrassing questions, will also be nonaggressive and ineffective in telling the planning board case to their peers.

The advisory committee meetings in addition to being well organized should not be overly drawn out in order to encourage attendance. The Author has frequently worked with such committees in the public arena and strongly recommends that the Chairman of the Planning Board or the board itself issue a written periodic report to the members of the committee. This report need not be a printed work of art but turned out as a factual document such as a chief executive of a corporation might send to the members of his Board of Directors.

One further device to secure the help and cooperation of the advisory committee is to advise them, preferably at one of their regular meetings, of news releases to be forthcoming in the near future. Advance knowledge automatically makes them participants. A case of the useful purpose served by an advisory committee took place recently in the author's own community when the town governing body, faced with a serious problem which had no pleasant solution, prevailed upon the committee to study the matter and come up with the recommendation. The solution, which really was quite obvious albeit painful, was then the recommendation of the group who represented the majority of the electorate.

CONCLUSION

The demand for and short supply of planners has created a situation in most cities where planning positions are filled, often in desperation or under political pressure, by inexperienced or so-called planners. Most of them, either through fear of losing their jobs or from lack of knowledge or by getting entangled in daily administrative duties, produce little, if any, planning. They are often protected by civil service regulations that guarantee an annual raise and protection from being laid off for nonproductivity.

Part of the answer to this dilemma is described above regarding a small, proficient staff with most of the planning being done by planning consulting firms. Another part of the answer is to employ a planning director who gets results from his staff, has guts enough to lay off nonproducers, and resists the temptation to build up a big staff and thereby more easily justify a larger salary for himself. The planning board should know what planning needs to be done in their community, schedule the work over a reasonable period of time, insist the planning director stays on schedule, and get another, if he fails to deliver.

In concluding this chapter it is important to bear in mind that virtually every community is going to do some type of planning. It can be good or bad. Bad planning wastes money and hampers the effective growth of a community. Good planning saves money and makes a community a pleasant place in which to live.

BIBLIOGRAPHY

1.   W. I. Goodman and E. C. Freund (eds.), *Principles and Practice of Urban Planning,* published for the Institute for Training in Municipal Administration, International City Management Assoc., Chicago.
2.   Jeanne B. Lowe, *Cities in a Race with Time,* (Random House, New York,)
3.   Donald H. Webster, *Urban Planning and Municipal Public Policy,* (Harper and Brothers, New York).
4.   Francine F. Rabinovits, *City Politics and Planning,* (Atherton Press, New York,).

14 | REPLANNING AND PLAN IMPLEMENTATION

Russell H. Riley

Many of the earlier comprehensive plans were seldom used and copies remained stored in closets, seldom examined or distributed. There were several reasons for this condition. In some instances, civic organizations had financed the preparation of the plan and neither officials nor citizens had participated in its formulation and were not familiar with the findings and recommendations. In other instances, the plan would be prepared by a planning consultant and the Planning Commission or officials would have limited opportunity to become familiar with the details. Many times, the Planning Commission would become inactive after the plan was completed. The major exceptions to this condition were the zoning regulations. The majority of the zoning ordinances were adopted, but all too frequently they were not revised to meet changing conditions.

As indicated previously, the comprehensive plan is intended to guide local growth and development, but unless it is closely related to changing conditions, trends and local needs, it cannot assure satisfactory results. Most urban areas are experiencing rapid growth. Changes are occurring in the types or patterns of urban development. New or additional services are demanded by the citizens and new regulations or controls are evolving. Finally, many new techniques in both planning and zoning practices are evolving. It is thus essential that the plan be revised and adjusted to these changing conditions and practices.

RECENT CHANGES

The following are among the more important changes occurring in the development of urban areas. Most of these were discussed in preceding chapters, but they are summarized here to indicate factors that should be considered in revising older plans.

Housing

Current housing problems probably reflect the most widely discussed needs in urban areas, with special emphasis upon the need for standard living facilities at medium to low prices or rental ranges and in desirable locations. Whereas much of the early housing was constructed on an individual basis, mass production of single-family homes and rental units now predominates. For maximum success, this requires large vacant tracts rather than scattered vacant lots. New construction practices and techniques are evolving—especially prefabricated structures. The rapid increase in use of mobile living units must be recognized and provisions made for such facilities (see Chapter 4). Urban renewal programs are resulting in many changes in housing and in residential areas (see Chapter 11).

Shopping

Whereas the majority of shopping was formerly done in the downtown business districts and in strip commercial developments along major streets, a large portion of retail sales now occurs at large shopping centers located in suburban and outlying sections or in smaller, but modern, neighborhood centers. The provision of adequate, well-improved, off-street parking areas and off-street loading facilities is now a necessity.

The growth of outlying and neighborhood shopping centers has caused much concern about the future of the older central business districts, not only in large cities, but also in many communities containing populations of 50,000 or less. Consequently, studies of the central area as well as plans for its redevelopment are being initiated in many cities and should be considered in a revision or updating program. Such studies are usually concerned with reducing volumes of through traffic, improving off-street parking facilities, providing convenience and safety for pedestrians, and improved appearance of the area (see Chapter 5).

Manufacturing

A large proportion of newer manufacturing structures are used for assembling and distribution purposes and, thus, are not seriously objectionable when located near residential areas. Admittedly, plants are still needed to process raw materials and to produce chemicals and to fabricate products, but new pollution controls are tending to make them far less objectionable than they formerly were. With the large increase in use of trucks, modern plants are much less dependent upon locations adjoining railroads. Industries are also recognizing the necessity of providing adequate off-street parking facilities for employees, as well as spaces for loading and unloading of trucks (see Chapter 5). An important trend in industrial development is the "industrial park" with deed restrictions and landscape treatment. Actually, its classification as a "park" is improper, for it is merely a planned and modern industrial district.

Transportation

The many changes in transportation facilities are so well known (see Chapters 7 and 8) that additional comment would be superfluous. Changes will continue in the future and new types of facilities will undoubtedly be developed. The current trend of providing mass transportation facilities in the larger urban areas should be encouraged.

Parks and Recreation

The shorter working day and increased private use of urban land has resulted in a marked demand for public open spaces and additional recreational facilities. Federal financial assistance is now available for acquisition and improvement of these facilities. It is increasingly imperative that a revised plan make adequate provisions for such facilities and early acquisition, if not complete development, should be encouraged (see Chapter 6).

Environmental Considerations

Chapter 9 discussed the pronounced trend toward new controls for protection of the environment. These will continue in number and detail and most urban communities must adopt some of them within the near future. Obviously, they must receive thorough consideration in any revision or updating program. The increasing prohibitions against septic tanks will require installation of collection systems and some type of treatment plants. These will have a major influence upon the development of new subdivisions.

Governmental Structures and Finances

The rapid growth and development of large urban areas, much of which is in unincorporated areas, has indicated the desirability of regional governmental agencies that can ensure properly coordinated and balanced growth. Regional planning is thus becoming increasingly necessary and an official administrative agency will probably be needed.

Preceding chapters, especially Chapter 10, have discussed the serious financial problems now found in most urban areas. Except for the financial assistance received from the federal government and some state governments, this problem will undoubtedly continue in the future. While government finances are not normally an integral portion of comprehensive planning, they certainly must be considered, at least from the standpoint of financing new improvements.

CURRENT TRENDS IN REPLANNING

During the past two decades, more replanning has been accomplished than in any previous comparable period. The major reason has been the financial assistance available from HUD's "701" program. However, the rapid growth and complex problems confronting urban areas, as well as new planning techniques, have caused Planning Commissions and city officials to develop a major interest in revising older plans.

The majority of the financial assistance programs of departments of the federal government are not available to communities unless an adequate comprehensive plan, or at least appropriate data, is available regarding conditions and needs.

As a part of the current agreements for preparing transportation plans in areas containing populations of 50,000 or more persons, the federal government requires that there be continuous planning activities after completion of the original program and that the plan be completely updated at least every five years. Thus, in many instances, it is becoming mandatory that comprehensive plans be revised or updated.

STEPS IN REPLANNING

In general, the revision of an older comprehensive plan involves the basic principles or steps used in the original studies. Following is a summary discussion of some of the more important analyses that should be made.

Changes in Conditions and Needs

The current comprehensive plan should have been based upon complete data regarding existing conditions and such information is equally essential in any program of revision. The essential items upon which the information is based are: (a) land uses, (b) amount, distribution, and characteristics of population, and (c) the several physical facilities included in the plan, such as transportation, and community facilities of various types. The development of data in the revision program should enable the compiling of valuable information regarding changes and trends that have occurred between the two planning programs.

Information regarding changes and trends in land uses is especially important [Figure 14-1]. This will indicate amount of land being occupied by different types of uses as well as the trend in location of uses. With similar information available regarding changes in the local economy and employment, much useful data is provided for developing future land use plans and the zoning district map.

When data regarding existing land use is recorded in an electronic computer, it is comparatively simple to obtain detailed information regarding changes and trends in local land uses at any time. It is expected that this method will be much more widely used in the future, especially by the planning staffs in larger cities.

It is particularly important to develop comprehensive data regarding changes that have occurred in traffic volumes upon individual major streets. When the existing volumes are compared to current capacities and related to major trends, the need for street improvements or new types of transportation facilities should be clearly indicated.

GLENDALE, OHIO
LAND USE 1944

SURVEY CONDUCTED BY
HARLAND BARTHOLOMEW
AND ASSOCIATES

▨ SINGLE FAMILY DWELLING   ▦ PARKS
▦ TWO FAMILY DWELLING   ■ COMMERCE
▨ MULTIPLE DWELLING   ▨ INDUSTRY
▦ PUBLIC AND SEMI-PUBLIC   ---- RAILROADS

SURVEY CONDUCTED BY
HAMILTON COUNTY
REGIONAL PLAN
COMMISSION

LAND USE 1969

Source: Harland Bartholomew and Associates, and Hamilton County Regional Plan Commission.

Figure 14-1 Changes in land use.

377

Any new or revised state legislation must obviously be carefully studied and any revised plans related thereto. It is expected that a substantial amount of new state requirements regarding protection of the environment, especially control of air and water pollution, will be enacted within the relatively near future. Thus, incorporation of new local regulations will be required in the revised plans and some will undoubtedly be required, even if there is no comprehensive revision.

Changes in Citizens' Desires and Needs

Changes are occurring within the social and economic structure, as well as in the physical structure, of urban areas. Integration, segregation, aid for education, health services, higher wages, and trends toward shorter working weeks are among the more important changes; with these has come the widespread demand to eliminate slums and blighted areas, as well as to provide more moderate- and low-priced living units in satisfactory neighborhoods. A detailed and comprehensive housing plan and program will be an integral portion of any revised comprehensive plan.

Changing social and economic conditions will also result in the need for additional and new types of public physical facilities, especially community centers and health subcenters. Facilities and opportunities for adult education and for retarded and handicapped persons should also be considered. Additional or expanded public services will also be required in the future and their requirements and operating costs must be fully considered.

Estimating and Planning for Future Needs

The preceding discussion reveals that most careful estimates must be developed of probable future needs during the period planned for. This will involve both the types of facilities, as well as their number, extent, and location. Special consideration must be given to the amount and major characteristics of the future population and the amount of different land uses that should be provided. A basic reason for many of the older plans becoming obsolete was inaccurate estimates of population and land use requirements. In addition, the older plans were not adjusted to changing needs or standards of essential physical facilities, such as schools or neighborhood centers.

In preparing revised proposals for the several physical elements of the comprehensive plan, full consideration must be given to changing standards, as well as to new planning techniques. For example, there is now much discussion regarding location of elementary schools to serve individual neighborhoods, which has been the practice in the past, but some are now advocating the grouping of all grades upon large sites which would serve large sectors of the community.

There are also new practices in planning techniques. A current practice in both land use and transportation planning is to develop alternative land use plans and estimates of traffic flows from each plan, which can in turn be tested upon different major street plans. Sound selection of each plan can then be made on the basis of efficiency and economy. It should be noted that a land use plan will show only the general location and type of uses as well as the intensity thereof; but the more detailed zoning district map can be closely related to the land use plan. Other new techniques and practices should be followed in developing the revised plan.

In large communities, the revision or updating of existing plans will primarily be done by the local planning staff. In some instances, such as the transportation and water and sewerage phases, the staff may engage consultants experienced in this work to make a study or to advise and assist. In smaller urban areas, usually those containing less than 50,000 persons, there is only a small staff, if any, and the normal procedure is to engage an experienced planning firm to develop the revised plan.

CITIZEN UNDERSTANDING AND SUPPORT

The increased discussion of urban problems and of the need for comprehensive planning has aroused much citizen interest. This is especially true of urban renewal projects and model cities programs where complete neighborhoods may be affected. It is only logical that citizens should have an interest and participate in planning for the redevelopment of the area in which they live. Thus, many citizens' committees are needed to advise upon the local planning of neighborhoods.

The development of a comprehensive plan requires much technical knowledge and detail. It is the responsibility of the planning commission and its staff, assisted by such outside consulting service as they may desire, to utilize close cooperation and consultation with heads of city departments. As the staff develops a preliminary plan for each phase, it is desirable to create an advisory committee consisting of local citizens who are familiar and experienced with that particular element. Each committee would carefully examine the preliminary findings and proposals and make suggestions deemed desirable to more closely adjust the plan to local conditions and needs.

The report upon the comprehensive plan is normally a relatively large volume containing much statistical data and complete discussion of the findings and recommendations. This is necessary since it will be reviewed and referred to by experienced officials and representatives of other governmental agencies. The major findings and recommendations should be publicized by the newspapers, radio and television stations, and by presentations before civic organizations. The individual reports need not be widely circulated, but adequate copies should be available for use by officials and representatives of other governmental agencies and organizations concerned with the growth and development of the area. These reports will, however, be of little interest to the average layman and a brief and more popular version of the technical publication should be prepared. These should be widely distributed among interested citizens and civic and neighborhood organizations.

Members of the planning staff should also meet with neighborhood organizations to explain and discuss the revised comprehensive plan. The explanation and discussion of the plan in the public schools, particularly junior and senior high schools, is a desirable procedure.

In brief, extensive efforts should be undertaken to secure widespread citizen understanding and support.

PLAN IMPLEMENTATION

This chapter has discussed the necessity of keeping a comprehensive plan abreast of changing conditions, practices and needs which are an important part of implementing the plan. Chapters 9 and 10 also discussed essential steps in implementing a comprehensive plan.

Because of rapid growth, increasing costs, and decreasing amount of desirable vacant land, the current major problem in implementation is protecting its proposals and standards. Continuous efforts are made by individuals, developers, or infrequently by neighborhood organizations to change zoning or subdivision regulations as well as other regulatory measures so as to permit a more intensive type or lower standards of development than currently proposed. Much pressure is placed upon the Planning Commission and the responsible public agency to approve the changes and the major reason advanced is that disapproval would stop or retard growth and thus the entire community would be adversely affected. Actually, the motivating reason is predominantly a desire on the part of the promoters to achieve a higher return from their investment and many court decisions have held that this is no legal reason for changing zoning regulations.

There are frequently instances when citizens organize to oppose initiation or construction of improvements proposed in the comprehensive plan. The construction of major streets, especially expressways, within or near residential sections, most frequently arouse this type of opposition, but some public buildings are also objected to. The desire to protect residential sections from large volumes of through traffic is certainly understandable, but because of the importance of vehicular transportation, the entire urban area benefits from an adequate major street system. Thus, the planning commission and public agencies must carefully appraise the needs and benefits of all citizens against the smaller number that would be adversely affected. The obvious goal is selection of a location and design that will afford maximum service and a minimum of adverse influences.

15 | COURAGE

Wm. H. Claire

The preceding fourteen chapters describe how to formulate a practical comprehensive plan for an urban area and how to implement the plan. Goals were mentioned at several points as the foundation for realistic planning and one of the difficult tasks decision-makers have is setting goals for planning. Goals that generate broad support from the public need more input from a wider cross-section of the people than presently.

GOALS

A new approach to arriving at goals is needed and emerging now. Priorities are changing as to what is important and what is not. Members of the younger generation are the instigators of the peaceful revolution is this drama of change. Their desires and goals are beginning to be heard, not only in the street, but in the political arena, as more fully and aptly related by Charles A. Reich in his account of Consciousness III[1]. Consciousness I was the frame of mind the founding fathers of the United States were in when they left the tyranny and class status of the Old World and founded the New World, based on a republic where the people were sovereign; Consciousness II, according to Reich, came into being as a consequence of the failure of Consciousness I and reached its peak in the twentieth century with "robber barons, business piracy, ruinous

1. Charles A. Reich, *The Greening of America* (New York: Random House, 1970).

competition, unreliable products and false advertising, grotesque inequality, and lack of coordination and planning." Consciousness III has liberation for its foundation where the individual is free to set his own goals. Power or status (as in II) are substituted in III for: be true to oneself. Competition is alien to III and brotherhood and honesty are in. Reich states that Consciousness III is new and may need to be reassessed in a couple of years. However, it is a change in philosophy worth watching and could lead to a simpler way of urban living, depending upon how widespread the movement becomes.

Environmentalists of all ages are influencing goals with disastrous prognostications, if their cautions are ignored. This is meant to apply to the practical adviser in environmental fields and not the meddlesome, partly informed, publicity-seeking, ecological lunatic fringe who are real stumbling blocks to progress.

A complete turnaround in values is beginning to influence goals, and more of this is needed. The attitude toward property ownership still has a long way to go in the United States to achieve a deeper social consciousness in use of privately held land in place of the fast-buck turnover in ownership or the selfish use of private property oblivious of and detrimental to neighbors. The time spent in commuting, considered a necessary evil for decades, is now being considered in a new light as less and less necessary. Escape from smog is altering values and bringing about trade-offs in places of living, places of working, and ways of making a living.

A new procedure is evolving in the political action process leading toward planning and development goals ever closer to the individual citizen's needs. Politicians are paying more attention to public opinion and insist on bureaucrats doing likewise. Highway location is an example, so arbitrarily determined previously and now more carefully taking into account environmental and other influences on the people. Yet, the likes and dislikes of the mass of individuals are not adequately taken into consideration. The decision-maker, often the politician or his backer, does this *for* the people in making a list of goals. However, a better-informed public is concerning itself more and more with public issues and goals. Alvin Toffler gets deep into this matter with his "social future assemblies" as a method for arriving at a truly democratic set of goals.[2] The technique is to organize groups or neighborhoods in a continuous system of opinion gathering and flow to public officials reflecting changes in desires and values. A complicated procedure but an effective way to know the will of the people in a complicated social structure. This requires planning, fairness, and courage.

COURAGE

The warnings of the effects of change at an increasing rate in Toffler's *Future Shock* are answered in his closing sections on the villain change being transformed into the hero change through appropriate planning. Change can be the hero of urban ills by solving them as the changes occur as mentioned earlier in this handbook, providing sufficiently courageous and intelligent plans are formulated to take the changes into account. Some trends and examples of this phenomenon are worth mentioning.

2. Alvin Toffler, *Future Shock* (New York: Random House, 1970).

Any Blight or Poverty Is Too Much

The gradual reduction in substandard housing units in Canada and the United States is an encouraging trend of great satisfaction to thousands of those who have worked diligently through the years to bring this about. On the other hand, those still in less than adequate housing, some 20 million in the United States, present a challenge of huge magnitude that takes courage to resolve. The pressure is on those in high places to resolve this irritating inconsistency and costly negligence.

Too often overlooked is the higher percentage of substandard housing units in rural areas than in urban ones, even though the numbers are smaller. Here again broad-scale, comprehensive regional plans are needed to attack with care and courage this widespread problem.

The human scale, so often ignored in planning and urban design, is being demanded by planners and architects with the courage to hold out for higher standards in this needed area.

The opportunities in future development for better urban planning and design may be grasped by inspection of the additional areas to be urbanized [Figure 15-1] and the completely new towns to be planned and built. Equal to the opportunities to create standard housing in future development is the opportunity to build comprehensive urban transportation systems.

Source: Wm. H. Claire (ed.), Urban Planning Guide (New York: American Society of Civil Engineers, 1969), p. 298.

Figure 15-1   Anticipated major urbanized areas in U.S. in 100 years.

Transportation Changes

The prospects for logical comprehensive urban transportation systems are tremendous—now! The need is no more nor less than for a school or a water supply system. When subsidized public ownership of rapid mass transit is as accepted and understood as public ownership of airports or streets, truly coordinated urban transportation will result. The opportunities in many areas are going to disappear as urbanization spreads and land values soar. A few examples of this are the urbanizing corridor between Cheyenne and Pueblo [Figure 15-1], Dallas and Ft. Worth, Miami and Jacksonville, St. Louis and Kansas City, Los Angeles and San Diego, Seattle and Portland, and Montreal to Toronto, to mention a few. The purchase of four-track right-of-way for high-speed local and express electric trains now would establish a transit system for new towns between the two major cities and connect with existing or proposed transit systems within the major cities at each end. Planning, foresight, and courage are the prerequisites. The long-term benefits are enormous—for air pollution reduction, for the human scale goal, for a balanced load on the transit system, for the major city at each end, and for a new dimension in quality of urban living.

The entire system would be built in stages as demand justifies. The Denver to Colorado Springs leg of the Cheyenne to Pueblo system would be a logical first phase. Rail right-of-way is already at least partially available. The Miami-Fort Lauderdale leg of the Miami-Jacksonville system is another example. Also, two tracks would be a first-stage rail requirement following with the other two when traffic warrants both express and local services. Planned properly, the added expense of an underground system could be avoided with an elevated system built into many of the buildings it serves.

The integration with each transit station, at the time rail service begins operation, of a complete community shopping center, high-rise apartments, office accommodations, and industrial establishments would help pay for the rail facilities. The maximizing of the capital investment for mutual benefit of both public and private facilities is the kind of comprehensive solution required. The broadening of the tax base should be planned to realize these improvements without raising the overall tax levy. Projects of such magnitude call for planning to open up opportunities for a more natural environment for the urbanite.

Natural and Urban Environments

One of the principal causes of the attraction of national parks and forests is escape from the strain of the urban environment. City parks, too, have furnished the setting for millions of emotional safety valves to cut loose and avoid a family blowup. Coupled with this relief mechanism or facility, the natural environment affords an inspiring quality of peace and contentment and a sense of balance and joy. The need for these attributes is not only on weekends or holidays but daily and hourly during each waking moment.

A national park in every city may be stretching the point a bit, but planning into new and old urban areas the degree of natural environment to attain these attributes is a psychiatric must. The dreary places where most people eat in the city can be transformed into pleasant gardens or outdoor picnic areas. The walk to work can be smog-free and planned to equal a tramp in the woods, whether the walk is from a transit station or parking area to the office or shop or all the way from home. The commuting trip by bicycle can be along a landscaped cycleway planned in a natural setting.

These amenities are easier to come by in new towns or urban areas to be built. The ingenuity of the planner, engineer, and architect are called upon here to preserve or restore the natural environment within and around homes, apartments, offices, factories, public buildings, and any other facility used by people.

Even more ingenuity is required of these professionals to plan the spread of the outdoors into the entire existing urban environment and not only a park every few miles. If a planner has any illusion about a city being built—virtually any city—and complete, he should look again carefully for the drab, the depressing, the stark stretches where people exist, and plan them over for people to live. Urban renewal presents a unique opportunity toward this goal and needs to be expanded greatly to fulfill the natural environmental requirements of the inner city. All this takes courage and faith in the future.

BELIEF IN THE FUTURE

One of the disappointing characterizations of some of the younger generation is their lack of confidence in the future. Hopefully, this applies to a small minority. Most young planners are eager to get at urban problems and understand how they came into being. They need more practical knowledge from their schooling to appreciate the forces behind these problems and more inspirational guidance assuring them that the problems can be solved. Encouraging young technicians in planning and development to believe in the future is a moral obligation of the educational community—to teach constructive awareness of urban problems instead of the hopelessness of this crisis or that dilemma.

The only way to solve any problem is first to have all the facts that cause it and then with sound goals to formulate a plan to solve it. The immense complexity of current urban problems necessitates an accumulation of enormous amounts of data and constant revisions of those data for a solution based thereon to be reliable and workable. Computerized data banks or urban facts are now being kept current, if only on experimental bases in some cases.

Such a comprehensive analysis has been in process at Massachusetts Institute of Technology (MIT) for years on a worldwide scale. Some of their findings might be considered disastrous for the future of mankind on earth regarding depletion of natural resources, population increases, and quality of life [Figure 15-2] were it not for the fact that they have formulated a course [Figure 15-3] for human events in the future that avoids the extremes originally plotted.

The MIT studies are relative only and based on broad assumptions difficult to prove or disprove. However, they provoke thought on values and priorities as goals are set for future urban plans. One critical aspect of the study reported in *The Futurist* magazine articles[3] may not have taken fully into account the shift from natural resources use, such as coal and oil, to nuclear power as projected by the Bureau of Mines [Figure 15-4].

3. *The Futurist* Vol. 5, No. 4, (Aug. 1971), published by World Future Society, P.O. Box 30369, Bethesda Branch, Washington, D.C., 20014.

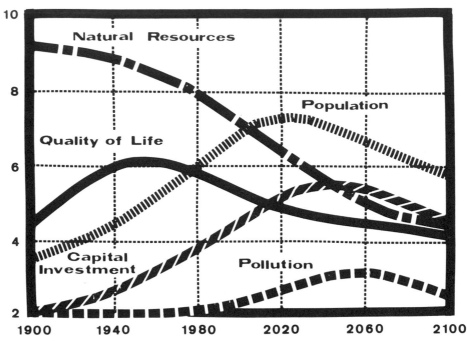

Source: The Futurist, Aug. 1971, published by World Future Society, Washington, D.C.

Figure 15-2   Quality of life forecast I.

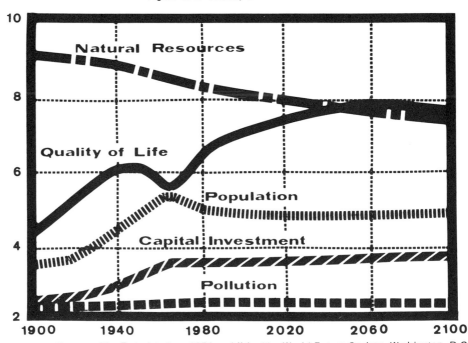

Source: The Futurist, Aug. 1971, published by World Future Society, Washington, D.C.

Figure 15-3   Quality of life forecast II.

Annual average generation

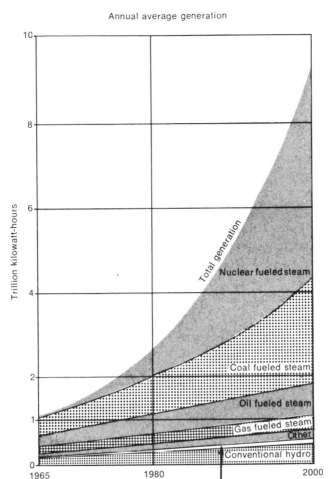

Figure 15-4 Projected electric generation by Source 1965-2000.

The encouraging developments by the Atomic Energy Commission have reached a new plateau in their breeder reactors. This tremendous new source of power may be the answer to power shortages already experienced in highly concentrated areas of power utilization. The cover of the booklet[4] states "Johnny had 3 truckloads of plutonium. He used 3 of them to light New York for 1 year. How much plutonium did Johnny have left? Answer: 4 truckloads."

Geothermal and solar energy are other potential power sources with promise well worth watching by the planner and others.

The planner would do well to keep abreast of these broader aspects of his profession

4. Walter Mitchell, III, and Stanley E. Turner, *Breeder Reactors* (Washington, D.C.: Atomic Energy Commission, 1971).

in order to more intelligently analyze day-to-day encounters with plans for cities, counties, and regions, and thus be prepared to gauge better how each fits into the whole scheme of things.

The whole world watches what the United States does at home and abroad. Never in the history of man has a country built a nation as affluent and powerful as this one in less than two centuries, an example of free men working together solving one problem after another and, yet, creating others along the way. In 1844 Ralph Waldo Emerson wrote in his learned essay, "Politics" "there will always be a government of force where men are selfish"; and selfishness is still here. Yet, a glimmer of light shows signs of less selfishness, a generosity for countless eleemosynary movements and institutions, foundations supporting a variety of studies of all kinds of problems, an enlightend attitude on the part of more property owners in the use of their property, and now the Consciousness III attitude—all spelling hope for the future.

The reliance of Canada and the United States and many other countries in their growth and development, on principles involving the importance of the individual, justice for all, personal freedom, and belief in God provide a basis for a strong faith in the future and a solid footing for the confidence the planner needs in preparing urban areas for fulfillment for all the people.

INDEX